D1587256

FORTY-SEVEN YEARS ALOFT

YEARS ALOFT

FROM COLD WAR FIGHTERS AND FLYING THE PM TO COMMERCIAL JETS

FORTY-SEVEN YEARS ALOFT

FROM COLD WAR FIGHTERS AND FLYING THE PM TO COMMERCIAL JETS

A PILOT'S REMARKABLE STORY DURING THE GOLDEN ERA
OF BRITISH AVIATION

BRIAN BURDETT

AIR WORLD

AIR WORLD

FORTY-SEVEN YEARS ALOFT
FROM COLD WAR FIGHTERS AND FLYING THE PM TO
COMMERCIAL JETS
A Pilot's Remarkable Story During the Golden Era of British Aviation

First published in Great Britain in 2019 by
Air World
An imprint of
Pen & Sword Books Ltd
Yorkshire – Philadelphia

ISBN 978 1 52675 303 8

Printed and bound in England by TJ International, Padstow, Cornwall, PL28 8RW
Typeset by Aura Technology and Software Services, India

Pen & Sword Books Limited incorporates the imprints of Atlas, Archaeology,
Aviation, Discovery, Family History, Fiction, History, Maritime, Military, Military
Classics, Politics, Select, Transport, True Crime, Air World, Frontline Publishing,
Leo Cooper, Remember When, Seaforth Publishing, The Praetorian Press, Wharncliffe
Local History, Wharncliffe Transport, Wharncliffe True Crime and White Owl.

For a complete list of Pen & Sword titles please contact

PEN & SWORD BOOKS LIMITED
47 Church Street, Barnsley, South Yorkshire, S70 2AS, England
E-mail: enquiries@pen-and-sword.co.uk
Website: www.pen-and-sword.co.uk

Or
PEN AND SWORD BOOKS
1950 Lawrence Rd, Havertown, PA 19083, USA
E-mail: Uspen-and-sword@casematepublishers.com
Website: www.penandswordbooks.com

Contents

Let's Get Airborne First

My time in Wymeswold was an opportunity for a really close call. On a Sunday I had been to Dolphin Square pool with Maureen, my girlfriend, and her flat-mate and, during the normal mucking about, her flat-mate pushed me into the pool. No big deal, except I was not prepared for it and went in awkwardly with water shooting up my nose. It hurt and was still uncomfortable the next morning when I got airborne with Nan Dog McEwan (those were his initials in the old phonetic alphabet), as my leader for a pairs ciné exercise, i.e. take pictures of our attacks which simulated the firing of cannon and was filmed for later assessment.

The Monday morning meteorological (met) briefing had forecast poor weather all day but it was within limits when we got airborne in formation in our Hawker Hunter F.2s and climbed through thick clouds to 40,000 feet.

Due to weather deterioration at base we were urgently recalled and immediately initiated a rapid descent through cloud to get home. Formation in cloud is no big deal: cloud is only water droplets just like fog and you can see the car in front can't you? Anyway, halfway down I had a massive pain in my right frontal sinus and just could not concentrate my vision. I was obliged to abandon my leader, turn away and climb rapidly to balance the pressure to a point where the pain ceased. I was between a rock and a hard place because I had to get down but had only a finite amount of fuel; the F.2 carried less fuel than other marks, so staying up for long was not an option. I descended again at a reasonable rate of descent but the pain returned and I could not relieve it. A fighter's pressurisation is not like an airliner where the cabin rarely exceeds 8,500 feet; it is much higher.

I kept tentatively, climbing again to ease the pain, then trying again. Eventually, I got below 10,000 feet but was experiencing much pain and the onset of disorientation. Suddenly, there was a moment of intense pain and, I think, but don't know, that I either lost consciousness or had a very momentary total disorientation. Whatever the circumstances, I suddenly

1

saw that I was breaking cloud. I was upside down and at about 200 feet! Fortunately, my sinuses had been forced to equalise. I could see the aircraft was in a gentle descent for a line of trees and, equally fortunately, the rate of roll of the Hunter is 420 degrees per second which saved me. I rolled the wings level and pulled back; to this day I can see the long grass, or wheat, flattening out as I went through a big enough gap in the trees on the edge of the field and across the crop. I went straight back into cloud and managed to level off around 3,000 feet. I was close to panic and my voice must have conveyed this when I called base; to my astonishment and relief they answered as I no longer knew where I was. All should now be well but I was garbling a bit and then my best friend in the mess, Murky Murkowski, an ex-fighter pilot from Poland, came onto the radio. Like so many Poles after the war they were thanked for their amazing contribution during the Battle of Britain and later by being only given ground duties, Air Traffic Control being one of the popular ones.

Murky was a lovely fellow who really missed his flying. However, he enjoyed mixing with us and giving us the benefits of his experience. For some reason, he and I hit it off and shared many an evening together. He had the fascinating habit of having soup to start his meal, then the main course and then soup again. He didn't like puddings.

He was officer in charge of the sergeants' mess and was off shift this particular day but wished to speak with the sergeant on duty in the tower. When he heard my voice, he knew I was in trouble and asked the controller to hand over to him, which he did. His voice came over the air just like in an American film, 'Hullo Brian, Murky here, what's the problem?' I immediately settled down and followed his instructions for identifying my position. He used basic maths, using my bearing and giving me 90 degree headings and a constant speed. He saw which side of the airfield I was and how far I would have travelled. This gave him a good idea of my position and he then gave a steer for base. I was now down to little, or no, fuel, so there was no chance of a full procedure of coming overhead, letting down outbound, etc., thus having a reasonably normal QGH (controlled descent through cloud), so he guided my descent based on his judgement. We just did not have anything like the navigation aids we had even three years later, let alone now.

As I passed 1,000 feet I had a decision to make as my fuel gauges showed empty – do I eject immediately or continue? The Mark 1 ejector seat was no good below 1,000 feet, especially in a descent, as there was no time for the ejection and the automatics to work. I stayed with the aircraft as I decided that, if it went really pear-shaped, I could do a forced landing. Stupid, but that's what I did. I broke cloud at 400 feet and just off to my right and a mile or so ahead was Wymeswold! I landed, taxied in and went to our crew room, which was actually a big marquee, as we were based there temporarily, grabbed a coffee and sat in a corner mulling over the last thirty minutes. My crewman, airframes, signalled from the entrance for a word in my ear. His message was that he thought I might like to know that when I shut down that I had only sixteen gallons of fuel left.

Pilots reading this are certainly saying what a lineshoot, what bullshine, etc., and I really don't blame them. However, it's as it happened and is still as clear in my head as when I sat in the corner of that marquee.

I could only fly four times in the next two months, each time with another pilot and each time the sinus gave trouble. By October all was well but, suddenly, mid-November, the sinus flared up badly and I was finally admitted to the Royal Air Force Hospital at Halton for repairs. I did not fly again until January 1957, but then all went well.

Take Off

I arrived at 0700 hours on 11 September 1936 in the hospital at Kingston-upon-Thames, Surrey, and after a suitable time went home to our flat in Hampton Wick.

My father, born in 1909, was the fourth son and fifth born of five boys and two girls, all born in Tottenham. His father was missing, believed killed in Gallipoli, and after a while the boys had to find work to keep the family going as his partner in their goldsmith business ran off with the cash and stock. Harry, the eldest, was already in the Royal Flying Corps as an air gunner, having lied about his age (he survived), the next two did part-time work when they could and Dad, nine years old, cleaned brasses for the milkman. In later years when we were enjoying a pint in a decent pub and he saw the horse brasses on display he would think of the hundreds he had thrown in the corner of the milkman's stable because they were scratched and of 'no further use'.

He was a fine sportsman and had been runner-up in the London schools' swimming championships, was a good amateur boxer and later played for the top amateur football team Walthamstow Avenue alongside Arthur Rowe who became the Spurs' manager. Dad had an England amateur trial but, before the team was announced, he managed to slide hard and end up with one leg either side of a goalpost, finished up in hospital and couldn't have been selected anyway. It must have ended OK or I would not be here to write this account!

My mother, née Beatrice Florence Strachan, was born in Fulham by a Scottish father from Auchtermurchty, Fife, and an English mother. Her father was a cabinet maker and his skills were well used by the RFC as an airframe repairer in the First World War. Mother was a secretary but, in 1933 and '34, had been one of the Brighton Belles dancing troupe in the summer. She won the 220 yards (200 metres) race in the London Schools' Athletics Championships at the White City and was really miffed at being presented with a doll as a prize, even though it was from King George V. They both encouraged their three children in their sporting endeavours but at school I played rugby and cricket without too much success but was quite useful at cross-country and athletics, especially 440 yards, 440 yards hurdles and the half-mile. The cross-country was the real McCoy with fields, ditches, streams, woods, etc.

My father regularly took me to Bushy Park to see the deer. In those days the pond was much larger than now and totally unfenced or walled. It is now much smaller and contains what I believe is known as The Princess Fountain. The deer used to stand alongside us to drink. One day a stag became aggressive and my father, the boxer, punched it on the nose and it ran off. Yes, I can remember it! I was in my pushchair at the time.

I remember going on the bus from Kingston to Central London and from the outskirts of Kingston to, probably, the other side of Richmond and it was all open country. I know Richmond Park is there but that now seems to be all that's left of real open spaces.

My memory of aged two to three is quite amazing. I remember the kennel of Becky, our spaniel, under the metal steps leading to our flat and the layout of the kitchen. My father used to enjoy a half-pint in the Swan and as I was in the pushchair he parked us on the lower level. Years later when I passed through Kingston en route from London Heathrow to Sussex, I thought to look in, already having a picture of the layout in my mind's eye. Bingo! The floor levels were exactly as I remembered them. My father told me that a neighbour was most inconsiderate with the way he revved his motor-bike engine at inconsiderate times. I rarely heard my father swear but he would say 'There goes bloody King again.' Apparently, I always thought his name was Buddy King.

We moved to Revelstoke Road leading to Wimbledon Park in late 1938. My mother's parents lived three roads along in Marlborough Road, now Stroud Road, and I recall visits to the park and the paddling pond by our nearest entrance. My father enjoyed a weekend walk with me in the pushchair to Wimbledon Common and Putney Heath where he enjoyed a half, or two, at the Telegraph pub. I remember him laughing and joking with his regular group of guys and, I believe, one of them was a well-known comedian, Sid Fields, who used to sit me on his knee.

In early 1939 we moved to Leigh-on-Sea, Essex, where my father was to be manager of the Co-op on Eastwood Road opposite the Woodcutters Arms. Our house was 200 metres down the road from the shops and my sister, Greta, was born there in July 1939. Dad had a snooker-room but I was never allowed in except to say goodnight.

By 1940 the war was well underway. There was an ack-ack gun emplacement just up the road in Belfair's Woods, and, because of the noise, plus falling shrapnel, we moved farther down the road to Byworth in early 1941 as Leigh was quite quiet at that time.

Being on the Thames Estuary and just up the road from RAF Rochford, now Southend Airport, we saw much of the Battle of Britain overhead. I saw a couple of bombers being shot down and occasional dogfights. So much for Leigh being quiet! At that age and time, of course, the sound of the RR Merlin engine was just a noise but now it's music to the ears.

One day the air raid warning sounded and Mum left the house with Greta in her arms and Dad walking with me to our Anderson shelter, an earth-and-sandbag-protected dug-out used all over the country. As my mother was entering the shelter a German fighter came down the back of our row of houses with guns blazing. My father pushed me against the wall as I saw my mother duck into the shelter and earth and cabbages leap into the air. I distinctly remember my father's wail of 'Oh, not my cabbages'. 'Dig for Victory' was well under way at this time.

In late 1940, after the Battle of Britain, Mum, Greta, Nanna and I were evacuated to Blockley, Gloucestershire, where we watched from the window of our house on the hill the glow from the November 1940 bombing of Coventry. Quite soon after that we returned to Byworth.

In May 1941 my brother Barry was born during the huge sound of bombers en route to London. The Battle of Britain had dented the Luftwaffe's day work but they still tried at night.

Although on the route for many bombers going to London and in the aftermath of the Battle of Britain my father felt he had to join the Army. Because of his civilian role he was in a 'reserved occupation' but he had never forgotten the white feather given, often unfairly, to non-serving-men in the First World War, or even serving on leave and in civvies. He feared that might happen to him.

Dad joined the Army around August 1941 and was drafted into the Royal Corps of Signals, Catterick, as a driver, thus making use of his, by now, huge knowledge of grocery, butchery and greengrocery. In fairness, he was about to be transferred to the Army Catering Corps, which was formed in 1941, when he was on night manoeuvres on the moors and, unknowingly, in the pitch dark, was right next to a powerful field gun which fired and ruptured his eardrum. This resulted in his being unfit for service and he was demobbed on 18 March 1942.

TAKE OFF

During his absence my mother had befriended an unmarried lady with a young child, who was having a hard time because, then, her status was frowned upon. Anyway, she was welcomed into our home as helper to my mother and the four children. We loved her and she stayed with us for the rest of the war, then moved to Bude in Cornwall. She was known as Auntie Dean; I never knew her full name.

From my Dad's return until April 1943, life was just the war, rations (yes, for us as well!), starting school at Leigh Hall College on First Avenue near Chalkwell Park, and visits to the beach – a normal young boy's life.

Me versus Lorry

To attempt to slow down the movement of tanks and heavy armour in the event of an invasion, tank blocks were built in many towns in England. A tank block was a solid 6-cubic-feet block of concrete. Several were placed across roads in a line with just one gap for reasonable-sized vehicles, including lorries, and smaller ones for pedestrians and bicycles. There was such a line between the Woodcutters Arms and the Army base next to the shops. Any decent tank-driver would have been unfazed and simply gone through the pub's fence and out the other side.

My mother was with Barry in the pushchair, Greta alongside and me free to roam. She stopped to talk with her friend, whose son and I set off to play 'It' (or 'He' or 'Tag' as you may call it). We probably chased each other for five minutes before I chased him across the road next to the tank blocks. As I passed the gap, I was struck by a lorry exceeding the permitted speed. The bumper fractured my right femur and pelvis and I flew through the air. On landing I fractured my skull and lay with my right leg under my torso whilst the front wheel traversed my left leg.

My father, by sheer luck, was the other side of the blocks and heard my cry of 'Dad!'. He came immediately and from then I remember five things: my father's assurances; his command to Mr Nunn his assistant to go straight to Caulkett's, the pharmacist, and get loads of pads, etc., and say he would pay later; a man telling my Dad 'to move the boy as this is holding up the traffic' and my father replying 'Touch him and I'll kill you'; and the ambulance arriving and me being lifted in. My father assured me we were going home but I saw a line of trees outside what was eventually to be my school and knew he had fibbed.

I remember nothing until post-operation before which my father had signed to agree the amputation of my left leg. I had my left leg in plaster up on a pillow, a blanket and sheet over my chest and midriff and my right leg in a sling attached to a pulley system. I cannot remember how long

I was thus restrained, but it was for a long time. Every morning the nurses came around with the breakfast trolley, and if I received none I knew it was another operation. The procedure is memorable because in those days the anaesthetic was ether distributed onto a gauze mask drip by drip until you went under. To this day the smell of ether not only takes me back to those days but causes me a little shudder but, strangely, I quite like it.

After three months I saw 'chocolate' (it tasted horrible!) on my left leg which turned out to be discharge from osteomyelitis which is a serious and rare infection of the bone or marrow. As there were no antibiotics available for civilians at the time it necessitated surgery. Again, my poor parents had to give permission for amputation if found necessary. In the event, it was necessary to remove some bone but the leg was saved again. In all, I had fourteen operations. It was a long time before I was able to be wheeled into the airy and bright conservatory at the south end of the ward, but how wonderful it was to feel a breeze and to have a view.

My surgeon was Mr Murray who saved my life and gave me the opportunity to live a fairly normal life.

During air raids the ward was evacuated, to where I know not, but I and a young girl on the other side of the ward from me were the only ones left. We each had a nurse sitting next to us holding our hands and listened to what noises there were. Mostly, nothing happened, but one night bombs fell really close and a couple of windows blew out and took the black-out curtains with them. There was the noise of aircraft, including fighters, ack-ack guns and searchlights roaming the sky. The nurses were very brave. The aforementioned girl had a wasting disease which required bananas in her diet so the Royal Air Force, apparently, brought bananas from Gibraltar on their runs home. She and I used to exchange messages by tying paper round our toothbrushes, attaching string and hurling them across the ward. As I recall, that and parental visits covered our time.

Sadly, during my sojourn of five months both my paternal grandparents died and my mother's oldest sister was killed in an air raid.

By the time I left hospital just in time for my seventh birthday, my mother's hair was white. I guess she blamed herself for my accident, although I have never thought to look at it that way. She was twenty-seven years old and white haired!

The next few weeks were spent in a wheelchair and occasional gentle pressure on the leg with crutches. My Dad used to wheel me at weekends to the railway bridge at the south of RAF Rochford to watch the Spitfires and Hurricanes of various squadrons. It was all very exciting, including a wheels-up landing. There were also some Lysanders there, presumably for clandestine operations. Strangely I'm sure this period was not instrumental in nurturing my desire to be a pilot. That came later.

Then it was crutches and learning to walk safely on my own. To this day I can hear my father saying, or shouting, according to distance, 'Brian, STOP limping!!' Although I was left with my right leg shorter than my left, his exhortations worked.

During my time in hospital there had been a major error on the part of a gun unit to the east of town and a shell went through the headmaster's study in the tower at Leigh Hall College. Mr Steggles, the head, was killed and the school was shut down.

School Days

In view of the fragility of my leg, in January 1944, I was sent to St Andrew's private school, Leigh-on-Sea, where it was hoped the rough and tumble would be less than the local school. Mrs Carney and her staff made life very easy for me but as the school had a predominantly girl population, I found myself playing netball and learning knitting. One of the most mortifying experiences of my life was standing in the bus to go home and, whilst searching for my fare in my satchel, my knitting fell to the floor. I refused totally to knit again and was demoted to raffia work. My sister and brother joined me at St Andrew's later.

Whilst I had been in hospital my parents had moved again, this time to Prittle View, on the south-west corner of Picketts Avenue and Eastwood Road North, now known as Mountdale Gardens. Over the road were woods and fields which for the next few years gave so much pleasure to the local kids. Our house was large and with a long and wide garden, quite enclosed by hedges and poplars. The owner of the field to the rear was a tyrant and we dared not set foot in it.

On the other corner was Bob Purle who, with his brother, successfully ran a business emptying septic tanks. My father helped him with his accounts and tax affairs and eventually he offered my father a permanent job. My father did not feel that such a business suited him and so declined. Later Bob sold his business to Redland, which became Redland-Purle for a while, and Bob retired to the Channel Islands with his millions. Dad occasionally kicked himself.

My good friend Malcolm and I regularly visited Mr Hyde down the road to be regaled with stories of his time as a despatch rider during the Boer War and to enjoy his homemade ginger beer. He had a few hives and he made us remove the honeycombs without protective clothing. The technique was to be gentle, slow and positive and show no fear. It worked as neither of us were ever stung!!

Georgie Knight lived up near Malcolm and, although he never gave Malcolm any grief, he seemed always to be with a brother who held me or helped Georgie to knock me around. It didn't help that my sister, having had trouble with him, told him that she would tell her brother. Ouch!

One day, turning into Malcolm's road at a corner shielded by a laburnum tree, we bumped into Georgie. He was alone so I set about him to the encouragement of Mr Hyde. I had no more trouble after that.

Sometime after my arrival at St Andrew's I became very friendly with Caroline whom I now consider my first girlfriend. Naturally, it was an innocent friendship between two eight-to-nine-year-olds. She had a lovely angora jumper which smelt nice and was so soft to the touch. It helped, of course, that she was sweet and pretty. I was invited to her house for tea and we ended up above her horse's stable admiring her apple storage; a young girl's equivalent of etchings maybe. Anyway, it seemed appropriate to enjoy a little kiss.

Later on, Caroline boarded at a school near Felixstowe and her doctor father would visit her in his single-seater Chilton aircraft, one of only three in existence. When I saw him after I got my Private Pilot's Licence in 1953 he said I could have a trip in it. Unfortunately, on his next visit to Caroline he had engine failure, did a successful field landing, but ended up in a ditch. This wrote it off and broke both his legs. It was very sad for him, and sad for me too.

During the war years there were a few exciting events, one or two of which are indelibly printed in my mind. At Leigh-on-Sea, whilst walking to see my Canadian friend Michael, a German fighter came down the road firing and I had to dive over a neighbour's wall. Later in the war I was in Michael's garden when we became fascinated as a V-1 'doodlebug' approached over the house. His mother came screaming out saying 'Inside, inside, into the shelter' at the same moment the engine stopped and it started its dive. I slammed my head on the metal of the Morrison shelter as I got in and saw many stars. We just made it before there was a massive explosion.

Soon we left the house through the kitchen where part of the ceiling had fallen down, some of it over the stove, and all Michael's mother could keep saying was 'Oh, my cabbage, oh, my cabbage.' I've heard that somewhere before, I think! She was shocked at our near escape. We went over the field and after about 200 yards came to the house where the V-1 had struck. The lady of the house, her five children and another six she was caring for were all killed. The fire engine arrived and, tragically, it was the home of one of the firemen. He had lost his entire family. My Dad's friend Basil Barley owned the factory across the road, the Southend Arterial, and every single window was gone.

Later, when the V-2 rockets started arriving, one landed on Eastwood School which my sister attended. It was the weekend so, although it did a lot of damage, there was only one casualty: the headmaster was killed! That's two headmasters we, the Burdetts, had now lost!

I cannot remember if it was that V-2 or another, but as the result of the shockwave our front bay window and wall to the roof was caused to crack wide enough to see daylight and pass your arm through. This explosion gave Barry, who was upstairs alone, such a fright and shock it was attributed to his falling ill with pleural pneumonia. He was in hospital for a while and my parents were very worried. They were having their share of concern for the family during this war.

Sometimes we would be at Nanna's in London and I can distinctly remember the feeling of adventure when we camped out on an underground platform. It would have been the District Line, I guess, but I don't know where. I think we would have only done that two or three times. We occasionally went into the coal cellar during air raids but, in retrospect, that seems a dumb place to be if your house falls down. Eventually, in the next road along, Ryfold Road, a huge communal air-raid shelter was built with the roof just slightly above road level.

One morning, after having had a good night's sleep, I was advised that a bomb had dropped less than 100 yards away. Sure enough there was a large gap in the line of houses, but there had been a survivor, a lady of about forty who, like my mother, went grey in a very, very short time.

Other memories of that period were horses everywhere pulling drays with beer barrels or coal which the men emptied through little man-holes in front of each house. The coal then ended up in the cellar. Rag-and-bone men were always passing, milk came in urns carried on carts and you had to take your jugs, or whatever, and the milk was delivered from pint or half-pint ladles. Men came on bicycles with large grindstones operated by the pedals and would sharpen knives and scissors. They had some sort of kit to mend holes in saucepans; nothing could be thrown away in those days. Every now and then there was even a man with a large tray on his head from which he sold crumpets and bread.

Such traders were to be found not just in London; they were a regular sight everywhere.

After the end of black-out the lamp-lighters returned; they would come with their long poles, use them to pull the gas-chains and light the lamps. In the morning the procedure was reversed.

Late in 1944 the vicar of the church over the road, the Reverend Percy Bates of St Michael's and All Angels' Church, came on a recruitment drive for choirboys. Two or three of us joined. There were two practices a week and two services on Sunday. During Lent there was an extra service.

Practices were paid at a halfpenny and services a penny and the money paid out every three months. Bonanza time!! Weddings and funerals were 2/6d (12½p) paid on the spot. Later, when my boy soprano voice was better trained, I sang solos during the signing of the register, this was also worth 2/6d.

Later on, I became head choirboy and during most Evensong services sang a solo. Mr Goldsney, the choirmaster, would not let me 'perform' 'Oh, for the Wings of a Dove' until I could sing all of it with a lit candle six inches from my mouth and never extinguish it!

Once during a rendering of 'Bless this House' whilst the wedding register was being signed, I deviated from my normal procedure. I always sang to the stained-glass window at the west end of the church but, on this occasion, I glanced at the congregation and looked directly at my mother and Nanna. The surprise was such a shock that I stopped singing, blushed, then sat down. I can still see Mr Goldsney's face looking down from the organ loft. I still got paid though!

Needless to say, nature took its course and my voice started to falter and by 1951-52 I gave up the choir. By this time I had already joined the Air Training Corps (ATC) but I had had a wonderful time with the choir and, although I have slowly lost the strength in my faith, I always find myself uplifted by much of church music, especially anthems. For many years afterwards, I knew many hymns and psalms by heart, as I had done as a boy.

I remember with great fondness my time at St Andrew's School and St Michael's Church. They were opposite each other and about fifteen minutes by bike from home.

There were three elderly ladies always in the front row for Sunday Matins and they smiled sweetly to us all and, as time went by and I rose through the ranks to Head Choirboy, they seemed to give me more and more attention. It was disconcerting but warming.

You could tell from far and wide if the Reverend Bates let me have a go at the bell as I managed to miss the occasional 'ding' or 'dong' during the five-minute session.

The choir was always well attended with at least six to eight boys each side, Decani, on the right as you look at the altar, and Cantori. Many men also attended and it was normal, for a couple of years, for my father and Barry to be in the choir as well. During the Christmas period the choir would sing in the town of Leigh-on-Sea for donations to the church and local charities. We always had a visit to the Corona and Coliseum cinemas to the accompaniment of the Wurlitzer organs which all cinemas seemed to have in those days. It was bit daunting to sing my regular solos in front of such large audiences.

When Mr Goldsney thought I was ready he had me sing 'Ave Maria' from the organ loft. He played softly and the congregation heard me but could not see me. Apparently, it was very moving.

Weddings were great occasions, if only for the money and my extra payment for a solo, but funerals were hard at first because of our age. You got used to being so close to the recently departed except when one of our choirboys died. Richard Thorogood was only nine or ten, so that was a difficult service.

When my voice was at its best I was keen to join Chelmsford Cathedral and was advised that I would be accepted. However, it was too far for regular attendance but I did get to sing solo there.

Also, had I been a member, albeit occasionally, it would have ruined my Dad's golf game. He was a member of the magnificent Warren Golf Club near Woodham Walter, south of Chelmsford and Malden. In those days it was very much a private members' club run by the Durham family, which continues to this day. You could only play as a member or a guest. Now, the course is just as good but things are a little easier.

I went along as my Dad's caddy occasionally and in the afternoons, after lunch, he would teach me. What a fool I am, because I could play well, one afternoon to handicap 14, but I stopped when I joined the Air Cadets and never recovered. My best since then has been 18, having started again at age thirty-one.

My Dad and his golfing buddy and best friend, Freddie Good, won quite a few competitions. The Warren was very friendly and actively social. As was the way in those days drinking was quite relaxed and it was not uncommon for people to drive home after a few games of snooker and a few beers. On one or two occasions Freddie, who was the Chief Constable of Southend, would decide that they had had too much to drink and call for a police car. They would have another beer or Scotch until the car arrived, then my Dad would be delivered home. In the morning a police car would arrive with Freddie in it as a passenger and they would go back to the Warren to collect their cars!

Dad got to know a lot of the policemen and one day whilst driving one of his Austin A60 vans (this was after he had acquired his own shop) to renew its tax in town he was stopped by one of the police who knew him. I should point out that in those days you could not renew tax or driving licences by post; it was an annual one or two visits to the appropriate offices.

Anyway, the constable said:

'Oh, hallo Mister Burdett, did you realise you were speeding?'

'No, officer.'

'May I see your licence, please?'

'Here you are, I was just going into town to renew it.'

'It's out of date!'

'That's why I was going into town.'

The constable walked round and said, 'Your tax is out of date and where is your C licence?'

'Oh, thank you, officer, I'll do that at the same time. Oh, here you are: the C licence has fallen off the windscreen and on to the floor.'

'Mister Burdett, this is out-of-date also. I suggest you get out of here before I get cross with you!'

It was obviously well known that Dad and Freddie Good were friends. It's the old story – it's who you know, not what you know.

In early 1948 I went to the Southend Town Hall to sit my 11-plus. Dad and I were early, so we joined the anxious and pacing fathers and offspring outside smoking and revising respectively. In the end I felt well-prepared and passed.

Westcliff High School

September 1948, I arrived with 100-plus other boys at Westcliff High School for Boys but with a Leigh-on-Sea address!

Although it was titled a high school, it was actually a grammar, as was Southend High. I was assigned to the A stream but ended up for the next two years in B as I was poor at Chemistry and Physics. I was put into the Arts stream in my third year, so my plans to be a doctor fell by the wayside.

In those days, to be a doctor, you had to pass GCE in Latin, which turned out to be my favourite and best subject. Because of my earlier singing success I now thought that to be a professional singer would be wonderful but it was becoming obvious I was never going to have a voice at all so that idea was ditched.

During the first rugby season I was not allowed to play because of my leg. I was still having regular checks from my surgeon who was happy with the progress. Anyway, after watching a few games in the 1949-50 season, I had had enough and begged to play rugby and, eventually, the surgeon agreed reluctantly. I was somewhat delighted, but my parents were less so. Incredibly, although my leg was hurt more easily than most boys, I finished school with only normal bruises. I was fast and good at tackling and spent most of the time at full-back or wing. I eventually was a regular with the second XV and by the fifth/sixth form was an occasional first XV player.

I loved cricket but was not much of a bowler or batsman so again a regular second XI player but never in the first XI. I wanted to keep wicket but was never given the chance. My main sporting problem was not that I was bad, but that I was a member of one of our school's best ever sporting intakes in our history; the London and Home Counties rugby team had eight of my year playing for them!

Where I did do well was in athletics being a good 440 yards (400m) and half-mile (800m) runner and, as I grew taller, a 440-yards hurdler. The school sports' field was tiered which meant a good view for the crowd as one came round the final bend and into the straight for the tape.

Westcliff High was a highly regarded grammar school in my time and for some while afterwards. I was later advised that we were third only to Manchester Royal Grammar and Bedford amongst grammar schools in the opinion of the recruiting officers of the armed forces.

Our headmaster, Mr Henry Cloke, was a formidable and great man. He would walk around in his cloak, 6-foot 2-inches tall, reduced by a slight stoop, and predatory walk as he traversed the quadrangles. His appearance was much like Lee Marvin but he made Lee look a bit of a pussycat.

Nevertheless, he was held in great respect. On one occasion I was taken to him by Gage, the least-liked prefect because he was a bully, as I had been waving my hands around whilst talking to my friend in the form assembly line. He had assumed I was making rude gestures at him. Despite my protestations, Mr Cloke told me to choose a cane from his large collection in the umbrella stand. It was difficult to choose as he had so many sizes but I was soon hurried along by the exhortation, 'Get a move on, Burdett, I haven't all day!'

After second year decisions were made by the school as to whether pupils were more suited to Science or Arts (Humanities, it's called nowadays, I believe). My chemistry was awful, so I ended up in Arts. I had already realised that to be a doctor was not my destiny.

By this time, I was cycling to school or walking more or less in a straight line through fields which took about twenty minutes, allowing for deviations to check the pond for newts or scrump an apple or two for break. The break meant milk; in good weather the milk bottles were delivered to the area under the head's balcony or, in bad weather, to some corridors. The allowance was a half pint each. Also, by this time I had made new friends. Malcolm had joined Westcliff one year ahead of me and we had drifted apart.

For the last three or four years we had enjoyed the open fields and trees opposite Pickett's Avenue but, eventually, development reared its ugly head and from living on the edge of town we slowly entered it. The development became Stonehill Road down to Broomfield Avenue and much to the east. A familiar sight in the earlier days was loads of young boys' and girls' heads bobbing amongst the trees and bushes heading for home at 1830 to 1845 to arrive in time for 'Dick Barton, Special Agent'. Parents knew their kids would be home. There was one field for cows in this area and when the occasional bull was in there we would jump over the gate and annoy him. When he ran at us we would dive back over the gate; on reflection, I cannot believe we were that stupid!

Fortunately, as the natural playground disappeared so opportunities grew for other adventures such as climbing scaffolding, using piles of earth to dig into forts and making lethal mud-balls to defend them.

School started to become more important and time consuming. I also had three jobs: choir, paper-round and grocery delivery-boy on Thursday and Friday evenings and Saturday mornings. This gave me a good income for my age. My father regularly gave me the shop's takings, put them in a canvas bag and I would take them to Barclays in the High Street, Leigh-on-Sea. He reckoned it was safer than him doing it but, as I recall, crime was pretty low in our area.

When we were young children my mother used to take us in the bus down First Avenue to the Crowstone at Chalkwell beach. The Crowstone was the marker for where the River Thames became the Thames Estuary. The beach was okay but the real pleasure came with the tide out. One could walk about half a mile out on the mud to a 'river' under the Thames which we knew as the Ray. It had gently sloping sides which made great slides by running and diving flat and slipping into the water – after a few times it became quite fast. Of course, one found a few mussels at the expense of a few cuts! On other occasions it was fun to collect mussels for the pot *but* always get back to the beach before the tide really turned or you could be cut off! Throughout my later school years I regularly used my lunch-hour to go to the beach – tide in, swim, or tide out, mud.

The Arts side at school had no Chemistry, Physics or Biology but Latin, French, Spanish, History and Geography. Both Arts and Science had Maths, English, English Literature and a choice of Music, Woodwork or Metalwork. I chose music but was very poor at the history part of it. As with all schools some masters make more of an impression than others. Mr Cloke, the head, stood in for Latin and taught Greek to those who wanted it.

Mr Harry Harden taught me Latin. His technique was to present you with the day's subject already written on the boards and you had to copy it faithfully. It was a fantastic idea because you ended up writing your own Latin primer. He was deputy head and a great disciplinarian. Tragically he committed suicide after his wife died from a long illness. 'Pip' Thomas, my form master and Maths teacher, was a gentle and kind man, but the subject never caught my interest early on but extra instruction by Mr Limbergh helped get me up to speed.

Mr Limbergh was a physics teacher who had been a prisoner of war on the railways with the Japanese. He and my father were quite friendly, which is how I found out that he had dozens of burns on his body caused by his guards stubbing out cigarettes on him.

Mr Claude Webber was a chemistry teacher and, although he had never played rugby, was the rugby master. He was good as the results showed. He had the irritating habit of shouting 'get up and run, laddie' even if you had two or three guys lying on top of you. Eventually, when the first XV scored they (we) would chant 'Pilae erga, mustulae vultum', which meant 'Balls to weasel-face'. Naturally in our naiveté I think we thought he did not follow it. He seemed amused anyway.

Mr Midgley was a very serious man who still lived with 'Mother' and took to wearing 'Empire-Building' shorts in warm weather. His only humorous act was, during our lesson on 'A Midsummer Night's Dream', to write players' parts on the board, which included Bot(tom) and Tit(ania) and then look round with a silly grin on his face.

Mr 'Moke' Morris taught Geography very well. He was known as Moke as he had been in charge of mules during the Great War. Every lesson he would give us an exercise and disappear behind the blackboard for a smoke out of sight of the peep-hole window which all the classrooms had. He was the man who arranged all school trips to theatres and circuses. We would go in coaches to London and always stop for the lavatories at the Gants Hill roundabout; he was getting on a bit. This was the junction of the Circular Road and the Southend Arterial Road which was a four-lane dual carriageway from Southend. Nobody in Southend could understand the incredible fuss made of the eight-and-a-quarter-mile stretch of four-lane round Preston, donkey's years later.

Mr Ivan (H.I.) Brown taught History. Much to my father's disappointment, it was not my subject. It did not help that H.I. lived 100 yards down Pickett's Avenue and we were always seeing each other. He was a stern and forbidding man in class but really kind away from school. Although he refused to let me take History in the GCE, he stayed our good neighbour.

In fact, he used to lend me his motor-bike, even though I had no licence, which I think was one of the first ever built, and that gave me the chance to visit my girlfriend Coral in an impressive way. I thought so anyway!

Mr Jones taught Art. I said earlier that I chose Music, but that was not strictly true as I started with Art. Mr Jones was an ex-boxer with many muscles he hadn't used recently; his face suggested a painful experience but he was kind and gentle. My art did not please him – not enough to cause a fight, but enough to suggest I move on. Woodwork was next but my tenon joints did not meet with approval. Oh dear, Metalwork or Music. I was fascinated by the Merlin engine outside the metalwork room but Music won.

Mr Davies taught Spanish – or not, as it turned out. In a class of twenty-five to thirty, only six passed the GCE. He had a poor delivery and no control over the boys who took advantage of his weakness. He was too kind and gentle to be in the classroom. However, he always redeemed himself as the very successful drama director for plays and concerts. In fact, I had a part in his 'A Midsummer Night's Dream' one year. Bot and Tit indeed!

French. I cannot remember who on earth taught me French. I think that is because I had at least three teachers. One was a stern French lady whose English was accented somewhat like in a Peter Sellers film and 'Jumbo Cowan' who left no impression except on cushions. His son was a less than popular prefect whom I met later in fun circumstances. More later.

Physical Training: Mr Brownley I think. He was always, winter or summer, in white vest and trousers. Every form had a basketball team and there were three groups as for every physical activity at school: junior, intermediate and senior. Every day there would be two or three matches for which you paid 1d entrance. Spectators hung from the wall bars or sat on top and also sat on the sills of the high windows of the large gym. There was massive noise in support of the teams playing proper basketball, i.e. as a contact sport.

Sport at school was taken seriously by staff and pupils alike, thank goodness.

My rugby was not bad but I was never a solidly placed first XV member although I managed probably 60 per cent of the games when old enough. I only ever received second XV colours. Cricket was fun but I achieved very little and received no colours. Cross-country was definitely good for me. Our route was always for real, i.e. fields, mud and ditches!

In good weather we were sent outside and allowed to use most of the school sports equipment. This was good but Health and Safety did not have its stranglehold on innocent pleasure in those days and athletics-cum-field events practice had its moments. Discus and javelins, although restricted to specific areas, could stray from the desired path. One day I was lying on a wooden platform doing some swotting for GCE and there was an urgent cry of 'Burdett, look out'. I looked up in time to see a javelin en route to yours truly and rolled away as it embedded itself in the spot where I had been lying. An apology, followed by amusement, sufficed and we all continued as if nothing had happened. Nowadays, the snivelling of people with 'rights' would be deafening!

Apart from a reasonable level of success at athletics, my favourite moment came in my last summer at school, 1953. During the war a former pupil named Brown had been killed and, in commemoration, his parents funded an annual sports event, separate from the normal School Sports Day. This followed the programme of all sports days. However, the winning house stayed on for a feast in the school hall followed by entertainment.

I was house captain for this event and one of the rules was that everyone had to take part. It was quite a juggle to get it right. Eventually, the finale came which was the 440-yards relay race. Our house, North, yes boring names, North, South, East and West – Gold, Red, Blue and Green respectively, were only a few points short of winning the Brown Cup. Our first off the blocks was Michael Cocks whose athletic prowess took a long second place to his high academic standards but he gave his all. He handed his baton the last and our second and third runners tried but I received it about sixty yards behind Shallot of South. Well, luckily, this was my sport and I was faster. To the acclaim of the cheering North house mob on the terrace overlooking the home straight I won by a whisker and, probably, for the only time in my young life I was hero for a day. H.I. Brown was our housemaster and, later, at the end of term I was awarded our annual Honours award for my contribution over the years.

No. 1312 Squadron Air Training Corps (Southend)

As my voice was less able to do justice to the music I began thinking of the Air Training Corps. By this time my interest in aviation was developing. I had seen the first flight of the Comet on Pathé News during the family's weekly cinema visit and had immediately commented that, surely, square windows were not a good idea. My father confidently pointed out the reasonable explanation that the experts knew what they were doing. Obviously, I had no special background of metallurgy and stress but I remained sceptical right up to the structural failure in January 1954 and the next, three months later; the reason for the crashes was, of course, not immediately known.

Also, the Hunter was in the skies and Neville Duke became my hero. The National Air Race was held at Southend Airport in early 1950 and I wandered from ATC onto the airfield – no need for heavy security in those days. Neville Duke was working on his Hawker Tomtit, I think it was, and kindly chatted with me. Of course, he was even more famous now as he was the Hawker Hunter test pilot whose exploits were regularly documented and filmed. He encouraged me to continue my plans to become a Royal Air Force pilot and I departed with his autograph and a positive desire to follow in a few of his footsteps. Soon afterwards was my first flight. An Anson, a twin-engined communications and navigator training aircraft, arrived at Southend and we were put into groups of six to await our fifteen-minute flight. As a corporal it was my job to decide who sat in the other pilot's seat, so I folded six small pieces of paper, one of which had a cross printed on it, placed them in my beret and we all drew lots. I got the pilot's seat as I drew last having kept the cross under my finger and inaccessible to the other cadets! I still have a slight twinge of guilt but not enough to lose sleep.

The flight was fantastic! We flew over my house, it was on the extended centreline of the then grass runway, out over the Thames and back via the Southend Pier, all one-and-a-quarter miles of it.

Behind the ATC HQ were dozens of old broken and discarded Halifaxes and, I think, Lancasters, which we raided occasionally for memorabilia, including altimeters, air-speed indicators and suchlike. The remains had been discarded by Freddie Laker who had originally purchased whole bombers at the end of the war and converted them to freighters. In 1947 he had formed Aviation Traders, based at Southend Airport, to do these conversions. Bond Air Services used the aircraft during the 1948-9 Berlin Airlift and Laker serviced them.

Later, and during my time at 1312, he designed and independently built a light, twin-engined transport named the Accountant which he hoped would be adopted by the Royal Air Force for tactical transport purposes. In the event, the government did not want it but, most interestingly, they eventually funded the Avro 748 Andover which appeared very like the Accountant but a little larger.

ATC was not just an introduction to the service, but, even for those not interested in a military career, a great way to develop character and discipline. No. 1312 had a good record for drill and, at the annual meet at Chigwell for squadrons in Essex and, I think, Eastern London, we always performed well. We were well known for our continuity drill, whereby we carried out a full range of marching, rifle drill and various tricky manoeuvres without any commands. There were also competitions in aircraft recognition, engines and more, to name a few. I actually reached sixteen words a minute in Morse which was not bad; the professionals normally can handle twenty-four words a minute. Eventually, I was promoted to sergeant and appointed as drill instructor.

At some time during the winter of 1952-53 I received a reply for my request to be considered as a Royal Air Force pilot. I was to report to the RAF Station Hornchurch on a Sunday afternoon for the four-day selection tests. In my possession I had a letter from Mr Cloke assuring the selectors that he was confident I would attain the requisite passes in my upcoming GCE exams.

The only times I had slept away from home were with relatives, so to find myself in a barrack block with dozens of grown-ups (i.e. eighteen to twenty-two years old) was a little unnerving. Their conversation and behaviour was a bit alien to me but I was accepted.

Day 1 was form filling and interviews. Various officers asked about background, school, sport, motivation, etc.

Day 2 was written tests and co-ordination exercises and reaction tests. We were also put into groups and took it in turn to be leader of an initiative and application test, which usually comprised of rope, logs, planks, barrels, etc. and you had to get from A to B using just these items; they were, of course, too short or inadequate in some way but you had to solve the puzzle.

Day 3 was the medical where every square inch, in and out it seemed, was checked. We went to all the departments in groups of four and stayed together except for the more intimate bits. As the youngest I ended up last at each of the examinations which helped me tremendously on one occasion: when we were in a small room just having our overall bodily reflexes checked, I was intrigued that the last item was to sit sideways on a long seat and, with the handle of that funny rubber hammer the doctors used, the leg lengths appeared to be checked. Well, as I knew my right leg was shorter than the left, when it was my turn I relaxed my left leg and extended my right. I was okay and off we went to the next check with my being very pleased with myself. Sixty years later my doctor friend advised me that it was just another type of reflex test to which I had been subjected. Oh well, I had at least sixty years being pleased with myself.

The oldest guy in our group, twenty-five maybe, came out and said, 'The doctor lifted my penis with his pencil and said "that's been in a few nests hasn't it?" and I said, "Yes, but it's the first time it's been on a perch!"'

Day 4 was more interviews and then the results. All those who had passed most of the tests and medical were offered various positions in the Royal Air Force, not necessarily as pilots. We were all in a large area watching each other going in and coming out with happy, moderate or glum faces. My turn came and, with much trepidation, I went into the lion's den to face the three officers. I was amazed and delighted to be advised that I was accepted at all flight crew positions and, that when I was old enough (seventeen and a half or later), I was to contact the RAF with the form they gave me and I would be called when they needed me.

I was particularly proud as I was one of only five to be offered pilot out of the 106 who had applied. Further, they recommended me to apply to the Royal Air Force College, Cranwell. This I duly did and went for their four-day interviews and assessment during the Easter holidays of 1953. The tests etc. were a tougher version of Hornchurch, especially the leadership ones. Although I had a wretched cold throughout the period I cannot blame that for the fact that I was not accepted.

Shortly after Hornchurch I was advised that I had been awarded an ATC Flying Scholarship which would give me thirty hours to qualify for a Private Pilot's Licence (PPL).

Spring and Summer 1953 meant GCE exams but during this period I received a letter from the appropriate department, and including a rail warrant, to report to RAF Station Kenley, to collect my flying kit needed for my flying scholarship training. The date was the same as that for my English Literature exam but, by this time, I was desperate to get going on my chosen career so, without telling my parents or school, I simply set off from the house to Leigh-on-Sea station.

Mr Cloke was not impressed and expected my father to pay the fee that the school normally paid for each exam. My father got his outgoings from me. Thank goodness they were both understanding and, I think, slightly amused. I know I would have passed the subject but I was not offered a re-sit.

I ended up with all the required passes and took time off from school, as you do after exams. I spent time at Southend Airport cadging flights with anyone who would take me and even got a bit of handling. One of the most interesting pilots was 'Laddie' Marmol, a Polish ex-RAF pilot. He had a little twin-engined 'box-car' as it was named. It had a box-like body and a single boom holding the tail-plane. He did small freight work and was to be seen regularly flying up and down the coast at 200 feet trailing advertising banners. His party trick was to get airborne and at 1,000 feet close both engines and carry out a landing such that he could roll to a stop where he had previously parked! He was amazingly accurate.

Holidays

In the summer of 1949 we set off with Peggy Renwick, our eighteen-year-old neighbour, for a camping holiday in France. Peggy was our excellent interpreter. We landed in Ostend where there seemed to be guns everywhere; Barry kept his head below the parapet. The effects of war were everywhere; rutted and potholed roads, ruined buildings, thin people in ragged clothes and little in the shops. It was like this all the way to Paris.

Dad had not been sure how the money would work out, so any free space in the car was packed with Player's cigarettes. This turned out to be a brilliant move as a good cigarette, or packet, greased our way many, many times.

Our first night in France was spent in a guesthouse untouched by the war. The people were amazed to see 'tourists' as they were very rare but made us very welcome. To our foreign eyes, the breakfast was strange but we had no trouble in enjoying it thoroughly; croissants, home-made jam and butter, the best I have ever tasted. Coffee to our surprise was in large bowl-like cups. We had been given a great introduction to a new country.

From then on we camped using two tents, ladies and gents. We kids had a wonderful time but I'm sure my mother would not agree. En route we stopped for fuel where there was a bridge from which a chap was fishing. Dad asked what fish could be caught and was advised to have a look. We went to look and found it to be a railway bridge! He was given a cigarette; it appears he was the 'village idiot'.

Just short of Paris a part of the suspension on the Vauxhall failed but we staggered into the main General Motors garage where, to Dad's astonishment, the manager was a chap he had served with in the Army. More importantly for the girls a Yank tank drew up behind and Errol Flynn stepped out. He spoke to us all and my mother was delighted.

At my Dad's Army friend's suggestion we found a cheap but clean pension in Pigalle. I asked Dad what the bidet was for and he said it was for washing feet! We did as many tourist things as possible and had a wonderful time. Unfortunately, the extended time due to the car repair meant we could only afford to camp our way back to the ferry, but this turned out to be more fun for Greta, Barry and me than the outward leg.

We camped on a hill next to the beach a bit south of Boulogne and we were amongst ruined fortifications from the war. We kids went down ladders, along tunnels and, everywhere, there were broken or rotted guns, ammunition, helmets and many military artefacts. It was paradise until Dad realised what was going on. Anyway, by this time I had a great collection and I was allowed to keep some, including ammunition.

The area was not a camping site officially, just open land. The couple near us got chatting and it turned out his father was the Maire de Boulogne and there was to be a fair that weekend. He invited us to meet his father with whom we enjoyed wine and cakes. Then, he gave we three a booklet of free tickets which lasted forever, it seemed. We rode on everything more than once, I'm sure.

Then it had to be homeward bound, nearly broke and ciggieless. At the customs we were thoroughly put through the wringer. However, apart from my sister saying, 'Don't forget the nylons Daddy' and then being charged duty, it went well enough. What a holiday; few Britons had done this, I think; certainly we hardly saw any.

Other summer holidays were spent as normal, i.e. Somerset, Devon and/ or Cornwall. In the earlier days we had camped all over the place but for the previous two years and this one we set off for 'The Marinero', a cottage in Church Cove near the Lizard, Cornwall. It was at the end of the narrow road which had no traffic and, surprisingly, very few tourists or ramblers. This meant that the pebbled cove beach, about forty metres wide, was ours. We were always quite put out if anyone turned up to use 'our' beach. We used to go out with Vivian Bosustow fishing for pollack and mackerel; amazingly, he was unable to swim and never took a lifejacket with him!

One day my father, Vivian and I went out to meet a small French fishing vessel about 500 yards off shore. We climbed aboard to be confronted by five fierce and rough-looking men who then conversed in a very strange language with Vivian. It seems that the Bretons and Cornish share an ancient language which was a mix of old French, old English and Celtic. Anyway, after Vivian handed over a load of lobsters he received a crate of brandy and we went back. Dad was delighted with his bottle. Actually, the brandy was probably Calvados, the apple brandy of Brittany.

We always set off on our holidays on Friday night and, on at least one trip, Dad turned up with a newly-purchased car; he did quite a bit of private trading. That time turned out badly as the roof leaked, it rained heavily and my poor mother spent a lot of the journey keeping us dry.

In those days, late 1940s and early 1950s, unless you could afford the best, the cars lacked acceleration and a decent top speed. The journey from Leigh to the Lizard took around thirteen to fifteen hours, even though it was overnight and even though Dad always got in a tizz whether to go A30 Staines or A303 Ilminster. Whichever he chose would turn out to be considered wrong!

The problem then was that there were no by-passes, dual-carriageways or motorways and, in any event, overtaking was quite tricky because of the poor acceleration. Furthermore, on arrival at any town or village, from dawn onwards, the high street, through which we had to pass, had parking both sides and two-way traffic. Imagine Ilminster, Honiton, Chard, etc. with no by-pass, traffic lights or controlled parking!

The A303 was favoured by the kids as one of our breaks was at Stonehenge and, as it was simply unfenced, we parked on the main road and just walked over to it. The only way to see it nowadays is to be willingly ripped off and look at it from a distance.

On the way back, it was always the A303 because, having left the previous night, we would arrive there at dawn or thereabouts. Just past Stonehenge by about 500 yards, going up the hill, was a terrific transport café and for 12s/6d (62½ pence) we had a full English breakfast for the five of us and unlimited tea and toast.

After our holiday that last year I went off to RAF Hawkinge on the hills above Folkestone to do a gliding course with other air cadets. The gliders were somewhat old-fashioned and nowhere near as graceful as the modern ones. They were named Slingsby Tutors but I don't know who made them or designed them. The means of getting airborne was to connect a cable to a release catch in the nose, the cable was then rapidly wound back onto its drum some 400 yards away and the glider got airborne. There was a critical point at which you released the cable or you would just get pulled down again. Once released we flew ahead a little, turned left downwind to parallel the runway then left again to line up and land. That was all we did and, although the cliffs provided some upward flow of air, we were shown nothing else as these craft were somewhat heavy and ungainly.

I gained my licence signed by Lord Brabazon of Tara, holder of the No. 1 flying licence. I had been to the Farnborough display on two or three occasions with my father but this time I was to go on my own. Yippee! However, I missed the bus to the Southend Bus Station and finally arrived five minutes after it had left for Farnborough. The fare was approximately £1.10s. (£1.50) for the journey, plus entry. There was no other bus that day, 17 August 1952.

There was a small hill at the airfield on which my Dad and I would stand; missing the bus probably saved my life. John Derry was demonstrating the DH110, later known as the Sea Vixen, when it broke up in flight. Its two engines smashed into the hill killing twenty-eight people and injuring many more.

Typical of the time, the show was continued the next day and I was able to get there. When my hero, Neville Duke, flew by in the Hunter it made my day.

Flying Scholarship – Southend

After the school holidays I was champing at the bit to start my Flying Scholarship but they could not fit me in until 18 November 1953. Until then I settled in to being a prefect and starting my A levels, English, French and Geography. I enjoyed the privilege and responsibility of being a prefect and decided that, although it was a normal and acceptable practice, I would not be administering corporal punishment. At that time prefects could use a slipper on the backside but not a cane. Whereas the staff using a cane were usually restrained, I'm afraid prefects could be quite unpleasant. My own experiences confirmed that.

When the weather was inclement we had what was known as an 'in-day'. This meant that boys remained in their classrooms except for lunch, basketball matches or other under-cover activities. To ensure adherence to this, and to control discipline, each class was allocated a prefect. This seems a good idea but, somehow, I ended in charge of my brother's class. Boy, did they give me a hard time and Barry was, as often as not, the ringleader. Minor punishment was to make the offender stand in the quadrangle outside the classroom which, although covered over the walkways, was open to the elements. Barry spent a lot of time outside.

At last! I had my first flight on 18 November 1953 in a Tiger Moth with my instructor, Dougie Proctor. He was a dapper moustachioed ex-Royal Air Force wartime pilot who put me at my ease. I already had my student pilot's licence, No. 41115, with my medical certificate included. Training followed the standard pattern, viz. briefing which included teaching as well as explaining the structure of the flight lesson, then the flight and then the debriefing.

The Tiger Moth is a biplane with the student sitting ahead of the instructor. I was wearing my sheepskin coat and wool-lined boots, a pair of gauntlets and a helmet. Forget your modern intercom and radios; each pilot had a mouthpiece in front of him with a tube running to the other's headset, it was forked to enable a tube to go to each ear. To talk to each other you shouted into the tube leading into the other pilot's ears and hoped he could hear you! It was called the Gosport Tube.

Since a lot of the words were new it was easy to misunderstand at first. This misunderstanding led me to believe that I was to 'follow him through', i.e. rest my hands lightly on the controls, whilst I felt what the instructor was trying to show. In the event, I was congratulated on a good landing when, in fact, I had merely been resting my hands whilst he made corrections. He had actually said I was to try a landing this time and he would follow me through! Oh well, I eventually got the hang of it and was sent solo after only five hours and fifty minutes' instruction.

Up to solo was just basic handling such as straight and level flight, climbing, descending, stalling and spinning (necessary in case of sudden loss of control), turning, take-offs and the main things at this stage, circuits of the airfield and landings. Naturally, engine failures were practised in case, heaven forbid, the engine failed on your first solo.

After that the circuit work was much consolidated, especially solo, with more stalling and spinning. Then came navigation which was mostly inland as our lovely coastline, plus the pier, made it too easy otherwise. By this stage I had a new instructor, Mr Quinn, and even had a lesson from Mr Bernard Collins, the airport manager. When my navigation was deemed adequate I was sent off alone and it was quite an adventure.

Mr Quinn, having checked the weather and forecast, briefed me thoroughly on the route, reminded me of aspects of navigation to be extra aware of and rules of arriving at strange airfields when you had no radios. There were two Tiger Moths at the school, G-AMSY and G-ANGD, and I was allocated GD. The route was Southend to Lydd on the Dungeness Point via overflight of Sittingbourne and Ashford as this was easier to navigate than going direct. Then Lydd to Shoreham, east of Worthing, which was dead easy as the coast was always in view, then Shoreham to Southend, overflying Royal Tunbridge Wells and Rochester.

My navigation was fine but upon arrival at Lydd I was dying for a pee so, as soon as I landed, having avoided regular traffic of Carvairs etc., I stopped at a derelict building in the middle of the airfield, put my helmet and gloves in front of the wheels and did what I had to do. However, having hopped back in and taxied to the check-in office I was given a rollicking for leaving the engine unattended. Well, I could hardly stop it, as there was no starter system other than having someone turn the propeller.

When this was amicably sorted out – I was, after all, only seventeen years old, which was far less mature than nowadays – I refuelled and set off for Shoreham. I joined the circuit in the non-radio regulation way and received the green light for landing. The downwind section seemed very quick and when I finally lined up with the section of grass shown to be the landing strip it took ages to get there. As I tried to land, the aircraft did not respond and just stayed airborne – I was at the correct speed of 28 mph.

Because of my lack of experience, and not working out what might be the problem, I increased power, climbed away and tried to work out what I should do. I noticed a vehicle had arrived at the landing point and a few men getting out. One was waving a flag and gesturing for me to land there. So, I continued to make another approach; again, as I tried to land the aircraft it would not stay down. However, on this occasion I had help! Men appeared at each wing tip and another grabbed the tail whilst the man who had been waving to me came alongside and said keep the power up and we'll go to the hangar. So, there I was, flying on the ground with wings held down, tail up and the marshaller alongside. As soon as we entered the hangar he ordered 'Power Off!'

When the aircraft was shut down and I was out of it, I was advised that the problem was caused by the wind being the same speed as my stalling speed, or just over, so the aircraft could not avoid flying even though my speed over the ground was zero. No wonder I couldn't land it. Of course, it's all obvious now but I was not sufficiently experienced to realise what the problem was.

I met the Chief Instructor, Mr Pashley, who advised me that I might be about to be grounded because of the weather. However, sometime later the wind dropped and he was happy to let me go back to Southend, having checked the weather there. I found out later that Mr Pashley was famous in the aviation world, having done just about everything and had a trunk full of logbooks to prove it.

Home safe and sound by dusk.

Three days later I took my final test and passed. I was a qualified private pilot!

During the course of the training which stretched over four months, due to weather, aircraft and instructor availability and the fact that I was low on the totem pole, there was a lot of time on my hands when I was at the airfield. I found myself helping to clean aircraft and generally helping in the hangar and environs. I should, of course, have been at school but skived off an awful lot. One task I loved, and which would be unbelievably unacceptable nowadays, was to drive the refuelling vehicle. I say vehicle because I don't know another word for a 1,500-gallon cylindrical tank with two wheels at the front and a steering-wheel and seat over a single wheel at the back.

Anyway, I used to drive this around the airfield and refuel light aircraft. I had only just obtained my car driving licence and had no official training in fuel management or safety procedures. The mind boggleth now, but it was all so laid back and relaxed.

During my training I had frequently been a passenger in the Auster aircraft but had not actually flown it. After I gained my licence I took my parents and family for a trip in the Tiger Moth but one rainy day a new instructor said, 'Why not take the Auster – have you flown it?' Well, in all innocence I said I had, so he said to take it. After that I flew it a couple more times and when I asked for it later Mr Quinn asked when I had done a check ride. I said, 'Never', and he went ballistic – not so much with me as the poor new instructor. I got checked out and was cleared to fly it in future.

I think it was £5 per hour to rent a Tiger Moth or Auster, so my flights were few and far between until I joined the Royal Air Force.

Because of my frequent sneaking off school to go to the airport, even if there was no flying, I got behind with my A-level studies but nobody seemed to mind. I suspect that they knew, as I did, that as soon as I could I would be off. I enjoyed a good rugby season which included mostly first XV appearances, but being only awarded second XV colours, though. Otherwise life was on hold as I approached the grand old age of seventeen and a half, the magic minimum age to join the RAF. As the time approached I was exhorted by my parents to get my A-levels as this would 'stand me in good stead', so I respectfully delayed my decision.

The Start of My Career

I contacted the address given to me back at RAF Hornchurch all that while ago and received a railway warrant for Leigh-on-Sea to RAF Cardington in Bedfordshire to arrive at noon on 10 May 1954; transport would await my arrival. Well, my parents were dismayed but understanding and, on Sunday 9 May, we packed what little I was permitted to carry, shed a few tears with my mother and listened to some fatherly advice. Dad had set me up with a bank account at Barclays in Leigh-on-Sea and the manager, Len Barnes, who was a friend, added a fiver.

On the morning of the 10th Dad drove us to the station and I said my farewells. I was just seventeen years and eight months old, and very nervous and excited at the same time; I had only been away from home a total of twenty-four days in my whole life.

So, Leigh-on-Sea, Fenchurch Street, and on to Bedford where transport was waiting as promised. It was not just for me but about thirty of us, all the same entry date. On arrival at RAF Cardington we were shown to a barrack block and allocated, or chose, bed spaces in the long dormitory. Nobody seemed to know anybody else so things were a little strained at first, especially for a few others and I who had not been to public school or boarded. The ex-boarders were comfortable immediately.

Nothing was expected of us that first day, Monday, and we became comfortable with each other and after supper one or two of the older ones managed a beer or two in the NAAFI (Navy, Army, and Air Force Institutes, which ran bars, shops and mobile refreshment facilities on all military bases).

Next day, life changed! Firstly, we all had haircuts whether we needed one or not and there was no choice as to style, short back and sides. Then off to the uniform store for the basics at this stage. Shoes, socks, underwear (called 'shreddies' as their pattern was like the well-known cereal), three shirts plus six collars, one pair trousers and one battledress top (i.e. fitted just to the hips) and a cap. As we were to be officer cadets our jackets had a white rectangular patch on each lapel and our caps a white band. We also had a beret.

From then on, we were to wear uniform at all times. I had never used collar-studs so I found it quite awkward to sort out collar and tie and not keep having the collar disconnect. I was helped by one of the cadets, Bo Plummer, who not only gave me his spare studs but put things together initially.

Then we were all assembled to take the Oath of Allegiance to the Queen. Prior to the oath-taking ceremony there was a comprehensive briefing to make sure we all understood the depth and permanency of the commitment we would be undertaking. For those of us who had been thinking more of the flying than the deeper responsibilities it was a sombre moment.

After the Oath came the paperwork. We were now Royal Air Force Officer Cadets and had to fill out many forms and, firstly, next of kin information, plus others to be contacted, and to write a will. Then we were offered the opportunity to open bank accounts; initials A-M were to join Coutts Bank and N-Z another bank, but I have forgotten which. I declined as I already had an account. However, I should have gone to Coutts as my family was distantly (very!) related to the Burdett-Coutts and it would have felt the right thing to do.

On the Thursday we were placed in the hands of two corporals and headed off to Royal Air Force Kirton-in-Lindsey, north-east of Gainsborough in Lincolnshire, the Royal Air Force General Duties Officer Training Unit. General Duties meant all those who were flying-crew members. Other officers were trained in Jurby, Isle of Man. Again, we were shown into our barrack block where we each had a bed, a wardrobe and a small bedside locker. We received our initial lesson in exactly how the beds were to be made for each daily inspection; sheets and blanket folded to the exact size and wrapped around with the last blanket to the exact size and shape. The pillow was to be on top. Our rifles, yet to be issued, were to be spotless and placed in the appropriate housing at the end of the bed and secured by padlock.

The wardrobe was to contain only military apparel and the side locker was to contain kit and other necessary military accoutrements, placed exactly as per orders. The drawer was our only private and personal place and was to be locked at all times. All items of value were always to be locked away because the military view was that if you tempted theft then you were also culpable.

THE START OF MY CAREER

The next day we received our No. 1 Uniform, i.e. trousers and long belted jacket, our work overalls and our boots. It was required that the boots, pimpled and dull upon receipt, should be smooth and mirror-like within a week! Actually, that was nearly impossible but it had to be your priority.

The boots were worn all the time, so each night after the chores of keeping the block spotless it was work on the boots: spit, polish, spit, polish, ad infinitum, or even ad nauseam. To keep the wooden floors clean there were piles of foot-sized rectangles of blanket pieces at the dormitory entrance and it was upon pain of death, or worse, if you did not slide around on these for every moment you were there. Walking around in stockinged feet was okay, but it still seemed safer to use the blanket bits.

Each morning the block was inspected, so it was constant pressure to keep the place spotless. There were weekly rosters, made out by ourselves, which covered everything from windows, cobwebs, washroom basins, toilets and even keeping a shine on the brass fittings in the urinals! The floors were a special duty, of course, but each individual made an extra effort round his own bed-space.

Every Friday there was a special inspection when the cadets and the block were given an inch-by-inch check. Whereas the daily inspection was before breakfast and carried out by the course NCOs, the weekly inspection was by senior officers and if there was any serious infringement or failing then we would be checked again on Monday. This meant extra work for the weekend; we only had time off from Saturday noon to Monday at 0600 hours.

At first, the emphasis was on drill each morning which was fine for the ex-Air Cadets but a shock to the others. My position was always behind a cadet who just could not keep in step and, if I had not the experience, it would have been a shambles. It was quite disconcerting. He eventually had a semblance of timing, but proceeded in such an awkward manner that I was always ready for trouble. When we appeared proficient, each cadet was given a few days in charge of the course and he marched us everywhere between classes, exercises, meals, etc. As those who have done drill will know, it's not just the ability to act on commands but also to receive them at the correct time and on the correct step. Some of the cadets took a while to master this, so there were quite a few commands which merely caused confusion.

Obviously, in any initial training in the services it is necessary to master the disciplines of drill, appearance and sundry other controls but it was not all bull. Most of the days were taken up with lectures on English and Maths, official, formal and informal, letter writing, officer conduct on and off duty, social service etiquette, rank structure and, of course, RAF history.

The Warrant Officers and NCOs (i.e. flight sergeants, sergeants and corporals) were hard but fair; I often wondered how they liked calling us 'Sir', bearing in mind their ages and experience compared to their wet-behind-the-ears charges.

I cannot remember the names of any of our officers except for the flight (course) commander, Flight Lieutenant Frank McClymont. He was a kind and understanding man who, for some reason, chose me as his babysitter, which suited me as it supplemented my 28s./0d (£1.40p) per week pay. He had been involved in some way by flying his Sunderland flying boat up the Yangtse river in support of HMS *Amethyst* after she had been fired upon and trapped by the People's Liberation Army of China. She was trapped in the river for some time and had needed re-supplying.

It was fascinating to get an insight into my new career as I looked at all his photographs of that incident and wartime exploits. He had been awarded the DFC (Distinguished Flying Cross).

All RAF stations and units have an annual Air Officer Commanding's inspection which meant 'spick and span' was taken to new heights. We not only had all our normal workload but, in preparation for the big day, we had to expand our range of chores. All stonework, walls etc. were painted white and, what took me to my lowest ebb at this point, I ended up trimming the grass edges around our block with scissors!! I eventually sat with my head in my hands asking myself what I was doing there and Derek Blundell, an older cadet (twenty-two!), then a serving airman, gave me a pep talk and I managed to perk up again.

At this time I did not smoke but Derek smoked a pipe and I thought this seemed a good idea. When we were given our first free weekend, after the inspection, I went into the village and chose an inexpensive pipe, an ounce of the same tobacco as Derek, a set of fluffy pipe-cleaners and a box of Swan Vestas matches. As I left the shop I tripped on the step and dropped the pipe which broke into three pieces and was quite irreparable. I sold the other items to Derek and cursed the loss of about a quarter of a week's pay.

One Friday afternoon we were all assembled at medical quarters for our TABT jabs, i.e. Typhoid type A and B and Tetanus. The reason for Friday was that, almost without exception, the recipient spent a miserable forty-eight hours of after-effects. We were in a line and, amazing as it would seem nowadays, we received the jab through a long and quite thick needle which was used for us *all*! It was not unknown that, on rare occasions, people would be seriously affected by the use of the same needle.

My friend Peter Hudson and I decided that if we were going to be ill we might as well try to distract ourselves. To do this we went out in the car his mother had lent him and had a few beers in Gainsborough. We returned to a barrack room full of complaining bed-ridden cadets and the next day Peter and I were fine and the others were still under the weather. Ah, the benefits of beer!

The best sleeper in our group was Doug (Puddy or Bodger) Catt who could sleep for England. We had church services once a month, but this free morning, using great care, we carried him to the middle of the parade square without waking him. He was what would now be called 'cool', as he casually returned after his full rest and asked if he could have some volunteers to help him replace his bed.

It was very fortunate that our period at Kirton was in the summer, the weather was good, off-duty periods were pleasant and life was good compared to how other courses had to handle bad weather.

Obviously, we had very little time to ourselves as the whole purpose of the training was to cover all aspects of service life, to find our leadership potential and to examine us under pressure and hardship. To this end we went for five days to Donna Nook near North Coates and camped out in the sand dunes. We had to be self-sufficient and to carry out various tasks and exercises to test us. Rations were provided but few of us had gone much further than boiling water before! Morale fell a little during the rain but those of us who had had camping holidays fared best.

After three months we had our passing-out parade, changed into our officers' uniforms with the thin pilot officer's stripe and, that night, dined in the Officers' Mess. We were actually acting pilot officers on one year's probation. The next day we all set off for a week of leave before starting our flying course. We were split into two groups; half to No 2 FTS (Flying Training School) at RAF Hullavington near Chippenham and the luckier ones to Canada at RCAF Gimli.

At Last – Aeroplanes!

August 1954-March 1955

No. 2 FTS, RAF Hullavington, near Chippenham, Wiltshire

After constant discipline, drill and chores it was a wonderful feeling of release to arrive at RAF Hullavington to learn to fly at last. We were taken to the traditional, large brick-built mess, but housed in large wooden buildings alongside. We each had our own small room and shared communal bathrooms. A batman looked after six of us, I think, which meant beds made and linen changed, uniforms pressed, clothes taken to the laundry and retrieved and sundry other services.

I was astonished and slightly uncomfortable that an older man, fifty maybe, was going to do all this for a lad not yet eighteen. It's amazing how quickly I got used to it. Obviously, there was mutual respect as we were all well behaved and well brought-up fellows, but it felt quite strange.

We were to eat all our meals in the mess for which we paid about 5/- (25p) a week, which also covered accommodation and we paid the batman a small sum also. My first beer had been in the rather rowdy all ranks' NAAFI at Kirton-in Lindsey but the Officers' Mess bar was a place of comfort and ambience. All the other officers, seniors as well, mingled and chatted with us and we felt at home. The walls were adorned with originals and prints of great aviation themes and stories.

The first day we were in classroom and were addressed by the Station Commander (Stn Cdr), Wing Commander Flying (Wg Cdr (F)), our Squadron Commander, Squadron Leader (Sqn Ldr) Rawlinson and a couple of other people. The thrust of it all was the usual buckle down, work hard, behave like officers, never drink too much and *never* be late paying your mess bill. The bill was for accommodation, food, bar and any mess damage, individual or collectively made during dinner-nights which could get a bit raucous

40

during games. The station commander had asked all those with PPLs to put their hands up; I think there were three of us and he said, 'Right, forget everything you have learnt as we do things differently in the Royal Air Force!'

We were to be No. 103 Course, flying the Percival Piston Provost. We were split into A and B flights and, once again, split into two. As with all training, one group flew in the morning and the other would do ground school and then swap at lunchtime. The p.m. group would then fly again in the morning and so it would continue.

After all the talks we set off to collect our flying kit, soft helmet, goggles (which we never used), flying-suit, chamois leather gloves, thick socks and fur-lined boots. The open cockpit days were over but we also received a lovely fur-lined pilot's jacket.

The excitement was now building as we set off for our crew-room to stow our kit in individual lockers and finally meet our instructors. Most of them wore Second World War medals and looked the part – 'old' and experienced. I was allocated with one other cadet to Flight Lieutenant (Flt. Lt) Lou Riley, a quiet and calm man. Normally, an instructor would have just two students but sometimes the course size meant the seniors had an extra. Lou, aka 'Sir', showed us round the aircraft (a/c), airframe, engine and, at last, the cockpit. A few safety rules were covered, not least don't walk into a turning propeller! That was it for the day and we were ready to head off to our new home for dinner for that new-found pleasure called beer!

Ground school lectures comprised aerodynamics, radio, meteorology, gyroscopic, electrical and air-driven instruments, navigation, aviation regulations both civil and military, air traffic control (ATC), parachute training (no actual jumps, thank goodness!), piston engines, aviation medicine (i.e. effects on the body of pressurisation changes, vertigo, ears, eyes, etc.). Last, but not least, the aircraft and all its systems both general and especially the Piston Provost. These included electrics, icing hydraulics, air conditioning, flight controls, fuel systems, pneumatics, starting engine systems, oxygen, suction for instruments, brakes, etc., etc.

The Percival Piston Provost had an Alvis Leonides 9-cylinder engine giving 550 brake horse power (BHP).

The wing span (W/S) was 10.7 metres (35 feet).

Length 8.73 metres (28 feet 6 inches).

Weight (WT) empty 1,523 kilograms (7,283lb); Take-off weight (t.o.w.) max. 1,995 kilograms (4,399lb).

Maximum speed 170 knots (200 mph at MSL (mean sea level)).

Range 560 nautical miles (nm) (650 statute miles).

In those days, all aviation measurements were in yards, feet, pounds and gallons, but gradually metric took over most measures. However, before my retirement we were using only metres and kilograms, except for height which was still in feet for most countries. A knot is one nautical mile (n.m.) which officially varies a small amount depending where you are in the world but is generally accepted as 6,040 feet, a statute (s.m.) mile is 5,280 feet and a kilometre (km) is 3,281 feet.

One discussion in aerodynamics, also known as principles of flight, was to do with Bernoulli's Theorem which basically deals with the change of fluid flow speed relative to pressure changes induced by change of the shape of the path through which the fluid (air) passes. I always understood the principles and its application to the wing air flow and in suction tubes but always got it wrong when quoting it. This problem never went away and it was always a source of amusement to the class when the instructor would say, 'Burdett, please give us Bernoulli's Theory of fluid flow.' Nevertheless, I have always found aerodynamics a fascinating subject.

Another favourite is meteorology but we got off to a difficult start as the instructor rarely looked at us and was constantly saying 'Er' and 'Umm'. On one occasion we all agreed to compare notes and at the end of the lecture our tallies varied between 120 and 140 in forty minutes!

There would be regular written and oral exams throughout the course with, of course, seriously hard exams to pass to go onto the advanced stage of training.

We continued our administration training with lectures on letter writing, filing, etc., all military, of course. We were too busy and involved to be allocated normal officer responsibilities such as being in charge of airmen or barrack blocks, but one task we all had to do was 'Orderly Officer.' On all normal stations there would be a (DO) Duty Officer, usually a flight lieutenant, who was responsible for proper running of the camp outside normal working hours whereas the Orderly Officer (OO) was usually a pilot officer or flying officer, who was more of a dogsbody. The OO would attend all meals to check that the men were 'happy' with them and ask if there were 'any complaints?' In the morning his duty would be to double-check with the catering people that all foodstuffs were delivered correctly and confirm that perishables were safe. The OO could be called any time during the day or night to settle small problems.

However, the one task that gave me most embarrassment was the 1800 hours and 2200 hours check at the guardroom where airmen and airwomen had to report in best uniform and in immaculate condition.

They would have been going there as 'defaulters' and the punishment was usually to do menial tasks but to present themselves on parade for the OO.

My first OO duty would have been close to my eighteenth birthday and I was very nervous. There were about eight defaulters and I was required to inspect them up and down and front to back. I managed to do this for the first couple or so and by avoiding eye contact it was not too bad. However, I came to this young and buxom airwoman, carried out the inspection including shiny breast-pocket buttons and, unfortunately, made eye contact. She had a cheeky grin which said, 'I know you are embarrassed!'

She was right and I blushed almost to death. Blow me, if the next airman caught my eye and he was an acquaintance from my area at home. He was grinning fit to burst at my discomfort. I managed a nod of acknowledgement and bumbled on. At the next evening parade, we actually had a chat and I managed the inspection of the airwoman with nary a hitch.

After our initial briefings and one or two lectures the real stuff began. Firstly, my instructor took the two of us round the aircraft ensuring that the strap-in procedures were fully understood and that we had absorbed what we had to look for in our pre-flight external check of the aircraft. We sat in the cockpit as most of the switches, levers and instruments were discussed and, generally, got a feel for the new life about to start.

On 23 August 1954 I got airborne with Lou Riley at last. The flight was known as air experience and the student was observed for his reactions and attitude and also allowed a bit of handling. Believe it or not, occasionally this air experience flight would be the student's first time airborne.

The syllabus follows a time-honoured and logical progression whereby the next flight is to be taught flying 'Straight and Level', i.e. no change of heading and no change of altitude – easier said than done but this is a logical starting point.

Next, the student has to learn turning, during which you must neither gain nor lose height. Obviously, at this stage it's all just learning; accuracy comes later. Then you have climbing and descending and use of power to achieve the desired result; the co-ordination of power, speed and altitude does not come easily.

Then comes stalling, followed by spinning. Stalling is the condition whereby the aircraft no longer has enough lift to sustain flight and will lose altitude. If during initial entry into the stall there is any outside influence such as misuse of the controls, or one wing losing lift before the other for any reason, then a spin can develop. The spin is where one wing stalls before the other and the aircraft spirals in that direction. The recovery from both stall and spin is easy in training aircraft but has to be learnt thoroughly as there is little time to recover if the aircraft is low, e.g. in the circuit.

On nearly every flight the student is regularly asked where the nearest field is for a forced landing. The reason for this is that should you lose the engine at any time then you have to have a bolt-hole. It is a constant necessity in a single-engine aircraft to be aware of this need. Obviously, therefore, the student must always be conscious of the wind direction as it is safest to land into the wind.

Throughout all the early training exercises the take-off and landing is included in all the lessons so that when the student is approaching the first solo stage he can make full use of the intensive take-off and landing exercises. At the point the instructor feels the student is ready for his first solo they will land and he will say something like 'I reckon you're ready now, do you want to go?' I have never heard of a 'No' answer.

Anyway, with a mixture of glee, anticipation and nerves, off you go. I remember it as a joyous occasion, both the earlier time in the Tiger Moth and now in the Piston Provost, and a massive lifting of the spirits.

During the landing phase it is necessary to keep the aircraft straight using rudder and, when too slow for the rudder to be effective, the brakes. As you may recall my right leg is shorter than my left, so when I applied brakes I was always wandering off to the left. Lou Riley kept asking why I did this but I dared not explain my leg problems in case it went against me. It was probably an unfounded fear, but I didn't want to put it to the test. On the Piston Provost the brake lever was on the control column and you controlled direction using the rudder pedals, so off to the left I went. I finally trained myself.

After first solo the next five solo flights are all take-offs and landings or landings continued into another take-off, i.e. circuits and bumps. These solos are interspersed with one or two accompanied by the instructor to ensure continuity and to see if any errors are creeping in.

As the hours progress so does the standard required and prior to any aerobatics training there is more emphasis on stalling and spinning as the student is more likely to get into difficulties than in basic manoeuvres. To get into aerobatics has been long awaited, especially as appetites will have been whetted by the instructors having shown a few during previous flights.

On one of my earlier flights Lou Riley showed me a loop having explained and done the pre-aerobatic checks known then, and probably now, as the HASEL check; mnemonics are well-used in aviation.

H.	Height.	Sufficient to recover from any manoeuvre at a safe height.
A.	Airframe.	Flaps and undercarriage (gear) up. (The Piston Provost had gear fixed down.) Test airbrakes (where fitted). Rudder pedals adjusted to give easy full deflection.
S.	Security.	Canopy closed. Harness secure. No loose articles in cockpit.
E.	Engine.	Temperatures and pressure good. Fuel state.
L.	Location.	Know where you are. Clear of controlled airspace. Not over populated area.
L.	LOOKOUT!	Clear of other aircraft and cloud.

These checks would apply also prior to practice stalling and spinning.

Well, Lou went through everything and off we went into our loop and when we were vertical there was the registration VP123 written on the underside of a Varsity (or Valetta) starboard wing! We were only 100 to 200 feet from it, yet two pairs of eyes had not seen it earlier. Lou cursed a little and took violent avoiding action. It was a great lesson to me that, however diligent one could be in an aircraft you had to be prepared for any eventuality.

Aerobatics are great fun but the intention behind the training is to ensure that the pilot knows the limits of his aircraft and himself and builds massive self-confidence for all military flying.

Navigation starts in the second or third month with simple there-and-back flights but with no landing. On the first navigation flight I found myself with a new instructor, Sergeant George Applegarth; these changes were normal and were no reflection upon previous instructors. On the way back from wherever, he said 'I chose this route as it passes my old school.' And with that he dived down and crossed the occupied playing fields at about fifty feet and maximum speed. I thought 'I'm going to enjoy this chap.'

The trip worked out well but that was because George (Sir) was flying. Next, and all subsequent flights, the student had to fly as well as navigate. We had no aids except the Mark I eyeball and map. If you concentrated on the map then you lost accuracy in the flying and if you flew to your best ability then the map-reading and navigation deteriorated. Furthermore, you had a pencil, a flight plan and a circular slide-rule type of calculator on your lap with the map, so not only were you trying to fly and navigate, you had to be able to juggle as well. The cockpit was small and there were no desks or ledges to place anything. The pencil could go in a slot on the flying suit and the calculator could be strapped on the thigh and that was it. If mental arithmetic was not your forte then you could be in trouble; fortunately, there were quite a few formulae for wind speed, drift, distance/time etc. which made life a little easier.

We never got lost as all pilots will tell you. However, we will admit to the occasional uncertainty of our position.

Slowly but surely, confidence rises, ability improves and regular tests both airborne and, in the classrooms, confirm the progress.

Before any flight, you, plus any other student about to do the same exercise, are taken into one of the few small rooms off the main crew-room and given a full briefing using blackboards, books and the inevitable manoeuvre descriptions using hands as aeroplanes. After the flight you end up in one of the rooms for a full debriefing and assessment.

The instructor will write up each trip using the PAT format, plus general observations: P = Progress, A = Attitude and T = Technique.

All instructors refer to students in general as Bloggs, unless referring to a known or specific individual.

Next in line for learning is formation flying – every student longs for this. Naturally all the aspects of training are continuous. You do not complete aerobatics, then navigation, then formation; it's a continuous process of learning new skills whilst still honing the others.

At first formation flying is fun because the instructor is demonstrating, but then you have to do it and tentative barely covers your handling technique. With wings only, perhaps six to ten feet apart, you tend to concentrate too much on that to the detriment of other things. Slowly, you learn to relax, use power changes gently and be especially gentle on the controls.

Each aircraft has appropriate reference points for maintaining the desired position. For example, it might be that you keep a line of rivets or, perhaps align with a gap between aileron and wing, and keep level with, perhaps, the roundel on the fuselage. These two references will keep you at the correct distance out and at the desired up-and-down position.

Once attained, minor adjustments only will be needed. This is fine for straight and level flight but the moment a turn, climb, descent or speed change occurs then adjustment is needed. The only need is to maintain the aforementioned position and the fact that you are now into another mode of flight is actually irrelevant – just keep position.

Whenever there is to be change the leader will call on the radio and at the command 'Go' you are ready to adjust. If all pilots can see the leader's cockpit, then, when you are more experienced, you will respond just to hand signals.

AT LAST – AEROPLANES!

At the end of most formation exercises, dual and solo, the leader might call for a tail chase; this is massive fun as you trail behind by about 100 to 200 feet and try to stay with him. It's even more fun if there are plenty of clouds for him to dive around, especially the larger cumulus with all their height and numerous bulges. It becomes even more exciting if you are hugging tight to a cloud and suddenly, there in front of you is another group of tail-chasers coming from the other direction!

At the end of formation training you actually do one or two formation take-offs and landings, albeit with an increased spacing.

By this time there were four courses in progress – No.1 Course had passed out and progressed to advanced training at Middleton St George near Darlington, County Durham, and the newest course, No. 4 on D Flight, was in the early stages.

During one formation flight our leader was asked if he could raise a student, callsign D6 (Dog 6 then, Delta 6 nowadays) as he was not answering the tower. Our leader called him and asked him if he could read (hear) him and what was his position. He replied, 'I'm upside down in a field and I cannot get out.'

During all the aerobatics, navigation and, generally, before formation flying there is instrument flying. Obviously by now one has a reasonable proficiency in reading instruments and using information given but, so far, there has always been an outside view and, therefore, reference. Always being able to see what is up and what is down has meant that one's sense of balance has never really been tested.

As much flying is conducted at night or in cloud, it is essential to do all necessary work with reference only to instruments. Therefore, all instrument training was carried out with large visors that obscured all but the instruments. Now, sense of balance can be upset as, with no outside reference, all movements can be misunderstood.

The reason is that the semi-circular canals in the inner ear register all movements to our brain via small granules of fluid in the canals flowing and acting on sensory hairs. Normally, this does not trouble us because our eyes tell us our position. However, in the air, when the aircraft moves around its axes, i.e. nose up or down or left or right, and if it rolls left or right it has quite an effect on the canals. If we have no visual reference then it is possible to become disorientated. So, by concentrating on your instruments you can satisfy yourself that all is well – the problem to overcome is that of not believing your instruments and then making unnecessary corrections.

It takes many hours of practice to finally be 100 per cent happy with relying on those instruments. Usually, if there are doubts then cross-reference will

47

either confirm all is well or assist in identifying a possible fault. At this time in aviation there were the occasional instrument problems so the training was very thorough; indeed, to confirm your total understanding and proficiency, unreasonable and unexpected attitudes were practised and then examined by flight checks. These attitudes were presented by the instructor and examining pilots throwing the aircraft all over the sky whilst the student had no view of the instruments. He would then say, 'You have control' and you would now have a view of the instruments, one or two having failed temporarily due to the excesses of abuse, and have to recover to straight and level flight. The aircraft would have been handed over in the most awful positions such as vertical, up or down, power on or off, spiralling, spinning, upside down, etc.

As a result of all this confusion you would have no idea of up or down or whether you were turning or not. The reason for this is that the semi-circular canals, in your inner ear, which assist you in determining gravity and movement, thus eye co-ordination of relative positions, are overreacting and giving false information. This is caused by the small granules brushing against sensory hairs telling you something that you can only prove by eyes or instruments. So as soon as you are given the instruments again you have to BELIEVE them.

However, in the earlier aircraft the artificial horizon indicator and the compass repeater indicator would have been unreadable as their gyroscopes would have toppled. This may/does account for some earlier crashes after take-off at night. The acceleration would move the same granules as would the act of raising the nose of the aircraft, thus exaggerating the nose-up effect, and, if the pilot was uncomfortable with the instrument readings, he may instinctively lower the nose with awful consequences.

The only instruments available to assist in recovery would be the altimeter, airspeed indicator, vertical speed indicator, i.e. climb or descent rate (VSI), and an essential instrument called the turn and slip indicator (T & S).

The T & S was a vital instrument as the slip aspect was basically a skid indicator regardless of whether you were falling sideways, upside down, or whatever. Just about the first thing to be done was centralise the little ball in its tube and then turn the aircraft immediately it had started to return to stability. Then you used the other instruments to return the aircraft to straight and level flight, i.e. if you pull the stick back and your speed increases then you must be upside down and vice-versa; turn indicator is used to level the wings and power is adjusted to compensate for rapid speed loss or gain. The VSI adds essential information. This training is remorselessly continued throughout the course and gives a very strong background to enable the military pilot to cope with extreme circumstances throughout his/her flying life. It is too expensive, I feel, for most civil aviation-training to afford much or any of it.

When you eventually receive your rating which is, initially, a white card, you are cleared for flight in weather conditions slightly more testing than before. However, visibility, cloud base, cloud tops and rain have to have very defined limits. Later, you receive a green card, which allows far worse conditions to be acceptable.

Once you are considered safe on instruments the night flying training starts. It provides an amazingly different perspective on angles of descent, sense of roll angle etc. as your visual references are mostly lights of different colours and intensities. Again, the instruments are essential.

Training at night follows the usual routine, albeit condensed, of straight and level, turns, climb, descent and take-offs and landings. Whereas it might be between eight and twelve hours training before first solo, at night it is usually just two dual instruction trips totalling about one and a half to two hours, then off solo. As ever, the next couple of solo trips would be pounding the circuit; it's called consolidation and provides that confidence so necessary.

At this stage of experience there will be no aerobatics or formation at night, although a few will try the odd loop or roll when solo and out of the circuit. Night navigation is practised thoroughly but, of course, perspective has changed. Towns are now seas of light and seem nearer than in daytime, and, unless there is a good moon, rivers are invisible.

During navigation you could, if necessary, call for a fix which was obtained by sending a lengthy transmission and two or three radio stations would transmit their bearings on you to a central station who could see where they all crossed and then advise you of your position. In view of the reduced visual information at night this was a very useful aid. Alternatively, you could call individual stations for one bearing at a time.

At this time training aircraft were not fitted with Aerial Direction Finding equipment (ADF) which you could tune to a ground radio station of your choice, a non-directional beacon (NDB), when a needle would then point in its direction.

The prime navigation tools were planning before flight, lines drawn on maps and dead-reckoning by knowledge of aircraft speed, wind velocity (i.e. direction and speed) to assess effect on aircraft drift and speed over the ground (ground speed – G/S) and a clock/watch. Of course, as important as all these was mental arithmetic, using known formulae and the irreplaceable Mark I eyeball!

I had a particularly close call one night at the end of my downwind leg on a left-hand circuit. The circuit is a rectangular procedure from take-off to landing. Initially, after take-off you fly straight ahead then turn left 90 degrees to the crosswind leg. At the appropriate distance you turn left again and continue downwind, i.e. paralleling the runway. Usually for most aircraft you note the moment you pass the landing point on the runway and time 40 to 45 seconds, making adjustments to that if there are significant wind speeds, then turn left onto base leg, then left again onto the final approach to the runway for landing. Well, this night we were actually flying into and out of cloud at circuit height, 1,000 feet, but were still able to see the runway and airfield often enough for accurate timings etc. There were no instructors in the air at the time, otherwise flying solo would have been cancelled as there was no positive forward visibility or clearance from cloud. The students, naturally, didn't mention the conditions as they wanted to keep flying.

At the end of my downwind leg, and just before my turn onto base leg, a red light went directly in front of me from right to left, followed by a whacking great bounce as I went through the slipstream/wake of this aircraft. This pilot had obviously gone too far crosswind and turned downwind way out. I knew he was in front of me but, as I couldn't see him and his radio calls were correct, I assumed he was in the right place. That was my second near miss so far!

Later on, in the latter part of my training, during day flying I returned to the circuit in the, then, normal manner by being given permission to rejoin. I flew along the dead-side of the runway, i.e. right-hand side if there is a left-hand circuit in progress, and realised there was a much stronger wind aloft than reported at ground level. I needed a lot of airspeed just to get a decent speed over the ground. Being young, adventurous and, as I was later advised, stupid, instead of turning downwind for my circuit after the crosswind leg, I turned upwind and slowed down until I was going backwards over the ground. This necessitated an airspeed close to the stall. Anyway, ATC gave me orders to turn around and complete the circuit correctly.

Upon landing, I was given a serious rollicking and it was pointed out that, since I was close to stalling speed and as the air was turbulent and capable of gusts and wind speed drops, I could easily have stalled with the possibility of being unable to make a safe recovery or, worse, enjoy the onset of a spin. It was fascinating to go backwards, though, if only for a few seconds.

Obviously, my period at Hullavington was not all flying and ground school. We had a good rugby team and, most Wednesdays, we visited other RAF Stations or Army units. Once, playing RAF South Cerney, our captain and squadron commander broke his leg and I was 'volunteered' to accompany him to hospital where I champed at the bit as I knew I was missing the aftergame beers; yes, I was eighteen by now!

There were mess dinner-nights every week where we absorbed the rules and rituals of the service in its formal moments. Much beer was drunk, many games played and some damage done as a few games were quite ferocious. Any damage was paid pro rata by rank, for all those attending, whether involved or not.

My favourite true story regarding mess games was about an officer being asked by the medic how he came by his broken leg and he replied, 'As I was getting down from the mantelpiece I was struck by a passing motorcycle.'

Strangely, although I had no experience with bow-ties before my service, I became the one to whom half my course came to have their ties fixed. Somehow, I had the knack immediately.

None of us could afford cars but David (Paddy) Hipperson, Tony Dunn and I bought an ancient Bullnosed Morris Cowley for £14 and had great fun on our excursions to Chippenham. Unfortunately, it would only work if one of us took it in turns to lie on the offside front wing and keep tickling the carburettor (for you newcomers to the world they had little buttons you could push to encourage fuel flow) to keep the fuel flowing! This was a particularly onerous task as it was winter and therefore cold or wet or both. We were more concerned with the weather than the, now obvious, danger. When we moved on we sold it to some other mugs for £10!

Actually it was not true that not all of us could afford cars. Peter Wild had been an apprentice at Halton and graduated as a qualified engineer and had been an airman before being accepted for pilot training. He had a beautiful Allard which was immaculate and his pride and joy; he was forever tinkering or cleaning the car and, later, was a great help to us when we finally had our own cars, albeit bangers.

I eventually acquired an MG KN, which was also called a Magnette. I'm afraid it was a bit of a banger but, even so, it got me to Middleton St George, near Darlington, County Durham, after I was finished at Hullavington. Peter Wild kindly helped me keep it on the road.

My good friend on the course, Brian McGee, and I travelled in his two-seater Austin one weekend to his home in Kenley en route to Twickenham for England vs I forget. Anyway, there had been a spate of students returning to camp overnight on Sunday and being tired for duty on Monday. As a result the Station Commander had decreed that we were not allowed away at weekends without permission. We, nevertheless, chanced our arm and set off early on Saturday. Passing through Slough on the A4 we espied an extremely shapely young lady wearing an all-leather outfit which, in itself, was quite rare. We were sufficiently distracted not to notice that the car in front had stopped at traffic lights and we ran into the back of it. Our first thoughts were that we were likely to be in trouble due to our absence from camp. The driver came back to us and apologised for stopping so suddenly! Brian said that as there was no damage he was happy. Phew! What luck. At his home his unexpected arrival was greeted with open arms and after the usual introductions and chat we were given a super fry-up.

After Mrs McGee had proudly shown us her newly-decorated dining-room, Brian and I sat down to our breakfast. The tomato ketchup was reluctant to leave the bottle so Brian re-capped it and gave it a good shake. His mother went ballistic when she saw all the ketchup on the wall where it had settled after the cap had come off. We ate hurriedly and fled to Twickenham.

Sadly, after our gaining our wings, Brian went on to Canberra bombers and, whilst on a low-level flight over the Mediterranean, his aircraft disappeared and he was never found. Three or four Canberras had crashed without explanation until one had a sudden and rapid nose-down action at high altitude and could not be recovered. The crew safely abandoned the aircraft and reported how everything occurred. It was finally decided that the electrically-trimmed tail-plane had had a runaway fault. All aircraft were fitted with or changed to a revised system and there were no more incidents. I guess that explains Brian's disappearance.

I think of Brian nearly every day, not just because of our friendship, happy but short, but because I keep my finger over the cap when I shake my Tabasco sauce for my breakfast tomato juice!

Shortly after this adventure we, as a course, were given one of the usual short initiative exercises, beloved by the military, and were bussed a distance from base and told to get home in time for tea, and carry no money. We were dropped in a village 'somewhere in England' and the driver went off for a cup of tea. Geoff Taylor looked in the driver's cab and noted the key number. In those days the ignition key position actually had the key number on it! Almost invariably it was MRN + three numbers. Geoff had some money on him (naughty!) (as did we all!) and bought the key at the nearby garage. We all piled in and he drove us back. This particular piece of initiative was not appreciated by the powers above, including the driver, and we were all given extra duties and confined to camp for forty-eight hours. Geoff got a bigger rollicking as he did not have a military driver's licence and, obviously, had been uninsured. However, he had shown initiative and the rollicking had probably been somewhat tongue-in-cheek. Unfortunately, Geoff was one of the guys who didn't get his wings at the end of our advanced course. Naturally, it was nothing to do with his adventure with the coach as, albeit foolhardy, it nevertheless had shown initiative.

One of the chaps on the following course was Tony Marshall who was as young as me; he took a great fancy to Joy, one of the mess stewardesses. They had the odd unofficial meeting off camp but, of course, this was frowned upon as an officer was not permitted to liaise with an airwoman. However, they were so smitten that eventually permission was granted so long as discretion was maintained. I knew Tony for many years in the service, more later, and was happy for them both. They were happily married forever, it seemed; sadly, they are now both gone.

A real eye-opener came when we made a visit to RAF Morton Valence to see Rolls Royce Derwent engines being made under licence. They were being built, certified, sealed for transport, taken from the hangar and destroyed! We were horrified to find that such profligacy was because, although they were no longer needed, the trades unions had threatened widespread disruption if they were not permitted to finish the months of work, even though compensation had been offered. Our minds could not encompass the thinking here.

It was inevitable that we would lose one or more trainees through exam failures or flight test failures and so it was. The guy behind whom I had had to march and could not keep in step failed to make it as did the guy who had nearly hit me in the circuit at night. There were one or two others but the strangest was Julian (Bunch) Dyer who declared that he would not fly on a Friday the thirteenth. He was duly asked, nay told, to leave!

Eventually, the final night instrument, navigation and handling tests were completed and passed and we were all sent on our final trip which was our first landing away cross-country. My airfield was Feltwell in Suffolk. Also, at the end was an aerobatic competition in which I managed to reach the finals! In view of our inexperience we had to be accompanied by our instructors but they would only intervene for safety reasons. It was great fun even though I did not win.

My last flight at Hullavington was on 17 March 1955 and, shortly after our graduation parade and party, it was time for two weeks' leave and on to No. 4 FTS (Flying Training School) at Middleton St George, County Durham.

Sadly, Hullavington, having eventually been taken over by the Army, was closed down many years later.

Jets

APRIL 1955

Middleton St George, near Darlington, County Durham No. 4 FTS

The nine survivors of the original fifteen on 103 Course, Hullavington, duly arrived in mid-April 1955 at RAF Middleton St George for our advanced training at No.4 FTS (Flying Training School). At last we were to fly jets, firstly the two-seat Vampire T.11 and later on the course, when more experienced, the single-seat Vampire FB.5.

The nine guys were David 'Paddy' Hipperson, Douglas 'Puddy' Catt, Trevor Betterton, Peter Hudson (our only National Service – two years – trainee), Peter Wild, Brian McGee, John Simmons, Barry 'Bo' Plummer and me. We were joined by two Australian trainees, 'Johnny' Johnson, and Ian Cadwallader, to make the regular students to number eleven.

However, our course was further enlarged by nine university graduates who had already quite a few hours when with the various University Air Squadrons around the country. Their leader was Neil Ferguson and he also became course leader.

We ordinary mortals had around 135-140 hours which I think were a few more than the UAS chaps but their more mature age and experience made us feel pretty young and green, I think. That's certainly how I felt.

Anyway, back to the old routine; school in the morning and flying in the afternoon alternating daily.

The Vampire T.11 was a two-seater, twin-boom, single jet trainer. The FB.5 was a single seat ex-fighter. They each had a DH Goblin 3 or 35 engine, I believe.

The nearest figures are for the FB.6 and show a wingspan of 11.58 metres (38 feet).

Length 9.37 metres (30 feet 8 inches)
Weight empty 3,304 kilograms (7,283lb) weight maximum
5,620 kilograms (12,390lb)
Maximum speed 476 knots (547mph)

Much of what we had learnt earlier applied in the main to our new aircraft but certain rules had to be learnt thoroughly, not least how to handle a jet engine. The Vampire had a DH Goblin (Mark 35, I think) which was pretty much the original type of jet: large, heavy compressor which did not accelerate well so we had to learn to use a much gentler hand on the throttle otherwise it was possible to push too much fuel in too quickly and actually put the flame out. Hence the term flame-out for a jet-engine failure. The main concern with such poor acceleration was that one had to keep enough power on during approach to land so that if it was necessary to abort the approach power was rapidly available. Furthermore, at high altitude there was less air available so it was necessary to be even more careful. These differences were hammered home by the instructors, so it took very little time to learn how to handle the engine and have confidence.

As the aircraft was a lot faster than the Piston Provost one had to think faster and plan ahead more frequently. Again, this readily came naturally within a short time. Apart from normal handling exercises the navigation was the most important to absorb as destinations arrived much quicker and the higher altitude meant that some of the smaller features were less recognisable than at the lower altitude. Stalling and spinning were a little more violent and recovery took longer but was straight-forward enough. Aerobatics were great fun due to the extra speed but used rather more airspace than we were used to.

The best procedures were formation flying and tail chasing because of the higher speed and the feeling that we knew we were getting the real feeling of operational flying. Also, after many sorties, formation especially, we would be permitted to come in and break into the circuit, i.e. come alongside the runway at the correct height and execute a hard turn hoping to hold the same turn all the way round the tight circle and only levelling our wings when low and lined up with the runway centre-line. You know, like real pilots!

You may recall that I had to work hard to keep straight on landing due to my different leg lengths; well, I had the same problem at first on the Vampire. My instructor, Sergeant Les Baker, would ask me why I couldn't keep the damned aircraft on the centre-line, and I would explain that I didn't know! It got better after a few landings.

Because of our altitude, many more of our returns to base needed assistance from air traffic control (ATC) as cloud frequently obscured the area. We would carry out a QGH which was simply a CDTC (controlled descent through cloud). This was achieved by calling ATC who would take a bearing on your position and give you a heading to steer for base. Once overhead you were sent on a pre-determined heading for a given time at a specific airspeed. You descended to a particular height and, after a certain time, would turn back onto runway heading, descending the while. Headings given all allowed for drift caused by crosswinds. Each time you spoke, ATC could tell by your bearing whether you were attaining the runway centre-line. If not, then new headings were given.

The aim was to guide you to a safe minimum height with accurate timings so that you would arrive at a point where the runway was in view and a safe landing would ensue. As long as the pilot flew accurately and adhered to instructions then it was a very good system.

Later, we used that system, the QGH-cum-CDTC, to position the aircraft lined up with the runway at a safe height but further away. The aim was to be given a GCA, i.e. Ground Controlled Approach. This was conducted by a controller with a radar-tube who, having identified you, would keep you accurately on the centre-line and advise you of the ideal height for the range he could see on his screen. As this was much more accurate than the QGH the height to safely descend was lower. This, of course, meant you could fly in worse visibility and lower cloud base.

This was all early days in aviation but aids to safety and navigation were improving all the time. As mentioned earlier, the Mark 1 eyeball was still very much an essential aid in every aspect of aviation.

One day I flew with Flight Lieutenant Moxam on instrument training over the Chiltern Hills. He initiated a practice QGH away from the airfield, giving me headings, speeds and descent instructions. I was wearing the traditional headgear for such training which meant I could not see outside. Eventually, he descended me to 11,000 feet from 30,000 feet whilst giving me the appropriate commands. When I had descended to 11,000 feet as instructed he asked me to look outside. Horror of horrors, I was flying along a valley between the Cleveland Hills at 1,000 feet, not 11,000!

I had misread my altimeter. It was not an entirely uncommon event; the altimeter had three needles, one for each 10,000 feet, one for each 1,000 feet and one for each 100 feet. It was possible in a rapid descent with the needles whizzing round to misread it. Much later the three-needle altimeter was abandoned for two needles for 10,000s and 1,000s of feet and the actual height in numbers on the face of the instrument. Meanwhile, I became the best reader of the altimeter you could wish for.

During my time at 4 FTS one of the students flew straight into the ground during a QGH. It was reasonably attributed to misreading of the altimeter; all his calls had been correct readbacks of instructions, including to start his turn inbound at 11,000 feet. Nothing more was heard after that so it would seem likely that he had actually turned inbound at 1,000 feet and as he broke cloud he would have seen the ground and tried to pull up but it was too late.

Whenever there was an incident or accident most of the students would phone home immediately to let their parents know they were O.K. There were payphones at each end of the long corridor in the mess and queues would form at each one and the calls would, of necessity, be short; any lengthy personal chats were frowned upon. Interestingly, the boundary lines for two telephone exchanges ran across the mess so, depending upon the destination of your call, you used the cheapest phone. Long distance calls to the North or South could differ by as much a shilling (5p) depending on which 'phone you used.

Talking of the mess, we lived in single-storey hut-like buildings alongside the standard RAF style mess. Prior to our arrival a pilot had crashed his Meteor aircraft into the corner of the mess nearest the runway. His spirit was said to live on and one or two of the staff had 'seen' his ghost! Others felt 'the presence' but, although I visited the area, I never noticed anything. I wonder if the people in what is now a hotel on Teeside Airport ever notice or feel anything.

One day I was about to walk out to my assigned T.11 for a solo flight when the flight commander called me back as he wanted to do a normal check ride with Barry Windsor. Naturally, I was disappointed but only for a short while. As they got airborne the engine failed and, as these T.11s had no ejector seats and it was too low to bale out, the flight commander was obliged to land straight ahead. This he did successfully and came to rest in a field alongside the river. They evacuated the aircraft which was basically intact and not on fire, but prudence rules, as you may imagine. They sat on the riverbank with their cigarettes and watched with amusement as all the fire and rescue vehicles roared around trying to find a way to reach them. Eventually all was sorted out and the aircraft recovered to be airborne again not too long afterwards.

Another incident occurred to Johnny Johnson when he was coming in at high speed for a break and landing. Just as he arrived at the overhead he was struck in the face by a bird that had somehow found its way through the windshield. He was unable to see anything so pulled back on the stick to gain altitude, jettisoned the hood and started to climb out so that he could parachute down. Unfortunately, his harness, or something, was trapped or entangled and he couldn't exit. However, the slipstream blew enough blood from his face and eyes so that he could see enough of the instruments and the world beyond. So, he sat down and then landed safely. He was awarded a Green Endorsement, which is a commendation written on a page in your logbook in green ink to indicate a job well done.

By now we had all been promoted from acting pilot officer (i.e. on probation) to pilot officer, receiving our Commission Parchments from Her Majesty the Queen exhorting us to serve God, the country and her. Actually, Your Majesty, that's why we joined! It was very pleasant to be addressed as 'My Trusty and Beloved Servant'.

As our rank progressed so did our salary; we were now on the heady sum of £14 per calendar month, from which mess bills had the first claim. To be late, or worse fail, in paying the bill was a serious offence and punishment could go all the way to dismissal from the service. The bill comprised a small sum for room and meals, personal laundry, bar, where technically you were not allowed to treat others to a drink, and each person's charges went into his own book (no cash) and, of course, damages occasioned during weekly dining-in nights.

Later on, when I was at RAF Lyneham an officer's cheque bounced and he was placed on a charge and a Board of Inquiry was convened. His explanation that he did not understand how it could have happened didn't wash with the board and his bank account did show that he was short of funds. However, in those days all bank accounts were hand-written by a large staff out of sight of the customers. It was eventually sorted out by the bank and they accepted responsibility for failing to enter his pay cheque and some other money into his account. The poor fellow had had a frightening experience, more than he had had in the air probably, and the bank paid him substantial compensation.

This extra money meant that one or two cars started to appear. I was still running my MG KN but it was actually a bunch of loose and noisy parts just occasionally all going in the same direction. Peter Wild with his beautiful Allard was always outside doing something to it, so I could always find him if I needed some help or advice. As years went by I became quite adept with cars but Peter's early help was essential.

Doug 'Puddy' Catt was to be seen, when in civvies, in deerstalker hat and a silver-topped cane. He bought an old Snubnose Morris Cowley which was remarkably reliable and, even in those days, quite unusual to see on the roads. Whenever we went to the cinema in Darlington his appearance, see-through monocle, fair moustache, dress and car, was always a head-turner. All this carried out by a chap two months younger than me. Quite a character. Unusually, for a pilot, he was frequently airsick but soldiered on to become a fighter pilot and eventually taught King Hussein of Jordan to fly the Hunter.

As was normal in the services, young officers were always being invited to dances, and other events, at nurses' training schools and teachers' training colleges. Eventually, we were invited to the trainee teachers' dance at Darlington. There I was to see and spend much effort to drag one young lady away from all the other guys and keep her to myself. Thus began my many years with Maureen Boyd from Lancaster. She was a typical Lancashire beauty and with no discerning accent. She had been a student at the Lancashire Girls' Grammar School and gone straight to teacher training rather than try for university. For the last two or three months at Middleton St George I was a regular visitor to Darlington and, on one occasion, rather impressed her by saying that I had seen her wearing a swimsuit, lying on an orange towel whilst sun-bathing in the college grounds. I had been at 10,000 feet at the time!

Throughout our training we visited various organisations to broaden our minds and one such visit was to a coal mine outside Middlesbrough. We were suited up in overalls, gloves and helmets and off we went in the lift for a few hundred feet. At the bottom were the pit ponies, who looked well cared for, and tunnels in two or three directions. We walked for what seemed miles and eventually crawled into a tunnel about twelve-feet wide and three to four-feet deep. To one side was a conveyor belt and, on the other, at the coalface, were men hacking with hand tools and some machines removing coal. This was then taken by other men and placed on the belt. We had barely enough room to manoeuvre our way along this route and came to a stop some way in. There we were talking to the miners who were saying that they wouldn't want to do our job and we were being positive that we wouldn't want to do theirs!

To give us a taste of sea rescue we were taken out to sea in the Redcar lifeboat and each dumped over the side with a one-man dinghy and left to experience the sheer discomfort of sitting in a pool of sea water in a space just big enough to sit and be subjected to the movement of the waves as the rubber distorted at every opportunity. You may well be comfortable on a boat even in a rough sea, but the feeling in a small dinghy is quite different and most unpleasant.

Anyway, while we were all in our dinghies and feeling sorry for ourselves the fog rolled in! Oh dear, I could only see for about 100 to 150 yards and felt suddenly very alone and vulnerable, as did all the others. Fortunately, vertical visibility was okay and the helicopter suddenly appeared, lowered a sling, no winchman, and I was pulled from the dinghy but left hanging there as I was hurriedly flown to the beach and dumped. Suspended below the chopper I had noticed half-a-dozen aerials, some of which were like a shark's teeth, and I realised that if there was an engine failure I would have been stabbed badly before being crushed then drowned! The helicopter went looking for the others.

Meanwhile, the lifeboat was collecting the other drifters. I wandered up to watch the lifeboat return and as it came alongside the jetty the swell took it below the level then lifted up with the nose of the boat having turned under one of the quays. The boat was quite badly damaged, so that turned out to be a costly experience.

The course was going well and nobody had been chopped, i.e. dismissed for failing a regular check-ride. Halfway through the course, or thereabouts, we were let loose in the single seat Vampire FB.5 (FB = fighter bomber) which made us feel we were in a real aeroplane. It was so small and the cockpit so confining that you felt you were putting it on and wearing it rather than climbing in and flying it.

The FB.5s were parked in a line right in front of the squadron offices with a narrow taxiway strip between the offices and the aircraft. Also, there was a slight slope up to the offices so, when returning from a trip, it was normal to keep the speed up a bit rather than have to use too much power for turning into your space. This always worked well until the time I returned using speed and verve only to find, as I arrived in my position facing the marshaller, that my brakes had failed. Neither of us had any means to stop the aircraft so he sensibly dived out of the way and I shut the engine down and waited. I went through the little picket and rail boundary of the grass/flower bed bordering the offices and stopped short of the wall. The squadron clerk's face in the window is quite memorable. Brake failures have been a feature of my flying and driving life; so far, I had had the brakes fail on my MG KN and now this. Eventually I would have three failures in cars and three in aircraft.

Low flying was particularly exciting at Middleton St George as we had interesting hills and valleys close by, namely the Cleveland Hills. The lowest height, to which we were authorised dual or solo, was 200 feet above the ground with no low flying over built-up areas. One solo trip took me up a valley and as the ground rose so did I in accordance with the rules. However, there at the top of the valley were two big trees with a very large gap between them. Despite being quite aware of the regulations to which I had resolutely adhered, this was too much of a temptation. I went straight between the trees at about 300 knots which was incredibly exhilarating. Not only had I broken the rules as any redblooded student pilot and fighter pilot would have done, I went round to do it again.

Just as I approached the gap a shovel appeared, climbing rapidly. I pulled back and disappeared heavenwards. The time was around 1300 hours and I guess I had really frightened and seriously annoyed a farm worker having a quiet lunch. For the next few days I was terrified that I had been reported and that, quite rightly, it would have been the end of my flying career. Phew!! Nothing happened. Lucky me, but it was not a very clever thing to have done. Mind you it was great fun.

The Royal Air Force changed its cold-weather clothing issue, so all those beautiful wool-lined boots and flying jackets were recalled and we received quite unglamorous but efficient windproof gear instead. Muggins, that's me, handed all the good stuff in and went off with the new stuff, only to find out later that nearly all the other guys had gone to stores without the old stuff and were not even asked for it. I was so angry with myself, especially when I saw how warm and smooth the other guys looked when winter came.

We all had our final navigation checks, instrument ratings and handling checks and, suddenly, passing out parade came. Normally, the parade is held outside, all parents and family are seated and cared for and the successful course does a march past. At the salute to the reviewing officer, the instructors of the other squadron perform a fly-past; it's all very military and impressive.

On 15 December 1955 it rained! So, we had our passing out parade in a hangar with a Vampire T.11 at one end and an FB.5 at the other. My parents were there with Greta and Barry but Maureen, now very much my girlfriend, was unable to get the time off from her teaching post in London.

The usual gathering in the mess followed all the ceremonial stuff and my mother eagerly sewed on my new wings. That evening was spent celebrating in the usual service style, i.e. in the bar and with much jollity. Unfortunately, my father had to be back for the next day so the family left very early. Dad left the car for me and they all went home by train. What a wonderful gesture as it meant I could move my now accumulated kit and acquired bits and pieces in comfort.

Later that evening, probably near midnight, I set off south on the A1 (no motorways then) for London and to see Maureen on my way home.

About 0200 with me trying not to nod off, the fan-belt broke. No big thing you may say, but I had spent the last eight months flying an aircraft which had a big red light in front of me to indicate engine fire. Well, the sudden appearance of the battery red warning light got a similar reaction to the one in the aircraft: it got my full and immediate attention and, for a moment, I was back in the cockpit! The surprise nearly sent me off the road, but in a couple of seconds (even ten!) I realised what it was, woke up and stopped the car. There was nothing I could do, so drove on hoping for a garage to be open; yes, in those days it was possible to find one even in the middle of the night.

Well, within a few miles – Bingo. Not only was there a garage open but the owner was there and fitted a fan belt within minutes and I was on my way. I wasn't to see a 'fire warning light' again for a couple of years but next time it was to be for real!

I stayed at Maureen's place for a couple of days, then home for a fortnight's leave before Fighter Training School at 229 OCU (Operational Conversion Unit) at RAF Chivenor near Barnstaple, Devon.

Faster Jets

Chivenor, January to March 1956

No. 229 OCU was a fighter training school using Vampire T.11s (this time with ejector seats) and Hunter Mk 1s. Both aircraft were used for training to fire cannon at targets. Upon our arrival we all congregated at our new crew-room and met our flight commander, whose name I have forgotten, who advised us that no matter what we had been known as before we would now have new nicknames. I had the pleasure of being renamed 'Douche' as my surname could sound close to 'Bidet'. Very funny! Naturally, I responded to this name whenever he, or other instructors, used it but my fellow students were ignored if they used it.

He, the flight commander, made it quite clear that if we did not satisfy the exam requirements, or him, then we would not progress to fly the Hunter. We would be taking written exams, tests in the cockpit and flying tests in the Vampire. I believe the standard required was 95 per cent written and 100 per cent in the cockpit, where you sat and had constant questions on all instruments and aircraft performance. The reason for such stringent rules was simply that there were, at that time, no two-seater Hunters, so you had to be utterly versed in all aspects of the aircraft before being allowed to play with it.

However, whilst all the preparation for the Hunter was underway I had around thirty-three sorties in the Vampire to learn gunnery, battle formation, close formation and methods of attacking. The way to look at fighter aircraft then was to regard them as a gun/cannon platform which had to be flown to the enemy and then fired, preferably accurately.

Gunnery was carried out by firing at a flag six-ten metres long by a metre, towed behind a Mosquito which would fly at varying speeds. Each of the three to six pilots who would fire at it would have their shells' noses painted a particular colour. After all had fired, the Mosquito would return and drop the flag which would be laid out on the grass in front of the crew-room. We would eagerly search for holes with our colour around the edges. I am very pleased to say that then, and on my squadron, I was rated high average.

If we practised gunnery air-to-air, as we called it, then there would only be film taken of our efforts. This ciné, as it was called, always activated when you fired the guns or not, as long as you pulled the trigger and you were aiming through the gunsights. The gunsight was a heavy metal-and-glass piece of equipment which was only raised when needed. You pressed your forehead against the rubber/sponge headrest and concentrated only on the target. You looked at no other instruments. It was necessary, for further accuracy, to set the sight for the wingspan of your target. To this end, after every morning meteorological (Met) briefing we spent ten to fifteen minutes identifying aircraft as they were shown on a screen for about two seconds at a time. These included friends and 'foes' and we had to recite name and wingspan.

Every afternoon after flying was finished we collected in the 'ciné' room where all the film of the day was shown. It could be quite embarrassing when your efforts were greeted with catcalls rather than appreciative grunts. The room was quite small so, with everybody smoking, it was often difficult to see the screen.

The best ciné was that shown one day for the course behind us. We all wanted to see it even though we would normally only see our own. Ian Cadwallader, whilst firing on the flag, did what we had all been warned against, namely, don't get so locked on to the target that you put the Mosquito in danger! Well, Ian got locked on and the ciné lovingly showed the flag and then, slowly, the Mosquito appearing on the screen. It continued until centre stage when the left engine disintegrated! Ian broke off the attack and fled home. The Mosquito, flown by a Polish pilot from the war, landed safely. The pilot stormed across to Ian's crew-room and was advised that nobody knew where he was. He was actually hiding behind the sofa! Anyway, all was forgiven that evening as the two of them shared a few beers, probably all paid for by Ian.

Eventually, the big day arrives. Having been examined and tested I finally sit in the Hunter with the intention of flying it. Final briefing given at the aircraft, and away I go. Intriguingly, at the aircraft next to me there is a very senior officer, Air Vice Marshal McEvoy, preparing for his first-ever Hunter flight. Intriguing for two reasons. I know he only had a quick run-down on the checks, etc. (experienced pilot, of course) and he had a seriously deformed back and I felt that if he had to eject it would cause serious injury.

Anyway, I followed him along the taxiway, revelling in the feeling of having made it to achieve my original dream and follow the great Neville Duke. AVM McEvoy took off and I was cleared on to the runway.

Cleared for take off: full power against the brakes, then release brakes. After the Vampire, the kick in the back was amazing (goodness knows what it's like nowadays) and I just hung on to the control column unable to believe the acceleration. Anyway, I raised the nose at the correct speed and she just shot into the air. I was so impressed that I forgot to raise the gear immediately but all became calm and a joyfulness came over me. The climb to 30,000 feet was swift and exhilarating.

At altitude I carried out all the exercises required, including aerobatics, and when the fuel reached 'Bingo', which is a pre-set fuel level at which a warning light illuminates, I set off home. At that point I suddenly thought 'Crikey, now I have to land this thing.' In the event, all went well and, upon arrival at dispersal, i.e. parking place, I was reluctant to get out. It had been a wonderful experience and more was to come. That afternoon I had my second Hunter flight and was cleared to go supersonic! It was Valentine's Day 1956.

After that I only flew in the Vampire one more time and that was for my instrument rating. All in all, there were twenty-three Hunter flights, all of which were for air-to-air ciné, dogfights, close formation and practice engine failures and safe landings.

We were allowed to go supersonic on a few occasions, but only over the sea. The first time is a massive ego trip as you think '*Wow, I've gone faster than the speed of sound*' and you have a great feeling of achievement. However, the Hunter was a great gun platform up to about Mach 0·95 but at supersonic speeds (Mach 1·1 for the Hunter) there was little or no manoeuvrability for practical gunnery. But, hey, it was great fun. Mach 1 is the speed of sound at your current position; for general use you could say that on a normal day it's 600 mph at sea level and 590 mph at 30,000 feet.

Another of the exercises we were given was to get airborne over the dunes, gear up and don't climb. Then with full-power try not to hit the sea whilst going alongside the Devon and Cornwall coast. Now this was fantastic because very quickly the speed was around 600-plus knots (690 mph) and the exhilaration was unbelievably high. I guess the height was between 100 and 200 feet, which was more than enough for safety. If you aim at the horizon you can't hit anything! Well, maybe a seagull with a poor lookout and hearing!

The time came for selecting the squadron or area to which you wished to be posted. If the command personnel department could assign you your choice then they would. At this time there were many squadrons in Germany (2nd TAF, Second Tactical Air Force) due to the 'Cold War' and many pilots bid for there, but I elected for 111 Squadron at North Weald, north-east London area. When the postings came out I was posted to Wattisham and another pilot was posted to North Weald, although I was the only pilot who had applied for there. It appeared that his first choice had been Germany, but none of our course was assigned that posting. Apparently, he was friendly with the station adjutant and a fiddle had been made. Sadly, I did not pursue this. I may have been in the 111 Squadron aerobatic team of the Black Arrows when they looped a twenty-two-ship formation. A record I believe that stands to this day. Had I been more mature and less concerned about being considered a 'sneak' I would have pursued what was obviously an injustice.

As it happens, this event probably helped change my future career in a very positive way by giving me only a short fighter career which guided me into transport flying. The course finished late in March 1956 and I started with 257 (Burma) Squadron in early April.

Chivenor had provided me with a few interesting experiences other than the joy of flying. One of our instructors had a car with the registration RAF 1 which the station commander coveted but was unable to buy. I mention this to prepare the way for an episode many years down the line.

Sometime during early March, the batman came in with my morning cup of tea, shook me and left. When I didn't turn up for the morning met. briefing the mess was contacted and someone came to wake me, but couldn't. As said earlier, our accommodation was huts with individual rooms. To keep these rooms warm, we all had coke stoves and a ration of fuel. During the night the back of my stove had cracked and the fumes had given me carbon-monoxide poisoning. I woke up in the station hospital (sick quarters) that late afternoon with a stinking headache and feeling pretty rough. It had been a close call.

On 4 April all servicemen got a massive pay rise which, in the case of pilot officers, was about 70 per cent. The actual figure I can no longer remember but it was about £28 per month which was very good then. Many aircrew set off to lay down their savings as a deposit on a car with ridiculously low monthly payments. I ended up with a 1937 1.5-litre Jaguar, black with blue leather upholstery and walnut panels.

Alongside Chivenor's Northern boundary was the GWR (Great Western Railway) railway line from Penzance to London. Halfway along the boundary was a little station called Wrafton which served the local rail lines.

However, the powers-that-be, whoever they are, had arranged for the London service to stop there at 1204 hours every Saturday. This was a magnificent perk as it meant that those with girlfriends in London, or for other reasons, could get away easily. However, it had to be arranged that those of us who wished to avail ourselves of the opportunity had to be in the flight's good books to arrange that we were free from the last flight. We would then rush to the mess, pack and change and run. Usually, we managed to get a lift to the airfield boundary, over the rails and across the track in time. The train was always on time! There were four to six regulars and we would repair to the bar to start the weekend off well. The GWR was undoubtedly the best rail service in England at the time with the best staff and carriage layouts. This was the general opinion of all experienced rail travellers.

In the bar there were four tables, each about three-feet square with fiddles all round. For the non-navy and younger readers a fiddle was/is a little wall or rail to prevent glasses et al from sliding off and on to the floor. By the time we arrived at Paddington all tables were full of bottles and we happily wandered along the platforms to our awaiting ladies. We might then separate or continue on to the Gremlin Club nearby which was very much a flyer's club.

Later some might go to the Captain's Cabin, which was a basement bar in a hotel in Norris Street behind the Haymarket. It was the first bar in London to serve draught Carlsberg lager which took forever to pour. At the bar was a book in which you could log your arrival and expected movements or search for a friend for a meeting, etc. The book was in regular use and very useful. It was a wonderful meeting place and bar.

The night train would drop us off at Wrafton in time to make the Monday morning met. briefing.

No. 257 (Burma) Squadron
Wattisham April 1956 – March 1957

I arrived at Wattisham early April 1956 and was allocated a room in a real, brick-built, old-fashioned officers' mess; no huts this time. As is normal on reporting to new units you are required to check in to appropriate departments such as stores, admin. offices, safety equipment, flying equipment, etc. Of course, the best of all was to report to my new commanding officer Squadron Leader John Steele, a bluff and burly Somerset man. He was most welcoming and led me to the crew-room of 257 (Burma) Squadron to meet the pilots. Most of them were young, albeit a bit older than my nineteen and a half, plus one or two old guys of twenty-six to twenty-seven! A day-fighter squadron in those days comprised sixteen pilots, two flight commanders and a CO and, usually, sixteen aircraft. The crew room was one of three or four rooms allocated to the squadron and part of the hangar in which our aircraft were stored and serviced. All rooms overlooked the airfield.

My new flight commander was just about to be replaced by Roger Purdue, who was slightly notorious. He had been based at the Central Fighter Establishment at RAF Raynham, Norfolk, where weapons training and trainers were based. He got airborne leading an eight-ship formation when the weather closed in rapidly. They were diverted to RAF Marham, also in Norfolk, but only two made it. The others carried out their own attempts to land elsewhere. Hubert Slaney managed to land at RAF Kenley, in Surrey (!), went off the end of the short runway but was unhurt and the aircraft flew again. Another pilot tried a landing in a field (or crashed into it) and was killed. The remaining four ejected and all survived with their aircraft crashing into open country. The loss of one pilot and five aircraft did not go down well with the Air Staff and it even got mentioned in the Commons. Roger had no real control over the events but I guess it affected his career.

NO. 257 (BURMA) SQUADRON

During the early part of the Second World War, 257 Squadron was down to a couple of Spitfires so the Burmese government gave the Air Ministry £250,000 to re-equip the squadron. In recognition of that generosity, 257 was renamed the Burma Squadron and the crest portrayed a *Chinthe*, the Burmese mythical king of beasts, and the motto became: *Thay myay gyee shin shwe thay*, pronounced I believe as *Thai my gee shin sway tie*. The shortened meaning is 'Death or Glory' but we all understood it to mean: 'Death, the earth-life the golden umbrella'.

The most famous of our wartime commanders was Robert Stanford Tuck (1940-42) who, when chasing a bomber away from Cardiff, forced it to jettison its bombs. By an incredible coincidence the bombs killed his brother-in-law at an army camp.

Because I was newly qualified, I knew none of the other pilots but was made most welcome. Cigarettes were offered and a coffee. Coffee was rated as NATO (we were part of the North Atlantic Treaty Organisation) plus, or minus, i.e. Nato Standard was milk, condensed or evaporated, and two sugars. So, a NATO one was standard but one sugar etc., etc. There was, of course, a coffee kitty and we took turns at being milk monitor, washer-up etc. I realised I was a member, albeit new, of a special club. My first flight was on 11 April with the CO in a Meteor 7 to be shown around the area, local rules and to put me at ease, even as he was obviously checking my handling.

The Hunter F.2 was powered by an Armstrong Siddeley Sapphire Mk101 engine with 8,000lb static thrust at MSL which made a distinctive hunting and haunting sound when idling. She carried 316 gallons (1,206kg) of fuel, some of which was in tanks wrapped around the engine.

> The wingspan was 10.26 metres (33 feet 10 inches)
> Length 14 metres (46 feet 3 inches)
> Maximum weight 7,410kg (16,300lb)
> Maximum speed 620 knots (713 mph) Mach No. – no limit,
> but you would be pushing it 1.1+. Initial climbing speed was
> 420 knots.

The Lightning, later on, could do brake release to 40,000 feet in 1 minute 40 seconds!

My first Hunter F.2 flight was on 16 April, an area reconnaissance and acclimatisation, also known as a sector recce. From then on it was regular formation, tail-chasing, battle plans and ciné, ciné, ciné. Every evening into the ciné room for the ritual cheering and, friendly, jeering as successes and failures were assessed by our peers as well as the designated gunnery instructors. We did the odd sonic boom over the sea just for the hell of it but, as I explained earlier, it had no real operational use; we called it 'Big Thunder!'

An early introduction to the joy of Fighter Command and the reasonable tolerance we were shown was one night when most of us went to the Pin Mill Inn in Ipswich. We had a great time and got really fuelled up on high-octane juice. On the way back, with the boss driving, he missed a bend and we entered a field via its open gate. Upon reversing to the road we were greeted by a policeman on a bicycle. The conversation followed the course you might expect but was interrupted by Hamish being sick on his back wheel! He regarded this with a somewhat miffed expression and said, 'Now drive carefully, sir, and keep out of the fields.' That was it! Hamish became a successful test pilot later in his career.

During this period of the Cold War there were dozens of Russian 'fishing trawlers' around the UK and Europe with an amazing array of aerials; they were, of course, spy ships and, usually, our sonic booms were aimed at them. It was also great fun to go past at sea level and high speed to annoy them. We were usually so low the sailors (spies) were looking down into our cockpits. I vaguely recall that the Russians whinged about this and that and it was stopped.

Sadly, in April we lost one of our pilots. I was walking out to the aircraft for my first night flight in the Hunter when Roger Purdue, my flight commander, called me back as he wanted a more senior pilot to get his trip first. I shall call him 'John'; he got airborne and almost immediately called that he was abandoning the aircraft at 10,000 feet due to engine fire. He was eventually found dead next to his ejector seat but his parachute was found some distance away. He had separated from the seat and parachute and fallen to his death.

Let me explain this early model of the Martin-Baker seat. There was a handle above the pilot's head which, when pulled down, provided a face-shield for protection, and another handle between the legs. The flying suit had built-in belts below the knees with a metal ring attached. When the pilot prepared himself in the seat he would take two cords which were attached to the seat, weave them through each leg restraint and fix them to the seat.

When seated you first secured your parachute straps into the harness box and lugs locked the straps inside. To release the harness you turned the front of the box and banged it, thus forcing the lugs to retract and letting the harness free. Then you secured the seat harness. (Modern ejector seats have a combined seat and parachute thus needing only one securing method.) Ideally, for comfort, the seat harness box did *not* rest on the parachute harness box.

Upon pulling either of the handles on the seat a train of action would be started. Firstly, the canopy was immediately jettisoned and the seat would fire and start up its ramp, the legs would be pulled back by the restraints thus avoiding damage on the hood surrounds and you were on your way. As the seat leaves the aircraft, a small drogue parachute about three to four feet in diameter deploys and stabilises the seat which now should descend in an upright position.

If you are above 10,000 feet, that's it; nothing else happens! The screen is protecting your face, if that's the handle you used, and your legs are secure and cannot flail around, and oxygen is supplied via a small bottle attached to the seat and your mask.

Attached to the seat is a barometric capsule set to approximately 10,000 feet and, as the seat descends through that height, many things happen more or less at once. The shackle to which the drogue is attached separates from the seat, the seat harness at its anchor points is released and your legs are freed. The drogue which is attached to your parachute now pulls and causes it to deploy, the seat falls away from you and that's it again; you are now a parachutist.

If you eject below 10,000 feet then what I described just becomes a continuous action and you are at the end of a parachute in seconds. The intention is, that however badly you may be injured, if you can pull one of those handles, you will arrive safely on the ground.

At the time of the accident we had no idea what had happened but a fellow pilot, Colin Buttars, and I started experimenting with harnesses and eventually hit upon a strange occurrence. We felt that the possibility existed that 'John' had placed his harness box on his parachute box and that the blast of air with ejecting at 420 knots (483 mph) could have created a sharp blow to the harness box. Sure enough, when we approximated the force of the blow, the parachute lugs moved and one or more of the parachute harnesses were released. We will never be sure if that is what happened to 'John' but a new device was introduced that, no matter how hard you hit the parachute box, it couldn't happen again. Incredibly it was a simple clip which could be made for pennies. I like to think that Colin and I contributed something good for flight safety but we never heard any more about it.

Another excitement we had then was to intercept the Russian Tupolev Tu-95 strategic bombers that used to cross the North Sea and approach our shores. NATO assigned codenames to Soviet aircraft and these as bombers were known as Bears; fighters had codenames beginning with F. All along the east coast of England and Scotland there were dozens of fighter squadrons based and at any time of day or night there were three or four on standby. At the end and to the edge of all fighter airfield runways was an ORP (operational readiness platform) which could hold four to six aircraft (usually four). Four aircraft would be parked there, each with a radio line attached. This line was directly connected to the Command Centre. Two of the aircraft would be manned and two pilots would be in the readiness hut next to the ORP.

On the command to the two manned aircraft, 'Wattisham, Yellow (or whatever) pair, Scramble', a few things would happen. First, a book which was keeping the pilot occupied would be thrown out. Second, all checks having been done, you'd raise a bar in front of the control column and press the start button; this connected all essential services. Third, you'd hit the close canopy switch and, fourth, as the engine accelerated you'd go to full power and go. Thirty seconds from call to halfway down the runway. Immediately at lift off, gear up, keep tight formation and call radar. You would then be guided to the advancing Russian bomber. The Russians were doing this to constantly check our readiness and we always obliged. The Hunter leader would fly alongside the aircraft and signal 'Go away' or similar and, as often as not, the Russian would wave or shrug his shoulder, grin and turn away. Meanwhile the other Hunter hung around at the back and eyeballed the rear gunner. On one occasion the rear gunner waved a bottle of Coca-Cola at me and grinned. I was surprised, because they rarely had enough to eat in Russia let alone import American goods.

At the time all this was going on it was rated 'Top Secret', so we could never recount our stories to anyone. Whenever we were on standby we were fully armed with the trigger lightly taped and you had better have a good explanation if you returned to base and the tape was broken. The intention, of course, was to avoid an international incident by accidental firing of cannon. Nevertheless, we were armed in case one day the Bears did not turn back and showed aggressive intent. As it was only a game for them, albeit annoying to the government, we hoped it would never turn nasty.

Other than the occasional standby duties the squadron was constantly practising fighter tactics, attempting to shoot each other, and others, with ciné, dog-fighting and often returning to base with the engine at idle, i.e. with engine throttled back, to simulate engine failure and emergency landing.

So, we would get airborne and hunt for trade, i.e. victims for our own ciné practice interceptions. The Americans had the F-86E or –F, known to us as the Sabre, which gave us good practice at dog-fights etc. as they had a similar performance. Also, we came against other Hunter squadrons, British, Dutch and Belgian, and the French in their Mystères. We had two radio boxes in each aircraft pre-tuned to VHF frequencies, usually No. 1 was the tower, No. 2 the approach area, No. 3 local radar, etc., etc. One of the frequencies was pre-set to NATO common, which was used by all NATO aircraft for various reasons.

At 1100 hours on any Tuesday if an aircraft over Brest in western France, usually a French aircraft, found that conditions were good for a dog-fight he would transmit the words 'Trapiste, Trapiste', and those with time or inclination or, more importantly, fuel would roar off to Brest for a great mêlée and some fun ciné. There were the usual suspects of British, American, French, Dutch, Belgians and, occasionally, the funny looking SAAB J-29 Tunnans from Sweden. It all added fun to the ciné session that evening. How there was never a collision I do not know!

On the odd occasion we called radar for assistance to find trade, we would often be given a heading that would take you straight over the radar. In those days the screen had a circle about five-miles-diameter where the lady (nearly always ladies) would advise you that you were approaching her dark area, i.e. for a short while there would be no sign of you. This information gave rise to numerous comments, always of a dubious nature, and pilots vied with each other for what they thought would be 'funnier'.

Needless to say, the ladies of all ranks were getting tired of our 'humour' and eventually all squadrons were visited by a senior officer and ordered to desist. All these radar stations were deep underground and, manned by fighter controllers, officers and other ranks, did a very good job, always calm and lovely to listen to.

In late 1956 we had a Belgian squadron visiting us and I was charged with showing half-a-dozen around RAF Trimmingham, one of the fighter control bases. Whilst down below and being briefed on all we could see of the North Sea and environs, a warning klaxon went off. This was an emergency signal of perceived threat to the UK, so immediately we were ushered out. However, as we were leaving, I saw the reason for the fuss, a return on the screen was travelling north from Holland at at least 1,000 mph and then stopped. Then it shot off again, but to the north-east at the same speed. In the time I watched it, it went from abeam the Wash to around Scarborough in just a few seconds. Okay, sceptics, what was it?

These Belgian pilots and their fellow squadron members flew theirs alongside us and independently. It was when they were alone they went hunting a little wildly. Their squadron motto was 'Get In' which they surely did; the ciné evenings were interesting as these guys had broken all the rules and had film of many civilian aircraft, including a Comet. They were having a great time!

When the time came to leave they were given a final dining-out, a farewell dinner and I and another pilot were told to entertain them until they wished to leave and that we were excused met. briefing and flying in the morning. Great, so we stayed up late, had a few beers and went to bed happy. In the morning my batman brought me a cup of tea and I advised him I was okay for a lie-in. About 0800 one of the pilots shook me awake and said the CO (who by now was J.B. Carruthers) was livid and wanted to know why I was not at met. briefing. I reported to the CO and we two late-comers were ordered to get airborne. Despite our protestations, he had forgotten last night's orders; we flew off to do practice interceptions which involve one aircraft flying straight and level (S & L) and the other making various approaches and taking ciné. Thank goodness, we did not have to dogfight. Anyway, I'm sitting there straight and level, mind in neutral, when the cockpit goes dark. I immediately looked up to my left and all I could see were oil slicks, rivets and a lot of Hunter. Fortunately, the rate of roll is 420 degrees per second, so I got out of there safely, but that was close. I told the other guy (I know his name but he's always denied this happened, he must have been in a worse condition than me) that I was returning to base. He landed immediately after me and burst a tyre. Oh dear!

At last the Belgians were ready to go home, so duly got airborne and we waited expectantly for the farewell fly-past that was a normal way of saying thank you. Well, what a disappointment! Slow and steady at 1,000 feet and off to Belgium. We stood around bemoaning their timidity when I saw little dots on the horizon and drew attention to them. It was them! They came across the field at zero feet and flat out. One of them passed the air traffic control caravan at the end of the runway so low that the airman inside was looking down into the cockpit. Another went between our hangars so low that the windows in the roof of the stores centre, EPAS, behind shattered and glass showered onto a female clerk. She was uninjured but the shock caused some 'personal discomfort'.

Shortly after this our senior guys went on a similar jolly (sorry, exchange training visit!) to a Dutch squadron at Leeuwarden, I believe. They were no fools! The Air Officer Commanding Fighter Command was to do his annual inspection the next week and the juniors were left to do all the 'bullshine' in preparation. Eventually, Dickie Millward and I had had enough; it was late Saturday afternoon so I called my father and suggested we all meet at his fantastic golf club, The Warren near Woodham Walter in Essex. After a week of cleaning, scrubbing, painting and trying to fit in a bit of flying it was a good evening.

Low flying was always great fun and no more so than when we 'played' Hare and Hounds. Canberras from Bomber Command would 'invade' the UK from the North Sea by coming in as low as possible and continuing inland. If the radar picked them up, which was not every time, then we were scrambled to intercept or find them. Usually, the only way to find them was to fly lower and see them popping up and down on the horizon. This meant flying on the deck and hoping they popped up whilst you were fleetingly down. The only real obstacles were wires and HT cables, although you had enough room to get under the latter. It was the best fun ever.

This low flying, and the general demeanour of fighters, had been tolerated for so long by the residents of Suffolk and, indeed, the whole east coast because, I believe, of the memories of the war and how much the Royal Air Force had achieved. However, slowly but surely the brakes were put on our noisier activities and the sheer freedom of expression we had so long enjoyed was coming to end. But not yet!

Throughout my time at Chivenor and the early days at 257 (Burma) Squadron we had not been allowed to fire our guns as the ejected shell cases were bouncing along the under-side of the aircraft and causing damage. A cure was underway. In the meantime, ciné, ciné, ciné. Wattisham enjoyed entertaining the Americans from Bentwaters near Ipswich and it was traditional that the guests would get up early the next morning and do a low-level Balbo against the hosts. This entailed the whole squadron at low-level straight across the buildings not the airfield. As a single man I had no idea what wives and families thought of it! Interestingly, the only Balbo flown by the Corpo Aereo Italiano (Italian [Expeditionary] Air Corps) against England during the war was seen off by No. 257 (Burma) Squadron. The term 'Balbo' is derived from Marshal Italo Balbo's name. As Italian air minister, he led a flight of twenty-four Savoia S.55 flying-boats from Rome to Chicago and then to New York, via Amsterdam, Londonderry, Rejkyavik, Cartwright, Shediac and Montreal. One aircraft crashed at Amsterdam. It was this flight that led to the term 'Balbo' being adopted for any large group of aircraft. Another word coined at the time was 'Balbada'.

The English Electric Lightning was about to move to Wattisham but the runways and facilities needed an upgrade so, in early June 1956,

257 Squadron was transferred to RAF Wymeswold in Leicestershire. As a junior member I had yet to get my own aircraft, so I flew up in an Anson whilst the aircraft came up in a gaggle. Ground crew and office staff came in a fleet of buses and trucks with all the gear we needed for three months away from home. On arrival it was found that there were insufficient rooms in the huts (again!!) for all the pilots, so the four junior guys, including me, were sent off to RAF Newton, near Nottingham, after a hurried phone call to confirm availability. The CO gave us his Land Rover and said he would see us in the morning.

We arrived at Newton to find a grass airfield, an administrative sort of establishment and a PERMANENT beautiful mess. We even had garages! We four were two to a room and in the morning what should I see but an apparition of beauty with a cup of tea in her hand. Yes, the batman was a batwoman! My room-mate, Chan Biss, never saw her as his hand was roaming over his bedside table hunting for his cigarettes. Every morning was the same, hand out, find ciggies and lighter, under bedclothes, smoke appeared followed by Chan, then drink of tea.

After a hearty breakfast we set off to Wymeswold on a twenty-five-minute journey to join the gang. Oh dear, much moaning about damp rooms, uncomfortable beds and even a rat, or rodent, on one bed. We were asked how we had fared and, with one of those wonderful telepathic and brilliant moments, we all declared that they should consider themselves lucky! We were at Wymeswold until mid-November and no-one bothered to visit us until two weeks before we returned to Wattisham. Boy!, were the CO and the other senior members disgruntled when they realised how much wool had been pulled over their eyes. We four juniors had visited their mess often because we needed to be a part of the team etc., but had managed to never let on how wonderful it was to live like kings and have the wonderful city of Nottingham on the doorstep!! And, yes, the prettiest girls in England were in Nottingham.

On one trip down to Wymeswold I was with Bill Dodds (or was it Jim Timms? Sorry chaps) being driven fast, of course, in his Jaguar when he was late turning his wheel as the dray lorry ahead braked suddenly. I realised, with about half a second to spare, that we would hit the corner. I ducked enough to the right just in time to avoid that corner as it tore through the windscreen and continued decapitating the car. Thank goodness for fighter pilot reactions.

One of our pilots was minding his business up at thirty-odd thousand feet when his seat fired unannounced. Fortunately, he must have been sitting in an upright position because he was uninjured by the action. However, he landed on the roof of a house opposite a local pub and broke his leg. There was a picture in the local paper of the pub owner climbing a ladder and carrying a tray with a brandy for the injured man. Whilst we were at Wymeswold, one of our fellow 263 Squadron pilots ejected whilst supersonic. He was Hedley Molland and, as he had used the firing handle with the screen, he was less damaged than he might have been. As it was, he had two beautiful black eyes!

As a farewell to Newton, Dickie and I did a beat-up, with their permission, followed by a really low fly-past in tight formation but Dickie hadn't mentioned that when level with the control tower he intended to do a very fast slow roll. His initial action was to roll towards me, safely but I was not to know that, so I immediately disappeared exit right at a great rate of knots. I was getting a bit tired of being attacked by my own side!

My time in Wymeswold was another opportunity for a really close call – see the opening chapter.

Generally speaking, there are three problems from which pilots, especially fighter pilots, can suffer: Sinus – we've done that; back problems due to posture when strongly strapped in and combined with high G forces; and 'piles' or haemorrhoids.

The ejector seat was a metal shell, as it were, with an area behind the shoulders and middle-back for the parachute and the seat area contained dinghy, survival rations and a really badly-positioned water container. The water was in a bladder about three inches in depth and acted as a cushion. This was very comfortable, except when on standby in the winter because they froze overnight! So the first crew, and even the second crew, would sit for an hour thawing them out with their bottoms. One or two guys had bad piles. Thankfully, I only had the sinus problem; mind you, that gave me occasional trouble throughout my career.

Whilst I was grounded we had our 'summer camp' at Strubby in Lincolnshire. We were taking part in the annual Fighter Command exercises to enable the Command to employ all, or most, squadrons on a war footing. Sadly, my only contribution was to act as an operations officer or co-ordinator whilst the other guys did the work. One day Lieutenant 'Freddie' Mills, our Royal Navy exchange officer, had to land with his left main undercarriage stuck in the wing. He carried out a straightforward landing but with the inevitable swerve to the left. He careered across the airfield, leaving a trail of dust and clods of earth, heading straight for the ATC building. Fortunately, he stopped before he got there but those on the ground floor were not to know that as they fled. The only injury was that of an airman who went through a narrow door at the same time as another; they jammed and when he got through he was found to have dislocated his shoulder. Lieutenant Mills was fine.

For security reasons all fighter squadrons were given new call signs at regular intervals, rarely longer than ten days and usually for less than a week. I recall my individual call sign was 11 (eleven, or one-one) but we were all mortified when a new call sign was DARLING. Darling one-one was not happy because you can imagine the ribaldry we received. Someone in the command security really had it in for 257 because our next call sign was DEAREST! This was too much to bear but it was not for long.

Prior to my sinus problems we had all our aircraft fitted with Sabrinas (those of you of my era will know who she was) which were bulbous protuberances under the cannon mountings. These caught the rejected shell casings thus avoiding damage to the fuselage. We all eagerly set off to the North Sea gunnery ranges to try out our guns. This was my first opportunity to fire the Hunter guns and I set off in a four-ship formation with Squadron Leader Steele. Unfortunately, the weather was quite unsuitable with low cloud base and poor visibility but the boss was not going to let that get in his way. We had radar guide us accurately to the safe area of the range and we dived in line-abreast (i.e. straight line next to each other) and at his command we all fired our guns. Whilst the recoil is taken up in the weapons it still causes the aircraft to decelerate about 40 knots, which doesn't matter. However, it mattered to me! My guns jammed after less than a second and I was now out in front; our wing tips had only been a few feet apart so I felt I was in the midst of trouble. It may sound improbable but I could see the other guys' shells going past, so I was gone – straight up! That was my one and only jam but it was enough.

Based in Germany were eleven RAF squadrons of Canadian-built North American F-86 Sabre fighters. The Canadair Sabre was excellent fun and pretty much on a par with the Hunter but not so pretty. It had an extra fuel tank which was wrapped around part of the engine! There were two fire-warning systems: one for the engine which was dealt with in the normal way and the other for the engine area fuel tank. The latter required an immediate departure from the aircraft, preferably by the Martin-Baker let-down system, i.e. the ejector seat.

An RAF pilot coming in for a break and landing had the warning as he approached the airfield, so immediately ejected and landed unhurt. The aircraft crashed at the edge of the field so, when the squadron Land Rover picked him up, he went over for a quick gloat. The last laugh was had by the aircraft as the fire heated the cannon ammo and shot him in the thigh! He survived.

Around this time John Steele had taken a few of us in groups and practised formation aerobatics. I don't know whether he had a secret hankering to form an aerobatic team or was just doing it for the hell of it. It was great fun, though. I could have made it in 111 Squadron!

Towards the latter part of 1956 the Americans changed from F-86 Sabres to F-100 Super Sabres. The new aircraft was not only faster in normal flight, it had an afterburner which created rapid acceleration. Whereas before you could, perhaps, jump an F-86 and have a bit of a scrap it was now near impossible. Once the F-100 got a whiff of you all that could be seen was huge fire in its tailpipe and it was gone.

Soon we were to hear the sad news that we were to be disbanded in the 1957 purge of the armed forces by Duncan Sandys, the Defence Secretary. On the day we were advised of our demise our photographers took pictures of us all as we got airborne on our various sorties. These pictures adorn many a wall, I'm sure. Certainly, mine has one.

Just after this news I was flying Nan Dog's aircraft and couldn't get the undercarriage down at first attempt. Upon landing, and before I had a chance to log the occurrence, ND turned up to the aircraft and I told him of the problem. Oh, don't worry, he said, it's always doing that. Okay, I thought, if he's happy, so be it.

Upon his return the left gear would not come down and when he landed he careered across the airfield, ploughed through the boundary hedge and stopped across the road. The local bus managed to stop just in time. It is believed that the lady sitting in the front row upstairs wet herself but that is probably just hearsay, but it would be understandable.

Three days before the end, i.e. on 28 March, I was flying the squadron hack, the Vampire T.11, with 'Steve' Stephens. His name was Brian, as is mine, but, as there were four Brians on the squadron, only the senior one was called Brian and the rest of us had nicknames; mine was Berney as my middle name is Bernard.

Anyway, I was flying a loop and, for no special reason, glanced into the cockpit and noted that the brake pressure had gone. We thought about it, checked what we could do, nothing, and returned to base, having advised them of the problem.

As luck would have it the wind was light and straight down the runway. I executed a nice landing, kept her straight (yes, I could do that now) and we stayed on the centre-line and trundled off the end of the runway. The ground was a bit soft and the right main gear stuck in the mud and we slewed right. We finished up at 90 degrees to the centre-line. No assistance arrived immediately and this meant it was game time for 257 and 263 Squadron. Every aircraft taking off came down the runway, got airborne about three feet, raised gear and flew straight over us with probably five to six feet to spare. Great fun for them, but Steve and I were getting sea-sick!

Eventually a Land Rover appeared and we were rescued. However, the Vampire took ages to be recovered because the constant bouncing up and down had buried the right wheel.

On 31 March we had our Farewell Ball in the Mess, which Maureen was able to attend as it was a weekend, and on 1 April we dispersed to our new units. As there were now fewer fighter squadrons and with only a few vacancies, the junior guys got various postings; I was en route to RAF Dishforth, near Boroughbridge in Yorkshire.

Time to Slow Down

No. 242 OCU, RAF Dishforth

There were six ex-257 guys posted to Dishforth and we were pretty fed-up with having had such a short time on fighters and all felt we were far too young to be assigned to these huge (in those days) lumbering machines. The Hastings was a four-engine piston aircraft used mainly in support of the Army carrying freight or despatching troops via parachutes. It was a tailwheel aircraft because, it is said, the Army had inadequate equipment to load anything into the aircraft if it has a nose wheel. The civilian version, the Handley Page Hermes, did well and looked much better with a nosewheel.

The ground school was somewhat dragged out with charts for weights and balance, load sheets and problems we had never envisaged with numbers. We were used to full fuel, full power and full speed. Transport aircraft need a little more planning, more attention to weight and load and, if you have full load, is there enough weight allowance for full fuel? No? Okay, how much and which freight should go?

My first flight was with a lovely chap, Flight Lieutenant Kirk. It was an air test, a new engine perhaps, and, incredibly, some stalls. My next and only other flight with him was a fun low-level tour of the Western Isles, although 150-200 knots at low level compared unfavourably with 600 knots. That was it! After he left the OCU, he was flying an Anson in bad weather, lost his radio and attempted a let-down in a 'safe' area to establish his exact position. Sadly, he appeared below cloud and before he could react he hit a drystone wall.

I had just the two flights, then off to RAF Colerne.

No. 24 (Commonwealth) Squadron

Our new base, Colerne, near Bath, had a real mess and access to Squadron HQ was a walk directly across the airfield and runway. We walked in summer, but used cars in winter. One day, having walked to HQ, I realised that my silver propelling pencil had fallen somewhere into the long grass! Help! A few of the guys and I did a search, police-style, line-abreast and, Bingo!, we found it.

Our new Squadron Commander was Wing Commander M.M. Mair, a bemedalled ex-wartime flyer, as were all the captains. Because the Hastings was quite a handful and because we new boys were so inexperienced, I'm afraid we were very restricted in our duties. The captain flew it, the flight engineer helped and guided with the throttles and the co-pilot (second pilot), that's me, was allowed to raise and lower the undercarriage and flaps and lock or unlock the tail wheel depending upon flight circumstances. On top of all this was the incredibly uncomfortable awareness that there was no ejector-seat! Eek!

I was explaining to Flight Lieutenant Lou Sedivy that I missed coming in fast to a break and landing and he said, 'Watch this.' He roared in (at 200 knots?) and broke into the circuit. There was this large and cumbersome beast playing at fighter aircraft and I was really nervous as it seemed quite unsafe. In fact, it was perfectly flown and very safe and put me nicely in my place.

My first overseas flight was to le Bourget, Paris, to collect a group of Maquis (wartime resistance fighters) to bring them to the UK for a re-union. We arrived about midday for a 1400 hours departure and the captain led us into the dining-room and all the crew started ordering a good meal. The prices put me off as I was broke at the time and, not wishing to talk about it, I said I was not hungry and wandered off.

Visiting the 'toilette' I saw a lady sitting between the entrances to the ladies and the gents. I chose to do the necessary away from her line of sight but was exceedingly surprised to be standing there having a pee whilst she was brushing down my jacket! Upon returning to the nourished crew I was in time to join them for cheese and biscuits, which I could afford. When the bill came I was mortified to hear the captain say, 'Please send it to the British Embassy.' No one had explained to me the finer point of travelling 'On Her Majesty's Service'. They had eaten well, dammit!

The Hastings had an entry-door under the aircraft near the nosewheel. On a flight from El Adem to Benghazi the Traffic Officer (TO) cycled out to greet and get the passengers on to the aircraft. Having finished his task, he put his bike in the hold and, using the nosewheel entry, joined the crew on the flight deck. At Benghazi he reversed the process much to the astonishment of the disembarking passengers. The reason was that Benghazi had no TO, so he would do the paperwork etc. for this aircraft and, having done the same for the next aircraft en route to El Adem, he would do the same again!

We had the occasional trip over Salisbury Plain to despatch paratroopers which was when I heard for the first time the expression that 'No pilot can understand why anyone could possibly want to jump out of a perfectly serviceable aircraft'. In the 1950s and 1960s there must have been many observers wondering why the Hastings could frequently be seen describing the weirdest manoeuvres through the air. Well, the Royal Air Force was extremely keen on training and, in particular, regular continuation training, i.e. qualified crews regularly, usually monthly, to practise those things they did all the time anyway. This could be a bit boring, so games were devised and a very popular one on the Hastings was performed with a tennis ball.

At the rear of the aircraft were two toilets; one was a 'ladies' but rarely used, as such, as ladies were not onboard too often. Forward of the two toilets was a large container (approximately 8-feet by 3-feet by a foot) which contained ballast according to the load and balance requirements. The game was for each crew member in turn to fly the aircraft and the tennis ball was dropped between the pilots' seats and the aim was to manoeuvre the aircraft to score two points if you got it in the ladies and one point for the gents. There were at least six crew members, captain, co-pilot, navigator, engineer, signaller, and despatcher, so it used up a reasonable amount of the two hours allocated.

Although I said the ladies was rarely used it was necessary when we transferred families to various overseas bases worldwide. A favourite way of passing the long hours en route was to have passengers up for a chat and give them a treat. Each crew member had an oxygen supply with a long tube designed to enable you to move around – so they stretched some distance. It was fun to get a passenger, a pretty girl for preference, and prepare the flight deck. Two tubes would be tied to the arms of the co-pilot's control column and then a pair of gloves tied over these. The passenger would be shown around the flight deck and would be fascinated by the movement of the control column tied in with the movement, i.e. turn, of the aircraft and the gloves expanding and contracting.

What was happening was that when the captain activated the auto-pilot to turn the aircraft the flight engineer would turn the oxygen on and off. The passenger could never refrain from asking what was happening and always accepted the explanation that the two tubes plus gloves was simply the auto-pilot.

At the end of June all the ex-257 guys on 24 Squadron received postings to 216 Squadron, Lyneham to train as co-pilots on Comet 2s.

How did this happen? Pilots, like police, doctors, Army, Navy etc. are a bit cliquey and at Wattisham and Wymeswold I guess 257 was, as well. However, welcomed into our ranks and parties was a similar-aged and likeable Admin. Officer, Len Dent.

Shortly after we went to 24 Squadron, Len was posted to Personnel Department P2 at Transport Command Headquarters, Upavon, Wiltshire. He was required to find half-a-dozen new pilots for the Comet and he repaid us in spades for having enjoyed his company.

So Pat Fleming, Chris Gill, T.A.M. 'Paddy' Smythe, B.I.L. 'Hamish' Hamilton and I found ourselves on a four-week course at the de Havilland factory at Hatfield to learn about one of the most beautiful aircraft ever to have flown.

De Havilland Comet 2

No. 216 SQUADRON, LYNEHAM, JUNE 1957

We arrived at RAF Lyneham, near Swindon, Wiltshire, in late June and were shown personally by Mr Quick, the Officers' Mess Manager, to our rooms. Yes! Huts again, and they were about 200 yards from the touch-down point of the main runway. However, as there were few movements at night, this was never a problem.

After meeting the 216 Squadron CO, Wing Commander Don Harper, we went through the usual process of signing in to all the departments including, of course, the obligatory visit to the Station Commander's house to leave our cards for his wife.

Formalities over, we set off for the de Havilland factory and airfield at Hatfield, near St Albans. We were billeted in the comfortable hotel opposite the main entrance which was an easy walking distance to the lecture rooms – huts again.

The course lasted one month which covered every technical subject on the Comet 2 and included many visits to the hangars, where, on one occasion, the jet ignition was demonstrated. Jet fuel needs a damned good kick up the backside to ignite so, instead of the little spark you see on your car, this is the size of a tennis ball. It's only used once to start the process and is not regular as in the petrol engine. Whereas before we dealt with one engine, one straightforward electrical, hydraulic, flight-control system, we now had to learn a multitude of systems and their inter-relationships. The instruction was excellent and relentless. The quality of the instruction made the exams reasonably comfortable.

During one lesson we were interrupted by the sound of machine-gun fire. We rushed outside to see the Comet sitting on the runway and the captain's head protruding from the small side window. Cruising gently down the taxiway was Sir Geoffrey de Havilland's Rolls Royce. The noise had been the bursting of all eight tyres as the aircraft had landed with the parking brake set to 'On'!

The Comet was the first ever production commercial jetliner and first flew on 27 July 1949. The original design team was formed in 1946 under chief designer Eric Bishop, who had designed the Mosquito before the Second World War, and the aim was for a thirty-six-seater, four seats abreast with a central aisle. It started out as the DH106 but was named Comet in 1947.

The prototype aircraft was initially to be fitted with Halford Ghost engines until the Rolls Royce Avon engines were ready. The aircraft was structurally tested in a water tank and no failures occurred despite 16,000 cycles which included pressures of 100 psi inside; 8.5 psi is the normal pressure difference between the interior and exterior – giving the cabin a height of 8,000 or so feet with the aircraft at 35,000 feet.

As the aircraft would be flying higher than any other airliner and, therefore, subjected to much lower temperatures and, as it was to be lighter, many new materials were needed for its construction. New alloys with riveting and chemical bonding were introduced, reducing risks of fatigue cracks.

The first production aircraft flew on 9 January 1951 and was lent to British Overseas Airways Corporation (BOAC) to enable them to plan future operations. On 2 May 1952 BOAC flew the first jet passenger service on the route London-Johannesburg. By 1953 BOAC had services to Johannesburg, Singapore and Tokyo.

In the meantime, the Comet 2 was being developed and many airlines were showing an interest. British aviation was roaring ahead of the pack. However, things started to go wrong when early incidents sowed seeds of doubt in one or two airlines. Two aircraft had been written off, one in 1952 and another in early 1953, put down as pilot error (of course!!!) but a design fault had caused failure to lift off when the nose wheel was raised a little too high on take-off. Then a Comet flew into a thunderstorm or a squall after take-off at Calcutta and crashed after its wings separated from the aircraft; it must have experienced massive turbulence.

The Comet had a new system of flight controls which were all hydraulic and considered to have less feel or feed-back than the old conventional cable controls. So the possibility was that the pilot had over controlled. Oh dear! As soon as pilot error reared its ugly head it was so difficult to find good excuses for them.

Then came the serious losses, on 10 January and 8 April 1954 two Comets, coincidentally after departing from Rome, both disappeared shortly after take-off without explanation. The Comets were grounded and the Royal Navy started to search for wreckage to help establish the reasons for the disasters. In the meantime, fatigue was finally considered as a cause and when pieces of the first crashed machine were found it was decided to subject an airframe to a test to destruction. It was placed in a huge water tank and subjected to repeated pressure tests.

I said again to my father, 'The square windows will be found to be the cause just as I said a few years ago.' Bingo!! It was not the windows, but something else was found, also square. On top of the fuselage were two square panels housing the ADF (Automatic Direction Finder) aerial which identified ground station transmissions and pointed a needle towards it. This had failed at the corner. Later on in my career, 1960, I did the Flight Safety Officers' course in London and, on a visit to Farnborough, actually handled that very panel.

All the Comet 1s were withdrawn from service and scrapped except for, I believe, one or two which had their square bits changed to match the Comet 2s which now went into the Royal Air Force to reform 216 Squadron in June 1956. Our Comet 2s had four Rolls Royce Avon Mk 503/4 turbojets with a maximum take-off weight (TOW) of 54 tonnes and our normal cruise above 30,000 feet was Mach 0.74 which is 74 per cent of the speed of sound, also known as the local speed of sound. The wingspan was 35 metres (115 feet) and the length was 29.3 metres (96 feet 1 inch). Range was 2,260 nautical miles, 2,600 statute miles, or 4,180 kilometres.

In the meantime, the Comet 3 was being developed in readiness for the Comet 4 which was to enter service with BOAC in September 1958. However, during the period when 216 got its Comets, to the much later inauguration of the Comet 4, we RAF crews provided masses of information to de Havilland. After every trip, be it training or inter-continental, we were met by the DH and RR representatives on our return. We would have to describe everything, good or bad, and this was transmitted to Hatfield.

Sadly, the contribution made by 216 Squadron is very rarely acknowledged publicly, in print or otherwise. I know for a fact that much of the anti-icing procedures stem from our/my experiences and changes were made to the fire-warning systems. There are countless other unheralded contributions. Furthermore, it was excitedly published that BOAC inaugurated the first jet transatlantic service on 4 October 1958. *No, they did not!* No. 216 Squadron had a regular transatlantic service from late 1957 to Christmas Island in the Pacific Ocean. Okay, it wasn't a fare-paying service but it was a regular passenger service on a jet aircraft. When you read about the Comet please remember the Royal Air Force contributions and achievements.

My first flight as a co-pilot (we didn't have first officers in the RAF) was to Bahrain on 1 August 1957. After landing, as I walked away from the aircraft, I remarked to myself that the heat from the jet engines could certainly be felt from a distance! It was my first venture South of Paris and I had no idea what such temperatures could be like. It was, of course, the ambient temperature of 40 degrees C in Bahrain! Actually, it was Royal Air Force Station, Muharraq; the British Empire was still in its near-entirety except for India and the Gold Coast (now Ghana) so just about everywhere I was to travel with 216 would be Royal Air Force stations: Malta (RAF Luqa), Libya (RAF Benina, Benghazi and El Adem), Cyprus (RAF Akrotiri, Nicosia), Iraq (RAF Habbaniyah), Sharjah (RAF Sharjah), Kuwait, Ceylon (RAF Katunayake), Singapore (RAF Changi, Tengah and RNAS Seletar), Northern Rhodesia (RAF Lusaka, Ndola, Livingstone), Southern Rhodesia (RAF Salisbury), Kenya (RAF Embakasi, Eastleigh), Ghana (RAF Takoradi), The Gambia (RAF Bathurst), Aden (RAF Khormaksar), Oman (RAF Seeb, Masirah, Salalah), Maldives (RAF Gan), Malaya (RAF Butterworth – later RAAF Penang), Sudan (RAF Khartoum), and, doubtless, others I never visited.

We had regular services to Edinburgh Field in Adelaide where we went with spares and scientists to service the Woomera rocket range. The route was interesting because the Comet started its cruise at or about, 30,000 feet depending on its weight and the outside air temperature. The upper limit of the airways at that time was 25,000 feet so we had no other traffic, and no constraints, other than international regulations or conflicts to restrict our routing. As we had no height restrictions either we could cruise/climb. That meant we set a constant power setting, 7,400 rpm on the Rolls Royce Avon engines and a constant speed of M. 0·74 (i.e. 74 per cent of the speed of sound at that point). This meant that as fuel was used and our weight decreased so we climbed. This was the perfect fuel economy procedure but, alas, is not possible nowadays.

The route Lyneham-Adelaide was fairly standard and could be: Lyneham-Nicosia-Bahrain-Karachi-Sri-Lanka (then Ceylon), Singapore-Darwin-Adelaide. Interestingly there were very few tracks, viz.: Lyneham-Frome (departure beacon), Ajaccio-Nicosia-Bahrain-Karachi-offshore India-Ceylon-Negombo-Car Nicobar (overhead due to no permit to overfly Indonesia), Changi-Darwin-Adelaide. That's twelve tracks UK to Australia!

As there were no crews positioned down route we stayed overnight with the passengers and continued the next day with the same aircraft. This was very civilised as we had morning only departures. Heading east we had the occasional night landing. The return flight was Adelaide-Darwin-Singapore (forty-eight hours off)-Car Nicobar-Negombo-Aden-El Adem-Lyneham. Just seven tracks Australia-Lyneham. Layovers outbound were at Bahrain, Karachi, Singapore, and Adelaide and inbound at Singapore (two nights), Khormaksar (Aden), then home.

Cruise climb plus direct tracks meant the aircraft's range was used to its maximum. Now, of course, the aircraft are allocated tracks and altitudes so they cannot be used to maximum efficiency.

Nicosia was very busy as the British Army was engaged with the terrorist organisation EOKA, led by Colonel Grivas, whose aim was to drive out the British. Its method was the usual terrorist system of targeting men from behind or women from any direction. This meant that when we were allocated accommodation off base, usually in the Crown Hotel, we were issued with side-arms. These comprised the Smith and Wesson .38 revolvers with five rounds and no holster. The Crown had a long bar and it was normal to see a line of ten to twelve RAF guys sitting on the stools and, in front of them, almost symmetrically, a pint of Keo, a Zippo lighter, a tin of 50 Woodbine Export (a great cigarette at 10s/- (50p) from the NAAFI) and a revolver. The guns were just too heavy for the pocket, unnerving in the waistband and looked silly if you just carried them. Just to add to the total annoyance, should you lose a round or, heaven forbid, the gun, then a court martial would be yours.

One night, after a few beers, one of our signallers went to bed, but finding an armed man in his room shot him. The door and mirror of his opened wardrobe cost him a few quid and he also had to face the wrath of the RAF.

In July 1958 King Faisal of Iraq was assassinated and the British forces went on to alert. No. 216 Squadron sent two or three aircraft to Nicosia to be on standby for troop-carrying into Habbaniyah if the need arose. There were also tactical aircraft, such as the Hastings and Beverley. On the way out, I flew with six or seven other crews as passenger for the purpose of being able to keep the Comets going on a twenty-four-hour basis, if necessary. The flight was very relaxed, so the captain, Roy Harling, left the co-pilot in charge whilst he came and joined us all for cards. Card games and Uckers, an evil form of Ludo invented by the Royal Navy, was played all over Transport Command squadrons and some games could last all day with people buying themselves in and out of games or moving in when someone else had to go and fly.

We had suitcases in the aisle to act as tables, Roy was halfway down the aircraft, when suddenly it reared up and rolled right. Panic! Everyone rolled into his seat and strapped in whilst Roy scrambled over the bags to get to the flight deck. It was all over in seconds but what a fright.

The co-pilot, the same chap who had nearly hit me with his Hunter a year or so ago, had felt the need for a stretch. Unfortunately, he had stretched his right leg only and put a lot of pressure on the right rudder pedal. The result was as described! This was the second time he'd frightened the life out of me.

There were also more tactical transports than ours, the Beverley. Apart from being a crew-member I was given the task of security officer for the airfield and to this end went to the transport depot for a motor-bike to make my task easier. My prize was a Triumph 500 and, when the airfield closed each evening, I used the runway as my extremely fast route between parked aircraft and their guards. No crash helmet or leathers then, just hair straight back. Arriving at one of the parking areas I found an airman, rifle over his shoulder, lounging against an aircraft tyre. I berated him for not demanding my identification at the point of his gun and explained that he should be more aware of the possibility of sabotage at this time (the airfield boundaries were only fences). This caused me a few shivers from then on as I was confronted by all guards with loaded rifles pointed at me. Oh well, I'd made my point.

BAHRAIN

RAF Muharraq was not just a staging post for Transport Command but a major base in the Middle East area. The Royal Navy also had a base there. Our accommodation was Nissen huts! In the amazing summer temperatures these huts were worse than saunas. The only way to cope with the situation was to lie on your bed and keep very still. The alternative was to move around outside which could be worse. In the evenings, after a sweaty dinner, there was always the bar, but cold beer does not cool you down. It was awful. The winters were okay.

Occasionally, if the RAF accommodation was full we would be sent to the BOAC rest-house in Manama, the capital, which was better but still no air-conditioning (AC). I believe that in 1957-8 the only AC's on the island was one in the Sheik's bedroom and one in the British Embassy. In the height of summer, imagine having a shower where the 'cold' water comes out tepid and you sweat whilst doing it. That was summer in Bahrain.

The runway at Muharraq was 2,000 yards long and the Comet needed all of that. One afternoon we took off for Karachi and, because it was so hot, our performance was only just good enough to go at the given temperature. Decisions to go or abandon the take-off were quite primitive compared with today's super accurate figures. We would time acceleration to 100 knots and, if it was at or below the required figure for temperature and weight at that airfield, we would continue with the take-off! If not, we would abandon it. On this day, we taxied out in maximum temperature, no air-conditioning, as it was not available on the ground, and started the take-off. The temperature in the flight-deck was 43 degrees! Full power and off we went. The captain, Geoff Bolton, was slightly chubby and prone to sweat. As we accelerated down the runway I was fascinated by his elbows from which was a continuous flow of sweat. We were all in a bad way but *that* was terrible. We reached 100 knots to the second but, to show the inaccuracy of this system of timing, we just stayed on the runway Eventually, Geoff rotated, i.e. raised the nose, and I still have a vivid memory of the gaps in the drystone wall which marked the boundary at the end of the runway. I believed our wheels were going to hit it!!

KARACHI

Temperatures and conditions were much the same as Bahrain but we were always accommodated in the Mina Sulman Hotel. Quite comfortable and food okay. Karachi also had a BOAC rest house at the airport but I never stayed there. However, there was a shop which seemed to sell mostly cricket kit and paraphernalia. The airfield itself was well-run but nobody could control all the hawks which circled the airport and always posed a threat to safety. Strangely, I never heard of a hawk-strike there.

The Mina Sulman Hotel provided good food and one night I was so pleased with the fish dish that I had some more. It's the only thing I ate. Next day I was in a bad way and, in the modern way of things, I should have declared myself unfit to fly. That would have grounded the aircraft as we operated one aircraft, one crew and one set of passengers, so there were no reserves anywhere. So, I flew. This was a seriously bad sector to Katunayake; we had to fly away from India, as they would not let us overfly, parallel the coast, then head into Ceylon after we were clear of India. It was the monsoon season and we were soon dodging serious Cumulonimbus (thunderstorm) clouds of the ITCZ (Intertropical Convergence Zone) which is a weather system moving north of the equator and back again in late summer.

Whilst traversing this area our radar failed. We could no longer find and avoid the bad weather. We were tossed around unmercifully and began to be concerned for our safety. Nowadays, all aircraft have very advanced radar and a back-up. On top of all this turbulence and being nearly thrown upside down, I had a massively upset stomach from the previous night's fish and needed to go to the toilet. The toilets were in the tail and I had to hang on for dear life, and other reasons! We eventually landed in Ceylon for our refuelling stop but took extra time to relax after our awful experience. We had to leave four passengers behind due to massive sickness and/or fear. The onward flight to Changi, Singapore, was uneventful. We had no radar as there were no spares in Ceylon. In fact, we never had the radar again for the whole trip back to Lyneham. That would not happen today but they were different times.

On my return, I drove to London and collected Maureen and drove down to my parents'. Along the Southend Arterial Road I felt so weak that I had to stop and rest. At home the family doctor, Dr Quinn, diagnosed dysentery but said he would not put that on the report as the RAF would give me a lot of tests and check on my progress. I had lost more than a stone in weight and was very weak. I remained in bed for about a week. It took me nearly a year to return to 11 stone 7 pounds.

CEYLON

RAF Negombo, also known as RAF Katunayake and, nowadays, Colombo Katunayake International Airport, had a runway too short for the Comet. To overcome this, the western overrun was levelled and PSP (Perforated Steel Planking) was laid down for about 300 to 400 metres. PSP was a section of steel about 50-centimetres wide and various lengths which were interlinked by hinge-like attachments. There were tennis-ball sized holes, to reduce weight I suppose. We would taxi on to this PSP and take-off to the east which meant hoping to clear the forest at the end of the runway. The trees were on rising slopes, so it was all a bit hairy. Those trees are now gone and the runway extended properly.

Taking off to the west was okay unless it was very hot or we were heavy in which case you might finish the last couple of seconds of your take-off actually on this PSP. It never felt right somehow.

We never stayed in Ceylon as it was always just a refuelling stop. It was not unusual to see the occasional very large snake wandering across the taxi-way. One pilot, Kim Kimmings, did not turn up to morning briefing for his flight. Eventually, one of his crew members went to see why and found Kim still in bed staring at a Krait which had managed to get inside his mosquito net and was directly above him. He had not dared move as the snake's position did not look very secure.

SINGAPORE

Changi airport had a single Westerly runway with a large bank along the northern side on which people loved to sit and watch the activity. The village itself was very Royal Air Force-orientated with its most welcoming shops, bars and restaurants. The all-ranks crew accommodation was in HUTS! again, but well appointed. Laundry was done in the day, fast and cheap. The food was free and the bar was good.

The main base obviously had officers' and sergeants' messes which welcomed the appropriate temporary members and there was an officers' club with a large and well-patronised swimming-pool, bar and club. This was a great posting and a pleasure to visit.

On top of all this was Singapore City itself for shopping and general sight-seeing. The Singapore Cricket Club was a huge block in the middle of town surrounded by buildings and a great place to feel home from home.

AUSTRALIA

Darwin was a fuel stop. Hot, dusty and a memorably huge water tower on the airfield. Most houses were on stilts for fear of saltwater crocodiles.

Adelaide. We landed at Royal Australian Air Force Station Edinburgh Field and stayed in the officers' mess. We only spent one night before returning to Singapore via Darwin. However, one night was most instructive. Only once did I go into town and visited a bar where the last drinks were, as normal, at 1800 or 1830 hours. There were a lot of guys really over the top and when we left I watched the staff hose the place down. This was normal and easy as the whole place was tiled. Then, as now, the beer was so cold you couldn't taste it, American beer is the same. No wonder they call our beer warm, at least it has a taste!

Back to Singapore for a forty-eight-hour layover, then on to Aden via Ceylon.

ADEN

Aden, or Royal Air Force Khormaksar, in the summer made Bahrain feel like spring. The climate is so stifling and painfully hot that you sweat twenty-four hours a day. Furthermore, it was so poor and there was much evidence of cruelty. There were beggars everywhere but so many were so young; I discovered that many were deliberately deformed to be the beggar of the family. It may not sound too charitable but is absolutely true.

The approach to the runway was along the north side of town which meant you were quite close to the hill to the South. Furthermore, the street lights to the right of the approach could, in poor visibility, be mistaken for the runway approach lights if you were new to the place. I do believe on one occasion an aircraft got quite low over the lights before he realised his mistake.

There was so much activity at Khormaksar as it was the busiest overseas staging post for some time. Also, it had its own transport aircraft and a squadron of Shackletons for coastal patrols out into the Indian Ocean. In 1958 a state of emergency was declared as rebels were making their presence felt north of Aden. By 1960 they were attempting to infiltrate Khormaksar and the immediate area, especially the Radfan. This meant that the long serving 8 Squadron at Aden gave much support to the British Army using their Hunter FGA 9s. Later, in 1961, they were joined by 208 Squadron with their Hunters. It was quite wistful to see that beautiful aircraft at work and wishing that I had spent more time flying them.

By sheer chance I saw 'Murky' in the bar and we had a joyous reunion. He had a flying posting at last. His aeroplane was the single-engine Pioneer; this could take off and land in very short distances and was ideal for rescue purposes out in the hills and desert. He took me for a ride, and, to demonstrate its short landing ability, landed across the runway and stayed on it!

EL ADEM

The departure from Khormaksar was to El Adem (Tobruk) or Nicosia. This required just two tracks; the first to Nasser's Corner, as we called it, which was simply the south-west bottom corner of Egypt, then direct to destination. Nasser's Corner was so named as the then Egyptian president was Gamal Nasser and he would not let the RAF overfly. Still cross about the Suez War, I guess.

El Adem was a few miles inland from Tobruk and was both a staging post and support base for the British Army who did many desert exercises in the region. On some trips we would stay in El Adem after an overnight flight and I cannot believe, now, that we drank beer and then went for breakfast, which is best remembered for the waiter's thumb in the grease of the eggs and bacon! Yuk!

de Havilland Comet 2

RAF Nicosia

On 11 November 1958 we were en route from Lyneham to Nicosia and halfway along the Mediterranean when we lost our VHF radio, shortly followed by the HF (long range) radio. Weather at Nicosia was known to be bad but our alternative, Beirut, was good so we continued as per the flight plan. We carried out a let-down on time stated in the flight plan (normal ATC procedure for radio failure) and carried out an NDB approach down to our minimum descent altitude which was probably 400 feet. We saw nothing ahead or down; we were in thick fog. What to do? It was not fancied to go to Beirut without a radio, although that was what was expected of us. However, the captain, Geoff Bolton, asked the navigator if he could get us to RAF Akrotiri, which was not yet operational but had been built and was being used although not open to transport aircraft. We let down over the sea to the south-east of Akrotiri using our cloud warning radar to highlight the coast line, then headed towards Akrotiri on the known runway heading. The cloud base was about 1,000 feet and visibility was about three miles. At three miles the navigator, Dennis Rance, said he was sure the airfield was dead ahead. He was right! Even as he spoke the area ahead became a sea of lights and we could make out the runway. Obviously, Nicosia had seen our route away from them and guessed our intentions. It took time to rake out the Duty Officer who then had to seek out airport and air traffic personnel. We landed safely but, due to the recent excessive rainfall, the runway was flooded and wind from the nearby embankments was all over the place.

The morning after our arrival in Akrotiri we were astonished to find we now had a reddish-white Comet. The mud and water combination had covered it all over. After two days we were able to continue our journey to Adelaide via Nicosia.

It was during one of these flights to Australia that I was about to experience my third serious near miss. En route from Singapore to Darwin we were doing our usual cruise climb and, as the sun was blindingly in our eyes, the captain and I had opened up charts and obstructed 90 per cent of the forward view. There was no bad weather but we had enough gaps between the charts for a regular peek out. As mentioned earlier, the airways were limited to 25,000 feet and we were always above that in clear skies. We had filed our flight plan in Singapore and Air Traffic Control had advised us that there was no conflicting traffic, which was normal. Our regular contact with Singapore and Darwin on long-range radio (HF) elicited no information about conflict, as was expected.

However suddenly, out over the Timor Sea, the flight deck darkened and the sun disappeared. Geoff and I threw aside the charts and there, spread across our vision, was the entire underside of a USAF KC-135 Stratotanker! We must have missed each other by mere feet; indeed, in the split second of sighting it then losing it I was quite sure our tail would hit its belly. The KC-135 was a Boeing aircraft, derived from the Boeing 367-80, which also led to the Boeing 707 airliner.

What it was doing out there without us having been advised of its presence I will never know. The incident was immediately reported but ATC claimed no knowledge of it and we heard nothing more despite the information being passed up the line. The only damage was a couple of torn charts and cigarettes all round.

On 28 August 1957, during my first Aussie trip, we went from Darwin to Adelaide via Amberley Field in Brisbane. Why, I cannot recall but it was the first four-jet aircraft to land there and our arrival had been notified to the local press. There was a large crowd to greet us and, as was the custom in those days, there was no special security arrangement. We parked in the usual place and within fifty yards, maybe less, were three or four three-foot posts in the ground with one long rope between them. The crowd behaved impeccably, of course; they were asked to stay behind the rope and they did.

This stop of around forty-five minutes provided a moment of great amusement to us. Our normal stopovers in Australia were frequent and the ground crews knew our procedures very well but, of course the man on the headset down below who was conducting the start-up had never heard our cockpit check list before.

For some reason we did everything via the intercom in those days so the ground man could hear everything. The navigator called out all the checks and the appropriate crew members replied.

DE HAVILLAND COMET 2

It is necessary to give a technical lecture here: the Comet 2 had hydraulically-powered flying controls with no manual reversion, i.e. no hydraulics meant no flying controls! There were three levers above and between the pilots which, when in the rearward position gave secondary control to the ailerons, rudder and elevators. Secondary control was provided by the GREEN system and, also, in this position you could activate a pump via a circuit-breaker next to them which would give you the emergency YELLOW system; this was your last resort. Green system was powered by Nos 1 and 3 engines and the primary, BLUE, via Nos 2 and 4 engines.

Anyway, the appropriate part of the check list went like this, C = Captain, P = Co-Pilot, N = Navigator and E = Flight Engineer. GC = Ground crew man who would reply, where necessary, and had a truly strong Australian accent, so you must use your imagination.

C.	Are we clear to start engines?
GC.	All clear.
N.	Start Nos 1 and 2 engines.
	Engines started and all parameters checked.
N.	Check controls green (yellow system would have been checked before engine start).
C.	Controls checked green.
N.	Change to primary (the levers would now be moved forward).
P.	Primary selected.
N.	Start 3 engine.
GC.	Clear to start.
C.	Engine started and checked.
N.	Check controls blue.
	The captain and I would now exercise the controls.
	But before anything could be said:-
GC said 'Controls look O.K. to me BLUE'!	

So the Aussies did respond to the name Blue in those days? He had not replied to the N. saying check controls Green!

A small word here about the crew composition: captain, experienced and found competent in all areas to command an aircraft carrying passengers. Co-pilot: awaiting his turn to be captain, may or may not be very experienced but will be learning the ropes from a good captain and from experience. Navigator: skilled in all areas of navigating – dead reckoning, map work, use of all aids, especially sextant used for finding position by the stars, ability to navigate even when the compass is unreliable, especially in the higher latitudes. Flight Engineer; incredibly knowledgeable on all aircraft instruments, systems, electrical circuits et al. Signallers: to keep in touch with base, destination and other aircraft by voice radio or signalling Morse code up to twenty-four words a minute. Quartermaster: on Comets they did a lot of looking after the passengers but that is not their real role in life; their training is to prepare them for despatching paras, loading and unloading aircraft, preparing the load sheet, i.e. weight and balance, a vital piece of paperwork.

With the advent of better and better radios with VHF tuneable and UHF and far more accurate tuning of HF long-distance radio, the signaller was no longer required. The navigator continues to be in the RAF transport aircraft as so much still relies on pinpoint accuracy over targets, etc. Whilst the pilot could perhaps do a good job himself he has many other demands on his concentration so the navigator is indispensable. However, with the early inertial navigational systems and then GPS carried in threes, the navigator became redundant in civil aviation.

The three-man crew in civil aviation was then the norm, captain, first officer and flight engineer. Navigation was done by all the on-flight aids and constantly checked by the pilots and the radios were of such good quality that area and long-range communication was fairly straightforward. The saddest event in civil aviation came to pass when nearly all the aircraft systems were so computerised that they look after themselves most of the time. Corrections to faults and appropriate check-lists appear on screens and books, easy to hand, can remind you of anything you may have forgotten since your intensive training courses on ground and in the air.

Result: No flight engineer. Two pilot operation.

The flight engineer was not only the most technically knowledgeable member of the crew but was also an extra pair of eyes and ears. He kept an eye on the pilots, reminded them of things, asked questions and was a most valued member of the crew.

Now there are just two pilots doing everything. On long sectors there are stand-in first officers to give one of the operating pilots a break and, of course, usually all three or four pilots are on the flight deck for take-offs and landings.

Nevertheless, his expertise and massive contribution to FLIGHT SAFETY has gone. The reason? Almost certainly financial. I can think of two recent fatal disasters that would not have happened if long-range aircraft still carried flight engineers. The obvious one has to be the Air France airliner, which, en route from South America to Paris, was lost in the Atlantic.

An excellent example of the value and quality, technically, of the RAF flight engineers occurred in Khormaksar in November 1957. There is a fairly complicated battery changeover switch in the underfloor equipment bay. This was normally selected to a position for the ground equipment to supply electrics for starting the engines. On this day it did not work so the flight engineer went and changed the switch for starting using our own batteries. This did not work either. The switch was unusable and so we could not start our engines. There were no spares available and it seems that de Havilland didn't have one either.

Our flight engineer removed the switch from the aircraft, went downtown and found an electrical workshop. He spent two whole days in the terrible heat and rebuilt it. The switch was the size of a wheelbarrow wheel and slightly wider; the switch handle was similar to the one ship's captains use to signal the engine settings. He eventually returned to the aircraft and the switch worked. What a player! He was praised on two counts, his skill and the fact we could get us the hell out of Khormaksar.

Naturally, the RAF have retained their flight engineers as they realise the technical expertise and safety aspects are essential. An added bonus of flying with them is the fund of good jokes, good humour, the unmerciful ribbing of new, even established, co-pilots and their off-duty companionship.

The return to UK usually involved an extra day off in Singapore (Changi) which was always a pleasure with sun, sea, sand and Tiger beer. The Officers' Club was always well populated with wives and their kids and the nursing officers of the PMRAFNS (Princess Mary's Royal Air Force Nursing Service). The pool was very large and one could eat, drink and be merry in the restaurant or around the pool.

Foolishly, Geoff and I did not use common sense one day and fell asleep on the beach. We were so sunburnt that we could hardly move. The next day our skin was like parchment and was really painful inside the shirt and with seat harness on the shoulders. We were reluctant to seek medical advice as we might have been grounded until recovered. This would have constituted 'Self Inflicted Injury', an offence which was subject to varying disciplinary action.

As mentioned earlier, the only real navigation aid was the navigator whose skills with the slide rule and sextant were superb. Even so, he was not shy of asking us to keep an eye open for various geographical features which would enable us to fix our position. For me, the most memorable was the regular 'Tell me when you see the fork' on the Nicosia-Karachi-Nicosia legs. This referred to the confluence of the Tigris and the Euphrates in Iraq. In normal conditions in this area there would rarely be cloud, so the fork could sometimes be seen between 100 to 150 miles away. At thirty-odd thousand feet, the horizon would be visible at up to 200 miles and, therefore, the sighting was usually easy. I doubt that you can do that often nowadays.

When I started flying, apart from real industrial areas you would be clear of pollution, smoke etc. by 2,000 feet. Over the years this margin rose and rose and by 2000, when I retired, it could often be around 14,000. If you were in the clear above it was quite rare to see a physical horizon, let alone identify anything on the ground at any decent distance. This observation was applicable, in my opinion, certainly as far north as 65 degrees. Northern Russia, above the Arctic and Northern Canada and Northern Territories, were usually quite clear.

The same applies to a lesser extent in the sea, to the naked eye, that is. It was quite common to see a serious colour change in the water at the estuaries and out to sea of many rivers. Now they seem to merge more. I realise that the British rivers are much cleaner than they were but in certain parts of the world the discolouration shows quite clearly. Poor sea creatures. Poor us!

As stated earlier, 216 Squadron started a regular transatlantic service to Christmas Island in late 1957. The route was Keflavik, Iceland, then RCAF (Royal Canadian Air Force) Base Goose Bay, Labrador (part of the province of Newfoundland and Labrador since 1949) then Offutt AFB (Air Force Base) Omaha, then Travis AFB California, then Hickam AFB Honolulu and Christmas Island.

Keflavik was close to the Icelandic capital Reykavik and had been used by the USAF for many years. We normally stayed for an hour or so which gave me the opportunity to shoot off and get my first ever T-bone steak. I've since enjoyed these cuts but that was a real disappointment. A later visit was in very bad weather and after a safe landing it was my duty to file the flight plan in ATC for our next sector. Having donned my cold-weather gear, I set off for the tower about 200 yards away. The heavens opened and I found myself in a blizzard and zero visibility. I bumped into a ground power machine and hid behind it. The blizzard lasted about fifteen minutes but I dared not attempt any movement. Eventually, when it stopped, I realised that I was in a snowdrift up to my hips.

Sadly, I only started two trips to Christmas Island and they were both in the winter of 1957/8. The second in March was amazingly eventful; we landed at Goose Bay on the evening of 4 March where there was to be a party. As we were travelling west we had made up time so when 6 o'clock that evening arrived it was actually 2200 to our bodies. We had enjoyed a few beers, but decided that we would give the party a miss as we were scheduled to leave at 0700 their time. What a great decision!

The aircraft had been in a hangar all night and was warm; the outside air temperature was minus several and we actually started engines in the hangar. When we were ready the doors opened and we taxied out into light snow. A few minutes later we started our take-off run towards the unseen hills. Just after the decision to continue take off we lost number one engine – we had to continue as there was insufficient runway left to stop. At lift off, number two engine failed and we were in trouble. Geoff immediately turned hard left to avoid the known but unseen hills which were dangerously close now; it was a Saturday and I was imagining the Sunday paper headlines. The order was immediately given to jettison fuel, we levelled wings and a miracle happened, we were in good visibility. We were flying and dumping fuel straight over the USAF married quarters at about 200 feet and we slowly climbed as weight reduced. We flew a couple of times up and down the river but could see more heavy snow bearing down, so the decision was made to land. Meantime, I had managed to restart number two engine.

As soon as we landed the snow hit us and before we reached taxi speed we could barely see fifty yards. We turned off the runway and waited for the lead vehicle. He couldn't find us for ages due to visibility. Eventually we were back safe and sound in the hangar from whence we had started. At first we did not know what had happened; number two engine restarted with no trouble so why had it stopped with the number one?

To give experience of the USA traffic conditions, these early trips had two captains doing leg-and-leg about. The other captain on this trip was Bill Kay and he had been sitting where he looked straight at the intakes of numbers one and two engines. RAF transport aircraft all had rear-facing seats, which is much safer for the passenger but needs slightly extra weight for the stress bearing structure needed. (Hence, forward-facing seats on civilian aircraft as it is cheaper!)

Anyway, Bill had watched ice build up on the intakes until the engine could not get enough air and stopped (flame-out). The warm hangar, therefore warm aircraft, caused the problem. As we went down the runway the relatively warmer aircraft surface allowed the snow striking the aircraft to melt, run back and then freeze. Fortunately, we had crosswind from the left which permitted some fuselage protection of the other two engines, otherwise it could have been a disaster. Hindsight suggests we should have known this could happen; we had no real experience of these situations and, more to the point, nothing in pilots' or operational notes gave any indication.

Bill Kay was a lovely chap and well known for his unfortunate nervous habit which was to frequently rub his thumb on his breast pocket. Needless to say, after we landed his thumb was going the proverbial nineteen to the dozen. I have known three flight crew with variously pronounced tics or other strange mannerisms, but these always disappeared when seated on duty and all three were top performers. All of them held A Categories which was the highest rating attainable in the RAF.

We had a four-day wait for both the weather to clear and for the go-ahead from the RAF and de Havilland having analysed our incident. We also carried out an air test.

Whilst there I bought a Zippo lighter for US $1 which I still have. Actually, it's a bit like Trigg's road-sweeping broom used in 'Only Fools and Horses'. Remember, he had the *same* broom for twenty years as man and boy and only had six new handles and fourteen new brushes. Well, Zippo honoured their lifetime guarantee and, eventually, changed everything, including the main case. I stopped smoking on 16 March 1977 but I still have it.

We left for Offutt AFB on 8 March in good weather and I looked at the hills thinking how close we were to having actually ended up there. The first time we went to Offutt there was no room in the BOQs (Bachelor Officer Quarters) so we ended up in the Rome Hotel in Omaha. Next morning Geoff and I stood on the sidewalk in front of the hotel and noted the ten-pin bowling alley on the other side. As this was our first visit to the USA and we had never been bowling, we crossed the road. Now this was difficult as it was very busy and a one direction four-lane highway. We made it safely to the other side to be confronted by a rather large policeman, slightly incandescent. We realised that he was a bit cross and he wanted to know 'What the goddam hell do you think you are doing?' Geoff said something about bowling and the policeman said, 'Oh Limeys!' He let us off with a rollicking and strict instruction about crossing at the lights at the intersections.

We watched some bowling, had breakfast in their restaurant, they all seem to have restaurants I've found, and generally looked around. That evening in the bar I got into discussion with a guy who would not believe that the UK was big enough to have built the RMS *Queen Mary*! We managed quite an argument and, as I thought it was going to get violent, I left. It was the thought of guns that prompted my departure as, only that morning, a policeman had shot some boy who had stolen a hubcap and then run away when challenged.

Prior to our departure for Travis AFB and on leaving the operations building, a very large American car approached and all the people were saluting. The car had two flags each about three feet by one and a half feet attached to masts on each wing. How the driver could see enough for safety was mystifying. It turned out to be General Powers who was commander of the Strategic Air Command (SAC) headquartered at Offutt. Not for him the little pennants flown here!

SAC were operating B-47s and B-52s. They were operating a round-the-clock watch from the air over Europe as part of the Cold War readiness. This meant that for twenty-four hours every day there were aircraft airborne ready for action. There were bases in UK, Spain and Turkey contributing as well. The aircraft at Offutt would get airborne for Europe and another would return.

Just before an earlier trip in January a B-47 had returned from its trip to Spain for technical reasons. One of the crew members went to grab a beer before returning home to his wife. Unfortunately, he found her at the bar with a man whom, apparently, he had suspected of carrying on an affair with her. He was, of course, armed so he shot his wife's lover!

Departing Offutt that January we picked up distress signals from a Beechcraft (twin-engined and twin-tailplane aircraft) who was having severe icing problems. I relayed his messages to Offutt tower but eventually was out of range. Sadly, we found on our return a few days later that the aircraft had crashed and with no survivors. The remains were right there next to where we parked for the night.

US airspace was divided into FIRs (Flight Information Regions) and it was a requirement to report position, time, altitude and souls on board each time you entered and/or left each one. Also, occasionally we were to report elsewhere as directed. So, you might report 'New York this is RAFJET 1234, position Able at 1410 hours at 32,600, climbing, with fifty-four souls on board estimating Baker at 1432 hours'. The reply would be a read-back of your transmission and, after a short while, 'RAFJET, say again ALDITOOD and souls on board'. We would repeat the information. A little later another voice might ask the same question with a tinge of disbelief coming through the ether. Sure enough, two to three minutes later there would be an F-104 on each wing checking us out!

Despite the regularity of our crossings, Atlantic and the United States, it never seemed to sink in that our progress and total on board was understandable. Also, they could never get used to our speed. Once when we were intercepted Geoff said he was fed up with fighters on our wingtips, so he slowed down. The Comet had a swept-back leading-edge and a traditional trailing-edge to the wing. In general terms, swept-back wings had a higher stalling speed than normal wings, but we had a bit of each so our stalling speed was quite low. The fighters were swept-wing and, due to wing size and shape, needed a higher speed for proper handling. As we slowed down so did the F-104s, their noses getting higher and higher as they matched our speed. They eventually started to wallow and show erratic movements. This concerned me as sometimes one wing can stall before the other and I reminded Geoff that an aircraft could easily roll towards us. 'Oh, Okay,' he said and increased power again. Even as he spoke the two aircraft had fallen away. Good fun, but perhaps ill advised. Who am I to talk!!

Travis AFB was mainly a transport base of MATS, the Military Air Transport Service of the USAF. As with most US AFBs it was huge and housed numerous squadrons and types including C-124C Globemaster, C-121A Constellation, C-54 Skymaster and C-97 Stratofreighter. These various types were all over the airfield and many lined-up outside the terminal building.

We were parked close to the terminal building and just about every passenger for the assorted four-engined piston aircraft had to walk around or past the Comet. We were unable to make Honolulu due to headwinds and, on the third day, were asked to go and move our aircraft due to 'congestion'?! When we got there the parking area had plenty of space but we ended up on the far side of the airfield. I guess that all the MATS personnel were embarrassed by the sleek and beautiful lines when compared to the 'old-fashioned' lumpy aircraft they were operating. In my opinion they all looked lovely and I still prefer the sound of a noisy but sweet piston-engine to the jet. However, the jet can be wonderful at full power – think of Concorde!

The pleasure of the long delay was that we could look around the area and our USAF liaison officer took Geoff and I, the only officers on the crew, to San Francisco. En route we visited the small township of Birds Landing. It was like going back a century; the roads were packed earth, motor vehicles were all just for farming purposes, there were hitching rails everywhere with the occasional horse and the main enterprise was a combined general store, hardware outlet, bar and café. Just about all the men were in various coloured lumberjack shirts and jeans. Outside there were trays of rusty nails, screws, wire and tools, all open to the elements and obviously there all the time with no cover.

We entered the bar, of course, and were given a muted welcome but a thorough scrutiny. I could barely understand a word said to me but a friendly conversation and meeting of some sort of minds ensued. Thirsts quenched we moved onto the big city itself.

Obviously, as we had come from the north of California we had to cross the Golden Gate Bridge. Wow! What an experience – remember I was still not twenty-two years old, which in those days was considered less mature than now. Some modern young people have travelled afar and, often, been involved with many more of the opposite sex, they have computers and mobile phones – so much is advanced.

Our first pleasure was a tour of the city including all those twisting streets and then a ride on the cable cars where, at each bend, those standing on the outside are reminded 'to mind the curve' at each bend. Next to Fisherman's Wharf but unfortunately not enough time to visit Alcatraz Prison. We had a good view of it nevertheless. I found a novelty stall which had the usual tourist stuff but I was amused by a card that said 'Excuse me, but could you help me out?' 'Certainly, which way did you come in?' Now that I write it, it doesn't seem as funny as it did then but it stuck in my head. This memory was to have some unusual and awkward consequences.

It was getting to twilight so a beer beckoned and, naturally, that meant the Mark Hopkins Hotel. I think it was the tallest in San Francisco then but not that tall by US standards; it was on the highest hill and its main appeal was the top-floor bar which rotated slowly so, as the sun was setting we were still in sunlight but you could see that down below it was night.

Access to the upper parts of the hotel was an outside glass lift which was quite unnerving as I do not like heights, unless in an aeroplane. Entry to the bar was closely monitored and I had to prove I was over twenty-one!

Long day, a few beers, need the loo (sorry *bathroom*) so off I go. Standing there, I glance at my neighbour just as he glances at me. What a surprise, it was my original flight commander on 257 Squadron whose name I regret I cannot remember. He had left the Royal Air Force and was travelling for his new company.

We shook hands, washed our hands and shook hands again! What a coincidence.

These were the days when officers had bank accounts; indeed there was no choice and other ranks were paid in cash. The airmen at Christmas Island were no different. This meant that the cash had to be taken to them and the muggins were the co-pilots on the regular Comet service. Usually, you were given a very strong, and heavy, box approximately a metre by a metre by twelve centimetres full of notes and you had to guard it with your life, or at least your career.

So, there I was dragging this damned box everywhere and, only occasionally, finding a secure place to leave it whilst off duty, such as the safe on the base. However, there were few safes big enough or people keen enough to give you the confidence to let it out of your sight. On top of that the co-pilot also carried the imprest, i.e. enough money in dollars to meet all allowances and expenses. Unlike the wretched box which remained sealed, the imprest had to be opened daily for payments and a record kept of every cent disbursed.

Eventually, the adverse headwind kept us at Travis for four days, by which time the next scheduled aircraft arrived. The problem with Travis to Honolulu was that the flight time was around five hours fifteen minutes with no wind, so any headwind could put us into our fuel reserves and, as I recall, there were no suitable diversion fields if we could not make Honolulu's Hickham AFB.

So, it was lovely to hand over the box of money, £6,000 I believe, to the next co-pilot; good job he had two arms. We returned to the UK quite disappointed and this happened on our next trip also, so I never got to Honolulu then, but later on I saw a lot of it.

Christmas Island's real name was Kirimati. The only story I have of the place will amuse the older readers. You will remember FLIT, it came in a metal tube with a canister at the end and was fitted with a pump handle. When pumped this flit was sprayed out and used to kill insects, but especially mosquitoes. The island being in the Pacific, and with many inlets and lakes, was hot and insect-ridden, so each night a light aircraft equipped as a crop-sprayer flew around the island dispensing the appropriate chemical, DDT perhaps. Inevitably, his nickname became Flit and stayed with him for the rest of his career, I believe.

Friday night in the Officers' Club at Travis was gambling night and I thought I'd join in. I was drawn to the craps game as I had no idea what it was about. The punters stand around an oval table with a one-foot wall all around it containing slots for silver dollar coins. I placed my $5 next to a USAF guy's $200 and watched and bet. The two dice pass from player to player in clockwise order and the bets go into the number or total of your choice.

The rules are a bit baffling at first, but rule No. 1 is that the dice hit the back wall and bounce into play. One or two numbers have more significance than others but I recall that 2, 3 and 7 and 11 are important. However, when it came to my turn on the first throw only one die hit the wall! This ended with no winners, including the banker. My second throw sent one of the dice clattering amongst the feet at the bar which caused much glaring and muttering and my third throw landed on the number that meant the banker took all bets to his kitty! I blushed and hastily left, clutching $1 for more beer.

Both journeys home from Travis were uneventful except for the first Goose Bay-Lyneham flight on 7 January 1958. At briefing for a night-time departure we found that there were huge tailwinds on our route, so we persuaded Geoff to put on extra fuel and cruise faster than normal. The flight time plan would have given us a record time across the Atlantic. In the event the winds dropped halfway across to a decent speed but were no longer adequate for our attempt. In the event we still made a time of four hours and fifty minutes to cover 2,396 statute miles (2,083 nautical miles) at an average ground speed of 495 mph (431 knots) which was pretty good for then.

For me the journey was a little disrupted by the captain and the rest of the crew. Halfway across and whilst we still believed a real record was attainable the signaller, Sergeant Gibson, asked to go for a break, followed by the engineer, John (?) Haley, and then the navigator, Denis Rance. When the captain said he was going for a stroll I thought nothing of it as I assumed (very bad in an aircraft) one or more of the others had resumed their places. I dutifully donned my oxygen mask, standard practice then if only one pilot was at the controls, and monitored everything, especially the trim (balance fore and aft) of the aircraft.

Although we had an autopilot (just one) there was no automatic trim so it was the pilots' responsibility to constantly monitor the indicator. This was just like a spirit level but, instead of a bubble, there was a small rectangular glass with a white needle which had to be kept in the middle.

The toilets were at the back, so we always knew when a front-end passenger went down there and came back; yes it was that sensitive. More importantly, when the indicator moved constantly and positively forward you knew coffee was on the way. The galley was at the rear so the quartermaster walking the length of the aircraft was really noticeable; you were moving the trim wheel for all of his/her journey. On one occasion, flying with one of our female quartermasters the trim indicated that coffee was on its way. When experience showed she was just about six feet from the flight deck there was an almighty crash and the autopilot disconnected. She had tripped and fallen; she was our largest lady on the crews and one of the loveliest.

Anyway, back to the scheduled crossing of the Atlantic: I noticed that the trim started constantly changing back and forth and eventually did so at an alarming rate. This was totally unprecedented and I turned round to ask the navigator to get the captain. He wasn't there and neither was the engineer. I looked into the cabin and there were the flight deck, plus the quartermaster plus our only passenger (a USN rating who had bummed a ride) huddled together in a group walking backwards and forwards in the aisle. They were laughing their socks off and I was trimming nineteen to the dozen. I guess it was a good jape.

At TOD (Top of Descent) into Lyneham we had a fire warning for No. 3 engine which got our full attention as you can imagine. The warning consists of a very strident bell and a bright red light appearing in a large press button indicating the appropriate engine. The action, as with all jet engines, is to close the throttle (now called more logically thrust lever), cut the fuel and fire the first bottle of fire extinguishant; in some aircraft there are more actions required, but those are the basics. Thirty seconds later, if you still have a fire, you discharge the second bottle. We did all of this, but the indications remained. Very unnerving, but made worse by the fact that the bell could not be cancelled. So, you have this chilling noise, the tension of having an engine on fire, in particular, an engine right next to the belly of the aircraft and the urgency to get on the ground as soon as possible. Modern aircraft, indeed the next generation and even the same generation, had bells that could be cancelled immediately. In the end there was no fire at all; it was an electrical fault. We had exactly the same happen to us a few weeks later! It was just as unnerving.

I did most of my flying with Geoff Bolton and, although he was a nice enough chap and good pilot, found it very trying. He was one of those captains who wants to do everything himself and *never* gave me a landing. I pointed out often that other co-pilots were having a great time but he was unfazed. I got the odd landing with other captains.

It is my experience over my career that captains who do not give landings are, apart from being mean and not contributing to the advancement of a fellow pilot, actually under-confident in that they have not the ability to sit back, monitor and guide the other pilot whilst at the same time relaxing as they are in command and may take over anytime. This happened a lot in the early days of certain airlines where a first officer's advancement not only took account of his hours flown but factored in were the number of his landings. Regrettably, many selfish and mean captains could also be quite unpleasant and self-centred, with a false sense of their superiority. This was not usual in the Royal Air Force.

Oh well, I still had the Meteor to play with. One of our fun trips was to go over to RAF Brize Norton, which was in the hands of the USAF at the time, and do circuits, with roller landings (touch and go to them) and finish with a beat-up of the tower. Obviously, we asked permission but we got so close we could see whether they were spilling tea or coffee. You may recall Tom Cruise in *Top Gun* doing the same thing!

One extra pleasure with having the Meteors to play with was being able to give fellow officers rides. There were admin, and other ground, officers who loved to have aerobatics, low flying and lunches away offered them. A particular friend of mine was Tony Quant the dentist, brother of Mary Quant, with whom I played a lot of snooker. He was really good and, although I was no slouch, thanks to Dad's teaching, he could beat me eight out of ten games. Eventually, it was about five and a half out of ten games and we were a formidable pair in the annual Sergeants' Mess vs Officers' Mess games night. Tony, much to his receptionist/nurse's annoyance, liked nothing more than a chin-wag about flying. He had a little habit of initialling all our fillings with his TQ.

Years later I got chatting to my female dentist in Taunton and asked if I had any initials visible on my teeth. She was bemused and when I explained she was keen to tell me that Tony had been her teacher at dentist school. When Mary Quant had a birthday party I was invited with one or two other of Tony's friends from the Meteors. He who had tried to kill me in a Hunter and, later, frightened me to death in a Comet met the lady who was to become his wife at this party.

Another great pleasure with the Meteor was to get airborne whenever you wanted to and just pootle around. As any pilot alone in any type of aircraft and with no specific task it is wonderful to just cruise around, go and find a special view, do a few aerobatics and just relax. I was doing just this just North of Boscombe Down and in clear airspace. I was flying level at about 1,000 feet above an incredibly flat cloud surface which stretched for miles in all directions. Suddenly, directly ahead, and straight at me, a Vulcan came out of the cloud climbing fast. There was no chance of a collision but, as he passed through my level, he would have been approximately 500 yards away. He passed straight over me at about 200 feet. It had been a massive shock, not, as you might expect, because of the possibility of collision, but the sight of this huge delta shape appearing to be a bird of prey. Just for a moment I had felt as all these little birds must feel as the hawk appears and they are the target. It was a rare occasion for me to actually have a noticeably raised heartbeat whilst flying.

The Lyneham-Calne road alongside the eastern side of the airfield was prone to flooding, as indeed was the hutted accommodation of the Officers' Mess. I was orderly officer the night before going on leave and the heavens opened. The road was blocked and the police asked if we could open one of our crash crew exit gates and allow traffic along the taxiway and out of the main entrance. When I had rousted out enough personnel for security purposes, we opened the gates.

I felt that, although all was under control, I could not leave things unattended. Eventually, the water subsided and normal traffic was resumed. I returned to my room and found that my RAF-issue travel bag was lying on the floor open and floating. In it were all my clothes for the week ahead. This was about 0500 and my train left Swindon at 0830! So I shoved it all in the laundry bin and repacked my remaining clothes in another but battered old suitcase. I left a note for my batman requesting he sort out my stuff and then set off for the train.

On the platform I leant over my suitcase to check the train time, as one does, and the case fell over. On the tube across London, I, and others noticed a strange smell! It was traced to my case. I had brought a bottle of good Navy Rum on my last trip, put it in the case and promptly broken it on the platform at Swindon. Now I had no clothes for my leave and had to buy a load of new stuff when I got home!

In view of my lack of hours and experience it was obvious that I could not become a captain for some time, so, rather than wait for the end of my tour with 216 Squadron, I applied for CFS (Central Flying School) at RAF Little Rissington in Gloucestershire. This was a four-month course to train as a flying instructor.

At this time Maureen and I were married and had a flat in a large house in Wootton Bassett. Another 216 chap, Terry Hillman, had the other flat and we became good friends. Terry had been training for helicopters and, before I was accepted for CFS, went off with wife Brenda and new baby, Graham, in one of our Comets to Singapore. On arrival at Changi, around 0900, they were allocated a room in the transit hotel, Changi Creek, but Terry was so keen to get going that he went off to his new squadron HQ. He met his new flight commander who told him that when he'd finished his work he would show Terry the island and then go to the Temple Bar in the Officers'

Mess for a beer. Off they went, but later on they had an engine failure. The rotors went into autorotate, so all was well and it descended safely but, it landed on a small slope and the helicopter rolled and burst into flames. They both died.

On Tuesday morning I was on the ramp when the Comet bringing Brenda and Graham arrived. They left Thursday and were back Tuesday, as by this time we were running a slip service, i.e. the aircraft had crew changes at each stop. It was so sad to see her grief and I was so saddened to have lost a good friend for the first time.

Later, on 9 December 1958, a Shackleton of 205 Squadron, which had very recently been based at RAF Changi, crashed in the South China Sea with the loss of all ten crew members. After the funeral services, families who had only arrived within the last few weeks all set off in a 216 Squadron Comet for Lyneham. The weather was so bad that, after a failed attempt at landing, the aircraft diverted to RAF St Mawgan, near Newquay. The customs officers there were totally lacking compassion as they searched all bags and started adding up duties to be paid on all items.

In that period, probably similar now, if you had bought anything overseas during the previous twelve months then duty was charged if you brought it into the UK. Fair enough, but these poor people had only been away for a varied time from one or two weeks to a couple of months having expected a two-year posting. The customs officers demanded full payment. Okay, so their demands were legal, but utterly lacking in compassion. A small nominal charge could have been made and all could have felt that the spirit of the rules had been kept.

The Officers' Mess, of which the customs officers were officially members, took a very dim view of the whole affair. I can no longer recall the actual mess reaction, perhaps not permitted in the bar or official functions, but I do know that when they entered the mess they were cold-shouldered by all. Quite right too!!

Meanwhile, Bill Alcock, a fellow Comet pilot, and I went for a pleasant evening at the USAF Hospital Burderop near Swindon. There we had a few beers before continuing our journey to London to watch the England v. Australia rugby at Twickenham the next day. During the evening he told me he had been posted to the Ferry Squadron, the lucky so-and-so. Just after leaving Burderop we had a cigarette and as he leant over to take a light he drove his lovely Jaguar into the ditch.

Now what? It was gone midnight and would cost a lot of money to haul it out, even if we could find anyone daft enough to come out in the awful weather. Bill had a brilliant idea (to him); let's call the orderly officer at nearby RAF Hospital Wroughton and see if he'll come in the Land Rover and pull us out. The O.O. was less than pleased but after much cajoling and pleading he agreed to come. To our amazement he arrived with a fire engine and a lot of disgrumpled firemen muttering something I couldn't quite catch but seemed very like 'Bloody officers!'. O.O. explained that he felt the Land Rover might have not been enough. The Jaguar was rescued, and all was good with our world; the damage was minimal to the car and we were on our way. How lucky that the O.O. was daft enough to take any notice of off-station problems.

Naturally, I was most envious as Bill's new role was to ferry many types of aircraft all over the world to various RAF stations. My envy turned very soon to deep despondency and frustration. After I had been at CFS for a few weeks I popped into the squadron to say hullo and visited the adjutant. He said it was a shame I had volunteered for the CFS as I was earmarked for the ferry squadron. I was furious and asked why he hadn't told me. His excuse was that it was confidential. Well!! There is confidential and 'confidential' and he could easily have helped me out by some subterfuge or other. I was so disappointed.

I was sad to leave Lyneham, it was a happy station and I had learnt a lot there. Also, I had made some good friends, most of whom are no longer with us. In particular, I had had a great time at rugby. I was early on made officer in charge and, having had a look at the players, made myself captain for the second season, 1958-59. It was a memorable season which started really badly. We lost the first four or five games and I was pretty fed-up with the way the guys' heads went down when it was obvious we were going to lose. So, I arranged more training and, before the next game, I made it clear that the Bristol Police were a good team and we had a fight on our hands. However, I emphasised that whatever the circumstances there was to be a confident battle to the end. We lost 22-7, I think, *but* everyone fought hard and I was free with my praise.

On the way back to Lyneham we stopped at the Shoe Inn for a few beers. There was much satisfaction with our game and it was obvious a bit of pride was felt. Outside, fireworks were being let off in the car park and, eventually, the proprietor asked who was in charge of the large group. I said it was me and he said that as we were misbehaving (i.e. the fireworks) he wanted us to leave. I assured him it was absolutely not one of us. Even as I remonstrated I was delighted to see all the boys down, or put down, their drinks and walk out. Hey, we were a team now!

We never looked back and continued to win. We played at St Mawgan in the quarter-finals of the RAF Cup in a blizzard at minus-3 degrees C and won; at least ten of us went down with cramp during the game and we played St Athan in the semi-finals.

RAF St Athan, the Technical Training School, in South Wales, were very sneaky. Whenever a famous or well-known sportsman was coming up for his National Service they would pull the strings to get him to St Athan. They were not necessarily students but were based there. As a result of all this skullduggery, St Athan had the best sports' teams in the Royal Air Force, certainly in most disciplines. We played them at home and our station commander, who had followed our success with great enthusiasm, ordered all non-essential personnel to support us. Oh dear, thank you sir, but you were too kind! We lost 40-3 (tries were only 3 points) and I never quite lived it down. They had three internationals, Malcolm Price of Wales, whom I was marking in the centre, Dickie Jeeps of England, and A.N. Other of whomsoever. In the first ten minutes I tackled Price in possession three times and decided he wasn't as good as he should be! I never got near him again and he scored some tries! I was subjected to much ribbing and complaints about wasting a good afternoon etc. Nevertheless, I was very proud of our achievements to date and sad to leave them shortly afterwards for my next posting at CFS.

To finish my time at Lyneham I managed a few fun Meteor trips, including a toddle around Dorset to have a final look at 'The dirty old man of Cerne Abbas'. During this trip I espied the Needles of the Isle of Wight and a surge of mischief overwhelmed me. I dived at them and went through the chosen gap at a few feet only. Oh dear, will that get back to the top brass? I heard nothing, thank goodness.

My last Meteor flight was the renewing of my green instrument rating; there were three grades: White the lowest, Green then Master Green, each permitting operation in different weather conditions with particular control on permitted visibility and cloud base.

My final Comet trip was to Nicosia and back on 26 February 1959.

My final log-book entry was an assessment, by my Squadron Commander, Wing Commander R.C. Churcher, as above-average as a co-pilot. Considering the zero landings Geoff had given I guess that was a generous farewell.

Learning to Teach

CFS, 9 March-30 June 1959

On arrival at the Central Flying School at RAF Little Rissington, Gloucestershire, the normal joining procedures followed: signing in at all departments, card to Mrs Station Commander, collection of books for the course, etc. The Mess was one of those lovely very old standard buildings; I was to share a room with Gerry Honey. The aim of Central Flying School, as it had been since 1920 (it was formed for pilot training), was to teach pilots to become basic and advanced instructors. Unfortunately, for the period of my course, No. 197, it was all basic instructor training as the runways were being worked upon and only the Piston Provost could be used as they were okay on grass.

We all met the instructors on our second day and, as with all training units, we split into two groups for the usual alternating ground school a.m. and flying p.m. and vice-versa. I recall that each instructor was allocated two students but, unlike flying training school, we did not do the majority of our training with one instructor. We flew with all of them which enabled us to learn the many different approaches to teaching. Mind you, it was to a set syllabus but open to individuality.

The general flying was pretty straightforward and without any particularly memorable incident. However, one of the very experienced instructors, Arthur Sunderland-Cooper, had only one eye, which would normally mean he would be unable to fly. However, so long as he flew with a qualified pilot, as all the students were, of course, he was able to impart his knowledge and test us as well.

Halfway through the course I was to have a night navigation test with Arthur. The route took us at 3,000 to 5,000 feet to Bridgnorth, Ross-on-Wye and back home. The weather was awful, with rain and turbulence which made for quite a test. I had a map on one knee and my flight plan on the other, a pencil in one hand and the control column in the other and juggled away as best I could.

Between points one and two Arthur asked if I would like some Kit-Kat chocolate to which I said 'Yes please'. He produced this bar from the knee-pocket of his flying suit to find it had melted and taken a knee-shape. At his suggestion I opened the canopy (it slid backwards not upwards) and he held the bar in the slipstream until it hardened. He then broke bits off, picked out the now embedded bits of tin foil, and we had a snack. Upon the return to base we carried out a left-hand circuit for landing which Arthur flew. However, as it was his left eye that was missing, I had to advise him when to turn downwind and on to the final approach. What fun and what a lovely man.

Another of our instructors was 'Cec' Crook, a real character of fun and outrageousness. Whilst he was stationed in Germany on a fighter squadron he missed the last train home to base. Undeterred he climbed into the cab of the train sitting on the set of rails that seemed likeliest to get him home and promptly drove it off. It worked. But the subsequent board of enquiry, or worse, certainly put the brakes on his promotion prospects for a long while.

We would often go to a dance in Cheltenham on a Wednesday night and Cec always assured us that he would find and dance with the least desirable lady present. This sounds cruel and ungentlemanly, but the lady never knew of his intentions. We had to agree that he was masterful in his choices but one night he was dancing with a lovely girl and we were all indicating that this time he was wrong. Next time he went past he grinned and raised her wig. We had to give him best again but found later that she had agreed to the game.

There was very little solo flying and, if we were not under instruction, we flew with fellow students and practised on each other and exchanged comments and suggestions about technique. On checking my log-book, I see that I flew solo only three times and they were when training for the aerobatic competition final in which the last six of us competed for the Clarkson Trophy.

The ground school training went deeper into all the subjects that are taught at flying training schools. In particular, Aviation Medicine was expanded upon and a new subject, Supersonic Flying, was thoroughly covered, even though we were almost all ex-fighter pilots.

Frequent tests were carried out to check our grasp of the subjects and we, in turn, had to give lectures on various items given to us or, occasionally, to make our own choice. As I was the only ex-Transport Command pilot on the course I gave talks relating to bigger aircraft, long-range navigation etc.

The final exams were pretty tough, for me anyway, but made easier as I had paired up with John Topping and for two or three weeks we had toured the area pubs for a good beer (or two) and tested each other for two or three hours each night. From this experience I found that this was a great way to learn and, from then on, I always found a willing partner with whom to study.

As with all life in the service(s) work can be hard, but the play with like-minded fellows can more than compensate. Evenings at most RAF stations could be made comfortable with cards, the bar, companionship and, of course, the camp cinema.

Camp cinemas were always named the Astra. The RAF motto 'Per Ardua ad Astra' translates as 'Through Adversity to the Stars'. This was always considered to really mean 'After work to the cinema'. One night a few of us went to the Astra to see a Dracula film. In the beginning there was the usual banter and laughter at the absurdity of it all but slowly, as we feared for the young girl alone in the woods etc., it quietened and I think we were all a little impressed by the 'horror' of it all.

When it was over we exited into the night, suddenly lighthearted, all the slight nervousness forgotten. Off to the bar for the usual levity and fun. The bar was off the main corridor and down a narrow and longish passageway. At the end of the evening I was ahead of the others and, as I entered the main corridor, Jack Pollard appeared from the side and pounced with fangs showing! I think my heart stopped and I know that, had I not bounced against the wall, I should have fallen. This really made me shocked, perhaps more than anything other than my Hunter incident. We all had a good laugh, mine somewhat forced, Jack apologised and off we went to our rooms.

The RAF issued all aircrew with a long, narrow and not too deep, metal trunk which most of us kept under our beds for the storage of rarely-needed items. I was so affected by this incident I couldn't bear to have this 'Dracula's coffin' under the bed and removed it to a storage room. I am embarrassed to admit that I was even nervous in the dark for the next two or three weeks! Thanks Jack!

I went home to Maureen and Wootton Bassett at weekends. Maureen was teaching at the local primary school in reception/nursery which was her speciality. Of course, in later years as headmistress, she covered much more. In view of her school holidays and the fact that the Royal Air Force College Cranwell kept much the same holidays I applied for the College and was accepted. I hadn't made it as a cadet but did as an instructor.

The last couple of weeks, after all final exams, including ground and air, were more relaxed. Normally, the pilots were given the opportunity to fly Hunter, Vampire and Canberra, from Little Rissington. However, with no useable runways, we were sent off to Kemble to fly just the Vampire and Hunter. For some of the pilots it was a revelation as they had not flown the Hunter. Of course, as qualified pilots of experience, they only had a couple of hours chat and they were let loose. A bit different from my hours of tests and study when just a new pilot. There was no Canberra to play with unfortunately. Anyway, I managed to get one 'Big Thunder' in and received a certificate to mark the event. I hadn't had one on the squadron!

In the last week those of us left in the competition competed for the Clarkson Trophy. The six of us were briefed by an Air Vice-Marshal of Flying Training Command HQ that we were not to go below 200 feet during the demonstration, which included the usual loops, slow roll, eight-point roll, barrel-roll, stall turn and other fun things.

At the de-briefing up in the control tower the AVM praised us all on our performance and pointed out that only one of us had not flown below 200 feet. I was confident that that was me and my hopes rose. However, the AVM said that nevertheless John Carter had flown the best display and was declared the winner. Well done, John.

Although each course has no passing-out parade they do have a dining-out night. After our course leader's speech he announced that we had our own 'Cluckson' Trophy for Little Rissington at which point some chickens were launched from the balcony at the musicians' mezzanine. They glided well and landed mostly on the top table. An incredibly good night was had by all and we set off for leave and then our new postings. The timing was good for Maureen and me as it was not far from the end of term and we could arrange our move with minimal disruption.

In the event, I found a pleasant enough semi-detached house at 249 Dysart Road in Grantham. At the town end of the road was a square with a most amazing baker's and pork butcher's where, on a Saturday, the queues would stretch for some way. In those days Grantham was more or less two towns as the A1 road with all its volume of traffic almost split the town into East and West Grantham. No motorways then!

Maureen easily got a teaching post in the town and we were all systems go.

Royal Air Force College Cranwell

On arrival at Cranwell I followed the usual routine, i.e. check in here, sign that, etc., etc. Then I checked in with the Wing Commander Flying. I was given the usual welcome, pep-talk and encouragement and off I went to RAF Barkston Heath, south of Cranwell and near Grantham.

The college is based at Cranwell near Sleaford in Lincolnshire and known by the cadets as Sleaford Tech, where there were (are) two airfields, a grass strip to the north and a proper airfield to the south. Here is where the advanced flying, i.e. Vampires, took place. Barkston Heath was for the Piston Provost basic training and was a lovely place to be. We had a station commander (a wing commander), two squadron commanders and an air traffic control. The airmen were permanently based there in proper accommodation and there were very few officers housed in a hutted mess. There was a cookhouse and adequate fire coverage. Otherwise, out of duty hours it was very quiet. The working day saw two squadrons of instructors with enough aircraft to cover all the students we looked after – a.m./p.m. alternate, etc., etc. They did ground training and only came to us for the flying. We weren't in a backwater but all was so calm that we felt we were. It all happened at Cranwell proper!

When I arrived, it was almost the end of term so I had only two weeks before the cadets left on their summer break or, more likely, their two weeks of adventure before going home. It was usual for most cadets to go on various courses or join army or navy units for some sort of experience before actually going home.

Day One: I walk into my new crew-room at midday, the cadets having just left and the next batch to arrive at 1300 hours, to say 'Hi, I'm the new instructor'. Seven faces are looking at me and no-one says 'Hi', 'Hello' or 'Welcome'. Two of them, however, say in unison 'Do you play bridge?' Ouch, I say 'No' and am greeted by some groans.

In the lunch interval between cadets leaving and arriving, the flight commander and the seven instructors made two teams and played bridge.

A book was kept and at the end of each term dues were paid and/or received. Needless to say, having done my introductory check ride with the squadron commander and done a solo flight to reconnoitre the area, I was going to have a crash course on the great game of bridge.

However, it was nearly the end of term so I had not much time. In between getting used to flying with students, who incidentally, were the senior course and at a very high standard, I was given a crash course in the game as it was obviously more important.

A week before end of term I flew with a cadet Willings, and we were doing aerobatics. I said that I would do some for a couple of minutes as it was a while since CFS. I tried a couple of stall turns but, to my astonishment and embarrassment, failed dismally (they can be tricky). Willings then proceeded to do a couple of very good ones much to my mortification! He flew with me a few days later and asked me how my stall turns were going. Cheeky blighter!

As usual at the end of term, the instructors stayed on for a week to tidy up and to give air cadets some flying experience. My log-book shows thirteen flights in the next three days with an average time of forty-five minutes, so they had a good time. Some asked for aerobatics, some of them actually found it wasn't really what they wanted! Sick bags were occasionally not used in time as the poor chaps couldn't unclip their masks easily due to inexperience. Mostly, though, it was a pleasure to give them the experience; I remembered how happy I had been as an air cadet to have these trips.

So came our first summer break and how wonderful it was not to have to apply for leave but to be given more than one's contemporaries. Maureen and I finalised our move to Grantham and went on holiday.

In September 1959 my instructing proper started. A new course of students was introduced to basic flying, having finished a full year of studies, drill and more drill, bull and more bull. Their excitement was palpable. At last they were on their way. I think the course number was 81 or 82.

There were sixteen-plus cadets and each instructor received two or three each: I had only two as I had not yet had any experience. My two guys were Pardoe and Dick Woodhead; sorry chaps but some Christian names are not in my log-book.

The programme took its usual course: familiarisation, straight-and-level, climb, descent, turns, stall, spins and circuits, circuits and circuits. A most important part of the pre-solo flight was, of course, engine failure after take-off (EFATO) which involved the decision to return to the airfield, height permitting, or pick a field. This was practised on most initial departures of the day. The cadets were shown and practised how to make a wise choice and then carry out the practice down to 200 feet. Then power up and climb away.

Students generally went solo after nine and a half to twelve hours and both of mine were okay. The first solo cannot be pre-planned but is arrived at sometimes quite unexpectedly. During one of the regular circuits and landing sessions it becomes obvious that he can be trusted to go alone and not kill himself. His delight when you say, 'OK, off you go, are you ready for it?' is obvious, then a little doubt shows, then it's all 'Too right I'm ready' all over his face. All you hear is 'Yes Sir.'

The instructor then grabs the squadron jeep and hightails it to the tower to see his student go through his paces. It is difficult to say who is the more nervous but my money is on the instructor. At all flying training schools there is a duty pilot, one of the instructors, in the tower throughout any period there are solo students airborne, even the experienced ones.

Normally, after a first solo the student and instructor would get together for a celebratory beer, or two, but the cadets' and officers' messes were different at Cranwell. Also, at the end of the flying day at Barkston, the cadets were on the buses and away. The ritual had to wait until I was instructing elsewhere.

By this time winter was setting in and starting the engines became more difficult. The starting system was to prime the engine with fuel via a button on the starting lever. Then raise the lever to fire a cartridge to start the engine turning and, hopefully, to fire and run. Okay during warmish temperatures but not always successful at around 3 degrees or less. It was not unusual, and always embarrassing, to use all three cartridges without success. This happened to instructors as well as students!

Partway through the course the students usually change instructors to give them a broader view of ways to perform. Unfortunately, Pardoe, who had been progressing steadily but less well than others eventually had to leave us. Despite repeated demonstrations and exhortations, he would carry out practice engine failures from altitudes, i.e. above 2,000 feet, pick a good field, fly accurately but forget to clear his engine. Every 1,000 feet it was necessary to rev the engine for a moment to clear the plugs. Well, this day, on a solo flight he failed to do so and, when he came to climb away from his chosen field and at 200 feet the engine quit. He carried out a safe landing. Unfortunately, he had chosen a field entirely surrounded by dykes, the watery types, and there was not enough room for a take off. The aircraft had to be dismantled. As is normal, he was then taken over by another instructor but, regrettably did not continue for long.

It was usual that if a student could not get to solo by eleven or twelve hours he would be transferred to another instructor. This change was not necessarily a criticism of either of them, just that it was realised that, despite teaching to a syllabus, there were variations of personalities, techniques, methods of explanation etc. The change worked more often than not.

Our instructors were a great bunch of guys. Peter Anstee, my bridge partner for off-base competitions, Max Pettey, the older and wiser of us, who had flown Washingtons, American B-29 bombers, on maritime patrols, Reg Drown, a terrific teacher on the blackboard as well as in the air, Trevor (T.S.C.) Jones who would become my No.1 son's godfather, Eric Denton and Ray (?) Milburn. I cannot recall too well but Warrant Officer 'Jacko' Jackson is most memorable as a character and because he had only one ear. There was no opening even, and I do not know how he lost it. However, he was unworried by it and, I believe, still had some hearing on that side.

He told a lovely story of being in a pub one night watching a game of darts where one player also had only one ear; the other side to his. When the game was over he suggested a game to this fellow, suggesting that they played for the pair. Apparently, the other guy went all frosty and had a sense of humour failure.

Time goes on and we pass through the usual stages including instrument flying, aerobatics, formation, night flying, etc. There are regular progress checks, which test the student but, of course, reflect on the instructor. Every flight requires a period at the blackboard in the small, designated briefing rooms, then the pre-flight where the entire aircraft is checked over, then the flying lesson and then usually, back to the room for a debriefing and questions.

Then, or later in the day, the trip is recorded in the student's file under the heading PAT. P is for Progress, A is for Attitude, not to his instructor but his approach to each task, his confidence etc., and T for Technique, i.e. how does he fly.

There is no room for flippancy in these reports but the old joke of 'He sets himself a low standard and consistently fails to attain it' is sometimes tempting. Actually, the students worked really hard and had great ambitions. Whenever the student was mentioned in any reports you naturally used his name but whenever instructors referred to students generally they were known as Bloggs, as in Bloggs did this and Bloggs did that, etc.

In April 1960 we, the basic training outfit of Barkston Heath, moved to RAF Spitalgate whilst our airfield was refurbished and made ready for the

Jet Provost. Spitalgate, originally RAF Grantham, was a training school for new entrants to the WRAF (Women's Royal Air Force) but they were always known as WAAFs (WAFFS) as the force was originally the Women's Auxiliary Air Force.

The airfield was grass and still had the usual huts which we used as crew-rooms. It was a wonderful summer of good weather, sunny skies and comfortable temperatures. Inevitably, a lot of our time was spent outside, blackboards and all. It had some semblance of how our great Battle of Britain crews were shown in their chairs, still in flying kit, relaxing before the scramble. It was a great period for us. I'm not sure that the WAAFs enjoyed our presence as we watched them going through their drill training quite near our huts. I am sure some of our comments didn't help their progress!

Spitalgate was on higher ground about two miles north of Grantham but, unlike most Lincolnshire airfields, it was not surrounded by flat ground. Normal take offs to the north were okay but the ground to the east and south-east dropped away and did not offer good terrain for an emergency landing. During the day this was no big deal but at night there was no satisfactory guide to a safe landing. It was a bit like flying over water, i.e. you were even more aware of your engine readings than normal. Being a grass airfield and such lovely weather, the whole experience seemed more normal as the Piston Provost was, after all, a propeller aircraft and suited to grass.

On one occasion, landing to the south-east, I was at 300 feet on finals when a USAF Voodoo flew through my approach path just below me. We passed each other at about 100 feet and his wake turbulence and jet wash sent me upside-down and losing height. Hullo, I've been here before. Anyway, all was well and despite Air Traffic Control logging the incident and investigating a search for the offender nothing happened. It was quite exciting though.

One morning, sitting on the grass outside our huts, we heard a banshee wail and knew it was a runaway engine due to propeller failure. To the north we saw a plume of black smoke trailing behind a Piston Provost at about 2,000 feet. Trevor Jones and I dived into my Austin-Healey Sprite and sped to the area we knew he would land. The fire teams beat us to it, having gone through the crash exit to the north, but they were too late to save the student.

He had carried out a copybook procedure and landing. Tragically, he had chosen a two-tiered field, landed well, and, almost immediately, hit the three-foot 'wall' marking the next level. The aircraft stopped dead and the fire continued from the engine to the fuselage. The nearby farmer arrived quickly but could not get near the aircraft and the student died in the cockpit.

August, 1954. The starting line-up for 103 Piston Provost Course at RAF Hullavington. *Station Photographic Department* (SPD)

September, 1954. First Officer's Dining-in Night for the new boys. I did most of the bow-ties.

Rear (L-R): Author, Peter Hudson (National Service Pilot), Geoff Taylor, Brian McGee, Doug 'Puddy' Catt and John Simmons (Flight Engineer).

Front (L-R): Peter Wild, Trevor Betterton, Julian 'Bunch' Dyer, Tony Dunn and Barry 'Bo' Plummer. (Author's own picture (AOP))

January, 1955. Start of night-flying. My instructor George Applegarth with us.
    Rear (L-R): Peter Hudson, Trevor Betterton and Author.
    Front (L-R): David 'Paddy' Hipperson, Peter Wild and Brian McGee. (AOP)

March, 1955. All that remains of 103 Course with a Piston Provost.
    Rear (L-R): McGee, Wild, Simmons, author, Taylor, Catt and Hudson.
    Front (L-R): Hipperson, Neil Ferguson (late joiner from UAS), Group Captain
Fields, Station Commander, Betterton and Plummer. (AOP)

December, 1955. Wings Parade.
Front: Author, Catt, Barry Windsor (UAS), McGee and Hipperson.
Rear: Plummer and Wild. (Courtesy of the Northern Echo, Darlington)

NO. 10 HUNTER COURSE.

P/O. JACKSON. P/O. FOYLE. P/O. BURDETT. P/O. WRIGHT P/O. WHITE. P/O. CARTER. F/O. HOWE.

P/O. CATT. P/O. LANGDELL. P/O. THURLEY. F/LT. GREEN. S/LDR. BARTMAN. F/O. HUGHES. P/O. CHRISTIE. P/O. YOUNG

P/O Vaughan

January, 1956. 229 O.C.U. (Operational Conversion Unit) RAF Chivenor, Barnstaple. No. 10 Hunter Course. (AOP)

Summer, 1956. 257 'Burma' Squadron at RAF Strubby, Lincolnshire, for the annual Fighter Command exercises. Author in uniform. (AOP)

4th. March, 1957. Immediately after our 257 Squadron photo we were advised that we were to be disbanded. The smiles soon left us.

L. to R. TAM 'Paddy' Smythe, Arthur Summers(Somers?)(ex-vice squad!), Tim Hannah, Tony Weedon, BIL (Hamish) Hamilton, Nick Carter, Geoff Jarvis, J.B Carruthers (The Boss), Roger Purdue, Dickie Milward, Brian (Bernie) Burdett, Bill Dodds, Hubert 'Slube' Slaney, Phil Champnis(s) and Pat Fleming.

Above: March, 1957. We had just heard all about our disbandment and the squadron photographer took pictures of as all as we went about the day job. This is the author and if you look closely you can see the tears in his eyes. (SPD)

Right: Artist P.N. Rooney toured Officer's messes doing his caricatures for £5. Good value, I reckon.

April, 1959. 197 Course, Central Flying School at RAF Little Rissington, Gloucestershire Author second row and third from left. (SPD)

October, 1964. The V.I.P. crew at Victoria Falls, Southern Rhodesia waiting for Independance in Northern Rhodesia.

Navigator, Jimmy Constanti, Co-Pilot, the author and the Captain, Ron Underwood. (AOP)

1966. Comet II nosewheel taking the load at RAF Luqa, Malta. That's not a can of beer in my hand, honest! (AOP)

Comet II XK696 is the gate guardian at RAF Lyneham. (AOP)

NIGHT STOP MUHARRAQ

October, 1967. RAF VC10 XR 810. We have just arrived at RAF Muhurraq, Bahrain. This VC10 was soon after taken for the purpose of testing the new Rolls Royce RB211 by-pass engine, later used by the early TriStars. (RAF Postcard)

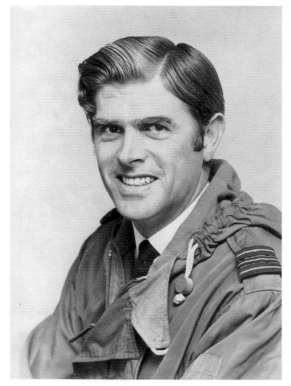

October, 1970. The author photographed for an article in the South Wales Echo concerning people with interesting jobs. (Courtesy of Media Wales)

Back to Barkston

We returned to Barkston Heath at the end of summer term and, having flown the usual air cadet contingent, we went on summer holidays. It was only to my parents' as Maureen was eight months pregnant.

I had bought the Sprite (the bug-eyed one!) on 1 January 1960 and a week or two later Maureen had told me her news. The Sprite had no room for a carrycot or child-seat, so I realised it would have to go. However, we had a good time with it for about fifteen months and, as a result, I have endeavoured to have convertibles as often as possible.

One night, en route Grantham to Cranwell Officers' Mess for a dining-in night, I was on the elevated level of the Fosse Way which ran past Spitalgate and Barkston to Ancaster. I saw a fellow officer's car hanging off the edge of the road. I braked to see if he needed assistance and discovered his problem; he had found the black ice on which I was now traversing backwards! His face was a picture, as indeed mine must have been. I had the hood down, I was skidding and I had a drop to the left and right. Had I left the road I could have easily rolled with awful consequences. No wonder my face was a picture.

As usual we returned to work ahead of the arrival of the cadets, got the aircraft ready and flew two or three flights to get our hands in again. Within a few days of starting the new term Maureen went into Grantham Hospital and Andrew Mark Burdett was born early in the morning of 15 September 1960. It was not usual in those days for fathers to be in attendance at the birth, which was just as well: I had been made Station Duty Officer on the 14th for some reason or other.

As Andrew arrived in the morning I was able to be there just after the event. I had been granted a week off by my flight commander which was generous bearing in mind we were normally only permitted absence during College holidays.

Excitement was mounting as we were soon to retrain on the Jet Provost (J.P.). This included the cadets we were currently training as there would be an overlap between courses. My current students, mainly Terrett, Thomson and Slade, had started in April/May and the next new group would be in January.

My J.P. conversion started on 11 October 1960 and who should be my first instructor but Lou Riley who had been my first ever RAF instructor. After two trips I did my solo and then most trips were with my fellow instructors, getting to know the aircraft and honing techniques for instructing on jets.

> Jet Provost general figures:
> Armstrong Siddeley Viper which had originally powered the Jindivik unmanned target aircraft for training ground-to-air missile operators.
> Wing span 10.77 metres (35 feet 4 inches)
> Length 13.36 metres (43 feet 10 inches)
> Height 3.10 metres (10 feet 2 inches). Maximum weight 4,173 kilograms
> Maximum speed 393 knots.

Part of the retraining included four-ship formations and one of the trips saw me at No. 4 in the box, i.e. the four were in a square and I was behind the leader and slightly lower. Unknown to me, my radio had failed just before the leader called 'Airbrakes, Airbrakes, Go!'

The other three immediately decelerated but, of course, I did not. Within a fraction of a second I was going under the leader and, if nothing happened, then my tail would hit him. Obviously, the instant it all happened I immediately stuck the nose down and got out of there. The leader was none other than Lou Riley, who at 2 FTS Hullavington managed to do a loop straight underneath that Varsity VP123, remember? Fair dos, I hadn't seen it either.

We continued our Piston Provost course to finish our current senior students but the junior ones had to convert to the J.P.

Shortly after we converted to the J.P. there was a passing-out parade for course 81 or 82 on 13 December 1960. Normally, the Vampires did a fly-past, timed to pass over the college at exactly the moment the cadets presented arms at the salute to the reviewing officer. The timing of the parades was meticulous and the present arms timing would be known to the second. The lead aircraft of the formation would carry a navigator to guarantee an accurate timing.

Depending on the wind velocity, i.e. speed and direction, the formation would use a known landmark of the required distance according to the wind. The aim was to pass over the chosen point exactly at the desired time, keeping a constant pre-determined speed. This was important for two reasons: the timing and to avoid the need for speed changes which could cause the formation to lose adhesion.

Well, this time we, in our J.Ps, had the honour. I had seen a couple of passing-out parades and had been both astonished and proud at the way the formation passed over the college at the precise moment the cadets presented arms. It was a great feeling to be in the J.P. fly-past which did exactly that. It was like you see the horses waiting for the start to the Grand National. We pottered about the Sleaford area in loose formation a while before the key moment and as the wind was determined so the leader went for the appropriate starting point. We closed up into tight formation and it went perfectly.

Every evening of passing-out day a ball was held in the College to which all cadets and officers were invited, with guests of course. Usually a well-known band was on hand for a splendid evening to be enjoyed, especially by the ladies. The cadets, obviously, had a great time. The band for this evening was Duke Ellington's.

Earlier in the term we had had a formal dinner for the visiting American cadets from the USAF Academy and, after the toasts to the President and Queen, they stood and sang 'Off we go into the wild blue yonder'. Regrettably the cadets and junior officers of the college decided that was a bit over the top and so responded with the song 'Why were they born so beautiful, why were they born at all?'

This went down like a lead balloon with our Commandant, Air Commodore D.F. Spotswood, and the cadets were punished in some way. We, the offending officers, received a shed-load of extra duties, including duty and orderly officers and other administrative tasks that normally passed us by. Fair enough.

After this we broke up for the winter holidays until the end of January. I recall that the normal leave allowance was two or three weeks a year, but I was getting around seven which gave Maureen and me plenty of time to spend with Andrew.

For the two rugby seasons at Cranwell I had played my natural, and now permanent, position of openside wing forward for the Cranwell Staff XV. Our captain was Wally Close, who later became captain of Malaya, as it was then, whilst based out there. We had a really good team and, in the 1960/61 season, reached the semi-finals of the RAF Cup. Our second-row man, name forgotten, was an early user of contact lenses and had to play with

125

them in. On a few occasions we heard the plaintive cry that he'd lost one. The ref would blow the whistle and the hunt was on; amazingly, we always found it despite the churned mud and unevenness of the old pitches.

Just after Christmas I went home alone, sold my lovely little Sprite and bought a Triumph Herald Convertible; it was a light green – the alternative had been mauve which I had not fancied. This car gave me loads of problems (Friday car syndrome) and when I was home a year later I saw the chap who had bought the other car. We compared notes and he had not had a single problem!

When I bought the car I also bought a pedigree yellow Labrador and we set off back to Grantham. En route, I let him out occasionally for a run and a pee and near our destination I found blood on the carpet. The poor thing had cut his foot which I had not noticed. The carpet or, more accurately, the floor covering was that corded manmade fabric popular in cheaper cars and I was unable to remove the stain. A later event didn't remove it either.

I was duty pilot in the control tower and, as was usual at Barkston Heath, was also Duty Officer, which meant staying overnight as officer in charge of the camp. I had left the hood down, as it was a nice day, with my No. 1 uniform and overnight bag on the back seat. During the morning with only four inexperienced cadets doing their early solo circuit exercises, I saw some heavy clouds appearing. There was obviously rain and likely to be some turbulence as they passed overhead, their apparent route.

It was obviously correct to recall these pilots so I requested Air Traffic to make the calls. Oh dear, two pilots landed with no problem but one made two or three attempts but I think nerves had the better of him. The real problem was that the fourth pilot could not get his undercarriage down and I was advising him how to proceed. He knew the drills, of course, but was getting flustered. Meanwhile, our nervous pilot had landed. By the time we had sorted out the gear problem and he had landed, the bad weather was overhead and had been for ten minutes. I had had the opportunity to peer down occasionally, and had all four pilots landed as planned, I would have had the hood up in time. Instead, the car was two inches deep in water, my uniform was soaked and the wretched blood stain was still there. The interior stank for weeks.

Pilots are privileged to see some wonderful sights. One morning to the west of Barkston Heath I saw Belvoir Castle shrouded in fog, or the area anyway. It stands on something of a hill which is somewhat of an island from its local area. As far as the eye could see there was just a flat white surface with the castle sitting on it. The fog wreathed, or writhed, around its base, making it look totally like a small island in a large sea. Sadly, as with far too much of my flying career, I had no camera with me.

Barkston Heath has a main NE/SW runway and shorter E/W runway. I was doing circuits with a student working up to his first solo. He was good enough except for one regular problem; in the event of an aborted approach, for whatever reason, the procedure was: full power, raise the nose, raise the gear, climb away and raise flaps at a safe height. Every time I called 'overshoot' he did everything correctly but, for some reason, occasionally, he put on less power than needed and then went through the rest of the procedure. Naturally, our speed would be reducing and by the time we got full power it was getting a bit hairy.

Eventually, we got it sorted out and I decided he was ready for his first solo. As we approached the short runway and at about fifteen feet I shouted 'overshoot'. He reverted to his old ways and applied a little power and immediately raised the gear. I grabbed the controls and we flew down the runway on stall speed, nose raised and the tail about four feet from the ground (ATC estimate). The only way to recover was to lower the nose but this would have put us on the runway. I could not lower the gear because the increased drag would cause a stall and we'd hit the runway before it was locked down. If I ordered him to eject, then the drag from the open cockpit could cause a stall and I would probably not make it; I kept that option as a last resort as we were still managing to fly. I hung on and willed it to climb, which it did for about ten feet, which was just enough to clear the fence and bushes at the end. Fortunately, the ground fell away quickly to the west and I was able to lower the nose, gain speed and start breathing again.

He went solo the next trip and continued to progress well.

ATC had hit the crash alarm and the fire crews had rushed to the west to pick up the pieces. The tower guys said when they saw us disappear downwards they were dismayed, then delighted to see us reappear climbing.

The word 'overshoot' was used in those days to mean carry out a missed approach but nowadays it means you've gone off the end of the runway. The expression, from the Americans who always seem to find the right word, is now 'go-around'. When we did a touch-down and continued with a take-off we called it a 'roller' but the Americans called it a 'touch-and-go', which I feel is much more descriptive.

The remainder of my time at Cranwell passed fairly uneventfully: my students, Terret, Thomson and Simpson, were doing well until one of them, Terret, I think, fell by the wayside. The next course of Milligan, Harding and, occasionally, Herring certainly did well. It was one of those three who did the gear trick on me but I cannot remember which one. Later on, Jones and Seyd joined my menagerie, as it were, so I was quite busy.

All good things come to an end and so it was that I was advised in August that I was to be one of eight instructors to reform No. 3 FTS, to be based at Leeming in Yorkshire. However, prior to that, I was to be joint officer in charge of a group of cadets visiting BAOR (British Army of the Rhine) on their annual adventure before setting off for summer leave.

We set off in early August to visit the South Wales Borderers based near Minden. There the regiment transported us to Sennelager where the Army carried out manoeuvres and training. On the first day there, the CO suggested the cadets might like to try out the new SLR (self-loading rifle) rifles. After a few rounds it was suggested that they could have a competition with the soldiers. Unbeknownst to the CO, almost all cadets were in the Cranwell Rifle Team and they jumped at the offer. They gave an incredibly good account of themselves and, from this distance in time I'm not sure, they either won or came very, very close.

After this we set off for the weirdest lunch I've ever had. It was raining and as we approached the food wagons we saw soldiers queuing with their mess tins. We continued past the soldiers and I assumed that we were either going to the head of the queue or to our own mess section.

To our astonishment there were tables set to one side, set for a three-course meal with napery and waiters! So we took our seats and, even though it was raining, I removed my hat and hung it on a convenient branch. We started with soup and soggy bread and continued for another half-an-hour. We had managed polite conversation whilst using napkins to keep the face dry, not just to daintily pat our mouths. Fortunately, we then went to a huge canopied lorry and fell on a few crates of beer. As we had an early start next day we were in our tents, suitably beered-up, by about 2100. I slept on a narrow safari-type bed next to the entry flap which was downwind and away from the direction the rain was coming from. We left the entrance open.

In the morning I was awakened to find myself two or three yards from the tent, still fully clothed, as we all were, and sopping wet. Obviously, I had rolled on the narrow bed, it had fallen sideways and I had continued rolling. Good beer, I guess!

The rest of the day was spent doing soldierly things and the end of the day was spent just as before. During the night I kept scratching my head and decided that having to stay in the same clothes for two or three days was best left to the Army. However, the scratching became more frenzied and I realised it wasn't just dirty hair. I sat up quickly to find a mouse sitting on my pillow. It wasn't perturbed at all, despite our staring competition but left after positive persuasion. Having turned the pillow over I had a good night's sleep.

On our return to the mess, and after a double shower and change of clothes, we retired to the bar. Bad luck, they didn't have one. As with many other elite regiments a bar was considered infra-dig and one had to retire to the ante-room and use waiter service.

Next day we were off to a battery of the Royal Artillery where we could play with big guns but not fire them. They entertained us extremely well. We were trashed by their basketball team and tennis team.

We finished our visit with a competition on Steinhuder Meer, a large lake north-west of Hanover. We were all paired off in dinghies for a circular race of some two or three kilometres. My sailing experience was quite limited, so I relied upon my skipper who was the other officer from Cranwell.

He was a naval officer on an exchange posting so I felt in good hands. However, we capsized early on and were out of it. That was my first and only capsize ever and it was with an R.N. skipper!

During our visit the Army personnel were looking very serious and concerned because the Russians were in the act of, or about to, start building the Berlin Wall. We were uncertain of how the West was going to react so we, the Cranwell lot, were glad to leave when we did.

After summer vacation/leave I had just ten days of instructing before transferring to Leeming.

RAF Leeming – 3 FTS Jet Provosts

September 1961 to November 1963

I seem to have used the old A1 main road as my personal RAF route, first to Darlington (RAF Middleton St George) in 1955, then Boroughbridge (RAF Dishforth), then Grantham (RAF College), where the high street was the A1, and now RAF Leeming with the road just to the west.

Until September 1961 the airfield had been home to 228 OCU for training Javelin crews as night-fighters. Now we were to reform No. 3 FTS. We were nine instructors and a squadron commander. Eventually there would be two squadrons of two flights each, meaning thirty-six instructors in total.

However, we were forming No. 1 Squadron. I was on B Flight and set about transforming our offices in one of the hangars into crew-rooms and briefing rooms. This meant making models, wall charts, diagrams and forming our own operations room where the flying programmes would be planned and all relevant paperwork, signatures and other legal bumf would be handled. The programme was laid out on a sort of whiteboard showing a grid with pilots' names, aircraft registration, take-off times and exercise to be performed over a five-day period. The programme would be written each evening in black or red wax pencils. The best way to remove or change entries was to use a soft cloth with CTC poured on it. CTC – carbon tetrachloride – had a pungent smell which permeated the immediate area and was forever associated with operations rooms service-wide.

The main bulk of administrative and station technical personnel remained after 228 OCU left but a large number of people arrived specifically for Jet Provost Engineering, Ground School lecturing etc. The important changes were the senior officers: the Station Commander was Group Captain Hyland-Smith, a Southern Rhodesian; Wing Commander Basil Lock the Wing Commander Flying; his deputy was Squadron Leader Paul Kent;

and the Wing Commander Engineering was Wing Commander Goodridge. They combined into the best group of men under whom I have ever served.

The atmosphere because of the excitement and interest in our endeavours was as much due to the senior officers as to ourselves. Now we were more or less ready but we needed aircraft. Paul Kent, I think it was, collected our first Jet Provost from Warton in Lancashire, then each new aircraft was used to ferry one more instructor to collect another. Soon we had eight or ten aircraft but no students. Our instructors were of varying ages and experience; the squadron commander was Squadron Leader Paddy Glover and B Flight Commander was Flight Lieutenant Al East, but I cannot recall their backgrounds. Jack Pollard, my CFS Dracula impersonator, was on the flight and the youngest, and greenest, was Roger Neal. Roger had graduated from Cranwell about four or five months before I left and had impressed everyone so much that he was sent straight to CFS to train as an instructor.

'Lofty' Lance, so-called because of his size, was the oldest and a South African. He had an amazing career; he started as a merchant seaman with the South African merchant service and then did his national service in the army. He trained as a pilot with the SAAF and during that time met his Australian wife. When he finished his contract, he joined the RAAF as a pilot. Then, as the money was really good, he transferred to the RCAF. Having completed his four-year contract, he joined the RAF. At the age of around forty-forty-three he returned to Australia for his wife and children's sake; they were Australian too. He flew for the RAAF in Vietnam where he was, sadly, killed. What a career, what a man!

The others were Wally Norton, Joe Hickmott, Bill Bailey, Ike Dawson and Tony Marshall of Hullavington days. By this time I was twenty-five years old and entitled to an officer's married quarter on base, so Maureen, Andrew and I ended up in No. 1 OMQ; it was a large corner plot with a badly-kept garden but, for now, it was better than commuting. As we were first there, all of the flight who so wanted, were in the married quarters. My neighbours were Wally, Ike, Tony and Lofty. The mess was a short drive away on RAF roads.

The students arrived in early October and, after joining procedures and instructor allocation, we were on our way. My first two chaps were Vere and Miller with my first instructional flight on 18 October with Vere. All the training followed the usual routine whereby more and more is learnt until first solo is achieved. Then it's hammer the circuit a few times, then on to aerobatics, instrument flying, formation, navigation and night flying.

The senior officers had encouraged flamboyance, with professionalism, of course, which led to the first aircraft airborne everyday being permitted to perform a low-level high-speed run after take-off. This was frequently done at about fifteen-twenty feet down the long line of parked aircraft. If the weather was slightly less than perfect the same aircraft then passed on all information on visibility cloud base and/or layers and any ice-formation on the aircraft and at what height.

The spirits were up and all was going well, so how about a party? The weekend was the obvious time but it had been found earlier that when the Javelin OCU had their farewell do, they had gone to town and spent *all* the funds in the mess account. So, our first party was to buy our own drinks and enjoy the small finger food and hamburgers! Never mind, it went off with a bang and, as Chubby Checker had just introduced the Twist, the dancing was terrific. One of the mess staff got so carried away by the event or purloined booze, he ventured to goose one of the wives. He got seven days' jankers and confined to camp; not bad in the circumstances.

When the school was at full flow, with four courses (flights) on the go, it was very important to try and keep a steady flow of traffic. Therefore, each flight was allocated times for take-off, to which we tried to adhere. Otherwise, there would have been bottlenecks and hold-ups for take-offs and landings. It worked very well.

The noise on the line from the Viper engines was very bad. Aircraft starting-up, departing and returning gave a very high decibel rating. For no reason we ever accepted we were not allowed to wear our helmets and bone-domes (protective helmets) to cancel the noise because we would not hear aircraft approaching as we walked along or across the movement area. True, but we had eyes. The airmen on the line all had ear defenders, so the ruling made no sense. Anyway, the RAF paid for it, literally, as many crews, including me, had early hearing loss and were compensated with one-off payments in our fifties and sixties.

At the beginning of my time at 3 FTS I was made officer in charge of ejector-seat training and progress and Squadron Flight Safety Officer. The Mark 3 ejector seat was a great improvement on the earlier models where there were serious limitations on their use. You will recall that the seat in the Hunter should/could not be used below 1,000 feet, especially if the aircraft was descending. Well, this seat could be fired even if you were on the runway as long as your speed was 60 knots or more. Upon pulling the handle, the hood went, the seat went and immediately the drogue pulled the pilot's parachute out; at the same time the harness separated from the seat. From pulling the handle to your feet hitting the ground was two-and-a-half seconds. All things being okay, you should have been able to walk away from it.

My duties were to give ground school lectures on the ejector seat to all the courses before they did any flying, then, as all instructors did, fully brief and teach the students the sheer necessity to know how to initiate the ejection and what to do if anything went wrong. They were taught that if they were told to eject then they did it within milliseconds. Further, they were advised that if they spoke to the instructor after the order that they would be talking to themselves.

My further duty with the seat was to test the students weekly and the instructors monthly, using an actual seat but not firing it, of course, to see that their knowledge was good enough for me to sign them off.

The main reason for constant testing was to ensure that the seat emergency drills were second nature. Should you be below 10,000 feet then the automatic system would cut in, i.e. the pressure capsule sensing the altitude would activate seat harness and leg-restraint disconnection from the seat and, at the same time, the drogue would leave the seat, pulling out the parachute. The seat would fall away and there you were on the end of the parachute, probably still holding the face blind and ejection handle as a souvenir.

However, if it did not work it was essential to carry out the emergency in exactly the right sequence, pull the first handle on your chest to disconnect harness and leg restraints, push clear of the seat and pull the parachute handle. It sounds easy but, if injured or panicky, the two handles were very close to each other and you had to be positive.

The ejector-seat harness also had a negative-G-strap which slotted into the base of the harness box and, if tightened properly, ensured that, when inverted, your bottom stayed on the seat. This ensured that should you eject inverted you would not be hanging from the seat and have it slam into your backside causing serious back damage.

On landing from an aerobatic sortie, before which I had ensured the strap was very tight, I parked the aircraft and released the harness. I experienced the most excruciating pain in my testicles, worse than anything that had happened on a rugby field, and could not move. The student called the ambulance and I was lifted out and on to a stretcher. By the time I reached sick quarters (the base clinic) the pain was easing off. The perceived wisdom of two doctors was that, as I hadn't had a pee immediately before departure, which is always foolish, I had probably forced urine in the wrong direction. I was given some gingery sort of powder and told to add it to water and drink four litres a day. Four litres!?

Despite terrible discomfort and pain, I continued to fly and even go to cricket training. However, around 0400 hours on the fourth day I was in terrible pain, so I went to the doctor at the earliest opportunity and said I was going to hospital with, or without, his authority. The reason I was so adamant was that he, or they, had kept dismissing my worries as unfounded. I had taken the precaution of neither eating or drinking that morning and, on arrival at Catterick Military Hospital, I was operated on immediately. The accurate medical term eludes me but the fact was that there was a lot of twisting or distortion there and this caused the cutting off or serious reduction, of the flow of blood to the area. The surgeon said that if the surgery had been delayed to later in the day I would have lost one or both of the testicles. No. 2 son, Nicholas, should be pleased about that, coincidentally being born later at Catterick.

There were four of us in the ward, an Army captain with pneumonia who spent every waking hour making flies to catch his beloved trout, the Chief Constable of the area who had several tendons damaged due to a dog bite and another Army guy. Needless to say, I was the butt of the jokes especially when, on the second or third day, I was allowed to get up and go to the lavatory unaided. I was exceedingly swollen and could only walk like John Wayne after a week in the saddle! I was released after about ten days and sent to the CME (Central Medical Establishment) in Goodge Street, London.

All aircrew after hospitalisation for certain injuries have to do a full medical to determine their suitability for current and future roles. For example, A1G1Z1 means top rating for Air or Ground duties and Zone for anywhere in the world. I ended up as A2G1Z1. I had been downgraded, because they found that I was high-tone deaf on one or two frequencies; it was nothing to do with the surgery. I was advised that it would actually not affect any future flying role but it would need to be monitored and, therefore, I would have to go to CME every year. The ENT specialist was a female wing commander and, on that occasion and all the following years, she wore a huge neck brace. Poor thing!

As Flight Safety Officer it was my duty to connect, collate and distribute all information relating to airmanship information and any technical or incident information about the Jet Provost in particular. If there were any incidents reported, either close calls or any damage or injury, I had to write reports and send them up the line. If the incident/accident was serious enough then the other Squadron Flight Safety Officer would be required to investigate it and, if of a serious enough nature, it would be handed to a higher level.

There were three flight safety officers on the unit; the Station FSO and each squadron FSO. When No. 2 Squadron had a bad incident the Station FSO and I were to investigate it. A temporary detachment instructor had been showing a local army officer the area and demonstrated an engine failure with forced landing at a disused area. Unfortunately, he left his go-around a little late and returned with some leaves and twigs in his undercarriage. The station FSO, the miscreant and I had all been at school together!

After a chat, a few coffees and a few reminiscences, we agreed that during his go-around at the correct and authorised height he had encountered a large flock of birds and had taken evasive action by diving under them and being unable to avoid clipping the top of a tree whilst doing so.

Very early in my time at Leeming I had one FSO course in London which included a visit to Farnborough, the home of so many accident investigations. There we all actually saw, and handled, the SQUARE panel that failed in one of the Comet crashes, the reason, eventually, why the RAF got to fly them.

I dealt with two very different incidents/accidents at Leeming. The sad one was when Bill Gambold and his student had an engine-failure just on lift-off and Bill ordered the ejection. They both got out safely but landed among trees at the end of the runway. Bill was quite badly injured but the student's parachute caught in the branches and he then swung strongly into the tree-trunk and was killed. I carried out the initial checks and made the technical reports but, quite naturally, it was taken over by the specialists.

At the other end of the scale was Tony Marshall's ejection. This was funny on many levels. He was No. 2 in formation with a student under training. No. 2 sits to the right of No. 1, or leader. Bloggs was not close enough and seemed not to be trying hard enough to get back in position.

'Get in Bloggs, get in.' 'Yes, sir but it's not working.' 'I have control.' Well, Tony did the usual manoeuvre by a rapid movement of the ailerons and a rapid return to neutral. Nothing! At that moment the engine fire alarm went off. Tony closed the throttle (thrust lever nowadays), shut off the fuel and pressed the fire extinguisher. He had advised No. 1 immediately and he and the other aircraft, No. 3, disappeared in half a second. Neither Bloggs nor Tony had been able to control the aircraft as the fire had burnt through the control in some way but had given a very delayed warning.

They were well up so when Tony ordered the ejection and then followed there was plenty of time for a safe descent. They were over the A1 (that road again) and Tony realised he was drifting towards Castle Howard. He couldn't see Bloggs, so concentrated on his own safe arrival. He landed comfortably in grassland and when he had collected his thoughts and unharnessed his parachute, looked around. He saw three estate workers about 300 yards away trimming a tree and walked towards them, dragging his 'chute behind him.

It should be pointed out that Tony was well-built and with a heavily-marked face as a result of some childhood illness. This did not make him ugly but his size and the very roundness of his face made him different. As he arrived at the tree, with bone-dome still on but visor up and oxygen mask dangling to the side he said 'Hullo'.

The three men turned as one, gasped in fright and fled! Tony said that it was like watching the finale of the Benny Hill Show. He turned round and set off back to the A1 and hitched a lift northbound. He was swiftly picked up but en route he saw the RAF rescue team's vehicles and transferred to them. The student was fine, too.

My other secondary duty was to run and captain the rugby team, with Tony as my vice-captain. Since all inter-station matches were played on a Wednesday afternoon it was occasionally difficult to get all the players needed as different departments had varying reasons to retain the services of the men I wanted. Fortunately, with so many young students it was always possible to get a few of them, so we always managed to put out a good team. Officers in charge of rugby were required to recommend players they felt could represent the Royal Air Force. The RAF team was very flexible for normal low-level games and used their best for special games, i.e. Army, Royal Navy, visiting top teams, etc. As a result, many of the people whose names I sent forward played for the RAF.

I believe, having seen the average team, that had I put myself forward I would have been accepted. I was now a better player than before plus I was in the position, wing-forward (now flanker), that best suited me. It has always been one of my regrets that I felt it would have been presumptuous of me to recommend myself.

In December 1961 at Leeming playing against Dishforth I broke from the scrum and crashed into their flanker as he did the same. I broke my leg at the thinnest point of my tibia, i.e. where I had lost most of the bone from my childhood accident. This meant six weeks off flying and having to spend all the time lecturing and looking after the programming. CTC never smelt so awful.

One year later, November 1962, I broke the same leg against the same side in the same way. The only differences were that it was an away game and the break was one of the spurs that had grown from my tibia over the years. Nevertheless, back to the drawing board, my CO said, 'Do you plan to fly aeroplanes, Brian, or walk around in plaster for the rest of your career?' The point was taken and my rugby-playing days were sadly over. Tony took over the team.

Our next course on B Flight comprised all University Air Squadron pilots, some of whom had qualified for their UAS Wings, i.e. having completed a certain number of hours and reached a certain standard. Their training would have been on the Chipmunk, which was a small and less powerful aircraft than the Piston Provost. At 3 FTS we were geared up to doing the basic and advanced training with just the Jet Provost as opposed to the earlier system of two courses, Piston Provost then Vampires. In view of their previous experience I believe the UAS students did a slightly shorter course.

Because they were all graduates with varying types of degrees their qualifications decreed their joining ranks. Whereas I, and all my contemporaries, had started as acting pilot officers these guys were already flying officers or, in one or two cases, flight lieutenants. This was a bit annoying to some of us, as we had done a reasonable amount of time and were fully-qualified pilots. One of the UAS guys had a degree in Drama and was a substantive flying officer and one with a degree in aeronautics had qualified for flight lieutenant. I was still a flying officer! It all settled down and life was pretty hectic and very enjoyable. I must say I missed my school holidays.

My days were very full because, apart from three or four regular students, I was filling time between flights making sure ejection-seat training was up-to-date, flight safety paperwork, which included information that had to be read by all and signed before flight, and trying to get a rugby team together. We had two training nights a week, as well.

In early 1962 I had a student who was regularly having navigation difficulties but, after a lot of hard work he settled down; his overall handling was fine. Having got all the way through the advanced side of the course with another instructor, there was always an instructor change halfway. He failed his final navigation test and final handling test by heading west from the Lancashire/Yorkshire border instead of east! He managed to do this twice and, having come so far, was suspended. Frequently, if pilots failed to get their wings they were offered the chance to change to training as navigators. I don't think this happened this time.

Calling other airfields and radio stations was a regular part of navigation in the pre-GPS and widespread ground radar days, so we got to recognise voices and where the best responses were. Lossiemouth was a station we all used when our navigation exercise took us well north. Indeed, some routes were chosen just to take us north. The reason was because the lady who gave us radio bearings had the sexiest and most beautiful sound you could wish for.

Eventually, it was inevitable that someone chose to use Lossiemouth for a landing-away navigation exercise. He bounded upstairs in the ATC building to meet this 'forces' sweetheart' and experienced one of life's great disappointments. Expectation had overwhelmingly exceeded results. Oh well, it never seemed the same again.

Another student tended to act too quickly, sometimes essential, of course, to react fast in certain circumstances, with poor results. For example, if he made a minor mistake he would try to correct immediately, and rapidly rather than in a smooth and calm manner. He finally calmed down and when he transferred instructors for the advanced part of the course I was happy with his progress. He was eventually awarded his wings and went on to fighter training.

At the end of one flight he joined the circuit and proceeded to do a turn left. He was reminded by the tower that it was a right-handed circuit. He rapidly rolled the aircraft to turn right but was too quick. One wing stalled immediately and the aircraft spun straight in. He was too low to recover and was killed.

The UAS course, as expected, progressed well, especially one of my students. However, he wasn't that pleased with me as his instructor and asked for a transfer to another. This was quite acceptable but unusual; there must have been a one-way personality clash!

The Royal Air Force mainstay of aircrew in the past had been non-commissioned officers (NCOs), i.e. sergeant pilot (navigator, etc.), flight sergeant pilot and master Pilot (equivalent to warrant officer). They were more likely than officers to spend all their time flying. As such, they were extremely competent aviators in whatever role they filled.

However, some time earlier the RAF had decided that all pilots and navigators should be commissioned officers. Suddenly, they decided to return to training NCO aircrew and we at 3 FTS had a few. After they graduated, the RAF changed its mind, I recall, and offered them commissions.

One of our students had been rated as D at the RAF Aircrew Assessment Unit, RAF Hornchurch, and had, despite certain shortcomings on the aptitude and leadership test, been accepted for training. The assessment required in the 1940s and 1950s had always been A or B for pilots but by 1960 there were fewer recruits for aircrew. They were right; although he started slowly, and needed more help than normal, he blossomed towards the end and actually won one of the half-a-dozen prizes for achievement.

As was normal at Flying Training Schools, at every passing-out parade the other squadron did a fly-past timed to pass overhead during the salute to the reviewing officer. One of the first for us was when Princess Marina of Kent reviewed one of the No. 2 Squadron parades. We decided to fly a letter M for her. This was tricky as the two top pointy bits had to be in line and the exact distance apart. The aircraft in the V of the M were vulnerable to any error of the two leaders so the pilots of the right arm of the V had to maintain position forward of their adjacent aircraft by looking over their left shoulders. By accurate flying this ensured the pointy bit on the left, viewed from the ground, was able to maintain position. I was in the V section and that was hard work.

Another fly-past we did was to form the number 3. This was much easier as the leader was the point on the right, as viewed from the ground. The take-off procedure with so many aircraft, approximately fourteen to sixteen, would be to depart in twos. The first pair would lift off and climb immediately and the next two would stay low. This way turbulence from the preceding aircraft would be felt for the shortest time. Each pair alternated. I shall be forever grateful that I was in a pair which had to stay low. How I failed to do it I don't know but I had not lowered my flap to the take-off position. To take off without flaps is a perfectly acceptable manoeuvre as long as it is deliberate and you are, therefore, aware. However, I was No. 2 to an aircraft with flaps down, so, when he pulled up immediately after we passed through the turbulence, I followed him. Except I didn't! I had felt a little turbulence on take-off but put it down to the expected wake affect. But it wasn't, it was an incipient stall, and as I tried to follow him up, I stalled.

Fortunately, my time on type plus experience, little shown up to now I must admit, stood me in good stead; I realised my mistake and hit the flap lever to full, lowered the nose a very small amount and, even as I skimmed the small (thank goodness!) trees and the A1 (that road again!), the aircraft recovered. I rapidly caught up with my No. 1 and all was okay. We had taken off on the runway to the south-west. I notice now on Google maps that all the trees are gone. It wasn't me, honest! As we had taxied out we all waved to the crowd, our wives and kids, etc., so Maureen had known my position in order of take-off. She had a few nasty moments herself.

In mid-1962 I started training a new student, 'Chuck' Turpin, who was from Tobago. He very kindly acted as babysitter for me quite often which gave Maureen and me time to use the mess facilities on Saturdays, the only days ladies were allowed in, or to go to Northallerton or other local places of interest. Unfortunately, I couldn't get him beyond the halfway point of the basic half of the course and he was given a new instructor. He was eventually suspended, or scrubbed as it was normally called.

Before he left, he tried to persuade me to come to Tobago at the end of my service contract and join him in forming a small inter-island passenger service. He was from a wealthy family and his flying standard was certainly high enough for him to progress with civil licences. After much deliberation Maureen and I decided to decline. I've often wondered if life would have been better in that glorious part of the world.

No. 3 FTS not only had students from the UK, but overseas as well. Also, although RAF Manby did most of the refresher training of pilots who had been on ground duties, we had a few, too. In addition, as a gesture of goodwill and co-operation, we gave many flights to local army and police officers to enable them to see overviews of their areas of responsibility. At the same time Turpin began his course we received about eight Jordanians for training. I was lucky to receive the most promising, and so it turned out.

His full name eludes me now but Khalad Barakat was how he was known. He was desperate to be the fastest to solo amongst his fellow countrymen and his enthusiasm was infectious. I was comfortable to send him solo, well ahead of the others, and he progressed well. We set off on his first dual navigation exercise from Leeming-Bridlington-Ripon-Leeming. Short of Bridlington, I was eyeing this very large cumulonimbus cloud and wondering what change of route to give him. No way were we going to fly into it but it was a shame to introduce the subject of route change on his first lesson. Anyway, the problem was resolved as we received a call from another aircraft advising us we were to return to base immediately. We both looked at each other as if to say 'What have I done wrong?' and Barakat took us home.

On landing, Barakat was whisked off in a vehicle bearing Jordanian diplomatic plates and I never saw him again. Apparently, his uncle, or senior relative, had really upset King Hussein and all the family were being interviewed, or worse. It seems that, in view of the uncle's behaviour, all the family's loyalty was in question, so Barakat could have been perceived as unsuitable for His Majesty's Air Force. Years and years later I heard that he, Barakat, was a captain with Alia, the Jordanian airline. He had been a great student and very promising.

On the same course was a student, John Proctor, who had eleven hours and the instructor could not send him solo. He was assigned to me for a further three hours prior to a scrub check. When students have this fear of the near future it normally affects their confidence and abilities and so it was with Proctor. After our three hours I had to hand him over to Paddy Glover, our Squadron Commander, as I had not quite the feeling he was ready for solo. However, I knew he had it in him and that he was very close. I asked Paddy to view the ride as a final check for solo rather than suspension and he said he would see what he could do.

I briefed Proctor really strongly about confidence, give it all you've got etc., etc. Paddy sent him solo and Proctor burst with pride. I was delighted and we celebrated that night in the mess. Having overcome what had been a large hurdle for him he settled down. However, his progress was slow and he was barely keeping up with the others. When the time came for starting the advanced part of the course and the regulation instructor change, he was really worried as he had become very dependent on me. I made a special plea to our CO, requesting that I continue with Proctor to the end as I felt any change now, even to the best of instructors, would unsettle him. The request was granted.

Actually, Proctor was lucky to finish the course with the others as he suffered a broken leg in the daftest of circumstances. Obviously, all aircrew learn how to use parachutes and how to land safely after a jump. However, there are no actual jumps, just work in the gym. One dining-in night, when most officers have a few beers, Proctor's course decided to really test their skills and proceeded to take it in turns to run along the upstairs corridor and dive out of the window at the end! Proctor's was the only injury.

Towards the end of the course Proctor started to catch up and hit all the targets. He received his wings with all the others and I think I was as proud as he was. At the family luncheon in the mess his parents could not thank me enough as they explained how all his fears and uncertainties had ebbed away as I had stayed as his instructor. Frankly, I never considered myself as a particularly good instructor as I was capable of showing impatience which is not conducive to keeping your students calm at all times. However, I regard John Proctor's success as my best achievement as a flying instructor.

John was not fighter pilot material and ended up on small tactical transport aircraft. Many fighter pilots ended up in Transport Command eventually, of course, but John was more comfortable in that role as there is normally more time to think and plan at the slower speeds.

I eventually ended up on 10 Squadron flying the VC10 and, on a flight from Akrotiri to Brize Norton, a friend from Comet days came up to the flight-deck for a chat. He asked if I'd heard about the Argosy crash in Libya south of El Adem. I said not.

Tragically John had delivered some troops and/or equipment to an Army exercise base and, on departure, did a beat-up of the strip for the benefit of the guys on the ground. Apparently, his squadron commander encouraged such flamboyance but perhaps John wasn't best equipped for it. As he flew really low he hit the wooden water tower with his wing tip, crashed, and all onboard were killed. So sad.

Late November 1962 I broke my leg and was in plaster until just before Christmas. The plaster came off in time for me to visit my parents for the break. It was a terribly cold winter and Leeming was nicely downwind from the valley effect of the Wensleydale Gap in the Pennines. This gap tended to adjust the wind direction to the side of my house. On my return I found a note on my door saying 'No Entry. Report to the guard room'. The postman had thought that the letters made a 'funny' sound when he delivered them and had reported such. The sound was caused by them landing in water. The roof tank had burst and the kitchen had become a pond and the water level had risen a few inches on the ground floor. Water was escaping from the French windows but nobody in the other houses had seen it.

All military bases in those days had decontamination centres, and probably still do, where anybody experiencing chemical, biological or, heaven forbid, nuclear contamination would be hosed down, etc. These were very warm and with pipes all over the place; this was where our carpets were. Luckily Ike, an instructor on my flight, and Barbara Dawson accommodated us for about six weeks whilst the house and carpets dried out. It was so kind of them and they were so patient; after all we had baby Andrew as well. Ike and Barbara had been awakened many times in recent weeks by a cat, believed to be feral, which yowled and carried on just outside their house on the field fence over the road. One night, many of us heard a bang which disturbed our sleep. Ike's patience had run out; he had shot it. Peace reigned; except it didn't always.

We, Leeming, were a dispersal base for the V-bomber force. Mostly at night, four Victors or Vulcans would arrive and park only 400 yards from the married quarters. This happened frequently. They would stay for a few days then go somewhere else. We never saw the crews as they were on permanent standby and stayed in their own mess and accommodation in the dispersal area.

In October 1962 Russia started supplying Cuba with missiles much to the distress of President Kennedy in the USA. At 0200 UK time on 22 October he made a broadcast to the world to make it clear that war was quite a possibility. Maureen and I stayed up to hear the speech which was made more chilling as we were expecting our son Nicholas in a couple of months. There had been an increase in the movements of the V-bombers recently which was now explained.

In the event the Russians backed down, but it felt as if serious trouble had been averted.

In view of the previous winter's woes, and to be sure that when Nicholas was en route I would be prepared, I got a new battery and four new tyres for my Triumph Herald. He was due on 11 December so I had been assigned a week's leave starting on the 10th. However, as all was calm on the 10th I did a couple of flights.

At 0800 on the 11th I was wakened by Maureen giving me a cup of tea. After a little chat she calmly said, 'No rush, but the baby is on the way.' I managed to not drop the cup, leapt out of bed and rushed around whilst Maureen remained calm and serene. Outside, the sun was shining, we had unlimited visibility and totally dry conditions. The new battery and tyres could have waited after all. Never mind, they saw us through the winter nicely.

We arrived at the maternity unit at the Army base at Catterick by about 0930 and I left Maureen in safe hands. Back at Leeming I popped into the flight to say 'Hi' and pass on the news. At lunchtime in the mess I managed to buy one or two guys a beer but, of course, most were aircrew so they had to abstain.

At 1230 I thought it best to check how things were going and, much to my astonishment, and embarrassment, Nicholas had been delivered at 1100. Andrew was in the capable hands of friends for the day, so I shot up to Catterick where all was just fine. Mother and baby were perfectly comfortable.

In the New Year our flight received a group of Iraqi students, many of whom had been trained earlier in Russia. The Iraqi Air Force decided that our training was probably better, plus English was an easier, and more used, language. They had learnt quite a few bad habits and they were hard work. Whereas the Jordanians had been easygoing and pleasant to teach, this lot considered themselves a cut above us. Sadly, they never proved it.

Three Sudanese flying instructors arrived to be trained on Jet Provosts so that they could go back and train their own pilots; I was allocated their commanding officer. After three flights, Paddy Glover asked why he hadn't gone solo yet and I explained that I was not prepared to put my signature to it. Paddy was pretty cross, flew with him and sent him solo. When they returned a week or two later the one I wouldn't send solo killed himself low flying. By this time I was an experienced instructor and knew what I was doing. Obviously, it was a sad event but I felt vindicated.

In March 1962 Ike Dawson and I had travelled down to CFS to take our A.2 exams and had passed. Instructors start as B.2 and are promoted to B.1 on the recommendation of their commanding officers. A.2, and the epitome of A.1, can only be granted by CFS. Our promotion meant we could now put *cfs* after our names.

Sometimes when a student was considered for suspension, being scrubbed instead of doing it in-house, he was sent for his final check to the other squadron. This task was assigned to me towards the end of my time at Leeming and I found it quite difficult. A young man would be delivered for briefing, followed by his last chance flight and I found it an awful responsibility. Almost invariably it was obvious he had run his distance and had to fail. It was very sad and stressful for them.

My counterpart on the other squadron was 'Bob' Bobrowski, a Pole. He would say after the flight 'Bloggs, what does your mother call you?' 'Peter, sir.' 'Well, Peter, you failed!' I like to think I was much gentler.

On 5 June I did a landing-away navigation trip to RAF Acklington in Northumberland with my student Buckley. When we called for start-up clearance to depart we were advised there was a thirty-minute delay due to Battle of Britain Day rehearsals. So, along with just about everybody from the hangars and offices, we watched a Jet Provost put through its low-level aerobatic paces.

Oh dear! I could see that he was too low, and maybe slow, at the top of a loop. Sure enough, he didn't make it by about twenty feet. He was still pulling through as he hit the ground going forward. The aircraft disintegrated and became a fireball.

The pilot's wife was there to collect him and was watching the display. The most terrible coincidence here is that she was John Derry's daughter; he had been killed on that day I had missed at Farnborough. She spent some time staying with her friends, Jack Pollard and his wife, after the terrible event. Jack lived up the road from me at Leeming married quarters.

My old base at Middleton St George was only a short way north of Leeming and was now a Lightning training base or a squadron base. An old colleague from 257 Squadron (Harry?) agreed to come down and give me a trip! Wow! I was going to travel at Mach 2, twice the speed of sound.

The Lightning had performance way before its time; apart from Mach 2, its most amazing statistic was that from the release of the brakes at the start of take-off to 40,000 feet took just a minute and forty seconds! I couldn't wait.

Mid-Friday afternoon, briefed, spurred and strapped in, the damned engine would not start! I'm sure a few of my envious fellow pilots were having a secret smirk. The upshot was that I never did get that ride. Harry's CO was less than pleased as, for operational reasons, the aircraft had to get back to base as soon as possible. This meant deploying equipment and a maintenance crew for the evening and the Saturday. This affected Leeming as well, as the airfield, normally closed at the weekend, had to remain on standby. Although it hadn't been my fault, I think I was lower in the popularity stakes than normal.

Our race to be first airborne to do the beat-up finally came to an end due to over-exuberance. Bill Bailey, who finished his career as a Qantas (Wantus!) training captain, flew down the line-up of aircraft, as was our wont, and pulled up into a vertical climb in front of Air Traffic Control. Unfortunately, he overstressed the aircraft and it had to have a wing replaced.

I was given the aircraft to do a flight test and was surprised to be advised that Chief Technician Sparrow (really!) would like to fly with me. When I asked why, he explained that, as he had been in charge of the work, he wanted me to know that he was utterly confident with what he had done. I would have been confident, of course, but it was a nice gesture.

Mid-1963 I was called to the Air Ministry in London but with no explanation. On arrival I reported to the appropriate department with some trepidation to be asked if I would like to do three years as an instructor in Takoradi, Ghana. I said 'no' as I had done two tours and felt that I had done my fair share. What an incredible waste of everyone's time! A phone call would have sufficed, or the same question asked by my CO.

Just after that I was called in to the Adjutant's office and asked if I would be happy to sign on to the age of thirty-eight? I said 'No thanks', unless I got the job I wanted which would be to return to 216 Squadron with the prospect of becoming a Comet captain. He said he would pass the answer along.

I thought little more of it as the military doesn't work that way. I continued studying for my commercial licence which I was finding quite difficult as I learn best with others and in a classroom.

Well, hoist by my own petard! I was advised two or three weeks later that my offer was accepted. I went home to talk it through with Maureen. We were very happy with the RAF and I knew that if I kept my nose clean I could make a full career to age fifty-five so I signed on.

We left Leeming in November and found a lovely house to rent in Eastwoodbury Close, Devizes.

216 Squadron Again – Comet 2
11 November 1963 – 29 February 1967

No. 216 Squadron was now equipped with Comet 4s as well as Comet 2s. Initially I was disappointed to find I was posted to the 2s as I felt I had done my stint there and was ready for the 4. However, I was soon to realise I had fallen on my feet.

The Comet 4 was now responsible for serving all the stations to the Far East as had been the role of the 2s in my earlier time. There was now a 'slip' in place whereby the aircraft flew continuously and crews would rest and fly on the next, or a later, aircraft.

Since my earlier tour the 2 had been downgraded. De Havilland and the RAF had decided that as it was a first-generation pressurised passenger aircraft, and getting on a bit, to reduce the pressure differential and take the strain off the hull. Whereas then, and now, the difference in pressure inside and outside was around 8.5 psi, it was reduced to 4 psi or thereabouts. The 8.5 psi difference meant that an aircraft up to 40,000 feet would give the cabin an altitude of 8,000-plus feet; we now had to fly the 2 at a height of 25,000 or 26,000 feet.

This meant that not only was the aircraft made to fly at a constant altitude due to the 'new' air traffic control regulations but, being lower, would burn more fuel. End result, reduced range, so shorter trips. The 2 was reduced to serving the Near East only which meant round trips to Malta (RAF Luqa), Gibraltar (RAF North Front), Cyprus (RAF Akrotiri), Tripoli (RAF Idris) and RAF El Adem (near Tobruk), often via Benina or Benghazi. We used to set off from Lyneham around noon or early afternoon and enjoy a night stop before returning. It was all very civilised but boring. Fortunately, I was flying with a real captain who gave landings, advised, taught and behaved kindly.

Before I retrained on the Comet 2, I was given one or two trips just as an observer, to get the feel again and also time to study the books. There was no plan to give me a training course until the New Year, so I was despatched as an Operations Officer to support an exercise in the Near East Command at RAF Nicosia.

Maureen was still living at Leeming with the boys, so I returned happily to mess life for a while. My snooker skills were still pretty good and I found that Mickey Mouse was now a very popular darts game; it is played by two teams of one or two players and the winner is the first to knock off the single, double and treble of all the numbers plus the inner and outer bull. I was playing Mickey Mouse with a group of fellow officers in the bar in Nicosia mess and desperately discussing where another officer and I had met. We covered school events, ATC cadets, various RAF units and other people we knew. Even as we realised that it had been in the mess at Lyneham the night I arrived, the station Commanding Officer entered the bar and called for our attention.

He advised us that President John F. Kennedy had been assassinated.

Thus, as for everybody in that time, I will always remember where I was when J.F.K. died.

In early February I and another 'new boy' flew to Nicosia with the two Comet 2 instructors, 'Mac' McLaren and Eddie Epps. There we each did twenty-four hours of training. It was marvellous. After all those boring hours with Geoff Bolton, I was now flying everything. During one take-off, the fire warning rang for fire in the equipment bay. I was admonished and advised later that the initial response was not 'bloody charming' but to call for appropriate actions.

In February the Mediterranean can produce some pretty spectacular cumulonimbus clouds (aka cumulo-bumpus) and it was not unusual to see lightning travelling in a series from one to the next for up to fifty miles or more. One day the weather looked pretty ominous, so Mac decided not to fly until it had passed. It was a good decision. We stood in the officers' mess and watched the biggest hailstones I have ever seen bounce on the terrace outside and then settle down to about a foot deep of carpet. A nearby village had many of its shanty-town type dwellings destroyed.

At the end of the week I was signed off with a C Category, having thoroughly enjoyed my time flying and socialising with Mac and Eddie. They were also the team who kept an eye on standards and did the regular route and categorisation checks. There were four categories in Transport Command: A, B, C and D.

D was freight only but most pilots started with a C, whereby passengers could be carried.

If you had a C then every six months you had to satisfy examiners for eight hours in a flight simulator, do a two-hour check flight and, worst of all, spend a whole day sitting at a table opposite the examiner and answer questions on every technical, meteorological, navigational etc., etc. subject he threw at you. When you finally made B Category this was an annual jolly. A Category was the crème de la crème and was held by but a few. This was awarded by examiners at Command level. Everybody had at least one check a year on an actual trip.

We all studied, knew and moderately understood cumulonimbus cloud but Mac had his own ideas about them. It was, therefore, easier to present his version to any questions he asked. Many a pilot had had his day's questioning extended if he argued with him. The check comprised observing handling, decision-making, crew co-operation (no Cockpit Resource Management (CRM) in those days, thank goodness), planning and, most important, adherence to SOPs, i.e. Standard Operating Procedures.

The SOPs are most carefully looked at because, in earlier days, when crews flew together all the time, it was not unusual for mistakes or irregular procedures to become commonplace amongst themselves and, thus, accepted. Nowadays, when people meet up in the briefing-room pre-flight it is possible that they have never seen each other before, let alone flown together.

Nevertheless, 216 Squadron still had the crew system some of the time, which is how I ended up with one of the best captains I've ever known and with whom I've had the privilege of flying, Ron Underwood.

Prior to my first flight with Ron on 8 April 1964, I flew with several of the other captains. Much as I loved solo flying, especially in the Hunter, and the joy of aerobatics, low-flying and formation, I began to realise that this was my favourite form of flying. All the captains were great guys and only too willing to pass on all their experience, and to share the sectors as well. I've been talking of landings a lot but what I should have said was sectors, i.e. you, the co-pilot, plan the trip, do all the flying and make all the decisions. The captain will change things or take control if he feels he needs to.

There were, however, three captains who were unable to relax however well you were performing. They felt the need to suggest alternative ways of doing things, i.e. their way, and could not relax during an approach and landing no matter how well you were doing. This attitude, of course, puts you on edge, so perhaps you end up not performing as well as you could. None of them had been actual flying instructors.

One of these captains had flown into unexpected turbulence one day and the aircraft ended up nearly upside down. This seemed to permanently affect his interest in Clear Air Turbulence (CAT) and his nervousness used to irritate the hell out of his crew. He seemed to think he had some divine ability to determine where CAT was lurking and would take avoiding action. Even today, it is impossible to be sure, although meteorological knowledge has improved way beyond those days.

My first month, March 1964, was an interesting introduction to my new, and permanent, role in life. From then until 31 December 2000 I would be in one of the front seats of multi-jet passenger aircraft.

I flew with Ron Locke, later a captain with British Caledonian out of Gatwick, to Gibraltar. This arrival had always to be done well if you were landing to the east as it was necessary to do a curved approach over Algeciras Bay. Spain would not allow us to overfly their territory so, having come down via the west coast of Europe and crept through the Straits of Gibraltar, we still had to abide by their rules; the reason, they were then, and still are, sniffy about the Rock of Gibraltar.

Apart from their childishness about making life difficult getting in via Algeciras Bay, the radar monitored us and if we even deviated by 100 metres a complaint was made to the British government and we got a wigging from Command.

Going into the west was no problem until the landing. The beginning of the runway was a raised lip straight off the beach and immediately the tarmac dipped away from you for the first few hundred metres and then came up to meet you. So, even if you made the perfect approach, you still had to juggle a bit to ensure enough runway was left for a comfortable arrival. Normally, it was not a problem but on occasion there was an interesting and exciting arrival.

The reason it was exciting for us was that we were a heavy multi-jet compared to the normal propeller traffic or small-jet aircraft. We used more runway than them and the slope at the beginning of the runway often resulted in a landing farther along the runway than desired. Also, we were not fitted with reverse thrust, so we had only brakes for deceleration. Reverse thrust is actually a misnomer; the process is by a set of panels which, when activated, close off the exhaust from the engine tail pipe and deflect the air sideways. The effect is not so much reverse thrust as cancellation of forward thrust. On some aircraft it is effectively sent slightly forward which does give some extra braking effect.

On a later occasion on an approach to Gibraltar the weather was really bad; there was lightning, heavy rain and turbulence. In the circumstances the captain, John Tulip, chose to do a full-instrument approach rather than just let down over the sea and go in visually. As we passed over the beacon on the Rock we were struck by lightning. This in itself was no big deal except that the Comet was an early-days design and was not as well protected as modern aircraft. I was adjusting the heading indicator and had my right arm resting on the air-conditioning delivery tube. I received an enormous shock and was unable to do any simple tasks until after landing as I couldn't get my fingers to function. John did a great job.

However, my problem was nothing compared to the flight engineer who had been controlling the pressurisation and air supply. The main control for this was a large valve control about three-to-four inches in diameter. His hand was gripping it when we were struck and he was unable to continue using the hand. Worse, he could not move his fingers in one direction, I forget which, and it took two-to-three months to recover. At one point he feared for his future flying fitness.

John Tulip did a good job all round. He was a really lovely man with an expression he used frequently: 'I have many faults but being wrong is not one of them.'

To add to the difficulties the Rock produced its own wind problems. Whereas it is best to land into wind, if possible, it was not unusual to have a tailwind at both ends of the runway due to the circulation around the Rock. Furthermore, if winds were strong, the Rock could generate quite a bit of turbulence.

The overnight stop was one of our favourites as, after a shower and change, we would head off to La Linea and the Spanish side of the causeway, unless, of course, they were having a serious tizz and delaying or stopping crossings. We would visit our favourite scruffy bar and have a sherry or two. Then back to the Rock for a meal. Most of us frequented a place which resembled an old converted barn which made the best paella I have ever eaten. Then, perhaps, to the casino to lose a couple of quid at blackjack.

One night I was there and two US Navy petty officers, 'The Fleet was in!', were at the blackjack table with a stack of money each and both the worse for wear on drink. After a while the manager turned up with a big smile and congratulated them on their success. He took over the table and played a couple of hands.

Meanwhile, we spectators were all agog at their skills, or luck, and eyeing a £50 (yes, £50) chip on the floor. The manager offered 'double or quits' to which they agreed and won. The manager offered double or quits again and they both looked at him, then at each other, then gathered their chips and one of them said 'We're not that far gone!' and left, taking that £50 chip with them as well.

My next trip to Gibraltar was my most exciting ever. The captain was flying the aircraft for a landing on the westerly runway, i.e. the one with a dip at the beginning. It was turbulent and we had a tailwind. We landed well into the runway and I had been thinking he would do a go-around. However, we touched down and he crawled all over the brakes. The Algeciras Bay end of the runway ends with a drop straight into the sea and we came to a stop with no runway in sight. There was total silence on the flight deck as we realised how close we had come to a watery incident. The silence was broken by ATC. 'Are you O.K. Ascot 2114? Do you need a tug?'

We advised him we were okay. There was enough room for a hard turn right to go back up the runway to the turn-off. Wow!

The ASCOT call-sign had replaced the RAFJET of my previous time on Comets. Transport Command was now Air Support Command, hence ASCOT. The OT was for Overseas Transport.

Each squadron, or rather aircraft type, had its own set of numbers so we started with No. 2. I think the Britannias started with No. 3 and so on. Starting with No.1 was reserved for special and VIP flights.

Next flight was to RAF Luqa, Malta, still British and proud to be so. Our parking area was just off the side at the beginning of the westerly runway so when we were ready to go it was start, do all checks including take-off check, taxi for a few seconds then go. Very convenient.

A night stop at Luqa was nothing special at the mess except that the barmen were an odd trio. There was a really tall one, a medium one and one so short they had decking behind the bar so that he could work properly. This meant that the tall guy was huge and so on. It was a bit like that sketch with John Cleese and the Ronnies Barker and Corbett.

We did not have much time for touring as we arrived rather latish and it was an early-morning start. Apart from the harbour, docks and port, it was the massive fortress-like structures I remember best. Along with the forts the only other impressive fact was that all the vehicles' tyres squealed nearly all the time, especially on corners. It wasn't excess speed but some constituent of the road material perhaps, which was polished like glass.

By the time I'd visited all our normal destinations plus a night stop for some forgotten reason in Athens it was time to see Cyprus again. This time with Ron. We hit it off straight away, and although I still had the occasional trip with other crews, I eventually did most of my flying with him.

The trip to Cyprus was to Akrotiri, by now our normal destination in Cyprus. Previously, all my landings had been in Nicosia with the exception of that emergency arrival after Nicosia was fogged in. We almost never stayed on camp at Akrotiri as it was busy and full, so were sent to the

Miramar Hotel in Limassol. This was a comfortable and pleasant hotel with easy access to the town and its eateries and bars. The hotel was probably the second or third building on the left as you entered town. Last time I was there, 1984, it was a mile into town and the area, once gentle and natural, had been ruined for, and by, the tourists.

Of the other captains with whom I flew at this time two stand out; Ned Neill who was not only a great captain but one of the most pleasant guys you would wish to meet, and Len Latham. Len was ditto the above, but he had a habit that always made me nervous. He frequently placed his coffee on the glare shield, the ledge above the instruments. This made me very nervous as any modest turbulence could have dislodged it and, perhaps, sent coffee into the area behind the instrument panel. He was immune to my entreaties to remove it. Simply, there was nowhere to put it. Modern aircraft are designed for safety to the *nth* degree but the Comet lacked many refinements.

One of the worst drawbacks was the method of providing air to the flight deck. It came from various sources, which included a perforated tube along the side below the windows. It blew air at temperatures and pressures which were sometimes at variance with those selected and spat water, i.e. condensation, too often. After we had been at high altitude for any length of time the hull and interior trim would be cold-soaked. At the beginning of the descent the quartermaster would bring two towels each for the pilots, one for the lap and one for the shoulders. As we descended, the ice that had formed would melt and continuously dribble onto us.

All pressurisation was controlled entirely by the flight engineer, no automatics or computers then. As the flight progressed he would adjust inlet and outlet valves to slowly advance the pressure differential to keep the aircraft cabin climbing, or descending, at a rate comfortable for the people on board. All power changes meant he had to be on the ball to adjust his valves as the air, taken from the cooler parts of the engine, would arrive at a different pressure. God help the pilot who changed power without telling the engineer.

Just after I first flew with Ron he was made a VIP-qualified captain which was okay by me. Our first VIP trip was to take Sir Thomas Pike, D/SACEUR (Deputy Strategic Air Commander Europe), around Scandinavia on behalf of NATO. This was an exciting trip as, on one or two occasions, we enjoyed typical Arctic weather even though it was June.

On 3 June 1964 we arrived at Orly in Paris (the airport at Charles de Gaulle was not even a twinkle in the government's eye at that time) as the

D/SACEUR presumably went to Versailles, HQ of NATO. Next day was Copenhagen to find that their own brew, Carlsberg, was twice the price you paid in the UK. This night was my first ever using a duvet.

In the morning Ron and I, in civvies, exited the lift at reception to be mobbed by a load of young boys demanding autographs. We insisted that there must be some mistake but they assured us not. In the end it was easier to start signing. As I started to sign the third book the boy snatched it away, glared at me and ran with the others. Upon turning around, I saw the England football team. Oh, well, fifteen seconds of fame is better than none at all.

We left Kastrup, Copenhagen, for Bardufoss that lunchtime. The weather was expected to be bad but, as a special approach and landing radar had been installed just for the NATO exercise, Ron was happy.

The approach to Bardufoss, way above the Arctic Circle, was across an island lake over a small hill and down the other side on to the runway. The missed approach was somewhat daunting as there was no escape dead ahead, so a hard right turn was to be performed with climb away from whence you came. No problem normally, but we arrived in a huge snowstorm and needed radar assistance. Once we were over the small hill on the approach and reached minimum permitted approach height we just saw the lights, so managed a landing. I think it had been quite tense knowing that the missed approach would be exciting as well, if needed. Obviously, the arrival procedure and missed approach was perfectly safe and had been done by many before but when it's your first time, the weather's bad and the hills look impressive on the chart, there's a tendency to tense up a smidgeon.

All went well, the aircraft was put to bed and off we went to the Royal Norwegian Air Force officers' mess for a meal and refreshment. The refreshment took a while and eventually Ron said he was off to bed and left. I managed to force myself to have some more, then I left. In view of the conditions prevailing up there, a lot of buildings are underground or almost so. When I left the bar and climbed the steps I stopped and was totally disorientated. I checked my watch, still going, I dredged my memory, still sort of going, and then 'Bingo', I was way north, it was summer here and it was normal to be in broad daylight at midnight! To we ordinary Europeans this was weird and eerie.

When I arrived at the room I was sharing with Ron, normal in the RAF in those days, I found him fast asleep with his sunglasses on. He wore them all the time, but this was a first. Incredibly, in such an environment, our room had silly, ill-fitting thin curtains. I went to sleep with my sunglasses on too.

The next morning Ron, Jimmy Constanti, our navigator, and I were taken in a Land Rover for a look at the local area. This included seeing the channels going up the side of the fjords to make life easier for the salmon. The forest, water and scenery were fantastic and at the end of the outing Jimmy gave the sergeant driver a bottle of whiskey. Liquor was very expensive in Norway and the fellow was effusive with thanks. I think a bottle was £30 to £40 in Norway which, in 1964, was *very* expensive.

Next on to Bodo, which is just above the Arctic Circle, flat, cold and windy. Then the same day drop D/SACEUR off in Paris and back to Lyneham.

This had been my first taste of VIP flying and I had found it exciting and interesting. Timekeeping was all, so departures and arrivals were rigidly adhered to. Depending upon who you were carrying various flags would be flown as we taxied out and in. There was a special flag holder inside next to the captain's window which could be opened. On occasion, if important enough, one could even be flown by the navigator holding one out of the sextant aperture in the roof!

The worst regular trip on our schedule was to El Adem, a hot and horrid staging post, situated inland from Tobruk. We always popped into Benina, near Benghazi, en route. The ATC tower was really tall and it was necessary to go all the way to the top to file the flight plan. There were no computerised systems in those days so, before every sector, it was mandatory to file the route time en route plus intended altitudes, souls on board, name of captain, etc., etc. At Benina, which in summer could reach 35 to 40 degrees C the climb to the top of the non-airconditioned tower was tough. I don't recall any captains doing it.

El Adem had a small compensation for me as my sister Greta lived in Tobruk for a while. Her husband Alex was an architect and surveyor and was employed by the Military Works Department, so he would drive me home after my arrival and get me back in time for departure. I reciprocated by flying them home at the end of their tour.

In July Eddie Epps gave me a route check into Luqa so I was on my best behaviour. The RAF, and for all I knew the civilian world, marked the runway with a line which indicated the last point of touchdown. Should you not be on the ground at that point you had to go-around.

I made a not so clever approach into Luqa and, realising I was going to touch down just past the line, I called 'overshoot' and proceeded to apply full power. Ron immediately called 'negative', closed the throttles, landed and brought the aircraft to a halt with plenty of runway left. I asked why, and he pointed out that had I done the overshoot we would not have got to the mess bar before it closed!

That may sound rather bad of him to have done that but he knew the airfield and aircraft very well, so knew what he was doing. I passed because, as Eddie said, I had made the right decision and he knew my landings were normally safe and well executed. We got to the bar in time for the de-briefing and refreshments.

Around this time I went on one of our monthly training trips and we were training a new first officer. It was the habit in transport aircraft to address each other by position hence: captain, co, nav, eng and sig. This is how this flight was conducted but our new, non-transport experienced co-pilot was furious that the NCO flight engineer hadn't called him 'Sir' and proceeded to berate him after the flight and in the hearing of all others. What a stupid start to a squadron tour. He continued even into captaincy as a disliked, distrusted and unpleasant fellow. Later he joined Dan Air where he was put in his place very quickly. What a pity the RAF couldn't have done the same. For some reason he seemed to get on well with the senior officers, so that's probably how he got away with it. Most of us were of the opinion he should have been given the heave early on. More of him later.

In July 1964 I flew with Barry Mills as captain and Mac 'Black Mac' McAllister the navigator to Akrotiri where I met Peter Anstee again. He had been my bridge partner and flight commander at Barkston Heath. For once we were accommodated on camp and Peter offered to take us to town for dinner. So, with Peter and his wife Anne, we set off in his car to Limassol.

On our way back around midnight we were stopped on a back lane by vigilantes with Sten guns, the most unreliable and unsafe weapons on earth. They demanded our IDs and, despite our obvious anger, we complied. Barry showed his ID at the left rear window and I mine at the rear right. Meanwhile, Mac was patting himself all over and said, 'Lend me your ID as I've left mine at the base.' Oh dear, he proffered it to the men at the left window and, by sheer bad luck, the man who had looked at mine had gone around there. He immediately realised that he had just seen that and we were all ordered out. This was crazy, of course, as this was totally unlawful but they did have Sten guns and they were waving them around.

As with all cowards they took great pleasure in pushing us around and asking stupid questions as if they had authority. It would have been almost laughable if it hadn't been for the guns. They had been known to fire even if you just knocked it against something. They refused to accept who we were despite the IDs (we knew them as 1250s) and demanded evidence.

They would not accept a call to the station at Akrotiri but only the air attaché! To this end they broke into a nearby school, phoned the consulate and, after an hour or so, Barry spoke to an incredibly angry and bemused wing commander. He convinced him who he was and the attaché, in turn, convinced the cowards. What a farce!

They eventually let us go about 0230 so we were pretty tired at take-off around 0730. It was reported, of course, but we heard no more.

What had not helped with Mac was that he was as bald as a coot and I had, and still have, a full head of hair. Had he had his 1250 he might still have been in trouble anyway as it showed him with all his hair and an afternoon shadow. He was Black Mac because his whiskers grew so quickly, but he had not changed his 1250 after he had suffered Alopecia.

When he passed an airman who needed a haircut he would say 'Airman, get your hair cut.' 'Yes, sir.' 'And send me the clippings!'

Talking of Macs: at this time I was doing general flight tests to tie in with my route check with Eddie. Mac McLaren had his girlfriend with him and she was from the Isles of Scilly. He decided that we should visit them, and upon our arrival at the airport, and with their permission, we gave them a beat up. That beats chat-up lines and a pizza down the road anytime.

As stated earlier, we had checks all the time and, to keep us up-to-date, we were obliged to fly two hours training every month, i.e. MCT or monthly continuation training. These flights were frequently used for other than let-down, circuit and other training.

We had a delightful and attractive adjutant, i.e. PA to the squadron commander whose home was near RAF Mildenhall, Bury St Edmunds. Every Friday afternoon, the last training flight always somehow landed at Mildenhall and, by an even bigger coincidence, our lovely adjutant was on it. The first training flight on a Monday always managed a landing at Mildenhall and our lovely adjutant hitched a lift to Lyneham.

Another very useful training flight was to call a day ahead to RAF Macrihanish in Argyll and Bute to arrange a landing. Having spoken to our officers' and sergeants' messes, and individuals, we would also have a shopping list. This list could include all types of fish and crustaceans, but especially salmon. We would arrive and as there were no proper boarding steps our fish would be delivered via an ordinary ladder. Money would change hands and the goodies were passed on an hour or so later.

Talking of training reminds me of the longest of them all. During my earlier tour on Comets our Commander-in-Chief Sir Andrew McKee went on a Near East and Middle East tour. On arrival at the first stop, El Adem, he realised that his mess kit (formal dining wear) had not been packed. The standby crew were called out on a training flight and prepared for the flight whilst the kit was driven from Upavon. The kit arrived in El Adem very early the next morning.

The best training flight was prior to our squadron station's 50th Anniversary celebrations. The station customs officers were approached to see how best to import stacks of champagne from Germany. Their answer was that if they were invited then they wouldn't notice. A 'training flight' was duly despatched to an RAF base in 2 TAF (2nd Tactical Air Force) and returned loaded.

The customs officers at Lyneham were actually reasonable compared to their counterparts at civil airports. Officially, aircrew in the RAF were allowed a miniature of Scotch and twenty cigarettes per arrival. However, we were eventually allowed to bring in a bottle and 200 cigarettes a month and they kept a list to keep an eye on it. This was a kind arrangement. When I was diverted to Manchester, those of us with our monthly allocation got short shrift from customs there. They were not interested in honouring their fellow customs officers' arrangements elsewhere.

Actually, customs officers were a breed apart. I suppose there could have been a decent person amongst them but they just loved to exert their power. They were rude, sarcastic and mean, they were a much disliked breed. I arrived at Gatwick one day in an RAF Comet and they kept us on the ground for three hours whilst they scoured the aircraft with about twelve officers. Why? They were training them to do full searches. They wouldn't have dared to do it to a civil company unless they had a damned good reason to suspect contraband. If we complained they would simply have said that they were looking for contraband. Things finally improved at the end of the eighties when crews were also authorised for a bottle and 200 but customs still had to keep an eye out for those who would spoil it for the rest.

The next interesting VIP flight followed Harold Wilson's success in the General Election on 16 October 1964. He appointed an ex-ticket collector trade unionist, Arthur Bottomley, as the Secretary of State for Commonwealth Relations. What had our once great country come to?

We positioned Lyneham-El Adem on the morning of 21 October and tried to get some sleep before Bottomley arrived from London in another 216 Comet. He was to attend the ceremony of handing over power to Kenneth Kaunda of Northern Rhodesia, now to be named Zambia. We left El Adem for Khartoum around midnight and on arrival there was no-one to meet us. It was usual for a cabinet minister to be met by a representative of

Ambassador or Consul or whoever. Nobody had turned up, probably as it was a refuelling stop only. On we went to Nairobi. It was now morning and, although beds in a bedroom had been fitted, Bottomley and his wife slept in their seats. We arrived dead on time and opened the doors as Jomo Kenyatta and his entourage strolled across the tarmac in their immaculate suits and crisp white shirts.

Bottomley and his wife descended to meet them in a most dishevelled state. Their attire was creased and in disarray and we felt deeply embarrassed. We had a four-hour stop, and, in the hope of getting a rest as soon as possible, I said to Ron that I was off to file the flight plan. He said 'No you're not. I'm not having my crew being seen on the tarmac with those scruffy people.'

We managed a couple of hours trying to sleep in the aircraft before preparing to continue to Lusaka. En route we realised the planners had misjudged the time and/or distance, because we had to lose thirty minutes. We were so tired having had no sleep worth talking about for about twenty-four to twenty-eight hours that Ron and I were doing ten minutes on and ten minutes off. Meanwhile, one or more of the cabin crew, two quartermasters and two stewards, were taking turns to confirm that enough of us were awake to perform. At one stage, if only for a minute, Ron and I were both asleep. Jimmy, the nav, would hit us with the flat part of his ruler if he saw us nodding off.

Eventually we landed at Lusaka where the embarrassment continued as Kenneth Kaunda arrived dressed as immaculately as you expect statesmen to present themselves. The Air Attaché dealt with us and Ron asked about our hotel as we were very tired. He was advised that all the hotels were booked for 'important visitors' and that he had managed to procure a marquee for us in the grounds of the university. Ron went slightly into orbit and advised the Attaché that this was not good enough. The Attaché said it was okay as it was partitioned, so some privacy, especially for our two ladies, was no problem.

Ron asked where the nearest hotel was and, with a smirk, the Attaché said 'Salisbury' which was of course Southern Rhodesia, about to become just Rhodesia. Ron said, 'Okay, we'll take thirty-thousand pounds of fuel, we're going to Salisbury.' This was quite in order, of course, as we were at and about to go to another Royal Air Force station in the Commonwealth.

We set off for Salisbury having received fuel and gained our second wind. We landed and set off for the Kilimanjaro Hotel, oddly named as Kilimanjaro mountain is actually in Tanzania, or Tanganyika as it was then. In the hotel we repaired to the bar in our uniforms, not allowed in those days, and had a drink to see in our twenty-four-hour duty day. We were actually something like forty hours without proper sleep.

The following morning, we all put our VIP uniforms into the hotel laundry/dry-cleaning, had breakfast and set off for the town swimming-pool as the hotel did not have one. There was a British Overseas Airway Company (BOAC, pre-BA) crew there, all tanned and relaxed next to the very white RAF crew.

Within thirty minutes a group captain, the Air Attaché, appeared and picked us out immediately; it must have been the dazzle from our bodies. 'Are you the RAF crew?' 'Yes, Sir.' 'Prime Minister Ian Smith has ordered you out of the country.'

Time for Ron to do his 'lack of interest in irritating senior officers act again'. 'Respectfully, Sir, he has no right to do that, so we cannot leave.' 'Well he can, and you're leaving now.' 'Why?' 'He is livid that Northern Rhodesia are getting their independence before him and the crew and aircraft who brought the Secretary to perform the act are not welcome.'

'Very well, sir, but we cannot leave without our uniforms.'

'I will see to it at once and have them returned to the hotel.'

We waited two to three hours and when they arrived all the trousers had turn-ups pressed very firmly into them. There was no question of wearing them so we set off to the airfield in civvies. At the airfield there was no particular concern at our attire and, after a brief check on our identity we got on with preparing for departure. But where to?

It was decided to take fuel up to maximum landing weight plus thirty minutes, which meant we could do a bit of scouting around. We could file no flight plan and endeavoured to remain clear of controlled airspace unless so authorised.

We tried Lusaka but still no joy, so on to Bulawayo. We hung around but they came back and said nothing available. Off we went to Livingstone who asked us to stand by. Whilst we were waiting, we pottered off to the Victoria Falls of the Zambesi river. They were just a few miles away. We circled them at 200 feet and, although they were not in spate, it was a lovely sight. Livingstone got back to us after a while to say they had four places in the hotel and four in the police station barracks.

Ron said okay; the cabin crew to the hotel and flight deck with the police.

We landed and were greeted by the personnel of RAF Livingstone with some bemusement as I guess they'd never seen a military aircraft flown by a military crew in civvies.

The next night was Independence celebration and, in his speech, Bottomley said how proud he was to be in Gambia! Prior to Independence we had crossed over the border to Victoria Falls and insisted that our passports were stamped. We did the same after Independence so now I have stamps showing entry to Southern Rhodesia, Northern Rhodesia, Rhodesia and Zambia in a period of twenty-four hours. I also queued for a couple of hours to buy all the new Zambian stamps, both unfranked and franked.

On the 26th we collected Bottomley in Lusaka and set off home. After a refuelling stop at Nairobi we headed for Khartoum, but before we entered their airspace we received an urgent message from Command Operations not to land at Khartoum as there had just been a military coup. Whoops! What to do?

We had enough fuel so we turned right and headed for RAF Khormaksar, Aden, where luckily for Bottomley, a Comet 4 inbound from the Far East was due at the same time as us. He was transferred to them and we went to the bar to celebrate his departure. On our return we found that we were on a training flight to the USA, with another crew alternating sectors. Ron had never been to the States as a captain and I had never been there using airways which were now up to 45,000 feet.

Just before our departure RAF Lyneham decided that we would have our Christmas card showing a line-astern formation of the three aircraft based there. No. 1 would be the Britannia, No. 2 the Comet 4 and Ron and I at the end. Well, it went badly; I think it was not until the fifth pass that we were all equidistant and the picture was acceptable. We constantly had to juggle the throttles to maintain position and, as a jet aircraft does not slow easily, we often had to use spoilers to avoid the aircraft in front. This was silly; Ron was a great pilot and had had plenty of formation experience.

Two embarrassed Comet crews discussed things afterwards with the Britannia captain. The intention was for the fly-past to be at 250 knots. Incredibly, instead of setting a constant power and accepting 250 plus 2 or 3 knots, the Britannia captain had been using his throttles to try and maintain exactly 250 knots. No wonder we had problems, because not only did the Comet 4 have to keep changing his power but our problems were doubled.

What a prat!

Ron Locke was to be our guide and off we went to Keflavik then Gander in Newfoundland. It was November, so obviously very cold but Gander Airport was eerie. It had been built for transatlantic traffic but had not been planned well. With the introduction of Boeing 707s and the Comet it was no longer needed. The modern aircraft had no need of an intermediary stop. So, the airport which was well designed with shops and the large assembly area was, to all intents and purposes, empty; wherever you went there was this sound of individual footsteps echoing around.

On to Andrews AFB, near Washington DC, then New York JFK. Although I had been to the States on my previous tour it had only been to air force bases which, although busy, were not hectic. JFK radio was a constant flow of high-speed talking and very difficult to follow for those used to the measured tones of London and, indeed, the rest of the world. It did not help that the accents were so pronounced either. It was necessary to concentrate hard and each crew member chipped in if I or Ron were not sure. The arrivals necessitated radio-frequency changes and then waiting to leap in with your call-sign and information or request. It was obviously not received well if you asked the controller to repeat anything.

Unfortunately, we were on the southerly of the two westerly runways, 22 L (left) and at that time, if the weather was poor, it was necessary to do an approach on 22 R (right) and, when clear of cloud, jink left and land on 22 L. Ron didn't quite get it right and we had to do a go-around. Immediately I called ASCOT2037 going round; instead of a rollicking and complicated instructions I would have been terrified to get wrong, we were told to stay below cloud and carry out a left-hand circuit and look for a blue and white B707. When we advised that we could see it, he said, 'OK, follow that and cleared to land.' It worked a treat.

Normally, our airfield charts were printed by the RAF and, occasionally, we used BOAC charts. However, I had a large taxiway chart produced by JFK and lent to me by one of the squadron pilots who had been there before. We were given somewhat complicated instructions, or so it seemed, but with my chart info I advised Ron when to turn left etc. At one point I said to take the next left and Ron, who had every confidence in me, was quite happy – however, Ron Locke, the instructor said 'No, it's second left, I know as I was here recently'. I disagreed and Ron backed me up but Ron Locke was insistent. Ron and I looked at each other, shrugged, and did as advised. It took us nearly half-an-hour to get out of the transport and general maintenance yard. Forklifts had to move all sorts of materials, trucks had to be moved, sets of steps under repair, etc., etc.

Actually, it was a good time to happen as it was early in the trip. We never had another peep out of Ron Locke after that. He was a good pilot and a nice fellow; it was a silly mistake, that's all.

As with every visitor for the first time New York was an exciting place as it is so different from anywhere else. We were accommodated in the Lexington Hotel which was used for crews from all over and the RAF used it for many years.

I had rough directions from a hotel clerk for Times Square. When I had gone a couple of blocks I saw a couple of New York's 'finest' and asked directions. The policeman's exact words were 'See that shop over there? They sell maps.' He then turned away and continued his conversation with his pal! Later experiences with NY Police were quite different and I found them helpful and pleasant.

Inevitably, we ended up in Greenwich Village at a well-known bar whose name now eludes me and Google rang no bells. It was very like the type of bar called 'Your Father's Moustache', of which there are quite a few around the States. They had banjo and trombone bands and showed cartoons on the walls when the band took a rest. They also served the best, and only decent beer around, Schlitz Draught.

This particular Greenwich bar had a statue of a man in the ladies 'restroom' with a fig leaf placed where you would expect it to be. Inevitably, the ladies would lift it to check underneath. The leaf was wired to a klaxon in the bar, so it was a very embarrassed lady who returned to the bar to the cheers of the drinkers.

Now I thought the approach into JFK was exciting enough but then we went to Chicago O'Hare. The radio transmissions were more frequent and faster than at JFK and there was more traffic. We were cleared for an approach to 14 L (15 L?) with the cloud base at 1,000 feet.

Just before breaking cloud I saw a flashing red light to my right and, sure enough, there was an aircraft on a parallel landing on 14 R (15 R?) No problem. However, on looking ahead, I could see an aircraft just touching down on each runway and one turning off from each runway. Okay, good controlling but, to my astonishment, there was an aircraft taking off across the two runways between the two aircraft. That's busy!

We then went on to Nellis AFB at Las Vegas for a night stop. We were accommodated on base and our hosts arranged a bus to take us downtown. At that time the airfield was outside the built-up area by a mile or so; now it's well inside the town. There were only a few gambling places then, so we all ended up at the Sahara Palace where, to our astonishment, there were lines and lines of one-armed bandits, half-a-dozen blackjack and roulette tables. There were probably other things but I don't remember. I rapidly lost the $10 dollars I had set aside to make my fortune and repaired to the bar and entertainment. The singer was once famous but only so-so, his name was Don Cornell.

Suddenly, there was a bit of a panic when the two captains realised that the other co-pilot was gambling with no success and about to dip into the imprest; for once I wasn't carrying it. We left for base. The next morning we set off for Los Angeles (LAX) via San Francisco (SFO) and in SFO we had an aircraft taking off across our runway just as we were about to touch down. This time we didn't turn a hair.

As all who know LAX, it is 100 per cent normal to land on a westerly heading. There are probably old hands in the area who have never done anything else. Well, we were routed out to sea for some reason and, as the airfield was not too busy, we were cleared to land straight in, i.e. in an easterly direction. That was my one and only time, even in all my later visits to LAX.

We were staying in the Thunderbird Hotel on Sunset Boulevard, so I could not resist the opportunity to visit the famous '77 Sunset Strip' of TV fame (it was actually No. 1365 or so). The interior seemed identical and I expected Efrem Zimbalist Jnr to walk in any minute. However, the side entrance to the car park, where 'Kookie', played by Ed Byrnes, looked the same but, instead of leading to a proper car-park, it was a small dirt strip with room for two yank tanks, if properly manoeuvred, and a scruffy shed. It did have a great view of Los Angeles, though.

Next day, 13 November 1964, we did just one sector to San Francisco and headed into town. We were there by noon, so off to Fisherman's Wharf to admire the boats, watch the fishermen and look out to Alcatraz.

That evening in the bar just down from the hotel there was a topless competition. The idea was that ladies would choose some music and render themselves nude from the waist up. This country was so full of contradictions; they thought that the 'f' word was part of normal English and that 'Motherf....r' was a normal way of showing dislike for someone. Yet, they could get quite upset if certain norms of etiquette and manners were not properly exercised.

So, this topless business was quite a shock. Naturally, we stayed. The system was that you applauded the girls when they finished and at the end their names were called out again and the girl with the loudest applause was declared the winner and, incredibly, went on to the next round somewhere else. Well, voters the world over are fickle, and so the biggest applause was for the ugly fat one. The other girls' faces were a picture; the winner should have been the dental nurse. I cannot remember what the other girls did but their jobs were a cross-section of any town.

Talking of 'topless', a Britannia crew was in a topless bar somewhere in the States and, after a while, were somewhat worse for wear. There's a surprise. Anyway, a very lovely young lady walks in wearing a leather suit that fits so snugly that nothing is left to the imagination. The guys make this the subject of much speculation and the captain, emboldened by the evening's fun, goes over to her and says, 'I do apologise for intruding but my friends and I are much impressed by your appearance. Tell me, how do you get into those trousers?' She replied, 'Well, you can start by buying me a dry Martini.'

The next two days were just visiting previous destinations to ensure that the tricky places were handled by both crews and then we finished at Kindley Field in Bermuda. We ended up parked right on the edge of the airfield with the beautiful blue sea only yards from the aircraft. The weather was balmy; everything was so obviously British based that we felt at home immediately.

I knew that Brian Scarsbrook, known as Scats, the school rugby captain had taken an accounting job out here so contacted immigration who advised me how to find him. I duly had dinner with him and his new bride. Afterwards I visited the RAF Association club and chin-wagged with a few Second World War guys.

We were staying in the Castle Harbour Hotel and, after breakfast the next day, a couple of us walked thirty yards from the entrance on to the first tee of their lovely golf course. It's a hard life sometimes. Then home via Lajes AFB in the Azores. Quite a trip from 8 to 17 November with only crews on board.

Shortly after this trip I had occasion to go to RAF Hospital Wroughton, near Swindon, for a minor operation to remove a cyst from my face. As is the wont of the RAF I stayed the night after it was removed. In the morning it was time for the Matron's round, so all was neat and tidy and those who could stood to attention by their beds. Matron would then walk up one side of the ward and back the other.

Opposite me was Flight Lieutenant McGarry and a fellow Britannia captain next to him; they were both unable to leave their beds and relied on bottles when they needed a pee. They had a small competition whereby the first to ask for a bottle in the morning had to buy their beer in the evening. Matron reached their beds and asked if they were still playing their silly game to which they sheepishly replied in the affirmative.

Further along was Squadron Leader Alec(?) Calder who, due to a stomach problem, was being fed rectally. This entailed a suspended bottle of nourishment fed through a tube and into his bottom. Matron said, 'How are you today Squadron Leader Calder?' and he replied, 'Fine thank you Matron, how many of these feeders have you in the hospital?' Matron looked at Sister and said, 'Three maybe, counting this one?' Sister agreed and Matron said, 'Three counting yours.' Alec said, 'Splendid! Would you and Sister care to join me for lunch?'

The ward erupted and McGarry and friend asked for bottles at the same time!

Such fun and camaraderie are a normal part of service hospital life, enjoyed by servicemen of all ranks and the hospital staff, and massively good for assisting healing, mental and physical. Blair did a massive disservice to the military when he oversaw the final closure of all service hospitals.

About this time I went to say hullo to Geoff Jarvis at Boscombe Down where he was a test pilot. Geoff had been the other flight commander on 257 Squadron. We had a chat and a coffee and then he showed me a TSR-2! 'Surely,' I remarked, 'didn't Harold Wilson scrap this aircraft and demand all models and jigs be destroyed?' He explained that it was such a magnificent aircraft that the local powers-to-be couldn't do it. Apparently, it was one of those rare types that more-or-less met all the requirements when first flown. Scrapping the aircraft cost the British taxpayer millions and even more when the government ordered a US aircraft that was to cost more, was very late in delivery and was then cancelled, costing even more. This was the F-111K, which could not match TSR-2, especially in technology.

Officers believed to be bound for higher rank attend various specialist courses. There is the Staff College and a similar course is held for specialist navigators. These courses are hard work and usually last a year; at the end they get a present of a trip to enable them to consolidate their learning and see how other air forces work. To this end the specialist navigators were assigned a tour of the US AFBs and major aviation companies.

I had returned from our USA trainer on 17 November and on 1 December I set off on a three-week tour of the States with these graduates. This time I was with Squadron Leader Roger Parker, one of our flight commanders.

The first day produced a very exciting flight. We staged via Lajes AFB in the Azores for Gander. When we had passed the PNR (point of no return) we were advised that the weather in Gander was deteriorating fast but that our alternate at Stephenville was already very bad and St John's airport's runways were too short. We were committed to Gander but at least we had enough fuel for a few attempts. When we started the approach, the weather was reported as 100-foot cloud base, and visibility, to the best of my memory, half a mile or less. These conditions were well below our normal legal limits.

In really bad conditions the RAF flew the monitored approach system, whereby the co-pilot flew the aircraft, the captain monitored and also kept a forward lookout for the runway and/or lights. This was much safer and more successful than the captain flying the aircraft on instruments and looking up and then down again. So, I flew and Roger watched and searched. The early days of such flying had nothing as accurate and slick and safe as nowadays. We received two signals from the ground rather like rays, one horizontal and one vertical. Very like the modern ILS (Instrument Landing System) but a wider beam. The instrument which interpreted these beams was known as the zero reader. It comprised a horizontal and vertical white bar which you tried to maintain as a cross or zero deflection. If you were above or below the desired approach angle then the horizontal bar would deflect and the vertical bar was to keep you on the runway centre-line.

It had a very sensitive response to deviations and was hard work but, under normal permitted limits, it did not matter if you were a little off-line because when you broke cloud there was usually time to jink around a bit to produce a comfortable and safe landing.

This night, however, there was no room for error so I had to really sweat it. All the way down I reacted really fast to all actual or anticipated deviations and, as we passed our normal minimum permitted height above runway, Roger advised that he saw nothing. At 100 feet he called 'I have control' as he had just seen an approach light underneath us. He carried out a successful landing with much relief all round. Immodest as I may sound, I had done a good job and the captain and the crew said so.

The cloud base was at or just below 100 feet and the visibility was much less than 500 yards. Had we not used the monitored approach we would never have made it.

BOAC did not use this method for another few years and, I believe, it was because the captains just could not bring themselves to rely on their first officers (co-pilots). From talking to many first officers with BOAC and BA over the years I know that many, if not most, captains did nearly everything themselves and gave very few sectors to their first officers.

The captains were treated like demi-gods and believed themselves to be so. The habit of accommodating captains in one hotel, having been driven alone in his own transport, the rest of the flight crew in another hotel in their own transport and the cabin crew in another certainly enhanced their belief.

Make no mistake, BOAC/BA have a deserved great reputation for service and safety (service was terrible in the 1970s and 1980s but changed for the better again) and, although the customers may like them, there was a time when most other pilots did not. Their captains' feeling of superiority came across very clearly in their radio transmissions and responses to other pilots. Every airline has a callsign to precede the number of their flight and BOAC/BA was/is 'Speedbird'. However, they always call themselves THE Speedbird 123 etc. It's damned irritating, no one else does it and most pilots laugh at it.

Quite a few RAF chaps, when relaying messages on behalf of BOAC/BA, if they were out of contact with the current radio station, would give them the callsign Birdseed.

You may think I have a down on BOAC/BA but I haven't, not now. But in the 1960s the pomposity and superiority was very irritating and they were unpopular with just about every airline pilot.

From Gander to Ottawa where we stayed for two or three hours whilst our passengers visited some aviation organisation and then on to Winnipeg for the night. When we travelled into very cold areas we were issued with some very good protective clothing and we needed it; the temperature was minus 30 degrees C.

That evening we decided to have a look at the town so we donned our cold weather kit and left by the main entrance. We went down the side street and straight back into the hotel by the side entrance. The temperature and wind-chill effect was so severe we realised it was stupid to stay outside.

At that time, in the bar, we discovered a strange Canadian law. Typically English, we got our beers at the bar and walked over to a table only to be accosted by a steward who demanded that we gave him our beers! Unknown to us, the law stated that nobody was allowed to carry a drink from A to B. It was necessary to have it done for you by an authorised member of staff. I think it was to stop men making unwanted approaches to ladies or something odd like that. As no lady was likely to enter a bar alone it was a strange rule.

From Winnipeg to Mather AFB near the capital city of California, Sacramento. We were there for four days whilst our passengers visited numerous aviation and defence facilities. Then to Los Angeles for two days, again staying in the Thunderbird Hotel on Sunset Boulevard. Then to Holloman AFB near El Paso. This airfield had the longest, or nearly longest, runway in the USA. It was used for all types of tests for rocket-propelled aircraft and other experiments where such a runway was necessary. We left after two or three hours for Carswell AFB.

Carswell AFB was next to Fort Worth, near Dallas, Texas. Here we found more strange bar rules; you could only order beer or soft drinks at the bar. If you wanted spirits then you had to bring your own and order fillers (i.e. soda, tonic etc.) from the bar.

Bill Adamson, our navigator, and I were in the hotel bar, The Key Club, guests only, and got chatting to a local guy who offered to show us around town. After a while he pulled up near a club and said. 'Let's go and get a decent drink.' I pointed out that I thought that spirits were illegal and, anyway, there was a police car right outside. He said not to worry as nothing would happen as they had raided the place only the previous night.

I was concerned as we were due to leave in two days and I could ill-afford to be in the local clink. Anyway, Bill and I were talked into it, of course, only to enter the noisiest place of my whole life – then and since. There was a group of two guitars, a wind instrument and drums and four six-foot-high speakers. The room was approximately twelve by five metres long and the band was not holding back. We had to sit on cushions at low tables and be served by lovely young ladies who regularly danced on the tables and were occasionally seen to go upstairs with a customer/client. We had to scream to make ourselves heard.

Our new chum said that this place was where some of JFK's secret service agents had been for a drink the night before his assassination. Obviously, I have no idea of the truth of that but he was adamant. We left after a couple of whiskeys, with sore throats and, probably, more damage to my already poor ears.

Next lunchtime Bill and I went for lunch in the hotel but before we ate we visited the small bar in the corner used by the waitresses to get drinks for the diners. It was not meant for customers but the ladies let us sit on their two stools and drink the only beer worth the name in the USA, namely, Schlitz Draught, the 'Beer that made Milwaukee Famous'. Nectar.

We forgot to eat as the beer and the ladies distracted us somewhat, especially when, after the diners were gone, we discussed what guns they were carrying. They all had them. Of course, in their line of work they often travelled home at night and they needed protection.

From Carswell AFB to Little Rock AFB Arkansas. There I enjoyed a game of golf on the base course and found that in the BOQ (Bachelor Officers' Quarters) a dime would make the bed vibrate to help you get to sleep. It didn't help.

Little Rock to Andrews AFB to park near Air Force One, the President's aircraft, not too near, of course. Then on to Navy Johnsville and a six-day stay in Philadelphia.

There's a limit to how much history and culture you can enjoy. Anyway, I did my best to visit all the historical sites and museums but it was a long time to spend in one place.

There was, however, a very pleasant interlude. On 19 December the BOAC station officer invited the whole crew to his home for the annual station staff Christmas party. We were made most welcome, the drinks flowed and we were all having a great time. The host eventually called out that it was presents time and all his team gathered to receive their gifts from him and exchange them amongst themselves.

We, the eight RAF crew, got together away from the jollity as we felt slightly intrusive at this particular moment. The station officer called over, 'Hey fellas, we haven't forgotten you, come here.'

We each received a delightful beer mug, sky-blue and with the BOAC crest. Normally these were a gift only for first-class passengers. What a lovely gesture.

Philadelphia is a lovely and peaceful city but it was good to get going again. By this time, our passengers were in New York, so we had to go to JFK, collect them and move on again to Gander. Johnsville to JFK was a thirty-five-minute flight, so little fuel was needed and the aircraft was very light. This was an ideal chance to show off the Comet so Roger climbed steeply and we reached 2,000 feet by the end of the shortish runway.

We stayed in Gander for the night having arrived in much better weather than nineteen days earlier, then continued via Lajes, Azores, to Lyneham. We did only fifteen sectors of which I had six. Thank you, Roger! Ron would have given me eight sectors, or more.

On the way back, we burst a tyre on landing somewhere which we did not hear or feel and the first we knew was when our on-board travelling ground engineer, Sergeant Ritchie, saw it on his post-flight inspection. On only one other occasion did I experience a burst, later when I was a Comet captain and we did not know about that either.

I mention this because, like all pilots, we are astonished to read occasionally that an aircraft had a tyre burst on landing at Heathrow, or wherever, but nobody was hurt. Again, like all pilots, I can only laugh with derision and despair at the sheer rubbish written by journalists about anything to do with aviation. I even read once that a jet aircraft on approach had its engines spluttering and misfiring; for a piston engine, possible, for a jet engine, impossible!

There are so many instances of lack of knowledge or attempt to gain some but the perpetuation of myths in the films is infinitely worse. It seems that if ever a single-engine aircraft has an engine failure it immediately plunges to earth with engine screaming, even though the propeller is not turning. What rubbish! All aircraft are gliders with engines; if your single engine fails then, if your attempt to restart fails, you find a suitable place to glide to and land. If you are a twin-engined aircraft, now on one engine, then you look for a suitable airfield to land. If you are a three-engined or four-engined aircraft then, generally speaking, you could carry on to destination.

If a Boeing 747 loses all engines it becomes a very heavy glider but could still cover a distance, wind velocity permitting, from a height of 35,000 feet of ninety to a hundred miles.

In the film of the Canadian two-engine aircraft which ran out of fuel and attempted a landing on a closed field (RCAF Gimli) you saw go-karts on the runway. This is a true story by the way. When the aircraft is on the approach with both engines out you see the pilot fighting the controls, gritting his teeth, sweating like hell and still wearing his uniform jacket (I recall). The controls would have been working well so fighting them was for dramatic effect, gritting teeth was unlikely, as was sweating; wearing a jacket on the flight deck is ridiculous. You might leave it on when the aircraft is cold-soaked and even until after take off but it would soon be removed. Anyway, most pilots carry a pullover, at least. Often you see a pilot still with his hat on which is even more ridiculous.

In my entire flying career, I've had a few stressful moments but I have never seen anyone fight the controls, except for severe turbulence, never seen anyone grit their teeth, maybe seen a bit of sweat in a heavy session in the simulator and only once seen a pilot who wore his jacket all the time.

The only way to cope with scary moments is to keep cool, show no panic and get on with it. This is how it really is.

There is another major irritation in films and TV regarding the use of communications terminology and this is 'Over and Out'. In radio-telephony in the air and on the ground, think police TV shows, this is frequently used and is always wrong.

'Over' means I have finished my message, over to you for your reply or further information. 'Out' means I have finished my message and I do not expect a reply. So 'over and out' is daft.

I think the second most stupid film showed Charlton Heston dangling on a rope from an aircraft being lowered to get into a Boeing 747 where a lady cabin crew member was valiantly trying to fly the aircraft into a mountain range. Heston was helped as his acting always consists of gritting his teeth and hissing when on screen. He eventually squeezes thorough a very small window used for pilots to see forward if the main windshield should craze over as they have been known to do. (Nevertheless, to give him due credit, he did serve as a wireless operator on B-25 Mitchells with the USAAF during the war.)

The stupidest film in history was *Concord* starring George Kennedy and Louis Jourdain. Louis is standing at the bottom of the steps as George arrives and says 'Hi, I'm your co-pilot for today.' Louis says, 'Have you flown this much?' (or something like that). 'No, but I've had a run through it with somebody today.' Any course on passenger aircraft takes a few weeks' ground school, simulator and route training, so how stupid was that?

During the flight a missile is fired at them and, by deft flying, they avoid it. As it goes by George actually identifies it as a specific type! After all the messing around, one of them says 'Let's have a checklist'! What checklist!? The after-missile attack checklist?

It gets worse, they night stop in Paris! Wow! What a fast trip to their destination Moscow. Anyway, the baddies get 'em and they crash land in the mountains! They all survive. I was watching this in my hotel room in Miami whilst the weather raged outside. If there had been a sofa in the room I would have cringed behind it. Unfortunately, those who are a little nervous of flying must have their doubts and fears badly affected by all this utter rubbish.

Back with Maureen and the boys in Devizes I was firmly advised by a policeman to get my car taxed. It had run out in my absence and I hadn't noticed. The fine was £5 I think. This was just one of those problems of being away for lengthy periods. They are nothing compared to the difficulties faced by wives and mothers, coping with the decisions normally made by the men and, of course, the physical duties were borne by the ladies. Children were a joy but hard work, and none more so than sickness, accidents, teething, etc. For Maureen it did not help that she was not driving at this time.

Our house in Eastwoodbury Close was just around the corner from the stores and other shops, so that was not a problem but the town centre was quite a walk.

In early 1964 I had been called away at short notice and shot off to the bank for some cash to tide Maureen over. We normally only needed £10 for a week's shopping and that is also the amount I usually cashed. I couldn't resist asking for a new £10 note, they had only just come into circulation, and rushed home, packed and fled. The next day Maureen went to the stores for a modest amount of stuff, proffered the £10 note and they did not have enough change. Things were cheap then.

My local was the Fox and Hounds which sold the Devizes brew, Wadworth's. However, my first visit was a bit of a shock; I had fixed my car and given it a run down Nursteed Road towards Etchilhampton to check it out. As I passed the Fox and Hounds I realised it was just about to close

171

so dived in for a quick pint. It was busy but very scruffy. The tables had linoleum nailed on them, the floors were wooden and covered in sawdust and the bar was a server about four-feet deep and ten-feet long. I thought I'll just have this one visit and find another place.

Well, in the short time it took to drink the beer before being obliged to leave at closing time, I managed some conversation with a few totally different types. Farmers, farmworkers, solicitors, businessmen et al frequented the place. It was amazing! Also, the beer was 1/3d a pint (7½p to you) and as good as it gets. It became my very pleasant local.

I used to leave Lyneham for Devizes at all hours because if you had no duties your presence was not expected. My route home was via Calne then over the Ridgeway down to home. The route passed through the North Wiltshire Golf Club which I joined as soon as I knew it was there. Naturally, I stopped off frequently for a few holes or so. Having played often with my father at the Warren Golf Club, I soon picked the game up again. However, I never, then or now, bettered an 18 handicap; although then I was a steady player.

On one occasion I was playing there with my father and brother Barry and we were being hassled by the following two-ball. It is polite to let others through but the three games ahead were all groups of four so there seemed no point. My father was addressing his second shot on the 16th hole when a ball went past him about six feet in front and twenty yards past. Barry said to stand back then he hit the ball back straight over the tee. The guys had to dive out of the way. What a shot! Not within the spirit of the game, perhaps, but their behaviour was questionable also.

We had a regular 4-ball group in Eastwoodbury Close; Ted Quinnel who lived next door, Cyril Glassett and A.N. Other. Ted was a pilot on a Britannia squadron at Lyneham, Cyril had his own company, surveying, I think and our fourth was an accountant. We each had 'pink chitties' from our wives which demanded our return home in time for lunch at 1330. This meant we were always the first to tee off. When we finished we always had a beer at the club to be good members then rushed to The Fox and Hounds until 1325. Then fled home.

Ted Quinnel had had a chequered career. Firstly, he had been a subaltern in a top British regiment and, because his father was a vicar, he was not accustomed to having much spare money around. So naturally, he always paid his mess bill on the dot so that he was aware of what little he had for the rest of the month. One month he went to see the President of the Mess Committee (PMC) to ask for his bill as it was a bit late in coming. The PMC said not to worry, all would be well. Nothing happened by the end of the month and again the PMC said not to worry. Well, after three months, Ted was desperate but knew he had done the right thing to keep in touch with things. However, he could stand the stress no longer and demanded, in the most respectful way, of course, that he could pay his bills. The PMC said, 'Look old chap I absolutely detest all the paperwork involved in this position so I have paid all the bills myself.' For the rest of this officer's tenure as PMC, Ted continued saving, in case, but managed to save quite a tidy sum, I believe.

Later Ted joined the Royal Air Force and served on Vulcans. On one approach, the aircraft was in serious trouble and the captain ordered Ted to eject. He didn't want to, as all the non-pilots in the crew did not have an ejector seat and he thought the aircraft would make a safe arrival. The captain ordered him again and Ted obeyed. Sadly, the aircraft crashed and all on board died. Ted said that he would always feel guilty about surviving in that way. The structure of the aircraft was such that an exit via ejector seat was not feasible for the rear crew members. Their only hope was to exit via a door/panel and hope there was enough time to open a parachute. What a terrible feeling to know that's your only hope.

Devizes is a beautiful market town and whilst we were there the film *Far from the Madding Crowd* was made. Quite a few locals played extras' parts and it was fun to both see people you knew in ancient costumes and even more fun to try and work out how lamp-posts, yellow lines, modern architecture and other modern items could be so completely transformed to fit the period.

One night about 0100, having been late from a flight, I left Lyneham, turned right and within 100 yards saw an upturned car against the roadside bushes. Worse, I saw an arm, against the driver's window, covered in blood. I stopped my car and went towards the other car with concern for the injured. I was about five yards from it when a voice said, 'Can I help you?' When I came down from my large leap of shock I found it was the driver who was waiting for the help that had already been summoned. What I had seen was a red scarf pressed against the window by a pile of other things thrown around when he rolled the car.

One summer in a carnival moment at the Fox and Hounds, a group of us decided to form a cricket XI and challenge the local grammar school. On the day I looked at the school pitch and pointed out to an umpire, a teacher at the school, that there was a round hole about the size of a golf ball, on the leg side on a length. I regarded this as dangerous but was duly pooh-poohed and the game started.

As I took a sweep at a ball on the leg-side I can still see it hitting this hole, acting as if off a slip-cradle, coming straight at my head. As I turned to avoid it I took a blow on my right temple. I don't think I lost consciousness but I was certainly groggy. The worst effect was that I could not see out of my right eye which was also hurting.

I was seriously frightened. Slowly my vision returned but the pain persisted for two or three days. I was in a quandary because, although it was only a friendly knockabout, I did not have the RAF authority to play for an outside team. One had to apply through the 'normal channels'.

So, I did not report it but, although the vision now seemed normal, I could not keep my right eye closed. It would slowly open of its own accord. I chose not to see a doctor but, after a few weeks, it was necessary. I said that I'd fallen down the stairs and I was sent to a specialist at RAF Hospital Wroughton where X-rays showed that I had cracked the skull along the sutures. For several years the eye ached when I was tired but eventually it stayed closed at the night times.

For reasons to be explained later I resigned from the RAF but, before I made it official, I arranged to see an eye specialist privately. I wanted his opinion as to whether he thought my eye would give no trouble or would deteriorate before I could finish a full flying career. If he said it would be okay then I'd resign or, if not, stay in the RAF where, if I were unable to fly, I would, at least, be retained for ground duties.

In the event he assured me that he could see no good reason why I should be concerned so when the time came I resigned from the RAF, albeit sadly. To this day the eye still aches if I'm really tired.

Ron and I did one more USA trainer, this time instructing, before we were given the VIP flights to cap nearly all others. Again, this was a trip at the end of Staff College training June 1965; it was a three-week tour of South America. Fantastic!

The system on the squadron was that when given a VIP flight it was guaranteed as long as nothing else came up before one week ahead of your assigned flight. We all had a lot of studying to do to really get to know our routes, local and national regulations and, for the pilots especially, the airfield approaches and weather patterns. The navigator had all that, plus the actual route planning.

All our work was well underway when we were hit by the bombshell that Harold Wilson wanted to be picked up from NATO HQ with a flight from USAF overseas base Evreux-Fauville. Boy, were we upset! This meant that all our work was for nothing and we would not go to South America; that trip was handed to Barry Mills and Tony Pearce.

We duly arrived at Evreux in foul weather, and mood, to wait for Wilson who, as was his wont, arrived late.

Barry and Tony had an amazing time; the hospitality was relentless, they hardly had to dip into their allowances, they were accommodated on ranches, ate wonderful steak everywhere, saw beautiful sights, rode horses and, oh yes, had a great flying experience. Whenever I saw Tony after this time, I think the last would have been around 1997, he always gave me a little grin because he knew how upset I had been about this trip.

Apart from a VIP trip to Arlanda, Stockholm, for Admiral Sir David Luce and a tour of the Middle East with Lords Shackleton and Shepherd on some sort of government inspection, that was my VIP time with Ron finished.

There was one other with Roger Parker to Berlin on behalf of the Chief of the Air Staff, Sir Charles Elworthy. This was memorable for only one reason; I was walking down Kurfurstendamm when a small sign for a bar down a side street attracted my attention. In I went, the time was about 1600, ordered a beer and sat enjoying it when a pleasant piece of music started. I thought nothing of it until I noticed in the bar mirrors that all heads were turned to the right. I looked and saw a small dance-floor about twelve feet by twelve feet was being used by an extremely lovely young woman dancing the 'Dance of the Seven Veils'.

This was not a seedy bar but, nevertheless, did not appear special either. The dancer was absolutely amazing. The dance was seductive and sensual but extremely tastefully done. I have seen many similar dances in and around the Middle East and, especially, Tehran in the Shah's time but nothing ever as good.

Sadly for me, Ron was posted onto the Belfast but as they were to be based at RAF Brize Norton, as I was too, we would enjoy each other's company in days to come.

Captain – At Last

In October 1965 I started my conversion training for captain. In view of my time on Comets I had just the one check ride flying in the left-hand seat and then went 'solo' with Tony Pearce (the grin) as my co-pilot. We did three trips of two-hour circuits, let-downs and general handling and then Eddie Epps gave me a quick test ride which I passed.

Then for the training and checks down-route with passengers. I did six sectors under supervision and I was cleared as a C captain. My first flight was with 'Tubby' Bower (I assume he has a Christian name) to Gibraltar on 23 November 1965. I was twenty-nine years and two months old and, having already talked with many US crews on KC-135s et al, I'm pretty sure that at that time I was the youngest four-jet captain in the world. There have been many occasions since then of younger captains but I was pleased to have held that honour for a while.

On 13 December 1965 a Comet 2 landed at Lyneham after having been unable to lower its flaps. The decision was made to ground all the aircraft until the solution was found. A quite correct decision, but muggins was in RAF Idris in Tripoli, which is not much of a place. Archie McIndoe, joint captain, and I were thinking of our fellow crews in New York, Gibraltar, Malta and Cyprus. It took three days to clear the aircraft to continue but to not use the flaps at all which caused no difficulty as it is always included in monthly training.

On 21 December I landed from a training flight and was told to report to the Squadron Commander, Squadron Leader Phil Walker, immediately. On my way I racked my brains for any misdemeanour or incident of recent days but could think of nothing. I entered his office, saluted and heard him say, 'I'm sorry, Brian, but I have some bad news for you. Whilst you were airborne your name was drawn from the hat to go immediately to Lusaka to help set up an operations centre for an oil-lift to Zambia.' Ian Smith had cut off their supply.

Well, with a start like that you can imagine how my heart nearly stopped with the reference to 'bad news'. I was expecting some bad family news. Leaving home for Christmas seemed acceptable. Then I remembered I had spent a fortune on food and booze as my family were joining us.

Naturally, Maureen was very disappointed but that's the Service – you go when and where you are ordered. I've often wondered if my name did come out of the hat!

I left that night for Dar-es-Salaam, capital of Tanganyika (before becoming Tanzania), and on the night of the 22nd there was much revelry and joy as all incoming personnel and crews of the Britannias, who were going to do all the work, had fun round the pool. Inevitably, some 'fell' in but many managed not to spill their beer. The next day we were all shipped on to our final destinations, Lusaka, Ndola, Kinshasha and/or Brazzaville.

Needless to say, the press had a field day telling their readers that the British servicemen were having fun whilst the poor Africans were suffering in Zambia, etc., etc. What dregs of humanity they are with all their distortion of truths. Every single time I've been involved with them in my career the press has always been wrong or malicious.

Anyway, for the next few months the Services worked their guts out loading, flying, unloading and distributing oil. I worked twenty-four hours on and twelve hours off at one time in Lusaka. Group Captain James was the senior operations officer plus three ops officers. We had set up charts for movements of aircraft timings and all other aids needed such as long-range radio contacts with aircraft and other bases.

Britannias were loaded with a large number (now forgotten) of 56-gallon barrels of oil and fuel into the normal area of the aircraft with just a row or two of seats for passengers and extra crew. They were loaded in Kinshasha, Brazzaville, or Nairobi and flown to Lusaka and N'dola.

The major difficulty was that Lusaka, in particular, had room only for three large aircraft. Therefore, not only was it necessary to plan the arrivals and departures very accurately, it was necessary to have contact well established to ensure no blockages, which could be created by aircraft unserviceabilities, held up the flow.

There were even one or two civilian companies with DC-6s getting involved. On one occasion one of them did a bad landing and left the end of the runway receiving some minor undercarriage damage. The captain decided to retire to the local hotel whilst the RAF ground crews tried to fix it. He had not expected them to have any success so when I shot off in the ops' Land Rover to tell him all was well he was as startled as me. He had a large whiskey on the go, and not his first.

Whilst I stood there not knowing how to tell him we had no room for his aircraft he saved me the trouble by downing the scotch and coming with me back to the airfield. Different outfits, different ways, I guess!

On one occasion Group Captain James was unable to raise a crew just about to leave and sent me in a hurry to catch them before they left. I ran out of the main doors of the Headquarters building we were using and there, on the paved area of the entrance area, was a Russell's viper with its head raised, just as surprised as me. I dared not stop as I would have been right next to it so I just jumped over it. It shot off to the nearest drain.

Later that day I needed to collect something from my room in the Law School; they were on holiday, and en route I glanced into the monsoon drain. There, about six feet below me, on the dry bottom was a long, over twelve-feet, greyish and thin snake. I was sufficiently intrigued to see it move so I scuffed some dirt onto it. It ignored me so I carried on. On my return it had disappeared.

That evening, when I was on my only night off, I mentioned this to a local chap in the bar. He was horrified. Apparently, I had perfectly described a black mamba which is the only snake able to rear itself up to two thirds of its length. Most snakes can only raise one third. He said I was really, really lucky because they can also be very grumpy and he could easily have hit me. Whoops!

The following April on the West Cornwall Golf Club at Lelant, near St Ives, I was looking for my father's ball. As I was about to move my left leg forward something made me stop; there, exactly where I would have placed my left foot, was an adder. What I had seen in my peripheral vision was the movement as it had drawn back its head prior to the strike!

These three snakes just described were the beginning of a reasonably interesting time I was to have with the snake world.

One creature which posed no threat was a chameleon we had decided was our ops-room mascot. There were plenty of flies and other insects to keep it happy for the three or four days we kept it. Its ability to change colour was of constant interest as we ferried it around the room. The best example was when it sat on our hats; the dark blue was a massive challenge and it took a few minutes to change whilst appearing to actually strain to do it.

Throughout the time in Lusaka I was very busy, especially on the signals network. Our title in Zambia was Combritzam which was service speak for Combined British (Forces) Zambia. I was known as Combritzambrian to many of the recipients. We also had a film company do a fifteen-minute film on the exercise which included shots of the Britannias and the Javelin fighters which had been deployed. I was even seen doing the usual silly thing of standing in front of my board holding a pen. Heavily posed. The film was one of many showing various stories known as *Look at Life* and were shown in cinemas between films and/or Pathé news. I returned to the family and Lyneham to find that everyone had had a Happy Christmas, thank you, and all the goodies had been eaten and drunk.

Some months later Maureen, the boys and I were walking along a road in Oxford and the boys shouted, 'Look there's Daddy!' There was a huge bank of televisions in the front window of the, then, popular television rental company. There I was on every screen and we stood watching my scene. However, it was pouring with rain and the passing pedestrians looked at us as if we were really sad people!

At the end of November and into early December 1966 I managed to get a trip as supernumerary crew with Maureen as passenger on a Comet 4 USA trainer. We went Lyneham-Gander-Omaha-Chicago-New York-Washington-San Francisco and return via New York. The time change and jet lag and late nights helped Maureen to realise why I was always tired, but it really knocked her out. She had a great time, though. As I was not operating crew I spent most of the flight time with her and it was splendid looking at all the views and explain much of them.

Our most memorable lay-over, I think, was in Chicago. We stayed at the Knickerbocker Hotel and visited the bar 'Your Father's Moustache' in Rush Street. They served only beer in pitchers, the waiters were constantly on the move, there was an Acker Bilk-type Oompa band with banjo, saxophone and guitar and when they stopped playing cartoon films of all types were displayed on the walls. Our ashtray became full on one occasion, after the local winning football team had joined us, and I asked a passing waiter if we could have a fresh one. 'Certainly Sir,' he said and emptied it on to the floor and replaced it on the table. It was a great place. Oh yes, I forgot, as you entered the ladies were given a garter and the men were given a moustache which you were expected to wear whilst in there.

Roy Chitty now entered my life as my assigned co-pilot. We mixed crews occasionally but I usually flew with Roy. He was a good pilot, his logs were quite immaculate but his major forte was his landings. They were the best I've seen and certainly better than mine. Eventually, one day at Lyneham I couldn't resist moving the airbrake lever a fraction at a couple of feet just before touchdown. The aircraft dutifully landed with a good old bump, nothing bad but Roy was mortified. He couldn't quite understand it as everything had, as usual, been correct on the approach. As we taxied in he looked so despondent that I had to own up. I hope he took my actions as a compliment.

From becoming a captain in 1965 until March 1967 when I left 216 Squadron I seemed to fly with very few of the several co-pilots; Roy Chitty mostly, Tony Pearce quite a lot, Brian Huppler and a new chap, John Redding. They were all excellent, as you would expect, and it was a pleasure to fly with them.

In February 1966 I wangled a trip on an Atlantic training flight and went as observer. The route was Lajes AFB, Azores-Gander-Bermuda-Piarco (Port of Trinidad, Spain)-Santa Maria-Azores-Lyneham. It was very pleasant to let others carry me around but I had two nice surprises. The first was at Lajes where, in the queue to be issued my room key, I put a quarter into a one-armed bandit as I filed past it. Jackpot! $50 or $60 provided us with a great night's stop.

At the hotel in Trinidad, the Hilton, I think, you entered the lift and it took you down to the rooms, all of which had lovely views as it was built into the side of the hill. The next morning, we were all lounging around at the pool when we were asked to move to the end of the pool. We were a bit annoyed to be dislodged from our favoured spots but did as we were asked. The reason we were moved was because they were having the finals of the Miss Trinidad and Tobago to select the lady to enter the Miss World contest. We were a very happy group of blokes and the icing on the cake was that we were next to the bar.

The RAF annual test of our capacity to return to UK via the Pacific and USA was next and 'they' got me to be an ops officer again. However, it was at Hickam AFB, Honolulu. I could handle that. The duty involved meeting every aircraft, ensuring maintenance and refuelling immediately available and being a general dogsbody. I had very little time to myself but on one occasion I was in the general base cafeteria at the entrance to Pearl Harbor. From the windows you could see the road and then the sea. I was talking to someone at the table when the room went dark. I was intrigued, so went to see the cause; for a moment I did not realise the view had gone. I could see no sky either. A huge aircraft carrier was entering harbour and not only was it incredibly high, but the outer part of its flight deck was passing over the roof of the building.

I was no longer involved with VIP flying, of course, so my life now revolved around regular flights to Gibraltar, Luqa, Idris, El Adem and

Akrotiri. There was the occasional 'treat' like a trip to RAF Gatow near Berlin, a trip to RAF Wildenrath, part of the 2 TAF (Tactical Air Force) of the British forces in Germany and just one, semi-VIP flight, taking senior officers of the Central European Treaty Organisation around the UK. My first officer was Hal Taylor who always took his leave so that he could attend the Olympics wherever they were in the world.

It was an interesting trip in that we went via Wattisham, my old 257 Squadron base, to Cranwell, my old instructing base. Furthermore, Little Rissington was also involved in that one of the landings was scheduled there. When I pointed out to the planners that there was not enough runway for a Comet they were rather miffed and asked if I was sure? Yup. In the event I had to land at Fairford and they were bussed.

The highlight of this trip was the arrival at Lyneham where they were given their own personal display by the Red Arrows. This display did not follow what the civilians see; it was red hot. They came across the airfield at zero feet and flat out. Their formation aerobatics were perfect, of course, but their extra stuff was exhilarating.

This had been in June and in late July I discovered that I had again been 'volunteered' for ops. duties overseas. This time I was very pleased as it was to be Nairobi. It was for the opening of a new base for an intensified supply of oil to Zambia.

We had to 'mill around' a bit until accommodation was found for all, the ops-room and communications established and aircraft handling and engineering set-up. My shift assistant was Sergeant Bob Brown, a Scot with fervent nationalist feelings; he was, nevertheless, a good servant of the Queen and one of the best men with whom I have ever worked. The hours were long and could be hard, but his enthusiasm and abilities never waned.

Our evening shifts usually finished around 2300 to midnight, which was long after the hotel bars normally closed. However, Bob invariably made arrangements with the Fairfax Hotel, not our residence, to let us in at the back door around midnight. There, revelry went on for a few more hours with the RAF going strong. Bob and I became good friends.

Naturally, when I had time to spare I played golf and managed, in the three weeks I was there, to play every golf course in the area. My aim was to keep the ball out of the trees and bushes as they were the homes of snakes.

On which subject I joined up with two UK teachers, hired a VW and we set off for Lake Naivasha in the Great Rift (i.e. 2,000-3,000 feet lower than Nairobi) to see the pink flamingos. It was a wonderful sight and we left the car on high ground and went to the water's edge. There, I saw many non-bird-like prints and thought, 'What am I doing here?' in the open in Africa with no guide!

On the way home I could not avoid a snake in the road; it was three-feet long, fat and seemed to have no discernible neck. I guessed puff adder. So, the next day I visited the famous snake park and the world famous herpetologist, name now forgotten and cannot find on Google.

I explained that although I could see many puff adders at the park I wasn't sure what I'd hit. He said 'Come with me' and took me through his huge laboratory into a smaller, but still large workshop. On the floor was a box similar to the old 36-dozen egg-crate. Each upper third was a glass screen and he asked if it was one of these. I pressed my face to the glass and could not be sure. I said so and he slid the glass aside leaving my face eighteen inches from this puff adder. I gently rose and said 'Yes' (I didn't want any more tests!) and he said I needn't be concerned as it was sick! How did he know that it hadn't recovered since his last visit?

We had a real administrative and technical disaster during my time there. A Britannia had its windshield cracked and I sent an urgent signal for a replacement. At Lyneham another Britannia was prepared to bring the windshield and other items such as mail, spares, replacement wheels, etc. A space was set at the front for the windshield and to the rear were placed two rows of seats for a few replacement personnel. At the last moment it was decided to send more personnel so a new row of seats was put in and a piece of freight removed.

You've got it! They made space by removing the windshield. The real purpose of the flight had been lost somewhere along the way. At least we now had a replacement aircraft so, in a way, it was quicker to send an aircraft even without the spare so that we were up and running.

Much of our spare time was spent at the corner of the New Stanley Hotel where we would sit, have a beer and watch the world go by. It was said that whilst sitting there you would always see someone you knew pass by. It worked for us as half the RAF seemed to be there.

Saturday midday the hotel opened its long-room bar and men, mostly farmers, would come from far and wide for a long and enjoyable drinking session. The bar was about sixty-feet long and fully occupied. I only managed to get there once but it was one hell of a good time.

Just down the road from the New Stanley I was strolling along and the most beautiful woman I have ever seen was coming from the other direction. She seemed to be Indian/African, was five feet ten inches, with a fantastic figure, totally elegant in a fine sari and walked like a dream. I was stunned into stopping and staring and she glanced my way and, with a hint of a smile, she seemed to be thinking, 'That's another one'.

Any girl who walks the catwalk should cry to think they have no comparison to real women; they appear stick-thin, po-faced and walking as if constantly suppressing a fart.

Around December 1966 I was given the wonderful news that I was to join the fourth VC10 Course in March 1967. Tony Pearce and Brian Huppler were to be on the same course as co-pilots, but John Redding was going straight in as a captain. This did not surprise me as he was obvious top quality; he had only flown with me on three occasions but I was impressed.

Maureen stayed in our married quarters with the boys and Barney, our Golden Retriever, bought as a Christmas surprise, whilst we waited for our new house to be finished in Wantage. The house had four bedrooms, garage and courtyard and cost £4,995; the mortgage was £44 per month.

Like many new house-owners, we had only essential furniture to start with as we could afford no more. We slept on mattresses on the floor until we had decided what we wanted and what we could afford.

The boys were enrolled in the Wantage Church of England Primary School and Maureen restarted her teaching career at the same school. She was, and always would be, a reception class specialist and eventually became headmistress before retiring.

No. 10 Squadron, RAF Brize Norton, VC10

March 1967 to October 1971

During my induction into 10 Squadron and RAF Brize Norton we moved into our house in Wantage from where I would start my weekly commute to London Heathrow for the six-week ground school, No. 4 course on the VC10. It was held at Cranebank which was the BOAC training centre. It housed the classrooms, flight simulators for all their aircraft types, the usual offices and a very good restaurant and cafeteria.

John Redding, Tony Pearce and I, using my car, left early Monday morning each week and stayed in B&Bs, then drove home each Friday afternoon. My bed was directly under the flight path to 27R (right) and on the dot of 0600 hours the first aircraft came in to land. At 1400 hours every day take-offs and landings changed runways, so I was only under the flight path every other day. The six-week course was very thorough; we studied the VC10 in depth. The navigators had their own course elsewhere but joined us for a few days when we were covering instrumentation and those subjects applicable to them. The flight engineers ran a longer and parallel course in Cranebank, but our paths only crossed in the restaurant.

The BOAC instructors were excellent but to absorb and reach the standard required by the RAF we had to add the extra work. John, Tony and I were a team and did everything together. There were six crews per course.

Each day when the lectures ended at 1700 we stayed and continued to use the models, films and audio trainers as we required. At 1800 we ate in the restaurant then returned to our B&B. More individual study followed until around 2000 when we piled into my car and went to our adopted pub in Shepperton. There, we sat round a table, drank our beer and hammered each other with questions, trick questions and more questions.

Eventually, when we had exhausted the day's subjects we wished to pursue we played darts. When we left the pub, I was happy that I more or less knew everything I needed to know from that day's lectures. I should have slept well but my landlady used nylon sheets. Ugh! I never had the gumption to provide my own.

There is little more to say about the course as it was a constant repetition of the foregoing. The exams at the end were pretty straightforward after the good instruction and the sheer hard work we put in, except of course for Jim Baldwin who had one of those infernal photographic memories. We all had lengthy notebooks, manuals with yellow highlighting and sleepless nights. His notebook fitted a top pocket and I guess he slept like a baby.

During the course our respective crews came together; my co-pilot was none other than my instructor at Middleton St George, Les Baker, my navigator was Eric Robertshaw and my engineer was Tony Boxall.

In late April 1967 we started our ground school and flying course with the 10 Squadron VC10 Air Training Squadron at Brize Norton. We did five two-hour flights and then we went 'solo', doing circuits and let-downs. Our instructors were Alfie Musgrove, who had flown HM The Queen on a few occasions, Bill Somers whose favourite words were 'Let's have a cup of tea', Andy Liddell, a New Zealander, Dave Ray and Jim Loveridge whose claim to fame was that he had reversed a Blackburn Beverley into its parking bay and had applied brakes too eagerly and it sat on its tail. The Beverley was a transport aircraft which looked like a massive box with a long tail poking out of the top. They were a great bunch of guys and life was good.

We did two or three more trips around the area and then, with Alfie Musgrove in the observer's seat, we set off on our first route trainer. I had requested Bob Brown, my ops assistant from Nairobi, to join my crew when I found he was also in 10 Squadron. My senior AQM (Air Quartermaster) was Don Martin, a Devonian with an unfathomable accent, so Bob became my translator.

At this time, Brize Norton was being overhauled and runway and other work being carried out. So, for quite a while the VC10s were based at Brize but being flown to Lyneham to collect passengers and to use its longer available runway for heavier take offs.

So, our flight started at Lyneham and went Akrotiri, Muharraq, Gan, Tengah, Hong Kong and return. The other crew on the flight was the one and only John Redding and his crew. It was a very happy ten days because we were all doing what we wanted, to fly, we were at the beginning of a new squadron's phase, flying a great aircraft and in good company.

The arrival in Hong Kong was particularly interesting as nobody is permitted to operate there until you have actually seen the approach from the flight deck. I was lucky as I was flying with Alfie in the right-hand seat, so this was my way of 'seeing it'.

However, for all the others to see it they had to be on the flight deck which only had five seats, four for the crew and one for the supernumerary crew member, instructor or whoever. Anyway, when I did the approach and landing into HKG there were fourteen on the flight deck. This was technically against the rules as there were only seats for five, but what the hell!

Hong Kong was a fun airfield for pilots because normally you do your damnedest to keep your passengers happy and do nothing to alarm them. But HKG Kai Tak was different. In those days you let down in a figure-eight-type of holding pattern over Green Island. At 1,000 feet you set off for the edge of Stonecutters Island heading for Lion Rock. Then you found a hill with a black-and-yellow-chequered board on it (the board was probably 100 feet by 100 feet) and aimed for it. As you got nearer you would see lights forming a curve slowly to the right of the board. You followed these and they led you to a runway which stretched out into the sea. You would normally only see this runway after you had finished counting the pegs on the rooftop washing lines. The runway would come into view through your right-hand windows at about 300 feet.

Having turned left off the runway you would taxi to an extraordinary large parking area. I bet that there are many readers who would be surprised to learn that this area was once the entire airfield with the runway being west to east straight at the hills/mountains, the base of which was just after the boundary.

This trip confirmed my belief that John was a great captain and companion but gave me an insight into his competitiveness. He was a mean player at Liar Dice. Unfortunately I would, perhaps, pass three aces to my right and it would progress to, perhaps, four aces or a full house to John who might then pass to me a better call. Muggins would accept and find that John had thrown, say two of the aces, and the hand was now worse than it left me. This just occasionally caused me to be seriously miffed because it seemed to me he did not do this to others. He just remained Sphinxlike.

John invented and, I believe, fitted to his own car, wiper interrupters such as we all have nowadays, i.e. on/off every few seconds. I bet he wished he'd patented it.

We returned to Brize on 3 September 1967 and on the 13th John and I set off with our crews and did exactly the same again but 'solo', i.e. without

Alfie. The taxpayers' money really stretched a long way in those days. Upon our return we both did two flights, several hours in the simulator and that dreadful day in a room being bombarded with questions and finally received our C Categories on the 27th.

We were released to the Squadron.

No. 10 Squadron had traditionally been a bomber squadron, having been formed on 1 January 1915 and disbanded in 1919. Then they reformed and disbanded two or three more times. It had a short period in Transport Command for four years up to and including the Berlin Airlift. The squadron returned to bombers with Canberras and then Victors until March 1964. The motto from bomber days was 'Rem Acu Tangere' – 'To Hit the Mark'.

In July 1966 it reformed, this time with the Vickers VC10 C.1, a purpose-built variant of the civil standard VC10. The C.1 (Cargo) had the wings and more powerful Rolls Royce Conway engines of the Super VC10, and also had fuel in its fin. As it was planned for the carriage of heavy military freight, there was a much stronger floor fitted and access via an upward-opening large freight door on the left forward side of the aircraft. Initially they were fitted with in-flight refueling probes but these were removed in late 1967.

RAF VC10:
Powered by 4 RR Conway Mk 301 axial-flow by-pass engines.
Wingspan   44.55 metres.   146 feet 2 inches
Length   48.36 metres.   158 feet 8 inches
Height   12.04 metres.   39 feet 6 inches
Max. weight 151,900 kilograms 334,876 lb.
Fuel capacity 19,355 gallons 70,222 kilograms, approx.
Max. speed 518 knots or Mach 0.9

Initially Vickers decided it needed to sell over seventy VC10s to break even, but only had an order for twenty-five from BOAC, so they needed many more sales. At the time only two or three orders were made for just a few aircraft by other companies.

The major airlines interested, but not yet ordering, came from China, Argentina, Mexico, MEA and Qantas. However, BOAC were dithering and showing a greater interest in the B707. Sadly, they changed orders and the new chairman, Sir Giles Guthrie, made it clear he preferred the 707. All of this lack of support for the British Aircraft industry was noted overseas and few orders were made. BOAC, with the support of the government, seems to me to have put the nail in the coffin of the British aviation industry.

Many years later I was browsing the BA technical magazine and, in the bottom right-hand corner of a left-hand page was a two-inch entry. It simply stated that over a ten-year period the VC10 had been cheaper to run than the B707.

In 1969 one of our VC10s was based elsewhere for Rolls Royce to use as a test-bed for their new RB211 engine which was to eventually power the L-1011 TriStar. It occasionally came to Brize and looked really odd with this large engine on the left side and the two smaller ones on the right. It just showed what could have become of the VC10 if it had had a better welcome into the aviation world. Two RB211s and a stretched body for a greater number of passengers etc.. Who knows?

The squadron offices were all alone on the southside of the airfield about halfway along the runway. Access was via a gate to the south or normal entry to the camp and then crossing the runway via traffic lights. It was a bit of a bind really.

However, a bigger bind was just behind the offices. There was parked a now-retired Comet 2 being used for fire-training. Within a very short time it was a pitiful sight and we old 216 men were so sad to see such an ugly demise.

Our new squadron commander was Wing Commander Michael Beavis. He had served mostly in Bomber Command and had set the record for the fastest non-stop flight from the UK to Australia in 1961 in just over twenty hours.

The VC10 being the newest, most beautiful and fastest aircraft in Transport Command (very soon to be changed to Air Support Command), meant we were known as the 'Shinies'. This was said, I think, with a bit of envy and some irritation. We were certainly the equivalent of the teacher's pet. (The same nickname was applied to the Army's 10th Hussars who had been dubbed the Shiny Tenth at some stage in their history. It's believed that their elaborate crossbelts led to the name 'Chainy Tenth' which was corrupted to shiny.)

There were many innovations on the VC10 but, perhaps, the most effective were the flight controls. There were two ailerons on each wing, two elevators on each tail-plane (left and right) and three separate rudder panels.

Each wing control or tail-plane had a master and a slave, the master being driven mechanically or by electrical signals from the autopilot. The signal causes an individual hydraulic system to move the control and the slave follows. If the hydraulic ram fails on the master then the other, the slave, just operates manually. This applies to the two bottom panels of the rudder. The upper panel receives mechanical only.

This system meant that, unlike conventional designs, if there were hydraulic system failures or malfunctions then the flight controls, being independent, were unaffected.

It also had a device called the Electrical Ram Air Turbine (ELRAT or, as Bill Somers called it, 'The Spanish Rodent') which, when selected, would extend from the underside of the aircraft. It comprised a propeller which, driven by the airflow through it, would supply essential electrics in the event of loss through faults or engine failures.

The performance was impressive for its time: maximum speed 337 knots, at sea level; close to 150 tonnes maximum weight with 70,222 kilograms of fuel available. Maximum operating height was 43,000 feet, limited only by the oxygen equipment available to the passengers.

The interior could be changed very quickly from just passengers to just freight or to pax-cum-freight. The huge side-loading door aperture (13 ft 8 in x 7 ft) enabled much military freight to be carried.

With two engines close to each other either side of the tail it meant a quieter cabin and, in the event of an engine failure or shut down, there was little or no effect if you compared it to the loss of an engine under the wing, i.e. Boeing 707.

As the engines were out of sight from the flight deck and not particularly easy to observe from the cabin there was access at the rear end for a magnifying periscope that enabled the observer to look closely at the engine air-intake guide vanes, intake area and cowlings.

On one occasion out of Hong Kong we hit a flock of birds just on lift off. There were a few thuds at the front and we were immediately interested in the engines. They performed without a problem. However, Tony went back to have a look and saw that some of the engine intake guide vanes had a long leg and foot jammed across them. The engine had eaten the bird without a problem. As the flight continued so the rest of us went back for a look; it had disappeared by the time we shut down in Gan.

In common with all passenger transport aircraft in the RAF, the VC10 was equipped with rear-facing seats. Sometimes for a VIP layout there might be a table with seats fore and aft facing.

The RAF transport squadrons have an enviable safety record for passengers; I'm not talking of combat or military operations but just routine A to B flights. The rear-facing seats have contributed to that record. One occasion the seats saved lives was when a Britannia went off the end of the runway at Khormaksar and came to an abrupt stop. There were three injuries; the two pilots hit their heads on the rubber-fronted glare shield and one passenger, who instead of waiting and obeying crew orders, opened a door and jumped out. As the escape chute was not automatic on that door he hit soft ground and stuck there. Before the crew could stop them, two or three other passengers jumped out also and landed on the first jumper. He was the only injured passenger with a broken collar-bone, caused by another landing on him.

I compare this incident to another of many years ago. I think it was in the 1950s that a DC-6 or similar aircraft ended up in some sort of car or equipment park and also came to a very sudden stop. The aircraft caught fire but some passengers managed to escape; there were many in there with broken legs and who died, which may have been avoided with rear-facing seats.

My first flight after receiving my Cat C was to Singapore, RAF Changi, via the usual route. The first sector was to Muharraq with my flight commander Squadron Leader Taylor as a squadron acceptance check ride, then we were on our own and finally carrying passengers. This trip was normally for eight to nine days.

On the 3 November 1967 I was in Gan en route to Changi. We had a pregnant lady flying on her last permitted day, i.e. I think thirty days to due date, who was in considerable discomfort. The Gan doctor agreed that she could continue but was to be given a whole row of seats to herself, thus enabling her to move around as she wished or to lie down.

The two vacant seats were because two airmen had been posted to Gan. A flight sergeant medic had been allocated one of the seats to go to Singapore for his son's wedding and in view of the urgency he agreed to travel by Shackleton, the four piston-engine maritime patrol aircraft, even though it would take much, much longer. The Shackleton crew and my crew were in the ops-planning room together and they got airborne just before us.

That evening in the bar/restaurant of the officers' club in Changi a senior officer called for our attention; he advised us that the Shackleton was missing and overdue. There was much dismay all round the large number of officers and wives, as some of them knew some of the crew members. My crew and I were stunned and I felt that irrational guilt people feel when 'what if?' comes into the mind.

Sadly, there were only three survivors, including the medic. The other two were the flight engineer and one of the signallers. The aircraft had an engine fire, which presumably engulfed the aircraft; whether it crashed or was destroyed during ditching, I don't know.

Interestingly, I heard that the engineer survived through the care of the medic and then later I heard the reverse. However, the engineer joined Virgin Atlantic whilst I was on the 747 but, sadly, I never got to meet him, otherwise I would now know who saved whom.

That month I had two such trips and the second coincided with Britain's withdrawal from Aden, earlier than planned but the NLF (National Liberation Front) had become too difficult to control despite the fighter squadrons and the army, especially the famous Argyll and Sutherland Highlanders led by the great Lieutenant Colonel C.C. (Mad Mitch) Mitchell.

Some of his soldiers had been killed in an area close to their HQ and Mitchell decided to go in and retrieve their bodies. Harold Wilson ordered him not to, but being a fighting man of honour, who would always put his men first he ignored the Prime Minister in a magnificent manner. He marched the men to the area, with pipes playing and flags waving. Not only did they achieve their objective but they saw not one brave enemy. What a man – what a regiment and what a bad loser Wilson was. Mitch was sacked. He became an MP but didn't last too long: too honourable, I guess! The Argylls were disbanded, although the Heath government rescinded Wilson's order and the regiment was saved, only to go under Cameron.

Anyway, since Aden was busy getting men and equipment back to UK they were using all reasonable military facilities including Muharraq. This meant that my flight was re-scheduled via Tehran. We studied the arrival charts assiduously as we had never been there before and it was seriously hilly and mountainous terrain. We arrived at night and in bad weather such that we did not see the runway through the rain until we were below 1,000 feet. The let-down procedure included the use of two or three beacons on the mountains or in the valleys.

The drive into the hotel was a nightmare; we were in a VW Combi and I was in the front. My knees were inches from the thin metal bodywork and all the cars beyond (the engine was mid-mounted). Every set of traffic-lights had its own personal traffic jam as the Iranians regarded all red lights as a challenge. Apart from Lagos, Nigeria, in 1973 I have never seen worse driving. We squeezed in at the back for the return trip as no one would sit in the front.

The morning after our arrival I opened the shutters of my room and went on to the little balcony. Thank goodness for the high railings as I could have fallen when I saw the view. I gazed, or gawped, in awe at the terrain around me as I thought 'Did we really let-down and around that lot?'

That night a few of us went to a night club of some good reputation for its vodka and its belly-dancing. They were both really excellent and of good taste. A truly artistic rendering of the dance is quite amazing. This was of course before the Shah was deposed.

When we returned to the hotel the driver did not think properly as he went past the ramp and parked next to a deep trench. I got out of the side nearest the trench and ended up in the bottom with a sprained ankle which swelled immediately and impressively.

I contacted Command HQ who said they would immediately send a replacement by civilian aircraft. The next day it subsided and, as I knew the departure would be delayed as the new captain would not be permitted to continue without official time off, I thought about it and realised I would be fit to fly. My message arrived just in time to catch Mike Hempstead as he was crossing the terminal at Heathrow for his BOAC flight. He was not pleased.

At this time I was still doing all the landings, so Les, my co-pilot, must have been getting fed up. The RAF rule for captains on a new type was for him to reach 100 hours without incident before allocating landings. Considering my transport and instructing experience it seemed quite unnecessary. I believe the rules became more flexible later on. They certainly are in civil aviation.

The crew plus another were sent to RAF North Luffenham, in Rutland, for Hypoxia training. All RAF high-altitude crews do this in their early career but refreshers are not unusual.

What happens is that you enter a compression/decompression tank and air is evacuated until the pressure and oxygen levels equal 30,000 feet or more. You are accompanied by a technician and an aviator doctor. In turn you start writing on a knee pad and then the oxygen is turned off to your mask and you continue writing. It takes only a few seconds for you to lose consciousness and then the oxygen is returned. The pad on which you have been writing shows clearly and progressively the period of diminished ability due to lack of oxygen.

Having completed this exercise, you return to ground level, i.e. pressure increased to about 14.7 psi and then, in a space of a few seconds the tank is sent up to 45,000 feet. If you survive you pass!

In January 1968 we did our first Hong Kong, where we stayed at the Park Hotel in Kowloon. Whilst waiting for Bob or Don to sort out the room allocation – they always took on that task – I noticed a small and elderly Chinese couple walk across to the lavatories where the gentleman entered whilst his wife waited outside. To this day I would like to know what happened in there as he had no arms from the elbow down.

NO. 10 SQUADRON, RAF BRIZE NORTON, VC10

It was on that trip we had the bird-strike I mentioned earlier.

Later in the month we had a flight to Gander and return as part of an army deployment exercise. On arrival at Gander we found the weather quite frightful with snow and very low temperatures, but not bad enough to create a problem for approach. However, there were strong winds, the runway was 90 per cent covered in ice with high snowbanks from runway clearance down each side. A departing aircraft pointed out that it was quite unpleasant. Oh dear, decision time! I decided to divert to Stephenville on the west coast of the island which had better conditions. However, upon arrival there, conditions had deteriorated to the extent that there was a snowstorm, low cloud-base and poor visibility. The approach was fine until we saw the runway and found that there was a white wall leading up from ground below to the runway lip and that, combined with a heavy snowfall, made for a white-out. Fortunately, all was well and we landed normally but it was my first experience of this phenomenon. The return to Gander without passengers and a much lower weight made the landing more practicable.

On 20 February, upon arriving at Muharraq, I was talking in the ops-room to Wing Commander Basil Locke, my wing commander flying at Leeming, and to Squadron Leader Malcolm Middlemist, a navigator from my days at 216 Squadron. I was handed a signal to congratulate me on promotion to Acting Squadron Leader. I could not understand why and said to Malcolm that I would stop calling him 'Sir' now.

On our return to Brize Norton I found that all VC10 and Comet captains had received the promotion. The idea bandied about from above was to give the captains more power over their affairs down route, and to reflect their responsibilities. This, to me, was a weak and weird argument as the RAF treated its captains with great respect and rank never seemed to come into it. At first, I enjoyed the privilege but it did not take long to realise that it was an unfair situation. All the captains on Britannias and Belfasts, many of whom had also passed their promotion exams and had greater experience and/or more hours, were being by-passed in favour of the 'Shiny Fleet'.

Worst of all, now being senior officers and wearing the extra stripe, all the flight lieutenants of the other squadrons were to salute us as per rules of rank. This was a bitter pill for them and, when regarding their demeanour and expressions, it was obvious that there existed mild contempt. Some just did not bother to salute so what are you to do if he's your friend? It was usually only when other ranks could see the failure to salute that they had to be corrected; but it hurt.

I decided that I wanted none of this but I felt if I made my feelings known to the wrong people I could be in trouble and in a ground job. So I went to see Ron who was a captain, and still a flight lieutenant, on the Belfast squadron. I asked if it was worth seeing his CO to request a transfer to Belfasts or what did he feel were my options. He was as angry as everyone else but he told me that whatever I did would just bring down a ton of bricks on my head. He said to think of my career and my family and to live with it.

In the end my principles, obviously not as strong as I wished them to be, were subjugated to getting on with it. I know I was not alone in these feelings but it was rarely talked about. I grew into the role but never felt superior to those who had not received this privilege. I cannot say that I noticed anything special from a captaincy point of view, before or after the 'promotion'.

The Britannias carried pretty much the same numbers of passengers, families or troops as we did. The Belfast could carry many troops and/ or heavy equipment and the Hercules carried out similar roles to the Belfast but, in addition, many low-level operations and 'special' operations involving much risk, especially, and usually, at night. The foregoing all had heavy responsibilities too. It was not unusual to be asked if you were a squadron leader or a VC10 captain!

On the next flight to Singapore I took what I believe was the only unsafe action in my time as captain; others may disagree that it was the only one. It was between Gan and Singapore and there was a long line of cumulonimbus and towering cumulus across our track, extending much too far for us to deviate round them. I noticed, however, that ahead of us and above, the cloud tops were lower than the rest and well defined.

I chose to climb over the clouds by climbing to our next permitted level agreed by ATC. This did not deviate from our safe flight envelope under normal conditions but was in the upper reaches and was not ideal in turbulence. In the event, we traversed the weather without a ripple but I have never forgotten that it was unwise and I certainly have never considered it again.

Had the conditions been at night it would not have been a problem as the lightning would have clearly shown the best route. This was very evident on the route Changi-Gan as we flew across Sumatra and over their west coast. At night the cumulonimbus clouds were well up to 45,000 feet and a chain as far as the eye could see. Furthermore, the aircraft radar, nothing like the later models, was just a sea of fuzzy white.

However, there was so much lightning activity that the gaps were firmly shown. I can honestly say that, frightening as it is to behold, we were always able to traverse the weather with considerable ease and little turbulence. One night we went through the cloud, not the actual cumulonimbus, into the usual clear sky except, on this occasion, there was a ginormous cumulonimbus sitting dead ahead at ten miles just waiting for us. We turned away and passed on its upwind side, safest normally, and carried on. It had not shown on the radar as the screen had been swamped throughout the passage. This phenomenon is called attenuation.

Arriving at Singapore, RAF Changi, one night I was advised when I was some fifteen miles out that I could continue approach, but I was No. 2 to another aircraft. I acknowledged and continued approach, searching with the eyeball Mark 1 but to no avail. At around five miles I asked how things were and if I was cleared to land? The reply was negative as the other aircraft was just approaching its final approach. Then we saw it. It was a Bristol Freighter just dead ahead of us about to finish its turn onto final approach. No wonder we hadn't seen it as its lights would have hardly been seen to be moving with the background of the town plus its ridiculously slow speed.

This aircraft was doing barely 90 knots and we were doing 150 knots. Fortunately, we saw him in time and did a go-around. This was ATC at its worst and I said so when I went up to the tower for that specific purpose. My new-found status didn't help much as he was the same rank.

Regularly there were departures from Changi as casevacs, i.e. *cas*ualty *evac*uation. Stretchers would be laid out at the front of the cabin and walking-sick or wounded would be in the first rows as required. The rest of the seats would be curtained off for the privacy of the patients and the nurses. The nurses, as ever, were a great bunch and did their work admirably. Sometimes the nurses, all officers, would be from the RAF Hospital Changi or nurses from the UK flown out especially.

Each patient, just before departure, would receive a goodies bag, they called it a *ditty* bag but I don't know why. It would contain a book, some chocolate or chewing gum, a magazine or whatever. I used to complain that I never received one, so eventually they surprised me. Mine contained a Snoopy/Charlie Brown book (they knew I loved them), a Kit-Kat and a card hoping I would get better soon.

We also did casevacs from Muharraq, many of which carried soldiers injured in Dhofar in Oman. Containing the rebellion there involved British forces on the ground and in the air. The explorer and ex-SAS man, Sir Ranulph Fiennes, was casevac'd by 10 Squadron. I doubt that he had a *ditty* bag though!

Although Muharraq was a major RAF base, and had many men accompanied by their families, there were too many for the accommodation

195

available. So, like Gan, there were many unaccompanied serving officers and other ranks. The unaccompanied personnel would arrive at Muharraq on the weekly scheduled round trip. The return flight was known as the 'Moonie' trip as all the passengers were mooning over seeing wives and/or girlfriends after a year away.

There was a company in Bahrain called Ross who caught, topped, cleaned and deep-froze large prawns. In those days eggs were not fresh but treated in some way and tasted rather unpleasant. So, 10 Squadron and, for all I know, other squadrons had a nice little 'earner'. We would take a crate or two of eggs, thirty-six dozen per crate, and exchange them for a large number of prawns.

This went well until a new AQM on the squadron heard of it and decided that she would like to get in on the deal. She telephoned the company and asked to speak to the person(s) who had traded eggs for prawns. Unfortunately, all company offices in Bahrain have their own individual number. She phoned the one at the top of the list and got the managing director. He was not daft. He asked her to explain what she meant and, of course, put an immediate stop to it. I know nothing of the internal discipline that followed but, as she had been unable to give any names, I guess the employees got away with it.

When we acquired the prawns we would keep them in the freezers at The Bristol Hotel which was actually the RAF transit accommodation for crews. Upon departure we would collect them and keep them in boxes of dry ice or in the aircraft freezer compartments. One night during the take-off run we went through the usual calls; 'V1' to indicate the point at which you must decide to go or stop, 'VR' the point at which you rotate the aircraft to get airborne and 'V2' which means you have reached the speed at which, if you lose an engine, you can continue to climb away. However, on this night the calls went: V1, VR, s—t we've forgotten the prawns!, V2. The prawns were not just for personal consumption or for friends but, like the others, I had a deal with a hotel which was most satisfactory, thank you!

The Bristol afforded me many interesting memories: I had not been in the UK to watch Neil Armstrong walk on the moon but I was up in the crew lounge one morning and put the old, rubbishy TV on and there, a month after the event, I watched it all alone.

I was on the roof one morning fearful of venturing outside as it was the day Bahrain changed from driving on the left to the right. Sure enough, it was funny and interesting. We all know how it is best if our driving seat is correct for the side of the road on which you have to drive. Well, they were having the same problems. However, I saw no crashes, just a lot of Keystone Cops incidents.

NO. 10 SQUADRON, RAF BRIZE NORTON, VC10

The drive from RAF Muharraq, which was an island at the upper north-eastern end of Bahrain, was joined by a long causeway to the main island. In my early Comet days this Sheikh Hamad causeway was easily between a half and three-quarters of a mile long with sea on the north side and on the south side sea and businesses on the left. In the height of the incredibly hot months, April to October, it was normal to see the small parapets about two-feet high, full of sleeping men. Here and there they were practically heads to feet; I never heard of anyone rolling in.

Today the causeway is basically just a main road, having only a small stretch with sea alongside it. There has been massive reclamation of land; even the old sailing club is now a few hundred yards inland.

One of my landings at Muharraq left a lot to be desired, viz., it was awfully hard. All pilots occasionally manage to do a bad landing, usually only once or twice a year. As we taxied in, the co-pilot complained that the passengers probably thought he did it as captains couldn't possibly be that bad. So, I went onto the passenger address and said that I had a whinging co-pilot up front as he thought you would blame him. I apologised and said I was the offender.

The RAF always off-loaded passengers whilst refuelling was in progress and took them to a transit lounge where there were snacks and a bar. The crew had to go through this area and would stop for a beer before going to the hotel. Well, when we arrived the passengers, much to my already embarrassed person, gave me a rousing cheer and a few ribald comments. Yes, it was a bad landing, difficult to do in a VC10 I might say, but there's the old pilot's adage that 'A good landing is one you can walk away from and a very good landing is when you can use the aircraft again.' By that definition I had, therefore, done a good landing.

In October 1968 I was given a States trainer (USA training flight) with Mike Hempstead's crew and Robin Howden, a flight commander, and instructor and observer. What I particularly liked was that I was to plan the itinerary. There were to be ten sectors, so I gave myself five, Mike four and Robin one. The route was over six days and went Brize-JFK-Boston-Chicago-JFK-Boston-Chicago-McLellan AFB (near San Francisco)-San Francisco-Toronto-Brize. Mike and I each had a JFK, Boston and Chicago, I had the McLellan and San Francisco and Mike had the Toronto-Brize.

I thought it would be a nice gesture to give Robin the San Francisco-Toronto sector to win myself some brownie points but actually the planning had an ulterior motive. My father's youngest sister, Rose, had emigrated to Canada years before and she lived in Toronto. Thus the schedule allowed me to visit her and have a good time without having to operate the next day.

By this time the crew system had fallen slightly by the wayside but I still managed to fly most of the time with my new navigator, Barry Wildin, and new engineer, 'Monty' Montague. The flying went well and there was little out of the ordinary to report, but the evenings were definitely planned and different. We decided that we would concentrate on visiting all the 'Your Father's Moustache' pubs we could. We were all just beer drinkers so it fitted us well. However, San Francisco did not have a 'YFM' but a bar called the 'Red Rose' (I think) had exactly the same system, so that was four consecutive nights of raucous singing and a little bit of beer drinking.

In the morning when Robin came to do the leg to Toronto his voice was virtually gone. We were all smokers or, if not, all subject to the atmosphere in the bars of those days. Robin was flying with Mike's crew and he just flew and the co-pilot decided what Robin might have wanted to say and radioed accordingly.

Why did we go via McLellan AFB you may be asking? Well, the VC10 crew and passenger oxygen was via LOX (Liquid Oxygen) cylinders. The LOX needed topping up at regular intervals and, although they would have been okay for this trip we went into there for a top-up. If we could get away with it we always popped in here as it had one of the best Base Exchanges in the USAF. They are the huge shopping complexes which are normal for American servicemen; there you can buy almost anything for almost nothing.

There were three on the crews of this trip with relatives in Toronto, so when we got off the crew bus and up into the terminal we were surprised to see virtually no one around. I went to the nearest desk with a member of staff and asked her to send a PA to our greeters and tell them where we were. Almost immediately there was a thundering noise from many footsteps echoing around the near deserted area and around the corner appeared about thirty people. It was a joyous meeting and a great evening.

I slept well on the aircraft next day all the way to Brize. Well planned, I say!

Before my next trip we had the VC10 naming ceremony; it had been decided that all fourteen VC10s would be named after RAF VC holders. It was further decided that only those who were no longer with us would be thus honoured. The ceremony was set for 11 November 1968.

Well before that all the relatives of those to be named were sought and invited to the ceremony. I was given the duty of caring for Mrs Kitty Hair, the sister of Arthur Scarfe VC, and her nephew. The ceremony was most moving for the guests and each main representative was given a plaque commemorating the occasion. Mrs Hair wrote me a lovely letter and advised me that, because I had been so kind to them and shown them around the aircraft, her nephew was now determined to be a pilot.

In February 1969 on the way home from our trip we were due to fly Akrotiri to Brize but the weather was bad with thick fog over England. I delayed the flight for an hour or so to plan arrival when the weather was forecast to improve enough for an attempt and added fuel for the possible diversion to Prestwick in Scotland. Whilst waiting in the departure lounge with the passengers, as was the system in the RAF, I heard one lady who was looking out at the lovely weather in Cyprus say, 'I don't understand it at all, the weather looks okay to me.'

Anyway, we got airborne and when we arrived at London control we found that Brize was socked in and Lyneham might be worth a try. I followed a C-130 Hercules on the approach to Lyneham but, when I saw him pop up out of the fog, I realised that if he couldn't get in at his slower speed and more aggressive attitude to limits then I certainly wouldn't make it. Anyway, he reported that he had seen nothing.

We duly diverted to Prestwick and when we arrived they were in the throes of a moderate snowstorm. I was comfortable for fuel so although the visibility was within limits but cloud-base indeterminable I thought it was worth a look. In fact, we saw the runway at a good height and distance but our main problem was a 40-knot wind which was about 60 degrees to the runway. The touchdown was okay but the landing run was eerie. It was the first time I had seen snow or sand blowing across the runway at such a speed and angle. It gave a very strong impression of skidding and, although we knew we weren't, it was all I could do not to take corrective action. Subsequently, I experienced this many times, particularly with sand, but that was the worst to date.

At the end of November we had the annual exercise whereby Transport Command practised their return from the Far East via America back to the UK. This was a contingency plan in case routes via the Middle or Near East became untenable. Unfortunately, I started the exercise by flying via the USA as a passenger in a Britannia. For two reasons this was a drag; firstly, it was slower than the VC10 and we went straight to Changi with only refuelling stops, and secondly, I could hardly get a wink of sleep on this trip.

We had twenty-four hours in Changi before we had to be airborne for Anderson AFB on Guam in the Mariana Islands. As we got airborne one of our doors moved slightly and jammed, which meant no damage to the aircraft but no pressurisation. We dumped a few tons of fuel into the South China Sea and landed back at Changi. There were no parts available for the repair so the engineering department set about making one. Meanwhile, I went to the medical centre and explained that I had not slept for three days; I was due to fly at midnight that night and please could I have a pill that would knock me out. He gave me just one and said I was to take it with water whilst sitting in the bed. It knocked me out; the time was 1300. Bliss. At 1500 hours Don Martin woke me up and said the flight was delayed to 1000 the next day, so to come and join them for a drink. I demurred but, after an hour of total wakefulness, I gave up and joined them. Next morning after a fruitful rest we got on our way via Guam, Honolulu, Omaha-Brize. Man, I was tired.

One week later I did a trip to Rome and Manchester for which reason I have no idea, but then off to Changi on our normal slip service arriving on the morning of Christmas Eve. The RAF always sent an aircraft along our normal routes and collected crews and sundry other pilots from other commands to get them home for Christmas and then, on Boxing Day, fly people back to man the various aircraft abandoned along the way. It was all very civilised and considerate.

So, I dutifully climbed aboard the VC10 doing the clean up and flew as passenger to Brize where the traditional barrel(s) was laid on to welcome us home on Christmas morning. I had two beers. I had now been around the world twice in opposite directions in four weeks. I had had an incredibly bad period of poor sleeping, poor sleeping patterns, too much passengering and I was utterly fatigued.

After greetings at home, present opening, etc., we, Maureen, Andrew, Nicholas and I sat down for Christmas lunch. At 1700 I woke up with my face in a plate of cheese and biscuits, the table cleared and everyone watching the TV. Apparently, in the middle of saying something, I had fallen asleep and just ended up flat out. It was nearly two weeks before I felt even half normal which meant still very tired.

To add to my woes a policeman was waiting for me as I left the hairdressers after a long overdue haircut. My car tax had expired in my absence and I hadn't realised it. I think the fine was £10. But that was pretty high then.

At this time, I was driving the Ford Cortina 2000E, which was not bad performance-wise and some motor correspondents reckoned its gearbox was only beaten by the Porsche. It was certainly smooth to use. Prior to that I had a Vauxhall VX4/90, which had tremendous performance for the time.

Nicholas loved the Ford so when I changed it for a Jaguar 3.4 (think Inspector Morse) he was pretty upset. However, when we visited Maureen's parents in Lancashire immediately after the purchase we had much trouble.

It failed to start next morning, it was running hot and I found water in the oil. A call to the garage where I bought it did not give me any confidence regarding assistance; rules for the buying public were not so strong in the 1960s. I called my solicitor friend who resolved the problem and on my return to Wantage exchanged the Jag for my Ford. The Ford was showroom spotless and Nick was delighted.

As I said earlier the VC10's oxygen system was to use liquid oxygen (LOX) converted to gas when needed. Unfortunately, the contents slowly decreased over a fairly short period of time and required replenishing fairly often. This was no problem as more or less all of our bases and other destinations stored it. However, it caused me a real problem at USN (United States Navy Base) Patuxent River in Maryland. I arrived on Wednesday 16 July 1969. I confirmed that they had LOX and, upon my arrival late afternoon, requested a top-up as, for some reason, the contents had dropped below permitted levels.

I was advised that this was no problem but would be done in the morning before departure, so we set off for our hotel. Much to our dismay the booking had not specified separate rooms or, at least, twin beds, and the male members of the crew were expected to share a bed. Apparently, this was not unusual in the US of A but to us it certainly was. All was eventually resolved and we settled in.

Sadly, the 16th and 17th was a weekend and on Sunday morning nobody could find a qualified LOX handler. All morning I was having to chase around, chase the ground crews and generally get annoyed. People assured me things were being done but I found that they had done nothing. The inefficiency was appalling. I worked my way to the highest rank who was the duty officer and, I think, a lieutenant and still no success.

Eventually, I dared to phone the Commanding Officer and then things got moving. Meanwhile, our passengers, all Coastal Command Shackleton crews, were giving us a hard time. In particular, they were being pretty uncomplimentary about 10 Squadron. It was all embarrassing and frustrating.

We were about five hours late in departing for RAF Ballykelly, Northern Ireland, and just to add to the woes of our passengers I managed a bad landing as I touched down late enough to cross the railway lines at a high speed. Yes, an operational railway line crossed the main runway, apparently the only such one in the UK.

Survival Officer

A few days after the Patuxent debacle I went to RAF Mountbatten in Plymouth Sound to start No. 157 Combat Survival and Rescue Officers' (CSRO) Course. The course, of nearly three weeks, started with lectures and demonstrations of sea, desert, mountain and jungle survival, and ways of escaping detection from the enemy but to be found by our rescuers.

The sea was the only realistic practical opportunity as it was right on our doorstop so to speak. We were all, about sixteen of us, taken out to the area out to sea and dumped from our lovely launch into single-seat dinghies. Every movement of the sea is felt through the very flexible nature of the dinghy and, although I felt queasy, I managed not to be sick. Slowly, in the way of wind and sea, we drifted apart. It was not helped that two air sea rescue (ASR) launches kept charging past us, and amongst us, churning the sea with their bow waves and wake. We were there all morning. At some time, there was a real fright as a submarine surfaced nearby looking very much like a serious predator. We were all glad to be back on dry land.

On the second Monday we were briefed for our five-day survival exercise on the moors which we knew would end up with us being hunted by the SAS. If caught, we would go through interrogation by professionals. At the end of the briefing a squadron leader came into the briefing and said, 'You must all look at me and remember my face, remember me.' The reason was that it was quite possible that due to sleeplessness and disorientation during interrogation we would distrust everybody. Him, we could trust.

The second Tuesday we were all given one day's rations, water-purifying tablets, a normal RAF survival knife and a serviceable, but out of date, parachute and taken by bus into the moors far away from civilisation. Firstly, we learned to make ourselves safe from the weather using natural sources, plus cutting and shaping our parachute for cover and bedding. Who should come but the 'Look at Life' team to make a film about the course. I was getting to be quite the film star. In fact, I went into a shop in Singapore a few weeks later and the little Chinese proprietor said, 'You film star!' He had seen the film and I could not convince him that it was a documentary.

I set a makeshift trap for fish in the river nearby and was astonished to find one waiting to serve as my breakfast in the morning. From now on food was to be foraged or forgotten.

The first day, Wednesday, was constant trekking, map-reading, purifying water and generally playing at survivors. Unknown to us at the time, this was the precursor to making us very tired by hard work and no sleep. Each night and day was occupied with keeping us awake.

Thursday, we were told to disperse and later to meet at a fixed point and we were to hide. The SAS would hunt for us, but we would then be released to get to the rendezvous; the nasty stuff would be the next day.

My hiding place was quite ingenious, I thought. I found an old tree with a large, narrow crack at the bottom which I could just squeeze through. However, my legs would have to poke out. So, I went around the area cutting ferns to different lengths and then backed into the tree 'planting' them as I went. It worked brilliantly as I saw two pairs of searchers twenty feet away who didn't see me and I managed a lovely nap. The ferns had wilted somewhat by the time I left!

Friday evening, we set off in twos to find an RV some distance away. However, now the SAS were after us. I was paired with 'Jumbo' Cowan, so called because he was somewhat larger than many. Regrettably, this slowed him down but not such to affect our demise. Before capture I had a terrible fright; I was feeling ahead with the long pole I had cut earlier, the fog was dense such that navigation was by just compass and listening for flowing water. Visibility was fifty metres at best had it been daylight.

Anyway, I felt ahead with the pole and my body angle, plus the 30-kilo pack, made me nearly fall forward. I had found one of the famous Dartmoor bogs. Had I fallen forward the SAS would never have found me. Later on, they appeared suddenly and set chase; the visibility was slightly better at this place but I still managed to run into some animal, a cow I think. It was night time and I guess it blended in. I continued to run and tried to crash through a hedgerow unsuccessfully. I heard the rumpus with Jumbo, so I kept dead still and stayed there for about ten minutes.

Eventually, I climbed out of the hedge and crept away but I guess they had been toying with me and they pounced. I ended up at a Land Rover with half-a-dozen other captives and we were slung in the back. The problem was that I went in first and we were shackled so I had two or three guys on top of me. I was quite frightened as I could barely breathe and things got worse as we were driven to the castle at Mountbatten. The vehicle bounced a lot and, although I yelled with what little breath I had, nobody took any notice.

At the castle we were dragged out of the vehicle and immediately made to strip to our underpants, a pillow case was put over our heads and we each had a man at either elbow and were propelled to the dungeons at a great rate. It is very upsetting as you dread that they are going to run either side of a pillar. Silly, I know, but we were exhausted and not thinking well anymore.

In the dungeons we had to take our weight on our hands against the wall and keep our feet apart. Any deviation from this and you were roughly forced to return to position. Throughout the time there was 'white music' being played; this is a strange and disturbing sound and does not enable you to think normally.

At regular intervals we were taken away, individually, for interrogation by professional men, presumably Secret Service or something like that, but I'm pleased to say despite all verbal, body language and physical tricks I managed to stick to number, rank and name.

One of the tricks was to make you sit on a two-legged stool stark naked whilst they carried out interrogation but with lewd and jeering comments. It's difficult not to respond to that.

Later I had my pillow case removed and was put into a cell of about twenty by twenty feet with a pillar in the middle. It must have been about 8 or 9 in the morning by now and I had been caught well before midnight.

I was cold, of course, so I started walking round the pillar noticing that in one corner there was quite a bit of horse harness and brasses and, incredibly, a shelf with some bottles on it, one of which was Drambuie. This was odd as I don't drink the stuff. I fell down occasionally but had to get up as it was so cold.

Later on, it was back to the wall and interrogation. As I left my pillow-case was lifted and there was the man we were told to remember! He said, 'You've finished now, come with me.' I was taken to a room containing my clothes, got dressed and was taken to the mess for a meal.

Two or three of us had decided, after our baths or showers, that we would go for a shave, shampoo and shearing in town. We had to hurry as it was now 1600. We got there in time and I noticed the clock was slow and pointed it out to my man. No, he said, it's correct. The captors had the last laugh – they had put our watches three hours forward.

That night there was a great party in the mess and at 2300 the barman had had enough and went to bed. We continued, on the honour system, but the party petered out quite quickly.

From 0800 Tuesday to 0200 Sunday most of us had managed about eight hours sleep. We had all hallucinated towards the end; I went to the dungeon with the pillar, Drambuie and horse stuff and it was completely bare and had no pillar! Seemingly, we had all been there and most of us had seen weird things there. It had been quite stressful but slightly unrealistic as we knew that we could not be really physically hurt as we were all quite valuable government property.

I passed with Merit.

Later I was expected to go to Norway to take part in a two-week winter-survival course. Sadly, I had to hand it to my deputy as I could not risk skiing on my weakened leg. Lucky him. However, on the last day and the last minute on skis as he went down the hill to the bus he fell and broke his leg.

After the course and back at the squadron, I initiated the addition of a loud-hailer to the safety equipment on board. The idea being that, since some failures could cut off the PA, then the hailer could be very useful in an emergency. Furthermore, in extreme circumstances, like ditching, information and orders could be passed to all. I'm certain we were the first organisation/airline to do this. I know that BA followed soon after. I'm certain that all airlines have this equipment on board now.

Back to the 'Shinies'

Shortly after this course it was the annual Officers' Ball when all the ladies get out their finery and the officers wear their mess kit, short jacket with gold-coloured buttons and gold-braided medals and rank markings with white shirt, bow tie and cummerbund. This year Maureen and I took our caravan with us, having arranged for my parents to babysit, and parked at the edge of the mess car park.

It allowed us to have a wonderful evening of wining, dining and dancing despite the evening's entertainer letting the side down. The mess had engaged the services of Jimmy Edwards, an ex-Dakota pilot who had earned the Distinguished Flying Cross over Arnhem, now a comedian, and mid-evening he started his show. Unfortunately, his jokes were quite blue and unnecessary with so many ladies present. Indeed, most of the men found it unacceptable. Maureen and I and many others walked out quite early and, shortly afterwards, the President of the Mess asked him to stop and advised him he would be paid, anyway.

The next morning, having had a very late night, we were awakened by a knock on the caravan door to find a mess waiter with a tray of tea and toast. How lovely.

1970 started quietly with just normal trips but it developed nicely by May. I had a New York trip carrying the 'Jackanory' team and their cameras were filming our approach into JFK. It was authorised by the RAF for them to be on the flight deck for the approach and landing. Also, Sandra Bisp, a journalist for the *South Wales Echo*, was along as well. So we had the crew of four, plus four others and their equipment.

It all went well and Sandra joined the crew for an evening out. During the evening she told me that she was doing a regular series on people with interesting lives. She had just had her last article printed and that was about Richard Burton. She asked if I would be happy to let her write an article on me. I said that would be okay if I or she could get RAF authority, which she did.

206

BACK TO THE 'SHINIES'

The next trip was a pleasant change from the normal; having arrived at Changi on the regular service we positioned the aircraft at RAF Tengah to the North of the island. That night, under cover, we were loaded with twelve or more Red Beard Tactial Nuclear Weapons. The next day we departed for the UK via the Pacific and the States.

First stop was Anderson AFB, Guam in the Marianas Islands where our six RAF Security Police stayed on board and the US military kept guard outside. Anderson was home to squadrons of B52 bombers which were regularly used in the Vietnam war. The runway had such a dip in the first quarter that, not only was it a difficult place to land well but the B52 would disappear from sight during its early part of the take-of run! It had eight jet-engines but with it's bomb load it still needed every metre.

On to Barber's Point AFB, now Kalaeloa Airport, Hawaii where the Base Commander met us with a carton of cold beer under his arm! What a lovely thing to do. Next morning on to March AFB, San Bernardino, California then Myrtle Beach AFB, South Carolina to gape in awe at all the golf courses we could see in the area. After landing our guide showed us the area but, sadly, there was no time for a game.

The last leg to the UK had a couple of interesting ATC 'incidents', whereby we were given a radar direct to a certain place in the USA and we had to refuse the offer, to the controller's surprise. Later, an instruction to descend by London ATC over the Atlantic was declined, and when he insisted, I advised him to contact his superior with a code number I gave him. We had strict orders to maintain certain height and the route as authorised and agreed by USA and UK ATC. Presumably, this was to give a clearer picture of where to find us if we 'disappeared'. It took quite a while to covertly unload our 'cargo'. It was good to get back to Brize and home to Wantage.

Upon return I was advised that I was to do my first flight as a VIP captain and would be taking Lord Carrington from Heathrow to Bahrain and return. This was the first VIP flight for the new Edward Heath government. As was normal with such trips an aircraft was allocated and it was my task as the captain to regularly check the progress on its lay-out and preparedness. Hardly necessary really, as the ground staff knew their job well.

The Friday afternoon before the flight next day I felt that I might be developing a cold, so I contacted Taff Williams, the standby VIP captain, to be prepared for me to call him in the morning if I was not fit. As, I think everybody is well aware, the risk of sinus trouble or ear blockage is not a good idea if you are flight crew.

The next morning at 0500 I got up and, sure enough, I felt blocked up. I paced around, knowing that early morning stuffiness was quite normal and hoped things would improve. One of my ears was slow to clear, so I made the decision to call Taff. I told him I would go to do the briefing and pre-flight checks and see him at the aircraft. He duly arrived and departed for London.

I was quite despondent as you can imagine and, although I felt maybe I would have been okay, I consoled myself with the knowledge that I had done the correct thing. This protected the flight and the squadron's reputation. To dot the *i*s and cross the *t*s I popped into the Medical Centre and, by chance, the doctor allocated as the 10 Squadron representative was on duty. I said what had happened and that, to my annoyance, I seemed okay. He did the necessary and I went home.

A few days later I was assigned a trip to the Italian Air Force base at Rimini. I checked the charts and said I felt it was a bit tight for the VC10 taxiing. I was advised that this had been considered and I should have no problems. The taxiing turned out okay until my departure when, obeying ATC instructions, I set off for the runway. We were quite close to accommodation blocks but the problem was that there was a basketball court outside and we were about to hit the pole and basket which were firmly bolted to a metal plate in the ground. We couldn't reverse or go onto the grass so we sat there for about twenty minutes whilst maintenance arrived and wrestled with the bolts.

Sometime in September, Sandra Bisp got back to me about the article in the *South Wales Echo* which was now authorised by her editor and the RAF. She had two seats for the opening of the new stand at Cardiff Arms Park. Would I like to come on 7 October to the match between Wales and the Presidents XV? 'No brainer' as they say nowadays.

I met Sandra at her parents' house where I was to be staying the night and we were then taken by taxi to a pub near the grounds and enjoyed a couple of drinks in the great atmosphere. We set off for the game where Sandra said we had seats at the halfway line. Wow. On arrival I was astonished to find it was in the press-box which was simply open and had four seats and a table.

In the corner was Alan Williams, the famous radio rugby commentator; next to him was the great Cliff Morgan, then me then Sandra! After introductions they got on with their work and we watched the game.

There were some great players to behold: J.P.R. Williams, Gareth Edwards, Barry John, T.J. Kiernan, David Duckham, Mike Gibson, Fergus Slattery, to name just the ones I knew best. The Welsh beat the Presidents

XV 26-11; there were only three points for a try in those days and Wales had scored 5-1.

Afterwards the box was besieged by autograph hunters and Williams and Morgan were very polite and very busy. Naturally, everybody thought I must be 'somebody' but in refusing to sign I could see that I was being looked upon as one of those snooty celebs. So I signed a few with my normal autograph where the two Bs could look like R, B or S, although the rest is quite clear. After the game, in the pub, of course, and having dinner I was browsing the very grand official programme and there in the list of past players was one R. Burnett, 1953. I guess a few people now think that they have his signature.

In December 1970 I did one of our early schedules into Washington Dulles Airport, which is in Virginia, and, at that time, had a road connecting it to the capital. It was about thirty miles and constant trees either side. Now it has been built up a lot. The schedule was in support of the Embassy and associated military posts involved with NATO etc. We also carried freight and diplomatic mail.

All flights between Hong Kong and Singapore traversed Vietnam during the war. We had USAF Major Ed Chivers on exchange with us and he was scheduled for one trip a month because, at that time, any American servicemen in Vietnam paid no income tax or, at least, there were terrific tax concessions. Because he actually flew once a month through the war area he received all the same privileges.

Although the air traffic control system was well handled by the Americans it occasionally occurred that communications were poor, even though I'm sure they could always see us on radar. When communications were bad it was, nevertheless, normal to make all position reports on the assumption that you could be heard. In any event they would have received our flight plan ahead of our arrival.

One night, en route from Hong Kong to Changi, I had no communication from entering Vietnam airspace to about thirty minutes later. Suddenly, the first words I received were 'Descend immediately to FL 310 (31,000)'. I complied and, wondering what all the fuss was about, looked around and saw little black dots ahead and left. Within a short while I passed directly under a wave of B-52 bombers.

In December 1970 it was my turn again for a VIP flight and when it was allocated to another I went to see my acting flight commander, Peter Isherwood, who had instructed with me at Leeming, to ask what had happened. He said he'd check on it. He came back to me later with the information that at the regular squadron Monday morning briefing after my Lord Carrington business the squadron doctor had advised them that there had been nothing wrong with me and I was fit to fly. As I said earlier, this was so, but my actions were entirely of a precautionary nature with the squadron's best interests at heart. So much for professional medical confidentiality and integrity. Furthermore, why had my commanding officer, Wing Commander D.B. Dowling, not spoken to me at that time? Another unprofessional and distasteful act.

Dowling was not very popular. Unlike his predecessor, who was too frequently absent on trips, including VIP flights, Dowling was around a lot. He rarely acknowledged your 'Good morning, Sir' in the building and was a dour man.

This was the moment that, despite having just been offered a supplementary commission to stay to fifty-five and have 'mostly' flying posts, I decided to leave the Royal Air Force. Indeed, I would retire the instant that I had enough time served to be able to receive a pension.

I toyed with the idea of applying for a 'Redress of a Grievance', which meant higher authority would address all the parties and facts and make a decision. Even if it had been in my favour, which I'm sure it would have been, it would have left me with the wrong sense of belonging I had always had. So I let it ride. Mind you it would have been rewarding to have the doctor reprimanded and the CO look even more miserable than he normally did.

Having made the decision, I set out again to study and work towards my ATPL (Airline Transport Pilot's Licence). This was a good time for me because, quite recently, the Civil Aviation Authority (CAA) had agreed that qualified Transport/Air Support Command pilots with a certain number of hours and transport hours could be exempt from Meteorology, Navigation and one or two of the minor subjects like instruments and radio.

All the other subjects had to be passed, plus instrument rating on civil aircraft (very expensive) and a test flight and pass in a civil aircraft (expensive). I started studying in earnest, booked leave for the last two weeks of July and booked a place at Kidderminster, Oxford, flying school for the instrument training and licence, radio operator's licence, et al.

In January 1971 I had the privilege of flying Sir Alec Douglas-Home from Brize-Muharraq on his way to the Prime Ministers' conference in Singapore. The aircraft was set up, at the front, as if for a VIP flight, although this was a normal scheduled trip. There was a table for four, plus a sectioned area for his staff and a small 'bedroom' for him to have a rest.

On the way one of his staff came to the flight deck and asked if Sir Alec could walk his dog. Dogs were normally not carried in the cabin, except on special duties when military dogs in special cages were carried. I reckon Sir Alec was on special duty with a black Labrador puppy in a cage as a gift for President Lee Kuan Yew.

Naturally, I said yes and was invited to go and meet the great man. I say great, because to me he was the epitome of all honourable gentlemen and how politicians should behave for the public. He was utterly charming and treated me, his captain, with great respect. We chatted about dogs and Labradors, especially, as I had had a couple including our current Golden Retriever, Barney.

Sir Alec went to his bed later and only woke up when I applied reverse thrust. The landing was obviously okay. Normally, in the RAF we always awaken our passengers at top of descent, so that blocked ears were less likely but no-one wanted to bother Sir Alec!

The year remained uneventful until I arrived at Kidderminster in July. I parked the family caravan nearby and used it as my HQ for study and living. Maureen and the boys went to her parents in Lancaster for their holiday.

The first week was spent in Link trainers and classrooms and on 26 July I had my first instrument rating ride. It was in a PA30 Piper Twin Comanche which was nowhere near as easy to fly on instruments as a VC10. Nevertheless, it went very well as indeed it did later and the next day.

There was a sad result from my good performance; the system was that the aircraft was used by the instructor and three students. Each student was required to do thirty minutes and there was quite a scramble to change seats in that cramped cockpit. One of the students had done many trips but was not progressing well and on the third day he failed to turn up.

The instructor explained that if I could fly like I had done from day one and he still couldn't get the hang of it, then he was giving up. It was natural that I had the ability because of all my experience but the instructor couldn't convince him.

After five half-hour sessions I went off for my one-hour forty-five-minute instrument rating test with Captain Sweet of CAFO (Civil Aviation Flying Unit). It went beautifully until my approach to Birmingham Airport when I inexplicably went one dot below the glide slope within five nautical miles. Failed! This meant I had to have at least one more practice before retest.

The next morning, my last day on leave, I went to Captain Sweet and explained my predicament. There were no training slots for me that day and, as I had done an otherwise good trip, would he make an exception and test me again. Thank goodness, he agreed.

The flight was terrible and I bounced off every limit I was so nervous. I think the limits were something like heading $\pm$ 5 degrees, speed $\pm$ 5 knots and height $\pm$ 100 feet. I managed to hit them all but never went outside, including the instrument approach into Bristol this time. He flew it back and agreed that it was not impressive but, as it was legal and I had done well the day before, he would pass me. Phew!

I explained to one of the instructors that I wasn't sure how to qualify on the VC10 aircraft and written exam to get my ATPL. These had to be done within six months. He, Mr Nowell, explained he could give me a ride in a single-engine Piper Cherokee and then a test and that would be acceptable. An ATPL on a single piston?

That morning I swatted the Pilot's Notes and took the exam that afternoon (it was a very small aircraft!). He was available the next day, Saturday, so gave me a thirty-minute instructional trip then a thirty-minute test, all within the same flight. I passed.

He also advised me on the Friday morning that the CAA would occasionally do a one-off permission for tests on military aircraft, so I had written immediately. The authorisation arrived the next week. I was due my six-monthly check ride on the Friday, so Dave Ray, the check pilot, kindly filled out the CAA Form 1179. I passed that.

A week later I had two days off and, having booked my final exam, which was to take place at CAA HQ in the Strand, off I went to London. The exam was quite tricky and you have to achieve a mark of 100 per cent.

The subject is recognizing lights and their implications, i.e. is the other aircraft coming towards you, away, left, right, up or down. You have questions and pictures. The examiner kindly marked it on the spot so I shot off to the licensing department with all my paperwork on exam results, 1179 (Cherokee) instrument rating etc. The VC10 would not be valid until I'd done the ground exams.

That afternoon I received my ATPL. I had spent three weeks, a lot of money, a mass of nervous energy and sleepless nights to get here. The relief was palpable. I had lost nearly a stone in that period.

My new posting came through whilst I was away and, bearing in mind that I had yet to tell the RAF my decision on the offer of a new type of commission, there was no reason to believe that I should not have been granted my request which was to join VC10 ATS. This was the VC training squadron, long taken over from BOAC at Cranebank.

ATS did all the ground school, the flying training, the categorisations and all the simulator training and all examining. The simulator was given great importance in the RAF and all crews did a minimum of four hours per month on top of all the time spent there whilst on annual or six-monthly recategorisations. C category was every six months and B every year with just a six-monthly check ride.

I had been requesting ATS on all my annual reports and it was reasonable to think I was in with a chance. I was a B category four-jet captain, I had recently been helping with the training of co-pilots and I was an A2 CFS instructor. Plus, on my last recategory, the instructor had advised me I could well make A category next time.

I was advised in advance that my next posting was to Air Support Command HQ, RAF Upavon, Wiltshire, as an operations flow controller. Dowling may have done this; I was deeply disappointed and it hardened my decision to leave as I had fewer prospects than I had worked so hard to achieve. Had I been posted to ATS, I would have signed on to age fifty-five.

I wrote to the Air Ministry to thank them for the offer of a Supplementary Commission but that I declined. I did not yet advise them of my intended early retirement.

As I was due to leave 10 Squadron in early October I went to see the main programming officer, Derek Adams, to ask for a decent swansong. Well, did I ever get one. I was assigned the 1971 Battle of Britain display at all the participating airfields in the UK, all seven of them.

Friday 17 September in VC10 XV101 I did a fifty-five-minute practice of my own devised display at Abingdon. This was to avoid disruption of traffic at Brize and had the added advantage that not only was it one of the designated airfields but it was where I could do a good display for my Air Support Command peers as this was our area, i.e. Lyneham, Brize, Benson and Abingdon itself.

These Battle of Britain 'At Home' displays take massive detailed organisation. There are dozens of aircraft from dozens of airfields criss-crossing the country to and from displays. Some go to only a few, some have to land here and there to refuel and all the routes have to be adhered to. Even the time between certain airfields is marked by times over certain features and this is for *every* aircraft. Any deviations can cause problems.

All of this has to avoid conflict or delays to civilian traffic, although civilian ATC do make many concessions and divert aircraft away from certain areas. There were 188 various aircraft or formations including helicopters and even gliders.

The crew comprised co-pilot Flight Lieutenant Wills, navigator Mike Webb, Master engineer Blackburn and AQM Flight Sergeant Bush who, apart from keeping us fed and watered, added the touch of flashing the landing lamps on and off as we approached the field. On board was Flying Officer Malcolm Hearn RAFVR (T), an Air Training Corps Officer; he was there because he asked if he could join us. Why not? We had 136 spare seats!

We set off for our first display at RAF St Mawgan, Cornwall, where the show went well but we were so heavy due to the extra fuel for low-flying, low altitude routes and high-power manoeuvres and seven displays, that it seemed a little ponderous to us but the Station CO's letter said it was excellent.

At every field it was our intention to arrive downwind, if possible, to give that little extra ground speed. We approached at 350 knots (402 mph) and just before the airfield boundary we closed the throttles and went past the crowd as quietly as possible.

After passing the crowd we turned 45 degrees away from them and extended the airbrakes (or spoilers), which are basically planks of metal that extend into the airflow and slow you down. As the speed became slow enough we extended the gear and retracted the airbrakes.

At the correct speed the first extension of wing flaps took place which further allowed a lower speed. By now we were turning back to the crowd with plenty of bank to give them a good view of this beautiful aircraft. Power would now be increased to avoid the speed reducing too quickly and full flap was selected.

Now the speed would be allowed to decay to normal final approach speed or lower, i.e. close to the stall and we would then pass in front of the crowd as low (200 feet legal) and slow as possible. This was impressive, as seeing such a big aircraft at such a low speed and making so much noise gets the hairs on the back of the neck rising.

Past the crowd, turn away again and turn back changing nothing. Back in front of the crowd, maximum power and start a climbing turn away from the crowd as steeply as possible. During the turn, flap and undercarriage was raised at the appropriate safe speeds; the aircraft was being flown at a slow speed but with enough safety margin in case of engine failure.

After one complete turn or two if time permitted, we'd then set course to the next airfield. I did all the displays and Wills (sorry I've lost his Christian name) would do everything else.

Next destination St Athan near Cardiff where all went well, then off to RAF Abingdon where I really wanted things to go well, and we were now light enough to let rip.

We arrived dead on time at maximum speed and there ahead of us at five miles were four Jet Provosts turning in front of us for a break and landing. This was not in their programme; they had done their display and were to hold south of the airfield until I had finished. If I carried on there would have been serious problems for them in my wake with probable accidents. I immediately carried out a 45-degree-banked turn left at 300 knots and 200 feet, which was both difficult and dangerous. At that time it was the most difficult and dangerous manoeuvre I had ever done in a large aircraft. When lined up with the airfield I continued my display but when it came time for my upward climb and grand finale the navigator said, 'No time, head for Biggin Hill.' So there I was in front of my peers and unable to show them our piece de resistance! I compromised with a really steep climb and lots of noise.

The failure of the 'Macaws' leader to follow orders so that he could 'show off' was reprehensible. He endangered his team, my crew and, maybe, even the crowd. I wrote to him and did not receive a reply; he would probably say that he never received it.

Aircraft Type:	Jet Provost ('**Macaws**')	Serial No: 109	
Planning Ground Speed:	235 knots	Call Sign: Display 109	
Number of Aircraft:	4		
Base:	Manby, deployed Abingdon		
Times:	All Times Alpha (i.e. BST)		
Remarks:			

ROUTE		ETA	LEG	LEG	LEG
FROM	TO		HEIGHT	DISTANCE (NMS)	TIME (MINS)
Abingdon	Take Off	1407	VC10		
	Display	1415½-26½	1427½-1432½		Macaws hold South of Airfield
	Land	1432½			
Abingdon	**Take Off**	1513			
	5142N 0114W	1514	ASC	3	1
	Odiham	1521½	3,000 ft	30	7½

	Reigate	1529	3,000 ft	30	7½
	5115N 0002W	1530½	DESC	6	1½
	Biggin Hill	1532	DESC	5	1½
	Land by	1533			
Biggin Hill	Take Off	1622			
	Display	1630-41			
	Land	1646½			

Aircraft Type: VC10   Serial No: 046

Planning Ground Speed: 275-300 knots   Call Sign: Display 046

Number of Aircraft: 1

Base: Brize Norton

Times: All Times Alpha

Remarks: 1. Lose 14 minutes between St Mawgan and St Athan.

                    2. Britannia (Serial No 047) under normal ATC, losing time St Athan – Abingdon.

                    3. Overtakes Andover (serial No 050) at 2,500 feet at approx. 1418.

                    4. Overtakes Spitfire and Hurricane (Serial Nos 014/015) at 2,500 feet at approx. 1531.

ROUTE		ETA	LEG HEIGHT	LEG DISTANCE (NMS)	LEG TIME (MINS)
FROM	TO				
Brize Norton	Take Off	A/R			
	5033N 0502W	1324	Normal ATC		
	St. Mawgan	1326	DESC	7	2
	Display	1326-31			
	5024N 0453W	1332	ASC	5	1
	5111N 0320W	1401	FL 90	76	29
	5119N 0325W	1403	DESC	9	2
	St Athan	1404	DESC	5	1

	Display	1404-09			
	5131N 0330W	1411	ASC	8	2
	5137N 0239W	1417½	3,000 ft	32	6½
	5139N 0135W	1425½	FL 35	40	8
	Abingdon	1427½	DESC	10	2
	Display	**1427½-32½**	**See**	**Macaws**	**Ser. No 109**
	5142N 0114W	1433½	ASC	3	1
	Odiham	1440	2,500 ft	30	6½
	Reigate	1446½	2,500 ft	30	6½
	5115N 0002W	1448	DESC	6	1½
	Biggin Hill	1449	DESC	5	1
	Display	1449-54			
	5153N 0033E	1502½	2,500 ft	39	8½

RAF ABINGDON

1. Static

VC10	from	Brize Norton
Britannia	from	Brize Norton
Belfast	from	Brize Norton
Hercules	from	Lyneham
Andover	from	Thorney Island
Canberra	from	Boscombe Down
Jet Provost	from	Manby
Meteor	from	Farnborough
Chipmunk	from	London UAS
Hastings	from	Farnborough

2. Static/Fly

Wessex	from	Culdrose
Varsity	from	Topcliffe

3. <u>Flying</u> <u>Flight Plan No</u>

Time	Event	Flight Plan No
1345-1402	'Red Arrows' Display	144
1402½-1406½	Alouette Take Off, Display & Land	090
1407-1408	'Macaws' Take Off	109
1409-1415	Hunter Aerobatic Display	122
1415½-1426½	'Macaws' Display	109
1427½-1432½	**VC10 Display**	**046**
1432½-1433½	**'Macaws' Land**	
1434-1439	Andover Display	050
1440-1445	Britannia Display	047
1446-1447	4 x Chipmunk Take Off	134
1448-1452	Canberra Photo & Display	011
1453-1458	Victor Display	008
1458½-1506½	Jet Provost Aerobatic Take Off Display & Land	115
1507-1512	4 x Chipmunk Display & Land	134
1513-1514	'Macaws' Take Off	109
1515-1520	Belfast Display	048
1521-1527	Phantom Aerobatic Display	069
1527½-1528½	Nimrod Flypast	024
1529½-1530½	4 x Phantom Flypast	051
1531-1535	PTS Parachuting Demonstration	056
1535½-1541½	Buccaneer Display	010
1542½-1547½	Lancaster Display	013
1548-1549	Comet Flypast	173
1549½-1550½	Vulcan Flypast	003
1550½-1613	Abingdon arranged Set Piece	
1614-1620	4 x CF104G Display	152
1621-1631	Zlin Aerobatic Display	180
1632-1633	4 x F-100 Flypast	160
1633½-1639½	Whirlwind SAR Demonstration	031
1640-1641	Victor and 2 x Lightning AAR	007A/B/C
1642-1650	Spitfire & Hurricane Display, Land	014/015
1651-1657	Lightning Aerobatic Display	018
1658-1706	'Falcons' Parachuting Display	052

Biggin Hill was fantastic! As we neared the airfield and surrounding hills we saw a sea of people. It was absolutely wonderful to do the show there.

BACK TO THE 'SHINIES'

We continued to Coltishall where my parents were watching, so that one was for them. Then Finningley, where my brother, Barry, was watching, and on to Leuchars.

By now, with no passengers or freight, we were light as a feather. The squadron there, No.43, was equipped with Lightnings, which had a phenomenal performance, so I thought we ought to play at Lightning. The final climb away was quite exhilarating.

Mills took us home and we were all exhausted as the constant chop and change of speed, altitude, direction and extra concentration for low-level flying had strained us all. It was a fine feeling of achievement, though. Mike Webb was never out by more than *seven seconds*.

Unfortunately, I got home too late for the news, so saw nothing of any of the displays but thought nothing of it at the time. However, I have decided I would like to see the show and have written to a few papers local to the displays requesting anybody who has film to contact me. No results so far, I'm afraid.

I received quite a few letters from Station Commanders thanking us for our displays and another letter from our newest CO at 10 Squadron, Wing Commander Lamb, praising my display and commiserating with me about the Macaws. He asked me to detail the practicalities of the performance for future use.

I understand that this display was used more than once and it finished with what I named in the letter 'The Burdett Screw'. I know it wasn't used the last time I saw the VC10 at Biggin Hill. The display was quite tame. Sorry, but it was.

'Auntie Flo' at
ASCHQ - RAF Upavon

One month later my time with 10 Squadron was over and I set off for Air Support Command HQ at RAF Upavon in Wiltshire. I was to be a flow control officer which was an arduous and important role in the safe and controlled movement of all overseas RAF traffic. We were not popular because, too often, we had to change schedules and crew movements due to congestion at airfields which may have one or two problems, such as unserviceabilities or weather changes. Those a few thousand miles away could not see the overall picture, so there was much muttering on the radio and the signals network. We were the Flow Control section of Command Operations, 'Auntie Flo' to the crews.

The operations centre itself was a very large area encompassing a sixty to seventy-feet semi-circular wall with spaces for all the Command's aircraft all over the world. The boards showed service call-sign, captain, aircraft and its serial number and other pertinent information. This area was lower than the rest of the set-up. Behind it was a glass-fronted office where the senior officers worked, room for three or four, and could oversee all the boards. The actual ops officers were on the lower floor, usually flight lieutenants, and at night were in full control. Next to the glass office was Flow Control.

We had a TV showing the weather at all the RAF Master Airfields, i.e. those permanently open and available to take anyone, anytime. There were two or three telephones: one, a normal internal connection, the second a connection to the long-distance radio communications controlled by the large radio room behind, and the third with about 100 buttons to connect to most of the free world's military and the UK air traffic system. My life was centred on these damned things and my own set of boards behind me. There were eight, one for each day of the week and the start of the next. They slid backwards and forwards individually, were about seven-feet-tall and four feet across. On these charts were records of the movements of all British military aircraft anywhere in the world, and I and my colleagues had to write the lot in pencil and every time there was a change, or we made a change, then out came the rubber (eraser to the Americans) and the new information was recorded.

As the world has varied time zones this was a twenty-four-hour task and we worked shifts of 0900 to 1900 and 1900 to 0900. There were five of us and we worked four days on, four days off, four nights on and four nights off. The handover usually took at least thirty minutes. Of course, in the morning the senior officers came to work, so they needed briefing as well. This made the night shift pretty long.

The worst times, i.e. the hardest, were during exercises as so much was going on, there were so many changes of plan, unserviceabilities etc., that we in Flow were hard pressed. The night shift was awful during these periods.

I was now living in the mess at Upavon as, sadly, Maureen and I had parted ways. Obviously, this was a major upheaval, especially for Maureen and the boys; it is said that such events are 50/50 but, in truth, I accept most of the responsibility and it has weighed heavily on me all my life. I had paid off my mortgage with my retirement gratuity and signed the house over to Maureen and departed with two suitcases, £300 in the bank and a tatty old car; it was all I deserved.

Sadness aside, I found mess life to be much as it had always been but quieter, as there were no flying units there.

ATPL – Air Transport Pilot's Licence

Having done my VC10 check ride with Squadron Leader Dave Ray in August 1971 I had until February 1972 to do the ground examinations to get the VC10 registered as entitled to fly and noted in my licence. To this end I went to Cranebank and paid £50 to rent the BOAC books as the exams would be based on civilian aircraft and there were many differences, especially weights in kilograms and not pounds.

All my spare time in Flow Control was devoted to studying and studying, off-duty also. Eventually I was ready and booked a date at the CAA (Civil Aviation Authority) in Southampton for the exam.

On the way, the windscreen shattered on my Triumph 2000 PI and I managed to get glass in my eye. Because of so much time in the service, and with no idea of civil aviation ways, I had no idea I could cancel easily and book another day. To me this was serious stuff, so I carried on using just my left eye. I noted that the eye hospital was directly opposite the exam centre, which was comforting. I collected my exam paper, winking away, sat down and completed the three-hour multiple-choice in an hour. I was experienced on type and had many hours swotting under my belt. The one thing that annoyed me was that all weights were given in kilograms and pounds, so I need not have memorised all the weights!

I hurriedly gave the adjudicator my paper and went to rush over the road. 'Hey.' he said, 'Where are you going?' I explained and he pointed out that my ATPL only contained a piston-engined aircraft and, therefore, I had to do papers on jet engines, hydraulics, electrics, air-conditioning and, maybe, flight-controls or fuel.

I was stunned, I had not done any reading on these subjects, so I went back to my desk with trepidation. However, experience counts and, in fact, I knew more than enough to complete them quite quickly. I think the adjudicator was quite impressed; I know that I was.

At last I was free to go to the eye hospital over the road and arrived at about 1115 hours. After a short wait, then into a room with four dentist-type chairs and some nurses. My nurse, a large and stern lady, proceeded to move my eyelids around and poke about. Unfortunately, the most unnerving thing for me is eye problems; even if someone points a finger towards me I flinch. After a couple of minutes, I was as stiff as a board and being told off by the nurse. Anyway, she removed the offending items and after another 'mauling' by a doctor I left intact and much relieved.

I passed everything and the VC10 was added to my licence; the ATPL was now for real.

Back Under Ground

Apart from normal duties we were often involved in round-the-world exercises, joint-service exercises and international co-ordination.

A particularly interesting event was the bomb scare on the *Queen Elizabeth II* in 1972. A telephone caller had claimed a bomb was on board and a $350,000 demand was made. We had to send a C-130 Hercules to mid-Atlantic with an SAS sergeant and three SBS men to parachute alongside the liner. The ship's lifeboat picked them up easily as, despite a 250-foot cloud base, the navigation was spot on. They got on board eighteen minutes before the bomb was timed to go off. It was a hoax.

Another interesting period was when Concorde did her round-the-world demonstration and marketing flight. All the signals were handled by the Royal Air Force and I was quite involved. We in Flow Control all received a commemorative tie.

Despite my previous experience as operations officer in Cyprus, Lusaka, Nairobi and Honolulu, I found this work tiring and too repetitive to gain any real pleasure from it. Previously I had been in the thick of things with aircraft, crews and hands-on tasks. I decided to get some flying.

Firstly, I managed to get two or three VC10 flights whilst my qualifications were still valid and also I offered my services to the VC10 simulator department each month. I had a trip to Puerto Rico and a couple to Malta to assist with the withdrawal of the Royal Air Force and the other forces after independence. This flying did not last long but I continued with the simulator.

How to get more real flying? I know, go to the Army Parachute Centre (APC) down the road at Netheravon. Sure enough I was welcomed by Captain 'Bob' Hughes, the officer commanding, and immediately checked out on the Britten-Norman Islander, a twin-piston-engined high-wing aircraft, ideal for crazy people to jump from.

There were usually eight parachutists on board and at 12,000 feet I would bring the power back on the left engine and they would jump in rapid succession, try to form a circle and then hold hands; odd lot! My fun was to try to land ahead of them but it was necessary to beware over-revving the engines as the air flow was driving the propellers faster than the power setting and I had not to hit them, of course. They usually won as they didn't open their 'chutes until 1,000 feet. I occasionally won but this game could not be played with the engines of the Dragon Rapide which we also used.

Bob and I flew to Germany on two occasions. I was the only pilot to be qualified for airways and instruments, which enabled him to see how other parachute centres worked and to do a bit of para-dropping himself; he was ex-SAS.

On 30 June 1972 I did my final RAF VC10 flight which was just training and prior to that I flew one more trip to Malta for the withdrawal. Some people who had worked all their lives for the RAF were crying.

Now it was just the APC with whom I flew in British championships at Weston-on-the-Green on 3 June 1972. The 'Red Devils' were also my passengers on one or two occasions. Much of the flying at Netheravon was done very early in the morning when there was little or no wind, especially important for trainees. To this end in the summer months, if I had no pressing problems, I would ask the operations officer if he could cover for me whilst I flew. This was usually granted.

Much as I had loved the APC, I wanted to use my ATPL and so I sent letters to many companies, medium to small, to see if they could use an experienced pilot. I had many rejections but one, Trader Airways, offered me an interview. Their head office was in Sevenoaks, their ops centre in Horsham and their aircraft at the light aircraft area at Gatwick (LGW). They operated two Piper Navajos, an HS125 and two Dassault Fan Jet Falcon Fs.

I was accepted and, having received clearance from the Air Ministry, I started training on the Navajo, appropriately at Kidlington, on 17 July and, on 23 August, flew my first civilian flight as captain carrying passengers.

I was now operating out of LGW so there was no point living in the mess any longer and I found a small apartment in West Humble near Dorking. It was actually a part of a converted stable as part of the house of Sir Carl Aarvold, the Recorder of London. I would use the mess when on my four days/nights duty and the apartment when using LGW.

During the period I was flying for Trader Airways whilst still in the RAF I flew many interesting people – it was an executive company – including Peter Townsend of The Who, Harold Lever, a Labour Cabinet minister, and many others who would not wish to be mentioned.

One to be remembered was a flight from le Bourget, Paris, to LGW. Shortly after take-off I saw the cowling on the right hand engine flapping up and down. During my pre-flight check I'm certain that it was secure. Anyway, an urgent landing was required so I went into Beauvais north-west of Paris and secured the panel. Unfortunately, life is not that easy; I had to write a report for the French authorities, I had to file another flight plan, uplift fuel, write another flight plan, do a new flight log (CAA law) and another outside check – all fastened. The passengers, former Resistance people going to London for a reunion, were quite happy, having raided the on-board bar and imbibed freely.

Another fun flight was to take a chap to Dornoch, way up on the east coast of Scotland, and land at a large grassy field. It was an official, unmanned landing strip on a farm and we had to fly over a couple of times to convince the cows it wasn't a good place to graze. It worked but the cows had left proof of their presence and the aircraft was covered in runny cow-pats. After this we were to go via Aberdeen for fuel and on to Frankfurt, Amsterdam, Paris and home, but it took ages to clean the aircraft in Aberdeen.

We were hired to fly all over mid and western Europe and there was never a dull moment, mainly due to the weather. Cloud once gave me one of the great frights of my life. The flashing white strobes had just been introduced and the Navajo had been fitted with them. I had left LGW in daylight for a round trip to Brussels and back and when I returned to London the area was in fog. I had enough fuel for a crack at LGW then, if it failed, on to Southend which was clear. I had been in daylight or clear skies since leaving LGW so, as I entered the upper level of the fog on my return, I was totally overwhelmed by the shock of this sudden blinding light. Of course, the normal procedure for evermore was to turn them off when necessary. Wow, what a shock. I got in though. I was chosen to fly Mr Harold Wilson and Marcia Falkender, his head of political office, to Leeds/Bradford, where they were to attend the wedding of one of his cronies. I waited patiently at Heathrow (LHR) and eventually, an hour late, Mrs Falkender arrived with two children and a nanny. Apparently, she had gone to the wrong terminal and, better, Wilson was not with her.

I was upset about his absence because I was going to tell him, lightheartedly, that because he had called for a Comet to take him from Versailles to the UK those few years ago that I missed a tour of South America. Anyway, he had gone ahead the day before. We got to Leeds in time, I checked flight plans, refuelled, got my book out and waited for our 1730 hours take off.

At 1715 Mrs Falkender appeared, but with no Wilson. We hung around. At 1745 Mrs Falkender rang a number and demanded to know where he was. Apparently, the other person did not know but would call back. He didn't.

Meanwhile, the airfield closed at 1800 hours and just one ATC officer remained, the fire crew, the duty policeman and the station manager.

No Wilson. More calls but now it was getting personal. At one stage I could have sworn that she and Wilson were married. She was yelling down the phone, 'Tell Harold that we are all waiting for him, this is not acceptable, when will he arrive, tell him I'm furious, etc., etc.'

We were all fascinated. Here was a member of staff, senior certainly, but yelling and ordering a past prime minister to do as he was told.

Eventually, she said, 'To hell with him, let's go.' So we did.

A week later I received a letter from Mrs Falkender saying that if I presented it at the House of Commons, there was a gift. I had a free day so I shot off, jumped the queue easily with my letter and received three, yes three, bottles of Chivas Regal. I sincerely hoped it had been paid for from trades union subscriptions.

The only other Navajo trip of interest was in April 1973 when I was asked at very short notice to take a spare TIA (Trans-International Airlines) crew to Malaga, but I had to be back at a certain time the next day as the aircraft was booked.

The outbound flight via Bordeaux was fine; I was rested and the weather was good. The hotel in Malaga was okay, but I was on minimum rest and I could not sleep for fear of wake-up call failure. Usual foolishness.

I got into the empty aircraft early morning and set off. The weather and flight to Bordeaux was fine but from Bordeaux home there was a lot of cloud. The auto-pilot was okay but not wonderful, so it was necessary to keep a more than wary eye on it. I was really tired and I had to fight to stay awake. I'm not sure, but I think I had a few seconds catnap at one time.

I was a little late and there on the tarmac was our owner, the lovely Mr Peter Bowles, his son and the next pilot and his passengers. They were a little miffed but they were lucky to have an aircraft at all. Single pilot operation plus fatigue do not mix.

At last it was time to leave the Royal Air Force, a sad and exciting day. My end of service was my birthday, 11 September 1973, but due to leave accrued I left on 30 August and headed to Bordeaux to do the ground school and examinations on the Dassault Fan Jet Falcon. I had simply gone from part- to full-time with Trader Airways.

However, prior to my departure, there was a serious personal mission. By this time, my new commanding officer in operations was none other than Group Captain Dowling of 10 Squadron lack of leadership. I went to see him and asked if I could talk without prejudice and he agreed. I asked him why he had not spoken to me about my failure to fly Lord Carrington and he said that the doctor had made a good point and he had accepted it. I said that had he spoken with me he would have realised that I had acted with the good name of the squadron in mind. He shrugged his shoulders and said he had done what he thought was right. I said that he was the reason I was leaving the Royal Air Force and that I believed he was a bad leader. I left sad and hurt. I left the Royal Air Force the next day, although my actual completion date was not for another week.

Trader Airways/Marcel Dassault

Four of us set out from Trader Airways to do the ground school course on the Dassault Fan Jet Falcon F and, upon arrival at Bordeaux, rented a small Renault for the period. It was from a company called InterRent who had started business that week. That night we had a head-on incident – it was whilst we were waiting to turn left on the ring-road (*peripherique*) and another driver could not wait. He passed the car for which we were waiting and hit us head on so hard that we ended back in the road we had just left.

I bent the steering wheel with my chest, broke the ignition key with one knee and the pull-out gear lever with the other, and went partly through the windscreen. Eric Tilseley in the passenger seat ended up with severe concussion and the guy behind him split his head open on the crumpled central support. The guy behind me ploughed into us at the front and was unhurt.

I was hanging through the front window watching the battery sparking away and, despite the power of my desire, I could not move. I feared fire, then a hand appeared and disconnected the battery! 'Merci,' I spat as I had a mouthful of windscreen, having probably screamed as I went through it. Also, my right hand was covered in cuts and splinters from the no-longer existent rearview mirror.

The emergency people arrived and I was lifted out, retaining the position in which they found me. They put me in a special seat with my feet in stirrups and my back and neck supported. To my embarrassment and mortification, I was then hung on the wall of the ambulance. My two friends were on stretchers and the fourth guy was ignored and never asked for a statement as they would not accept he had been in the car. There was not a mark on him.

As I was the only one who spoke a modicum of French, the doctors kept coming to me for information – all through the night. My knees were stitched in the A&E room by a doctor smoking a cigarette and I was quite fascinated by the length of the ash and wondered would it fall into my knee.

I swear that's the truth; even a nurse came in smoking! I hasten to add that I now regard the French health system as nothing short of amazing. In the morning there were so many beds in there that it was difficult for the staff to move around.

A voice next to me said, 'How are you feeling?' He had been there when we arrived so I asked him if he spoke French. He said he did, so I said, 'Why did you not help me?'

'I would have done if necessary but your French was too entertaining to interrupt!' he said.

Eric was kept in hospital for a week and, although I could barely walk or breathe, my intercostal muscles had all been bruised on the steering wheel. I went every evening to the hospital, having scrounged a blackboard and chalk, and gave him the day's lectures. He had been studying during the day according to the syllabus. As you can imagine the other patients were fascinated. During the course I was officially out of the RAF on 11 September and we had a few celebratory drinks.

On the 25th, having all passed the course, we returned to base. I carried on with the Navajo as we were waiting for the Falcon flying course. During the waiting period I enjoyed three trips with Jimmy Hill, John Motson and Barry Davies for 'Match of the Day'. I took them to the venue and then at the end they would come running across the tarmac with the film of the game. I would have an engine running and, as soon as the rear door closed, I would start the other and we would be off! Those of you old enough will remember that Jimmy Hill had a quick five minutes at the end of the news to talk about the match of the day. He did this from a small cubicle at RAF Northolt in Middlesex before roaring off to London for the programme proper.

I had to get them from the game to Northolt as fast as possible. Leeds and Bristol weren't so bad but Newcastle to Northolt required a bit of extra speed. Barry Davies always liked to sit in the other pilot's seat whilst Jimmy and John had a lot to talk about and enjoyed a small raid on the bar.

Fan-Jet Falcon F Training

In January 1974 I did my Falcon flight training with none other than M. Henri Suisse, the great test pilot. What a charming man and what a great instructor. One of his amazing tricks was to make me fly at 200 feet over the trees of the Aquitaine forests, 45 degrees of bank, speed 5 knots above the stall, and pull the stick back firmly but not harshly. This is not what pilots do but, as he was who he was, and with me, I did it. What an aircraft. She flew beautifully and, although close to the stall, the ailerons responded without a problem or an aggravated one-wing stall. Wow!

Having made me do this two or three times he said, 'Now you know that on approach you do not need to add 5 or so knots for your Grannie!' For those of you who do not understand, many pilots use the book figures which were arrived at by experts but still added 5 knots 'Just for Grannie, or whoever'.

A highlight of the course was a take off at le Bourget when my windshield cracked with a massive bang, just as I started to get airborne. I couldn't see anything through the window so had to peer out of the little DV (direct vision) window on the curve of the nose. Henri Suisse could have flown it from his side but he made me do it.

The course took four days and seven flights and I was qualified as captain, subject to some hours en route with other captains. I also continued with the Navajo. The Falcons were not permitted on the British register by the CAA (Civil Aviation Authority) as they were not satisfied with one aspect of the hydraulic flight control system but we had dispensation to fly on the French registration. The pilots all had to qualify for a French licence.

I went to Beirut with our owner, Mr Peter Bowles, which became quite interesting when he was held at immigration as he had an Israeli stamp in his passport. His visit was to deal with a significant person so it was eventually ironed out.

Next trip was to Nigeria, via Algiers and Tamanrasset, for Ashland Oil Co. We arrived at top of descent with insufficient fuel to make an approach, miss and go to an alternate. Surprisingly, the French system at that time allowed this. As long as you were sure to get into the destination you could begin descent. If not, you went to your alternate from top of descent for destination. Weird but flexible.

Unfortunately, when it came to leave next day there were many obstacles to our departure; not the least our flight plan kept being rejected. We had an army major as our liaison and he kept saying it would come soon but he wasn't sure what was happening. I had kept the oil-men in the loop and eventually their leader said, 'Give him this and let's get the hell out of here!' it was US$100. I said you can't do that, he's a military officer. Oh dear, Mr Naïve. I gave this corrupt officer the money and we were airborne twenty minutes later. This was my first but not last experience of the disgusting way in which so many countries work.

Upon our return I was asked if I would be chief pilot as Captain Oliver had moved on and I was happy to accept. The CAA authority came soon after. Sadly, having been investigated, analysed and then accepted by the CAA, my 'reign' was severely halted.

The son of our owner had a PPL (Private Pilot's Licence) and enjoyed dealing with pilots; however, his ability to deal with aeroplanes and the law left a lot to be desired. In my absence he had bought a Falcon from the USA and still with the N-registration. Instead of waiting for it to be given French registration, he rented it out to a customer, a friend, I think. Anyway, our licence to operate out of the UK was restricted to our French licence. HM Customs, I think, were less than pleased, so when it returned they attached a tractor to its nose-wheel. Furthermore, a grass-cutter managed to knock the wingtip off another Falcon. Then Geneva airport grounded our HS 125 due to money owing.

Ouch. Suddenly, we were in trouble and we ended up in administration. No flying, no customers and nowhere to go except down. I was really sorry for Mr Bowles because he had put his heart and his wealth, from quarrying, into this lovely little outfit and his foolish son and rotten circumstances ruined it.

We were in limbo for a few weeks, turning up occasionally to talk, drink coffee and keep our ops officer, Ravi Pathwardhan, company but nothing was happening. Out of the blue I met Nick Nicholls, one of my fellow ex-VC10 captains, and he asked what I was doing. He heard my sorry tale and told me that Gulf Air wanted VC10 captains. Wow! I went for an interview that day, was accepted, resigned from Trader Airways and set off on my next venture.

Gulf Air – Muharraq, Bahrain

On 8 May 1974 I climbed aboard a BA VC10 with BA Captain Phillip Hart-Lovelace and many other newly-hired pilots and off we went to Prestwick for training. At the hotel I unpacked and sat at the table with my VC10 manual to start again the ritual of studying. It was open at the index when the phone rang and Phillip said, 'Briefing in the bar in ten minutes.' He spoke my language.

Some of us had our golf clubs with us and Phillip found out there were just three of us plus him so, after a couple of beers, off we went to the nearest course. The next four days we flew and golfed. We all went up together and took it in turns to re-hone our skills. I fell into it as if I had never left. On the last day whilst packing I realised that my manual was still at the index. Oh well, it had all fallen into place so all was well with the world.

Later in the month I flew to Bahrain with Gulf Air (GF) in the company of Ian Stewart, a fellow new boy. At 300 to 400 feet in a turn left after take-off, the captain was talking on the PA, telling us about the flight and so on. Ian and I looked at each other and thought '*What the hell is he doing?*' Here we were in special airspace on a designated precise departure and his eye was not on the ball. The captain was one of the ex-BA pilots who had started the VC10 with Gulf Aviation now Gulf Air, one of the nicest guys you will ever meet fifty yards from an aeroplane.

This period was when we started using less power for take offs, weight permitting, and even reducing power at 1,000 feet to reduce the noise 'footprint'. We had a specific power reduction on the VC10 but this guy always tried to reduce it further. It was difficult for him because the flight engineer locked his hands on his set of throttles, so he gave up. He occasionally won but at Dubai there was usually a temperature inversion (increase in this case) at 1,000+ feet and if he selected his preferred reduction the aircraft would actually stop climbing or even descend. As soon as we were on our way he would go and see how the cabin crew were doing, which meant that the first officer and engineer could get on with the main task.

There was no line-training necessary for those of us who were VC10-qualified so off I went as a passenger to Abu Dhabi with Captain Neville Dowding, ex-BA. I saw this quite handsome chap with all these girls and reasoned he was the chief steward (or whatever: the titles change all the time). I later realised he was gay, as were nearly all the senior stewards. A bit of a shock for RAF blokes. They were all great guys and great fun as I was soon to find out.

I enjoyed my flights with Neville which were just around the gulf and up to Beirut and back. A good introduction to the airline. The airline had been known as Gulf Aviation Ltd until April 1974 and then went independent from BA as Gulf Air. They had been flying VC10s for a while. Most of the captains were from East African Airways (EAA) who had left when it was taken over by the local aviation authority as it was obviously going to deteriorate. There were five BA captains, Jack Payne, Jim Peers, Neville, Harry Nicholls, the Chief Pilot, and Dennis 'Bismarck' Briggs.

It was interesting flying with Dennis because he hated being called by his Christian name. He was one of the so-called 'Atlantic Barons' and decided that God was OK as long as he listened to BA captains. He thought that putting your landing lights on in daylight on approach was 'wasting electricity and unnecessarily burning out of bulbs'. Oh dear!

Dennis was known as 'Bismarck' because, on 26 May 1941, his aircraft had spotted the German battleship, which had sunk the British battlecruiser HMS *Hood*. Briggs had been a member of No. 209 Squadron, equipped with the newly-arrived Consolidated Catalina flying-boat, and was the captain of Catalina WQ-Z, which was deployed from RAF Lough Erne in County Fermanagh to search an area in which *Bismarck* was believed to be steaming towards safety. Since the Catalina was new to the squadron, US Navy pilots were assigned to assist in familiarizing the RAF crews with the machine. Alongside Briggs in WQ-Z was Ensign Leonard B. 'Tuck' Smith, who made the actual sighting while piloting the aircraft. Smith jettisoned the Catalina's four depth charges and dived for cloud cover to avoid the intensive anti-aircraft fire unleashed by *Bismarck*. Although WQ-Z lost contact with the battleship, two other US Navy pilots in RAF Catalinas spotted her later. The sightings led to the destruction of *Bismarck*, for which Smith was decorated with the Distinguished Flying Cross. Since the United States was officially neutral, no mention was made at the time that the sightings had been made by US airmen and it was Dennis Briggs who reported the sighting on the BBC. (Briggs was one of many RAF pilots who, at the end of hostilities, were automatically licensed for civil flying.)

Gulf Air was soon expanding and mostly with retired RAF VC10 pilots, EAA pilots and the five BA pilots. The fund of experience was truly magnificent. However, when I reached the top of the first officer list within one year of joining, Harry Nicholls decided to enlist half a dozen of his mates from BA as direct-entry captains, none of whom were current on type.

I went to see the chief pilot to ask why he had brought in his buddies, who had not flown for some time, when I and other experienced RAF VC10 captains were here, current and heavily qualified? His explanation was that we had insufficient civilian experience! We had not only been flying civilian routes for years but other more skill-testing flying as well. It was a really lame explanation for what was a form of nepotism.

This was looked upon as a pretty nasty and sly move, especially by me. Four of the guys were superb: Doug (Jumbo) Jarvis, Harry Mills, Lindsay Reynolds and Geoff Gray. The others were less so; one was rather superior (in his opinion), and the other a laugh if it wasn't for the fact this was serious work.

The 'laugh' had the ridiculous habit of engaging the autopilot in the climb to maintain speed but did not engage rudders or ailerons. What he did was to maintain heading or make small turns by using the rudders. This made some passengers a little queasy and the girls and boys down the back received sore and bruised hips. I asked him why he did it and he said, 'Because I can.'

What a prat!

He was also particularly agitated that GF used the long-established RAF tradition of monitored approach in bad weather. The BA system had always been that the captain flew the aircraft down to decision height, usually 200 feet, and the first officer would call 'runway in sight', the captain would look up and if he saw the runway then we would land. If not, he would carry out the go-around procedure. The RAF felt that for the captain to transition from panel focus to outside focus was slightly unnatural and a fraction of a second wasted.

The monitored system meant that the first officer flew the approach, the captain had the radio (therefore, no instructions to first officer for replies), could read the charts comfortably, monitor the first officer's accuracy and could keep an eye on the panel and outside. When close to decision he would concentrate only on outside and call 'I have control' if he could see the runway, or 'Go-around' if not. The first officer, already full on instruments, having never looked out, simply carried out the procedure. This scenario simply means that the captain was doing his main task of management and the first officer was doing what he did best and loved, i.e. he flew it.

Later in my captain's career I always let the first officer fly into any airfield I had never visited before, regardless of the weather, so that I could read the approach chart easily, monitor the first officer, handle the radio and *manage* the safe conduct of the flight. The alternative was to fly the aircraft, look from chart to instruments, tell the first officer what to say or reply to ATC and, generally juggle the handling. It's a no-brainer.

If you know the field well and the weather is fine then, of course, if it's your sector you fly the approach quite safely. The 'laugh' was so concerned that the monitored approach took control from the captain and that the first officer did the handling that he went round all the pilots to petition for the BA system. He was unlucky as the majority of captains and first officers were ex-RAF or EAA.

The monitored system is now used by most airlines, although I believe that, in those countries where 'face' is still important to the people, the captain still does everything and the first officers are reluctant to question his actions or decisions.

The Gulf Air route structure was mainly all the Gulf area, plus Shiraz, Bandar Abbas, Bombay, Beirut, Paris, Amsterdam and London. Later on, Cairo, Karachi, Athens and Larnaca (Cyprus) were also regular destinations. Bombay was probably the most frequented airport after the Gulf airports with sometimes as many as three flights a day from various places such as Bahrain, Dubai, Doha, Abu Dhabi and Muscat. There were huge numbers of Indians working in Bahrain and the Gulf.

Long-haul flying is very tiring due to overnight trips, time changes and the difficulty of sleeping either in daylight or when the circadian rhythm is too interrupted. Bombay, now Mumbai, was the worst of all because most trips, if they did not terminate in Bahrain, would end up there. Almost all arrived late at night or during the night and departures were early morning; sleep was hard to come by. You would eventually get home to Bahrain completely washed out and have only two or three days to get your act together before you were off again.

Life was good for me as I was in the Gulf Hotel for my first year. As I had no family with me or about to join me I refused all offers of an apartment to allow others to go ahead. Anyway, it was great to have my room cared for every day, a restaurant where my allowances covered good eating and a bar with decent beer. No-brainer, as they say.

As always, Bahrain was hot and humid and acclimatising was difficult. The most I had ever stayed before was a couple of nights but eventually one became accustomed to needing two or three showers a day and changes of clothes.

Although we only had four VC10s they managed a massive amount of work and, until we were up to strength with crews, it meant a lot of work for us. However, it was a joy to belong to the airline, the regular flight-deck crews were great guys and the cabin crew were superb. Everywhere we went it was party time. The girls were a marvellous bunch of fun-lovers, gorgeous and efficient.

In the early months, i.e. May-August, there was intensive cabin crew recruitment and training as we had fewer than needed for GF expansion. This meant that those already trained worked hard. As there were so few we got to know them all very quickly. The most senior are best remembered: Sue Murray, Jan Luck, Lynne Biddle, Joan John, Sue Jones, Rori McGrath, Linda Clarke, Mary Singleton, Linda Foster, John Redding, Angus Robb, Jean Jeffrey, Ding Sadler, et al. There were too many to name them all, sorry girls and boys.

Jaki Webb was on my flight to Bombay on 20/21 September but I don't remember her. However, in February 1975 we got chatting around the pool in Doha and our friendship started then. By this time my girlfriend Pat had gone off with a 'semi-friend' of mine, a BA traffic officer. Jaki was no longer a stewardess as she resigned over a really bad business with her seniors. She was the purser on a trip to London and on arrival found that some items were missing from her duty-free trolley. They had obviously been stolen, as so often happened. Anyway, it was not looked upon too kindly and she lived with it. Next payday they had taken it from her pay cheque without any warning, leaving her with nothing. She resigned on the spot and came to live in my apartment in the Sunflower building.

Jaki and I eventually married in July 1976 in the British Embassy on the North Coast road where the sea was the other side of the road. Now it's about a mile inland after island-wide reclamations. Years later I asked them for a copy of our marriage certificate as the original was lost in the post and the reply stated they did not do weddings. After one or two phone calls I managed to convince a senior member of the establishment that I was telling the truth and eventually received a copy.

Our best man, Peter Sheridan, took us to the Embassy in his white Merc and, with friends and some family, we started. Immediately Peter realised he had forgotten the champagne so had to shoot off. He returned as the ceremony finished and the party started. We left after the first glass for the usual photos and all gathered in Jane Burden's (white man's Burden) apartment.

Our honeymoon came later but, as I had no leave, Jaki came with me on my next trip with stops in Bombay, where she danced backwards into the bushes surrounding the floor and I didn't notice! Then we went to Paris and Amsterdam.

Bahrain

The airport was on an island, Muharraq, off the main island joined by a very long causeway. In the hot summer months, i.e. April-November, it was normal to see the two two-foot-high walls each side accommodating dozens of men sleeping. The yacht club is now half-a-mile inland; the British Embassy, where later on I was to remarry, was on the beach-front but now well inland and the customs house and port for the fishermen is also well inland. The house I eventually lived in, out in the countryside, i.e. desert, now has a four-lane highway above and next to it. The highest building in Bahrain was probably five to seven storeys – now there are skyscrapers everywhere.

There were just three proper hotels in 1974, Dilmun Hotel, Bahrain Hotel and the Gulf Hotel, which is now business offices with the new hotel next to it. If I was in the hotel for the weekly arrival of the French UTA crew, I would go to reception to watch them arrive. I was not alone. The girls were, without exception, trim, beautiful and sexy. Their uniforms enhanced their allure; they wore white angora sweaters, snug pastel-blue skirts and calf-length blue leather boots.

One morning I realised I was standing next to Michael Bentine, the famous comedian, Goon and writer. We got chatting; he was waiting for a taxi, but was quite happy with his fortuitous timing and I found out that he had trained as a Lancaster navigator during the war but, before he could join an operational squadron, he received a faulty anti-typhoid injection and, after a six-week coma, his eyesight was damaged and he continued service as an Intelligence officer (IO). His predecessor in the queue for the injection died as a result of the error.

He really was a lovely man with no 'celebrity' hang-ups, just natural. We said our goodbyes as his taxi arrived at the same time as UTA but he smiled at me to show he appreciated my reasons for being there.

Doha

Qatar had no skyscrapers but did have one of the three or four longest runways in the world. It did not need it but they had it because they could; three-plus miles long I think it was. We stayed in the Gulf Hotel and the only pleasure was room 501 which had been converted into a bar for non-Muslims. The barman was a charming Indian, the room had a view of the Marina and sold all you could want. The hours, however, were only 1800-2230.

The Marina had room for many boats and there was a slipway up to the huge maintenance workshop. There were only two or three engineers under the control of an Englishman. I wandered up there on most trips and this fellow was subject to joy and sorrow. He loved working on beautiful boats, some just speed-boats, some up to 40-metres long, but the sorrow was the constant damage done by the local owners. They would get in the boat, select full power and go screaming out of the port, usually showing off to the female passengers. The passengers were the local ex-pats or our stewardesses.

Sadly, this behaviour did regular damage to the engines despite the owners being constantly advised to let the engines warm up.

Abu Dhabi

We stayed at the Hilton which had the coldest swimming pool I've ever used. The only way to go in was an inch at a time – few of us dived in. All the crew would be round the pool eagerly awaiting a first-timer to arrive. Normally it would be a visiting businessman, white all over and eager to show the girls his perfect dive. As soon as he hit the water we knew there would be a heart attack or a brave attempt at walking on the water. We never saw a heart attack but, by golly, we saw some brave attempts at divinity. It was most entertaining!

As we were not on business accounts we ate out at one of only two real places. The city was probably 10 per cent of the size it is now and the corniche was only a few hundred yards long. One of the restaurants had lazy-susans on the tables and when we arrived we surreptitiously handed the head waiter a bottle of gin and of whiskey and received two tea pots, one with G & T and the other with whiskey. Water was, of course, provided. Great food too.

The other restaurant, opposite the hotel, was a rickety and wobbly wooden structure of two floors but served great seafood. No tea pots, though. I hear it is still there but I'm certain it has had structural work on it because I was always concerned it was going to collapse when I was in there.

Dubai

The airfield was suitable for all aircraft but had quite a small terminal, i.e. about 100 yards long with a spiral walkway at each end. The runway ended with just a two-lane road at the end, a beach of fifty yards and then the sea. Now, I think the end of the runway is quite a few hundred yards inland.

The spiral staircase was for the passengers. There were no tunnels etc. for them to use and board the aircraft and, like crews everywhere, we were always interested to see the various types as they walked out.

Dubai was often subjected to fog and we had to carry out missed approaches when coming in from the south. However, we had enough fuel before going somewhere else to have a go at the other end which usually had the first one or two hundred yards visible due to sea breezes, which are normally a daytime phenomenon in cooler parts of the world. It was quite usual to land and just have enough view of the centre-line white strips to maintain direction. Great fun.

From Muscat/Seeb Airport to Dubai was practically a straight line down the runway and one of our little pleasures was to get descent clearance early enough to delay the descent until ready. The idea was to close the throttles, establish centre-line of the runway and carry out approach procedures, i.e. gear and flap, in such a way that no power was needed until as late as possible. Naturally we always had to have power by 500 feet to ensure proper engine response if needed nearer the ground. It was always satisfying to reach 500 feet, adjust the power and make a landing with no further deviations from the norm.

We always stayed down the road in Sharjah and one night we used my room for drinks as, being the captain, I had a suite. I ordered beer, fillers and plenty of ice. It was ages coming, and most of the crew were there when the room service guy arrived with the order. However, instead of ice there was a huge bowl of rice.

Off the beach sailfish were a frequent sight and some brave swimmers ventured into the sea despite the sharks. I'd had my fill of sharks by now so I held their coats.

My encounter with sharks at Gan was eclipsed by my experience in the bay at Bahrain. I was water-skiing behind my friend Peter's boat and my girlfriend Jaki Webb turned to him and said something. He looked back, signalled to the beach and took me back. Fortunately, I showed off and skied onto the beach. It was explained later that I was being closely followed by a shark. A Korean sailor was taken by a shark the following week; needless to say, my water-skiing days were now over.

Muscat

Not too long before my first flight to Seeb Airport in 1974 there had been only a few miles of paved road. This road led from the airport to the Sultan's palace. However, there was a great improvement and, what was most remarkable, the moment building or roadmaking or any type of construction work was finished the entire area was spotless. This was so unlike the rest of the Gulf where detritus could remain for months and, occasionally, years.

We had the pleasure of staying at the Gulf Hotel sited on a promontory outside the city. The pool had its own café/restaurant and was where the crews spent all their time. The favourite drink was Pimms No. 1, usually to be found at the pool edge as the water was much cooler than the air temperature.

Whilst all sitting around the pool one day a Lebanese captain of Middle East Airlines (MEA) was teaching one of his lady cabin crew to dive. Frankly, he wasn't very good himself but he enjoyed being the centre of attention. His pupil was a quick learner despite his demonstrations. As if by telepathy, the GF crews picked the menus off the table and drew low numbers on them. Every time the captain dived, each table held up two cards, rather like the ice-dancing judges, awarding him low points for technique and skill. His student and the rest of his crew found this hilarious but the numbers disappeared as soon as his head came to the surface. He eventually realised what was happening and took it in good part.

One or two or so of the BA captains felt that having fun with the crew was a bit below their self-appointed dignity. The others acted as if they were really happy to be with us and able to abandon the hidebound rank structure of their previous employer. The only fly in the ointment for the 'ordinary' first officers was, that if you flew with a BA captain and flight engineer together they never stopped talking about pensions and some called us 'Goof Air', which was a little unfair as they had an extra salary to support their pension.

The manager of the hotel, Alan(?) Bodger, was very well known in the Gulf having been in and around for many years. He called me to his office one morning to ask if my crew and I would like to attend a five-course lunch which marked the culmination of the training of palace cooks and waiters and was their final test. I pointed out that as we were only on a two-day trip that none of us would be smart and, indeed, I only had T-shirt and shorts. He pointed out that it was totally informal and just an opportunity for the staff to show their new-found skills.

'Okay,' I said and advised all the crew. At the duly appointed time, I wandered down the curved corridor to the special dining-room and was asked by the man on the door to identify myself. I was then announced into the room 'Captain Brian Burdett, Gulf Air', whereupon I entered to see my crew in the corner all dolled up and various Ambassadors, VIPs and ladies drinking sherry, champagne, etc.

I was mortified. Before I could turn and run the manager greeted me with a glass and walked with me to my crew. They were in stitches as they had been briefed before leaving Bahrain as to what was to happen but were sworn to secrecy. Regrettably, no one else seemed to have been let into the secret, so I will never forget the frosty stares of the elegantly-dressed VIPs. I hid amongst my crew and when we sat at the tables with the amazing setting I chose to drink little because I had no desire to need the loo and walk past all these people dressed as I was.

The meal was, of course, magnificent and, afterwards, with me still seated until all had left the manager gave us a bottle of brandy and said that I hoped it was a good jape. Maybe, but I'll never be more embarrassed, I hope.

Later one of the girls in the crew came to the pool and explained she had gone to the beach and then swum out to a wreck (rocks?) about 300 yards out. She was excited to have seen so many rays. I asked if she had seen any sharks and she replied 'no'; I explained that they had probably seen her.

The Station Officer at Seeb Airport was an Indian gentleman called Mr Prince. He was very efficient, charming and polite. He always waited until our nose-wheel started moving and he held a very military stance and saluted. This he had learnt from BOAC and I found it most touching.

On 10 May 1975 I was being checked for my licence on the VC10. This involved the simulator at BA Cranebank and was conducted by Geoff Gray and monitored by the CAA inspector. I was normally calm with Geoff but pretty tensed on this occasion.

During the ILS (Instrument Landing System) approach I managed to very temporarily go out of limits below 1,500 feet. This is a no-no so, at the debrief, Geoff had to fail me. Geoff explained later that he had no choice as he was being checked as well. Usually, if the recovery is quick, well-handled and the check pilot knows your normal standard then you just do another ILS. The CAA man then made the chilling statement that 'I have to advise you that, until a satisfactory check, you are no longer able to exercise the privileges of your licence.'

Two days later when the simulator was again free, I did a satisfactory but scrappy check and received my licence again. The elevators had been hard work on both these rides. To my astonishment and anger, immediately after the ride the simulator was grounded for some time, i.e. days or weeks, as the elevator control system had serious defects.

I was never comfortable in simulators or, indeed, flight checks, maybe because in the early days the check pilots were there to try and force you into errors and give you a hard time. They were known as 'Trappers' and were much feared. Slowly, the system improved until check rides and simulator became much more relaxed but still taken seriously, of course.

Geoff Gray was actually someone who instilled confidence during checking but the best pilot I ever knew as a checker was Blair Boyle in Virgin Atlantic. Sadly, he left VS to move back to Scotland and fly for a lucky outfit there.

In August 1975 I did my command training, again with Geoff Gray, at Shannon, and we stayed in the Grounds Hotel in nearby Ennis. The weather was foul for two of the days but we pressed ahead, even doing circuits at 300 to 400 feet just to get the required exercises done. All my experience on the VC10 came into play. Not so fortunate was my fellow trainee, who had never sat in a captain's seat before and found it too hard for him. He made the grade later.

I passed comfortably and then bided my time until I received my command on 1 September that year. At the same time, I received an invitation for an interview with Cathay Pacific, to whom I had written earlier. I cancelled the interview, although I was sure to be employed – all ex-RAF had been – but I felt that another six to seven years as a first officer was not a nice thought. What a mistake! It turns out I would have probably been a captain within three years on a fantastic salary with ridiculous annual bonuses. I would even have ended up senior to the man who would eventually be chief pilot at Virgin Atlantic. Ah, hindsight.

Nevertheless, it was a wonderful time being a civilian captain at last. Strangely, I have met quite a few pilots who did not want to be promoted to captain but when I asked 'why', I don't recall one answer that really helped me to understand. To me, the responsibility was deeply felt and proudly accepted.

Actually, before my promotion I had had a bit of unexpected captain time. En route Beirut-Bahrain the captain, Murray Douglas, suffered a ruptured vessel behind his left eye; there was so much blood and pain that I had to assume command. We were midway, so I asked where he would like to go to hospital. He plumped for Bahrain where the treatment was successful.

In July 1975 one of my last flights as first officer was with Harry Nicholls – Bahrain-Paris via Baghdad. The main passenger was the Ruler of Qatar, who wanted to pick up a friend on the way. It was just a normal flight until an aide to the Ruler came on the flight deck and gave each of us an envelope. The captain put his aside, so I followed suit. However, the flight engineer, Danny Duffain, and the ground engineer, carried to look after the aircraft in Baghdad, opened theirs. They had each received 150 Bahraini dinars.

I decided to open my envelope but to my astonishment I had only 100. This caused much hilarity among the engineers as the ground guy had obviously received mine. I could not ask for it, he didn't offer it and I could hardly complain; so that was that.

My new captaincy differed very little from the RAF days, except I was now called Brian instead of captain or skipper. Unfortunately for the first officers I was not permitted to give them a landing until I had fifty hours in the LHS (left-hand seat). I gave them sectors leg and leg about but had to do the take off and landing.

One of my first LHS flights was to Karachi which was a pleasant stopover. In those days the crew could sit round the pool, drink beer and have a good time. There was a very British style restaurant nearby, i.e. formally-dressed staff, excellent service but old-fashioned British food; we enjoyed their offerings.

Eventually, the pool was closed to ladies, there was no beer in public and only available in your hotel room if you were non-Muslim. There was so much glycerine in the beer it was undrinkable.

We were still using the BA VC10 simulator, so every six months off you went with first officer and flight engineer for the checks. It was never included in a normal trip, so we went as passengers, normally in first class. There were usually four people: training captain, captain, first officer and flight engineer, so as soon as we were airborne we went to the bar and sat at the four-seater table and played cards for the six-to-seven-hour flight.

In the early stages of Gulf Air, the first-class section was superb, the seats excellent, the service world-class and, at the back, a proper bar with bar stools (fixed) and one or two tables. Before departure the passengers were offered orange juice or champagne and, immediately after take off, caviar and exquisite vodka. GF were really in the top league then and for a long time.

One of my simulator sessions was interrupted mid-flow by a message from base that the Sheikh's wives were in Paris and wanted to go home immediately. So we sped to the aircraft that would be taking the London-Bahrain flight that night and flew to Paris/Orly. We were scheduled to take them to London departing Paris 1400 hours. We arrived at 1300 and I told the crew to relax as they were bound to be late.

Suddenly, a cabin-crew member said, from the comfort of her first-class seat, 'Gosh, look at all those limousines!' Panic! They were early. Anyway, we got back in time for the evening scheduled service.

Until the Royal family acquired their own aircraft, it was not unusual for a flight to be cancelled just so that the aircraft could convey whomever to wherever. It was quite normal to disembark passengers and let them see others board and the aircraft disappear.

On Christmas Day 1975 I was called out to take an aircraft to Doha to pick up the Qatari minister of education for Cairo. The aircraft had been on scheduled service and many people were unable to get to their destinations that day, especially as there was a weather delay on arrival at Cairo and we were on the ground for four hours.

Earlier in that December I was en route LHR-Doha when a stewardess came to tell me that she had seen a baby that was not on the passenger list. The mother had concealed the baby under her abaya and nobody, including ground staff, knew of her.

The stewardess, a former nurse, said the baby was slightly blue and was probably oxygen deficient. I suggested one of our oxygen bottles but I was advised that neat oxygen was dangerous for babies.

So, I got ATC clearance to descend to 22,000 feet which meant the cabin environment would be at ground level and asked the stewardess plus her fellow nurse, who had now joined us, to see how it went. They came back shortly with some astonishing news; not only was the baby not responding but the mother had confessed that only three or four days earlier the baby had had heart surgery at Great Ormond Street Hospital. She further said the doctor had made an appointment ten days hence, but she wanted to get home.

I immediately requested clearance for an emergency landing at nearby Istanbul and we landed shortly after. An ambulance was standing by but the mother refused to leave the aircraft with the baby. The father took the baby off and entered the ambulance.

We continued on our way and the cabin crew re-started the lunch service.

A few days later the crew were all interviewed separately and unknown to the others to give their accounts of the incident. The baby had died almost immediately.

The father was claiming the pressurisation was at fault and blamed the flight engineer. It was claimed that I should have made the decision earlier and the two stewardesses were given such a hard time that they both resigned. The people making the waves were from the indigenous side of the airline management. Needless to say, it was all very unfair as the flight engineer had handled the pressurisation correctly throughout and I made the decision to land as soon as we knew the baby's circumstances.

The parents sued GF and won damages!

There were many instances of such unreasonable and unfair judgements. I was cleared to parking Bay 1, one night, and as I put the brakes on I was advised that I was in the wrong place and that they were going to push me back immediately. I said okay and we were pushed elsewhere. All three on the flight deck agreed we had definitely been given Bay 1.

The next day Dick Woodhead, who was now our chief pilot, called me to his office and asked me why I had taxied into the bay awaiting the arrival of King Hussein of Jordan. I explained it was because I had been told to and suggested checking the tapes in the tower. He advised me that they had not been working properly, so there was no proof!! He knew as well as I that this was all a set-up job to cover the inefficiency of the Bahraini controller.

Eventually, I ended up in an apartment in the Sunflower Buildings at a quiet(ish!) crossroads and set about giving it a new coat of paint but as the paint went on so it disappeared! They must have been the most porous walls imaginable. However, it was free with all services included which was wonderful. To this day I believe that all major Middle East companies still look after their employees this way.

Jaki and I were going down in the lift immediately after it had been serviced and it ran away. It was terrifying for only a few seconds as it didn't fit well and wobbled about. This movement meant that a bottom corner of the lift jammed against something and it stopped dead. We had only gone one and a half floors but it seemed like forever. The worst bit was getting out because half of the gap after the doors were open was below floor level. The fear was that it would drop again and cut us in half as we clambered out. It had been serviced that morning but was 'nobody's fault', of course.

As I became captain, so GF employed a few first officers from BA. These guys had been navigators until inertial navigation systems (three per aircraft) made them redundant. BA retrained them as first officers, which was very generous; their time in aviation may not have included piloting but their experience plus their depth of airmanship made them good trainees.

They were all charming fellows but knew they would never have enough experience or desire to be captains. However, one of their number, Peter Young, did get a command on our B737, so well done him.

Doha

Tony Mitchell, captain, was sitting quietly on the flight deck during a long turn-round when he felt a bump so he went to investigate. The fork-lift truck had been driven into the skin of the aircraft just below the door to the underfloor baggage stowage.

The soldier/policeman guarding the aircraft demanded his driving licence as this was a traffic accident. When Tony couldn't produce a Qatari licence, he was arrested and placed in the airport jail. It took an hour for our traffic officer and manager to spring him.

Doha again

I was sitting waiting for passengers and watched a light aircraft downwind who asked for a touch-and-go landing. He was cleared to land after the approaching TriStar. No mention was made of wake turbulence (think of churned-up white water behind a powerful boat) and, at about 300 feet on approach, he flipped upside down and struggled to regain safe control. He didn't bother with touch and go; he just cleared the runway and parked. What a fright.

Doha again

We captains were always signing for valuable items being transferred around the Gulf, such as diamonds, watches and especially gold. The transfer was always manual and on the flight deck; the captain signed the top copy of the manifest as a receipt and on handing on the valuables also received a copy. This continued until the addressee signed.

Gold is surprising with its weight; you can receive a parcel of it no bigger than a cigarette packet and initially your mind cannot comprehend weight to size ratio. One morning one of our B737 captains signed over the gold to the station officer and upon his return to BAH he was quizzed and given a hard time by the police. However, his receipt proved he had handed over correctly.

The station officer could not be found and it was surmised that he had received the gold, changed into civvies and boarded the Air India flight to Bombay within about thirty minutes. He would have had a chum in Bombay customs and gone into India untroubled!

Dubai

Dubai duty free was started around 1974 and business handed to the best bidder and the prices set by the government. Black Label Whiskey was £1.10p, a carton of Benson and Hedges £1, Gin 80p and so on. Heaven!

Eventually the lessees raised the prices by about 80 per cent and the government told them to return them to the original price as travellers thought of Dubai as the best duty-free in the world. Heaven revisited!

One day sitting in the flight deck waiting for one passenger I eventually decided to offload his baggage. This was a lengthy process as all bags were loaded by hand and stacked in the hold. The bags were all unloaded and the passengers left in single file via the front door, identified their bags and returned through the rear. Eventually, there was only one large bag left so we battened the hatches and prepared to start. At this moment a little man came haring down the spiral walk-way and sprinted to the aircraft. He skidded to a halt as he saw the bag; as if in a cartoon, you would have seen a large bubble with the words 'What's my bag doing there?'

He was advised that he was not going to London as he was too late. He was so crestfallen and sorrowful that I took pity on him and ordered his bag to be stowed and that he board. It was only a few extra minutes and we were on a long flight to London, so what was a minor delay?

It transpired that he had checked in but he had to pay a large sum for excess baggage, so he trotted off to the appropriate counter and his bag was sent airside. Normally, the Gulf airports are thronged with passengers' friends and family to see them off but our man found that he had insufficient funds for his excess and nobody to turn to for money. So, he got in his car and drove a round trip to his home to get some cash. When he returned, as he had his boarding pass, he fled through immigration and found a door to get to the aircraft. Security was still in its infancy but we were learning.

My caution about the baggage was as a result of one of our captains earlier who had offloaded baggage in Karachi. The staff there were angry at the extra work and took ages to do it. The offending case was dumped in the airport where it exploded fifteen minutes after the aircraft departed.

That captain, Keith Webster, was one of the first, if not *the* first, to start this procedure in GF. At that time there had not been any orders as terrorism was not deemed significant. It *was* after that.

I was put in a tricky position later at Doha when the first class in the VC10 was filled with many government ministers being given farewells by many friends and relatives. When they had finished and disembarked, a spare attaché case was found. I was now in the unenviable position of asking all the 'VIPs' to check their personal belongings and to identify the case. I was, of course, well aware that much of Royalty and high-ranking officials have achieved their positions over the years with a little bit of eliminating of the opposition.

This is what I was worried about but, as they accepted my decision well, I think that they knew that they could have had a reason to worry also. The attaché case was never identified and was offloaded.

Muscat

There were no buses for passengers or airstairs, so it was all shanks's pony. So, you would see a long line of passengers waiting to climb the steps to the forward door. One night I saw a large piece of white paper blown into the queue and was amazed to see everyone jumping about and showing concern. I found out later that was a camel spider. It could have done them no harm as it needs you asleep.

What it does is inject you with its anaesthetic and when you are 'ready' it quite simply eats your flesh. Many people have been disfigured by them. Fortunately, it is a desert spider and unlikely to trouble 'Upset of Tunbridge Wells'.

Bombay (now Mumbai)

We used to stay in the Oberoi Sheraton which was on the seafront and, in the morning, you would see hundreds of people having their morning walk. In the distance one could see the crows et al feeding on the bodies of those poor persons who had not been claimed by anybody. These people would be placed in the disposal site at the top of a hill overlooking our hotel. It was not unusual to find the odd human bone in the street, I have heard.

The hotel would be described as definitely first-class, i.e. Five Stars, but for one major problem: the fire escape was lethal. The doors were next to the lifts and went around the lift shaft. It was not a circular route but square and went between floor and ceiling of the respective floors. It was dimly lit and you were obliged to go through one door which opened towards you. Can you imagine the multitude of people all pressing against those trying to open that door?

I was quite nervous in this hotel because I knew that in the event of a fire many, many people would die. So I was in the habit of using the emergency route at least one time each visit. On one occasion it was impossible as renovations had used the escape stairs as a dumping ground for stone, wall panels, et al.

I eventually got to the reception and advised the duty manager of the blockage and the massive danger to the guests. Had he shown any interest I would have left him to sort it out but he just shrugged and said it would be finished at the end of the day.

I told him that if it was not cleared by the time I had finished breakfast I would be going directly to the fire service and the police. After breakfast the fire escape was ready for the appalling chaos that would occur in the frightening situation if there were to be a fire.

Later I was staying in another hotel (name forgotten) when it started to shake quite frighteningly; I was on the top floor so I grabbed my bag with essentials in it, money, passport, licences, etc., and prepared to run. As I passed the window I saw hundreds running towards me, and then realised they were going to the skyscraper next to me, I was on the thirty-second floor.

The disturbance was the collapsing of the entire scaffolding structure from the thirtieth floor. In India and most parts of Asia, scaffolding is made using strong bamboo and other wood tied with rope. There must have been tons of it, and many casualties. As I was off immediately on a trip I did not see much more or hear about it again.

We eventually ended up in the famous Taj Mahal but, although we received excellent service, we were never looked after in the way the truly wealthy were. There is a very sad story attached to this hotel. In front is the sea, Elephant Island and Queen Victoria's gateway to India.

The architect designed this beautiful hotel with all its public and best rooms facing the sea. The back was a flat, boring and almost windowless wall. He left the manager and builders to it and went home to England. When he heard they had finished he went to see it.

June, 1975. Gulf Air. The lovely Maggie Tarrant handing the traditional crew gift to captains on their final career flight. Captain Colin Butler receives the gift as the author looks on.

1976. Gulf Air 5-STAR TRI-STAR in the livery I loved. (Courtesy of Propfreak Photography)

16 March, 1977. Movenpick Hotel Cairo with Gulf Air. This is the day I stopped smoking forever. The hotel burned down shortly afterwards but it couldn't have been my fault, could it? (AOP)

August, 1979. The remains of the Cyprus Airways B707 which the family were in when it was slammed into the ground. The engines were hitting the runway as the wings flexed so much. Strangely, neither I nor any pilot witnesses were allowed to give evidence at the enquiry! (AOP)

1982. My children; Andrew with Josh(ua) aboard and Nick with Gemma. (AOP)

2002. The mob; Josh, Gemma, Nick and Andrew at our house in France. (AOP)

1982. At home in Pont's Green (please note the 'T') with my first and only beard. When I finally shaved it off, my mother, who had not liked it, did not notice for a whole day! (AOP)

Night loading at Khartoum with Saudia. Where are my mangos?

October, 1985. Geoff Uren seems to be saying, 'I took your photo now take mine'. (see rear cover). Note the vertical strips on the engine instruments. I'm a needles man myself. (AOP)

1992. Saudia TriStar L10-11 arriving at Frankfurt. (Courtesy of Paul Link)

2006. Jacki and I on the Merry-go-round at the Virgin Atlantic annual party at Sir Richard Branson's house, near Oxford. (AOP)

Early 1994. The author at about 200 feet before landing at Kai Tak, Hong Kong. No, I'm not about to land on the airport car-park. (Courtesy of Captain Christopher Wren, Virgin Atlantic (retired) One of the best!)

September, 1996. Yesterday, I was captain of this aircraft but now I'm too old! The company have kindly retained my services as a Senior First Officer; I don't know if the title relates to my age or my place in the order of things! (AOP)

June, 1997. Gemma and I during a night flight to Tokyo. Note the skyline, it's supposed to be night but we are at 72 degrees North. (AOP)

Airbus340 flight deck at night.

Summer 2016. At home in S.W. France with Gemma, Archie, our hairy Dashchund cum Fauvre Bretagne, and the most beautiful of our past six Dobermanns, Tallulah a.k.a. Tula. To me she was Toots. R.I.P. you beauty. (AOP)

Horror of horrors they had built it the wrong way round. The 'front' overlooked a narrow road off which were other roads with houses for the poor. The back was just a bare slab of nothing facing the beautiful view. He was so devastated he threw himself from the roof. When I visited in the 1970s it was as described above but by my later visits as a guest it had been converted with a beautiful entrance at the side nearest the 'gateway' and the 'back' was now a beautiful 'front' overlooking the sea.

There was a great restaurant in Bombay called the Berak. Upon entering there was a courtyard effect of 100 square metres of dining and for about five or six floors the interior all had balconies and walkways filled with tables. They must have had 200 covers. I dined on a fifth-floor balcony and it was a great vantage point to enjoy seriously good Indian cuisine.

We all regularly visited a popular furniture store in Hughes Street to get small pieces of beautifully-made furniture and hanging seats or garden things. One day I hailed a taxi and asked for Hughes Street; he advised me that there was no such place. After much bickering and that nearly impossible to imitate Indian head shake, we agreed to proceed and I would show him the route. When we got there he turned round and said 'No Sir, this is Huges Street.'

The poverty in Bombay was terrible to behold. Each early morning departure we would drive through streets with little or no traffic but many men with wooden two-wheeled flat backs collecting bodies of those who had died during the night, i.e. the homeless ones.

We would taxi parallel to the runway, turn right and hold until cleared to enter the runway and backtrack, and turn at the end so that we had the full length for take off. The hold before entering could be quite unpleasant because the area to the left was five acres of waste ground used for morning functions for the hundreds of people of the ramshackle buildings abutting it. The smell was pretty awful and was known to all aviators as 'Crappers' Corner'. You could smell Bombay from several miles downwind and up to 300 or 400 feet on final approach to the runway. Once on the ground you got used to it.

Amsterdam

We stayed at the then Hotel Sonesta just north-west of the upper end of the Damrak. It is now renamed but I cannot find the new name. It was well placed as the Damrak is the main road through Amsterdam.

On my first visit I just strolled around the canals and I was fascinated by a beautiful woman on the other side. I could see her through a large picture window, elegantly dressed and drinking tea. It was not until she looked at me as well and gave that professional smile that I realised who/what she was. It was quite a disappointment. Shortly after that, of course, I saw many more women behind windows and on view to the public, a quite normal sight in the end.

That night the girls all insisted we went to the local porn cinema. Believe it or not, the flight crew preferred a few beers, but we went with them. Within fifteen minutes the three flight crew were all asleep; it's a tiring job you know.

Another time walking down the Damrak in the afternoon I heard one of the world's unmistakeable sounds, Merlin engines. I turned round and looked up to see a Hurricane and Spitfire flying straight along the road at about 400 feet.

What is that all about, I thought, and proceeded on my way, uplifted by the experience. Then I heard military music ahead and thought it sounded like the Royal Air Force band. It was! They were in a square off the Damrak and I had a pleasant hour listening. When I visited the odd bar that evening I found that people wanted to buy me a drink. Why! It was Liberation Day and because I was English that was good enough.

Amsterdam Schiphol had the cleanest airport I have ever visited and that includes Singapore, Shanghai and Tokyo. The place was always spotless. Taxiing in one day I saw a cigarette packet on the grass next to the taxiway; I pointed it out to the first officer and engineer and they were both as surprised as I. It was always truly spotless.

As a matter of interest I rate the area ATC, Maastricht, as second only to London. They are so calm and clear; also, the Dutch speak the best English of all countries for whom it is not the mother tongue. Their accents are easily noted, though.

London ATC is so calming and efficient that after a long and, perhaps, rough, night it gives you a feeling of coming home. They had one particular lady having a tantrum one day on the Ground Control frequency; she had given clearance to USA flight to clear the runway, take the outer to Echo, proceed via the inner and go to Parking Bay 34 via Golf (or whatever). Unfortunately, he took a wrong turning and blocked another taxiway.

She berated him somewhat like, 'USA I told you to take Golf and now I will have to reroute other aircraft which will cause hold-ups down the line. Hold your present position and do not move until I call you back. Do you understand that?'

'Absolutely ma'am. Weren't we married sometime back?'

Another humorous recording was when an Air France pilot was asked his in-flight conditions. This was not unusual before radar was so good that, generally speaking, the conditions did not matter anymore. However, if the pilot had favourable conditions he could be given freer instructions.

VMC was visual flight conditions i.e. 1,000 feet clear of cloud, or better, and visibility 3,000 yards, or better. Occasionally, you might modify your response of VMC or IMC to, 'Becoming VMC or IMC,' or even 'In and out of the tops.'

The AF pilot responded, 'In and out of ze bottoms.'

Before ATC could respond a BA pilot transmitted, 'Vive le sport!'

Cairo

Cairo was a popular place for a layover. We stayed at the Movenpick Hotel quite near the Pyramids. Just up the road was the famous Mina House Hotel which also had a good golf course.

During the day we would do the normal tourist bit, go on camels, rent horses to go up to hills beyond where there was a good bar and restaurant, tour the Pyramids, meanwhile avoiding those who wished to sell you anything from 'local' paraphernalia to their sisters. En route to the Pyramids it was necessary to keep your eyes open in case you fell over a sleeping soldier and to avoid many beggars, professional or otherwise.

Sitting on the flight deck in the parking area one day I watched an Egypt Air B707 make a rather erratic approach to the runway. After landing (arrival more like) he left the runway and careered towards us. We fled the aircraft, we had no passengers on board, and watched the 707 swerve and make it back to the runway. Phew!

One of our UK handling officers from Bahrain was with us in Cairo. Unfortunately, for the Cairo baggage handlers he spoke perfect Arabic and overheard two of them saying they would load three or four bags onto our aircraft from a massive backlog of lost and/or mishandled baggage they had accrued. It came out in the investigation that they had been doing this with as many bags as they could and for months.

Abu Dhabi

Abu Dhabi provided me with the start of an attempt to understand the local idea of justice. One of our captains was sent to AUH to replace a sick captain. On arrival he hailed an airport taxi to take him to the hotel, boarded and the driver promptly reversed into the car behind. The driver berated the other driver and the captain, Len Midgely or Ted Whalan, demanded money for the damage. Len/Ted (RSA and Aussie) refused and insisted on going to the hotel. A few days later the captain was called to court in AUH and fined and told to pay for the damage to both cars!

The 'logic' to this is that if the foreigner (i.e. infidel) had not been in their country then the accident would not have happened! This reminds me that in my first month in Bahrain a lorry came out of a side road and hit me. I called the police and promptly ended up in court and was fined; I raised my eyebrows and was about to argue my case when a court 'clerk'? gave me a universal look of 'be careful' and a movement of his head. I paid the fine and left bemused; there were no damage payments as the lorry had only a mark in the scuffed, centuries old, mud on the bumper!

Later in AUH I was en-route to the airport in a taxi accompanied by a male and female flight attendant. The driver was a bit fast until he was cut-up by another taxi when he went all Lewis Hamilton. The two of them were shouting at each other, swerving in and out of lanes, nearly causing accidents etc. The lady in the back was screaming and all my demands were ignored. At one stage we were in the inside-lane and slightly slower so I switched the ignition off and threw the keys into the desert alongside! As Terry Wogan would have said, 'He went beresk!'.

We alighted, grabbed our baggage, hailed another taxi (with fingers crossed) and continued to the airport leaving 'beresk of the desert' scratching around for his keys. I heard nothing about it.

Our new driver lightened the mood by twirling his finger by his temple and saying, 'He crazy! Why you go with him?'

Jaki

Jaki is a great negotiator and persuader, so she managed to get us moved from the noisy city centre to a twenty-four-bungalow unit on a quiet main road to Buddeiyah on the west coast some four miles distant. The east coast was a mile away. The units were Swedish prefabs and ideal for Bahrain. They were designed to keep the cold out but worked perfectly keeping the hot out. There was central air-conditioning and heating from a big boiler-cum-heater and little vents in all the doors to allow the air to circulate. The house was on supports which kept air flowing underneath and the wooden walls were covered by six-by-six-foot sections of small white bricks joined together.

The group of people was a real mix: the Deputy General Manager Ops, P. Bruce-Souster, a few pilots, a few engineers, freight and ground and one or two administrators. It was very peaceful except for Mike Davies who roared home in his BMW at the end of a trip. It was a narrow road between my house and Bill Gopsill's but the company would not put in a sleeping policeman to slow traffic. We were concerned for our children.

So, while Mike was away Bill and I dug up the road, cemented a tree trunk into the channel and covered it with asphalt 'acquired' from a passing council vehicle using the universal currency, money. When Mike returned next day or so he probably got airborne in his car and in his anger. He eventually settled down and all was calm.

We all took over our houses from new so, for some of us, there was a fast learning curve for gardening. I put down grass on most of it, and planted tomatoes outside the bathroom; to my astonishment they thrived and after a while I started weighing them and exceeded 32lbs, which was the then British record, in Britain, of course.

Later I realised we had a leak in the underground pipe from the lavatory which explained all. I also took a cutting, with permission, from the only Flame of the Forest tree in Bahrain. In four years it grew to twenty feet and when I saw it again in 2011 it was huge.

It was wonderful to be back in the LHS of the VC10 after four years out of it. Although we now used first names instead of navigator, engineer, etc., it all felt just the same, camaraderie, respect, help whenever and wherever needed. Of course, the cabin service was different and we could always have first-class meals; the pilots, of course, ate different foods at different times. The cabin crew were different as they were mostly women with fewer men. Bahraini men were becoming more and more plentiful as cabin crew but the Bahraini girls no longer worked in the cabin. Originally, it was fine for us and I'm sure they enjoyed a bit of emancipation. However, parental and family doubts meant they all left.

The cabin crew were a great bunch of people, always up for fun and games. Sheikh Isa bin Salman Al Kalifa, or Jack, as the girls called him, had parties every weekend in one of his places or his yachts, and girls were always needed for decorative purposes. A couple of our senior male cabin crew acted as go-betweens and organised the invitations. The girls were nearly all keen, as the presents for just turning up at the parties were worth quite a bit. Many of the girls were regulars and did very well financially and had large watch collections!

Life in Bahrain was good. I had a third share in a twin-engined dhow and we frequently went cruising and fishing. It was moored to the west at Buddeyiah. The other two guys sharing were Ian Stewart, with whom I had joined GF, and an administrative officer. The admin guy had first dibs at weekends as that was his only time off and Ian and I liaised with each other for the rest of the time.

Jaki was a very good swimmer and loved the waters in the Gulf; after my shark experiences I was not keen so I would stand on the highest point of the dhow and act as lookout whilst Jaki swam. The biggest danger was actually the sea-snakes which were often over 1.5 metres long and would poke their heads from the water up to a foot above the surface and peer around.

Naturally, we would have our friends along occasionally, plus the appropriate beverages. I caught quite a few grouper fish, my best was 10lb, but one of the other crew caught a 32-pounder. The flesh was white, firm and delicious.

One night there was a massive storm with furious winds so the admin guy and I went to check the boat. It was gone! It was obvious that the mooring chain had not been secured to a heavy enough object as everything was gone.

We drove down the west coast for three or four miles and found it jammed against a jetty but undamaged. The admin guy had to get to work so I secured a line to the boat, jumped into the shallow water and started pulling it to deeper water where I could safely start the engine(s). That was the most frightening walk I've ever taken as I was stumbling over rocks, getting stuck in crevices and constantly petrified of finding a sneaky sea-snake. All was well and I rode her back to a temporary mooring.

Meanwhile, I acquired an abandoned 'yank-tank' engine of about 6 litres and we dropped it into our mooring position in about eight feet of water. The next day I set off in the rubber dinghy, moored it and dived down to the engine and breeze-blocks pile with some chain. As I threaded the chain through the engine a sea-snake shot up my arm. According to witnesses I left the water like a Polaris missile and landed in the dinghy. I was extremely lucky because sea-snakes have only small jaws and cannot bite easily – *but* the webbing between the fingers is a perfect spot. Snakes and sharks have given me quite a few frights in my time!

Our route to Amsterdam was via Paris/Orly inbound and outbound but we never stayed in Paris. My first flight into Paris Charles de Gaulle (CDG) was shortly after it opened. On the return flight from Amsterdam Schiphol, on 3 November 1976, the weather in CDG was foul, totally on limits with heavy rain, cloud base 200 feet and quite low visibility. It was my first chance at a genuine down to limits monitored approach for some time.

The first officer was John Davidson, an ex-BOAC navigator who had converted to pilot when navigators became redundant in civil aviation. This was his first ever monitored approach where it really counted and he did well. I took over at about 180 feet having called 'I have control' and having seen enough to carry out a safe landing. John was now converted from 'captain does everything' to real team flying.

Apart from my 'dhowing and fishing' my other great interest was cricket at the Dilmun Club. There was a Britannia club but they had no cricket team, as I recall. Cricket in Bahrain was only on concrete tracks covered in matting but quite true and effective. Most of our opponents were Indians, who comprised a large part of the work force on the island, and a few Pakistanis.

In early January 1977 Jaki told me that she was pregnant the day before my flight to London where I was to bring my parents back on the return flight.

My father turned up without my mother as she felt too tired to travel and was staying with Greta, my sister. I talked to her and she was her usual cheerful self but I did not mention her next grandchild as I wanted to tell her in person.

Two days later in Bahrain, my brother contacted me to pass the awful news that Mother had died. I have always regretted not giving her the news about the baby; she was such a splendid grandmother she would have been so happy. My father and I, with the help of the chief pilot, got seats on the next flight home. On arrival, my father's suitcase was missing. It was delivered the next day and we were advised that it had fallen from the carousel airside and nobody picked it up.

The Lockheed L-1011 TriStar or as GF called it, because of our superb first-class service, '5-Star TriStar', was in service with GF in early 1976. It was a little underpowered for hot conditions using the three Rolls Royce (RR) RB211-24B engines and at hot temperatures and MTOW (maximum take-off weight) she could just make an initial cruise altitude of 29,000 feet (FL290). Around the same time as the first L-1011 arrived in service I took a VC10 to London. Unfortunately, we had unacceptable vibration on an engine, so we returned to Bahrain. After inspection and some maintenance we took the same aircraft again but, unfortunately, I had to turn back once more. The crew and our passengers were transferred to a London-bound L-1011 and I was in first-class with a few of my ex-passengers.

There was one obnoxious man who clicked his fingers at the cabin crew, demanded vodka martinis shaken not stirred(!), had his feet up on top of the seat in front of him and throughout the journey behaved badly and ridiculously.

Meanwhile, the cabin crew did their best with the service, but as it was their first L-1011 flight they were slow and erratic here and there. Nevertheless, they did a good job in the circumstances.

After landing and the seatbelt signs had been switched off, this moron said in a loud voice, 'Well, that has to be the worst first-class service I've ever seen.' I said, 'And you're the worst first-class passenger I've ever seen.' He went mad and in a ridiculous posturing manner said, 'You're the captain of our last trip aren't you? What's your name?' meanwhile bending over to read my flight-bag label. What an ass! Anyway, two or three passengers gave me their cards and offered total support should there be a problem. I reported to the chief pilot, Dick Woodhead, upon my return but nothing more happened.

Sometime mid-1977 the crew were just settling down for a few drinks in my room/suite in Muscat when I received a call to re-route us to London instead of return to Bahrain. I pointed out that we did not have our European uniforms with us etc., but that was the order. Party over, early to bed and early start to London. En route I realised my bottle of whiskey, three-quarter-full, had been left behind.

Oh well, too bad. On arrival at customs LHR we had the usual hassle. Customs officers, with one or two exceptions, loved to exercise their power and position by hassling crews, being sarcastic and generally unpleasant. We were allowed twenty cigarettes and a miniature of spirits. Fair enough, but their attitude was always intimidatory and condescending.

This trip all went well and, in my room, I emptied my flight bag to give me room for my overnight kit to visit my sons and, to my horror, lying flat under my books was the bottle of whiskey. I truly did not know it was there and hadn't realised my manuals were sitting higher than normal.

Had a customs officer found that I can appreciate that all my protestations would have fallen on deaf ears. When I found it the hairs on the back of my neck actually stood up.

I have never, ever, tried to fool customs but I've known a few who have so I guess they spoilt things for the rest of us.

In 1977 we added Shiraz and Bandar Abbas, both in Persia, to our destinations but generally nothing had changed.

At last it was my turn to convert to the TriStar, starting the course at the BA training centre at Heston in August 1977.

However, just before that there was time for one last adventure on VC10s. I was en route LHR via CDG from Abu Dhabi when I had the failure of one rudder unit which, if I landed in CDG, would ground the aircraft. I announced to the passengers that for technical reasons we were going direct to LHR and CDG passengers would be flown there at GF's expense.

Shortly afterwards two large gentlemen from the Gulf arrived on the flight deck, without invitation, and suggested I went outside. There I was very strongly advised that if I did not land in CDG I would be extremely sorry and even my family were mentioned. I pointed out that I was the captain and they had no right to threaten me or to dictate to me about aviation procedures.

They became even more forceful with their argument and made it quite clear they would carry out retribution if I did not land at CDG. By this time, we were nearing descent time for CDG and Rick Richards, who had no idea what was going on, was pressing me to make up my mind. I said we would land at CDG. My mind was in turmoil and I was seething with rage, but only those who have worked in that part of the world would understand why I complied.

The tech problem turned out to resolve itself and we continued to LHR on time. I spoke to a Bahraini officer in London about what had happened and he said do nothing. So, I did nothing but I'm still unable to forget being threatened in that way.

Apparently, they were police or agents or whatever acting on behalf of someone highly placed.

The L-1011 Lockheed TriStar Course

The TriStar course started early August and comprised four weeks ground school and another four weeks simulator training. The ground course was the usual: engines, limitations, hydraulics etc., etc., but we had to learn and understand a new system, especially what to do if it went wrong. It was a new navigational system called ISS (Inertial Sensing System).

Very basically, it used a large gyroscopically-controlled platform at the corners of which were four vertical tubes. In each tube was a pendulum with an electrical coil in it and every time it moved from the vertical, left, right, forward or back, an electrical signal was sent to the appropriate receiver.

Before departure the ISS would be started and the latitude and longitude of the present position would be inserted, and would take fifteen to sixteen minutes to be fully stabilised, at which point 02 would appear in the selector-box window. It was not available for use until then, so the aircraft could not be moved.

From then on, every movement of the aircraft would cause the penduli to move, thus sending an electrical signal to show change of track, groundspeed, wind velocity and constantly recording current latitude and longitude. Further instructions were sent to various instruments but especially the artificial horizon (attitude) indicator.

The system was quite accurate but best checked whenever possible with radio aids, if available, to see if there was a rogue ISS. Even the Mark 1 eyeball was worth using. Most of us did our own navigating as a back up but the system worked remarkably well. At the end of an eight-hour flight the three ISS would be within a fifteen to twenty nautical miles accuracy. Their positional accuracy was not too important at destination as ground radar and radio aids took over.

At the end of the ground school there was a mock exam on 23 August and the real one on the 24th.

I was in London and Jaki was with her parents in Sussex and I received a wake-up call at 0700 on the 23rd from Jaki to say we had a daughter.

She was phoning from Brighton, the East Sussex Hospital, where her father John had taken her at 0100.

We were allowed three hours for the mock exam which I finished in one hour and off I went to see Gemma and Jaki. They were both beautiful and I was in awe of this little girl in my arms or should I say on my hands.

John and Irene, her parents, and I went back later to the family home, Mount Ephraim near Uckfield, cracked a bottle or two of champagne, had some gin and tonic (they were ex-colonials after all) and retired to a great sleep. However, the real exam was the next morning so I was off to London bright(ish) and early and did the official CAA exam. We all passed.

We all did about thirty-five hours in the simulator going through all the let-downs, looking at all the systems, doing all the emergencies and, of course, learning the newest thing, the ISS.

On 1 October all six crews went to Prestwick to train on one of the GF TriStars with Ian Savage, an ex-BA captain, as our instructor. At the briefing he talked about the programme and said he would not bother with the ISS navigation but just set it up for Track and Ground Speed and Wind Velocity indications. He also said the rest was just PFM.

Rick Richards and I were not the first crew to have a go so we sat in first-class and hunted the books for PFM. There are so many abbreviations we learn and use in aviation but we could not find this anywhere in our manuals. At the debriefing I asked Ian what PFM was and he explained that ISS was Pure F*****g Magic. He was right but we were embarrassed that we were so naïve that we'd never heard the expression.

Our TriStar was the Mk 100 with the early RR RB 211-22 which, for the hot conditions, were a little underpowered giving us a starting altitude at maximum weight of only FL 290.

Wing span	47.35 metres 155 feet 4 inches
Length	54.17 metres 172 feet 8 inches
Height	16.87 metres 55 feet 4 inches
Maximum weight	200,000 kilograms 430,000 lbs
Maximum speed	Mach 0.95

Training complete after three trips it was back to Bahrain and eleven sectors with passengers and training captain. On 27 October I did my first official trip as captain from Bahrain-CDG-LHR and on the return my two girls came with me.

Back to Bahrain

Jaki's parents had acquired a Bassett hound but the resident Doberman, Trampas, was pretty miffed so we agreed to take Fred, obvious name, with us to Bahrain. He was slightly drugged to relax him so Jaki checked in with a baby in a basket, the inevitable hand baggage full of baby's needs and a tranquilised puppy round her neck like a scarf! He was still barking and it resounded round Terminal 3 departures until he was taken away to his aircraft cage.

Our little house went from Jaki and me to baby's noises and barking but life was good. The garden was improving after the fierce summer heat, the tomatoes were good and the oleanders were forming a useful hedge.

Flying the TriStar was a great experience and, now we had the splendid automatic landing, it was at the time the most accurate aircraft in the world for maintaining glide-slope to landing. It would pass over the outer marker, an NDB, at plus-or-minus twenty-seven feet on average; this was way ahead of its nearest rival, the Trident.

One of the reasons for its accuracy was the Direct Lift Control (DLC) which was a system whereby some of the spoilers would lift to 7 degrees when flaps were selected. They would move between 0 and 14 degrees to augment elevator inputs so that those inputs were necessarily reduced. More importantly, under autopilot approach or autoland conditions it made for a smoother and more accurate approach, the most accurate in the world.

The DLC worked well for experienced and/or sensitive handlers but those pilots who were constantly chasing airspeed and correct flight path would be over-controlling and causing more trouble for themselves.

The TriStar also had an extremely accurate airspeed deviation doughnut. One set the desired speed and a small circular indicator would appear on the left side of the attitude indicator and when you were at the correct speed and the correct power setting for that speed and that set of circumstances, i.e. climb, descent, it remained steady. The moment it sensed you had too much or too little attitude or power to maintain that speed it would start to deviate from central. This information was spot on and if you kept a regular eye on it then the power change was immediately made, but a little at a time. It worked brilliantly and meant a very quiet approach for landing.

However, inexperienced or slightly inept pilots would chase it and all the passengers would hear was power going up and down all the time. Most pilots would be better off without this 'aid'. I spent a large part of my time in Gulf Air teaching the new local pilots to be easy with the power.

Because we were the 'Gulf' airline many of our trips were short haul around the various states and emirates, mostly to collect passengers to go to Europe. A typical trip might be Bahrain-Abu Dhabi-Muscat and night stop. Then Muscat-Dubai-London. Or an area trip like Doha-Dubai-Bahrain-Cairo.

Although she was a lovely aircraft she was long haul, not short haul, so occasionally on a quick climb, short cruise then descent it was busy. Especially so if you received descent clearance a bit late or they changed runway at the last minute then it became necessary to throw her around a bit and manoeuvre tightly here and there. She was not a B737.

Off duty I continued to enjoy my membership of the Gulf Hotel swimming pool, play cricket for the Dilmun Club, go dhowing and, of course, get as much social life which Jaki and I could enjoy as we had a lovely Indian lady, Nettie, who not only acted as occasional housekeeper but loved to babysit.

In June 1978 I finally gave up tolerating a nasal problem and was sent to a doctor in Devonshire Place who, despite my suggestion that I was qualified for service treatment, sent me to an ENT specialist in the London Clinic. I explained to the specialist that every time I lay on my right side the right nostril completely blocked and that it felt as if some membrane at the back was moving across.

Whilst I was in his little room off his office and he was checking my nostrils a lady barged in and demanded his attention; it was his previous patient and she wished to clarify something. I was astounded that he should stop my examination and chat to her. She was obviously very wealthy and he was quite obsequious; money talks.

Anyway, he turned back to me and said I can see your problem and can operate next week (or now, I can't remember). I foolishly agreed and subsequently had the operation. Afterwards he explained he had removed projecting pieces of bone from my lower nasal passages and all would now be well. What?

A week later I was back in Bahrain and still the blockage was occurring and, upon my letter of concern, he assured me all was well and it would soon clear up.

Well, I was overseas, rarely went to England so let it pass. Until, one day some time later when effects of the operation had definitely worn off, I realised that I had no sense of smell and my nose was still blocking up. This man had seriously failed his professional standards but in those days life went on. Now, I would sue him for as much as I could get. I never smelt my children's hair after their baths, my wife's excellent cooking, etc., etc.

Years later I gave Mr Mills, an ENT specialist in Taunton, my tale of woe. His eyebrows raised but he said nothing; obviously, more professional than the other one. He operated, removed a small piece of surplus membrane behind my nostrils and I've been fine ever since!

The London Clinic man was unprofessional in allowing that woman to interrupt and, obviously, temporarily, negligent and incompetent as well. I'm sure he was normally first class but he really spoilt some of my life.

Sometime around August 1978 Jaki told me she was pregnant again. Hooray! But on no account was she going to England; she was having the baby in Bahrain at the American Mission Hospital and with a Pakistani doctor.

The reason for her decision was that, as she was born in Malaya, we were advised that her child born overseas would have problems getting a British passport. That was the reason Gemma was born in the UK. Jaki disliked her time in Brighton so she decided 'to hell with it' and let bureaucracy take its course.

In November 1978 I was appointed as Line Training Captain on TriStars. This simply meant I was tasked with teaching new first officers (accompanied by a back-up first officer) to fly the aircraft on the line. They had already had their initiation on type with other training captains.

The majority of the new first officers were Gulf nationals, in particular, from Bahrain, Abu Dhabi, Dubai and Oman. They had been trained in the UK to commercial pilot standards of the CAA and were, therefore, good quality. Having spent so many years as a flying instructor in the RAF, I fitted easily into the role.

The best of all the students at the beginning was definitely Sulman Maidan and the rest were good too: Jassim Najim, brothers Habeeb and Adel Al-Ansari, Jameed Al-Matrook, Ebrahim Al-Gaoud, Mohammed Ghuloom, Ahmed Yaqoob, Ali Marhoon and many others with whom I had not flown.

Later the new batch of first officers had been trained in the USA where examinations were different in that most papers were multiple choice but the CAA required written answers to show that you had a deeper knowledge of the subject.

BACK TO BAHRAIN

There was quite a difference between the two intakes for a very interesting reason. Muslims study the Koran by rote and their ability to learn is amazing. However, the CAA requires you to really know the subjects but the FAA, whilst also teaching well, allow multiple choice which falls into the laps of those who learn by rote. It was obvious that the second batch could not put their knowledge into practice as well as the earlier first officers but, with hard work, they did well too.

In February 1979 the Dilmun Club was all ready for its cricket week on Kharg Island. This was an oil terminal for an Iran refinery and a port where oilmen (Oilies) would live for short periods, say two to three months, then have one month off. Needless to say, they were regulars on the GF routes.

Unfortunately, the Shah of Persia was overthrown and by 11 February 1979 he had gone into exile before he could be killed. Chaos reigned and, of course, our cricket was cancelled and we all had leave of absence about to go to waste.

HM The Queen visited Bahrain a few days later, from the 14th to the 17th, and toured the island and did her usual stately things. She came down our main road and we were all out there waving and she returned a wave. That evening I was in the bar at the Gulf Hotel chatting to the manager with whom I was on friendly terms due to my year-long stay there.

I noted that there were many journalists there and he advised me that most of them had been there all day. I said, 'What about reporting on the Royal Visit?' he said, 'Oh, each day two or three follow the Queen and then come back and report to all the others. Then they make their reports with their own twist on it and file the copy!' An even bigger reason than any to wonder how much truth gets distorted in the papers.

During the Queen's visit, having arrived in that beautiful ship *Britannia*, we played their cricket team. Seemingly, wherever they go, the crew try to get to know the locals through sport or other activities. The locals in our team were all Brits, but I'm sure they managed something more in keeping with the area.

The next week we played one of the few Pakistani teams in Bahrain. The batsman coming off said, 'Careful, he's good,' he was talking of the leg-break bowler who had got him. He was good. I missed three balls and was bowled round my legs by the fourth. Upon walking off the pitch, I said to one of the fielders, 'By golly, he's good is he not?' and he advised me that he should be as he had played for Pakistan many times. He was Pervez Hajiid Hassan!

I played often and regularly for Dilmun Club until management twigged that three or four pilots nearly always had Thursdays off (the Muslim equivalent then of the UK Saturday) and found that the rostering officer, also a Dilmun cricketer, was tweaking the rosters. Sadly, they were very harsh and sacked him. Oh well, I still got the odd game.

On 1 March 1979 I accompanied Jaki to the American Mission Hospital where I was privileged, overwhelmed and tearful at being present at the birth of our son, Joshua James. Jaki was happy to stay in her private room for five days and each afternoon receiving friends bearing wine or champagne. I usually took in a wine we enjoyed called Duck! (honest!) and a spicy kebab or shawama.

During one of the nights she was in hospital I received a telephone call and on leaving the bedroom tripped over Fred our Bassett, fell on him and broke his front left leg. The Australian vet patched him up and when Jaki came home she was delighted to be greeted by Gemma and astonished to see Fred waving his cast. I had not thought it a good idea to tell her about Fred whilst she was in hospital. On her return we held a party for people to see Josh but Fred got equal attention as he wandered around waving his foot in the air and demanding sympathy.

In July it was arranged that Andrew and Nick would come to Bahrain and then come on to Cyprus for our holiday. We had booked a cottage in Lower Paphos where we had the sea, a pool and a tennis court to hand. Andrew was to leave the UK later due to schooling but Nick joined me for our departure from London-Bahrain on 24 July in TriStar A40-TX. First Officer Abdul Al-Gaoud, a newly-qualified first officer, was doing the sector and a new first officer, Ali Marhoon, was observing.

As we reached the decision speed V1, No. 3 engine failed and I called Abort (or Stop or Reject, whatever it was at that time) and closed the thrust levers (throttles) and crawled all over the brakes, i.e. braked hard. I have never ceased to be amazed at the power of aircraft braking systems; we were forward in our straps and unable to sit back at first. The brakes became very hot as you can imagine and we left the runway (28R) after slowing down and had to wait in a marshalling area well away from other aircraft.

A fire crew stood by as the possibility was always there that a tyre(s) or brake could explode, sending pieces everywhere. After forty-five minutes we were towed to the normal area; the offending item, a fuel valve, as I recall, was changed and we continued to Bahrain. Quite a start for Nick; more frights for him later.

Eventually, we all met up and had a great time at Paphos. Nick kept beating me at tennis which was annoying but pleasing at the same time. Once again, Andrew had an easy ride because he had to leave early to do something in the UK about university. I took him to Larnaca for his flight to Bahrain, where friends met him and eased his journey on to the UK.

On 19 August we all boarded Cyprus Airway CY278 to fly Larnaca-Bahrain in a B707. The captain or first officer had to be replaced by the standby so we left about an hour late. As we turned left after take off, I felt the handling was jerky and, later, I thought pitch control (i.e. nose up or down) was also erratic. The level off at top of climb was quite abrupt. So far nothing had been smooth and I was not concerned but definitely unimpressed.

As we were in autopilot (AP) for the cruise all was well. As the aircraft had fewer passengers than normal, I was able to move back to the right overwing exit with Nick and give Gemma, two years old the next week, more space to play. Jaki remained at about row 7 with three seats to herself with Josh in his Moses basket. At top of descent I began to be annoyed by the pilot flying. I found out it was the captain, as our entry was quite abrupt and quite unnecessarily uncomfortable. The descent had to have been in AP as it was quite smooth but, once clear of any cloud and lower down, I could see we had a strong tailwind, probably up to 25-plus knots.

We levelled off at 1,500 feet and flew down, paralleling the runway about one to two miles out. So far so good, and normal. However, I suddenly realised that our nose attitude was getting higher and higher as the auto-pilot tried to maintain selected height, but there was no power. Just as I was feeling quite nervous the power was poured on and slowly the nose returned to normal position. By this time, we were alongside the landing end of the runway and, by the sound of engines being handled and the return to erratic handling, I knew the AP was now disconnected.

Normally, the procedure on a downwind at 1,500 feet, and pilot handling is as you pass the touch down end you allow 45 seconds and then you turn onto final approach. If you have a strong tailwind then you reduce the 45 seconds as necessary. I timed the 45 seconds which ended up at over a minute, so we were much farther downwind than necessary. This is not clever, but it means you have to adjust the descent rate of the turn and approach as you now have further to go. Not this pilot! He turned base leg, losing height at the normal rate, and I could see through my window that he was getting really low.

At about 400 feet and three miles out (i.e. should have been 900 feet) he deigned to add power and maintain height. We continued at 400 feet until the correct point for continued descent. By this time I was decidedly uncomfortable and Jaki turned round to look at me as all her experience on B707s told her this was not normal.

I sensed the nose was too high and the power movements too frequent. As we crossed the threshold it was obvious we were not in a good position. I gripped Gemma tightly and told Nick to sit straight up, head back against the headrest; this was good advice from my ejection seat days.

Sure enough we slammed into the ground with all wheels and bounced into the air. Most of the overhead lockers burst open, including over the centre aisle where dinghies were stored.

We now got airborne again with nose high in the air and crashed down again nose first. I don't know how much elevator control was left but I could sense the pilot was trying to fly it but was too late with his inputs or out of synch.

On the second arrival I saw the No. 4 engine, i.e. the outboard right engine, slam into the runway and I greatly feared its breakaway or, at least, fire. After a total of four major bounces, we came to a stop with smoke pouring back into the cabin. I immediately removed the overhead wing panel and threw it out ready to climb onto the wing and at the same time realised the smoke was actually only from the collapsed nose-wheel's tyre.

So I changed my mind as I was still doubtful of the engine's integrity, and headed for the front. The only two cabin crew I saw were at the two front doors, L1 and R1, so I headed for them. En route, a very large woman was blocking me as she bent down to look for her shoes. I slapped her backside really hard and, as she stood, Nick and I went past.

Near the front I noted that Jaki had gone, so I carried on and went for the left door. The stewardess screamed at me to go the other way, correct procedure, as the slide had not deployed. The R1 was blocked by a man too frightened to jump so I pushed him out.

I ran across the tarmac and sand to Jaki and Josh who were waiting for us to appear.

I looked back and guessed there would be no fire so we stayed at a safe distance and had a huge family hug.

There were two things I particularly remember from this moment and one was that Nick's knees were really banging together in aftershock. I didn't realise this could actually happen. The other I did not understand at the time, viz., from the moment we hit the ground I went into total survival mode and was so concentrated and determined that I never heard a thing until the stewardess's voice reached me. I had seen people screaming, mouths open, arms waving but not a sound.

Later I read that in serious situations like this the hearing is the first sense to go.

As we had our family embrace, I noticed that all the crew, bar those at L1 and R1, were further away than we were. The flight crew had no choice but to leave the flight deck through their own emergency exits but the fact that no one was near the aircraft and helping distressed passengers was shameful. Some had been injured jumping from the wings.

Our very good friends at the time were actually watching this from the departures area as they were to fly on the same aircraft to Larnaca and rent the same cottage we had. There was also another pilot friend waiting at the holding point for take off after we landed.

At the subsequent enquiry we all offered to give evidence but, as it was obviously going to be damning, we were not called. The verdict was given as wind shear, but our opinions would not have supported that verdict. The enquiry did show that the captain had received inadequate training for that position and, subsequently, training standards and hours required were raised. The captain was demoted to first officer.

A year later a letter appeared in *Flight Magazine*, name not shown, stating that the enquiry was wrong and that it was pilot error and there was a cover up. That's how I remember it anyway. People occasionally congratulated me on 'my' letter. Eventually, I had to write to *Flight* and ask them to confirm that I had not written the letter, which they did.

To this day Nick won't fly and Jaki is not entirely comfortable when she does. I say that they've had their 'incident' and the odds say it won't happen again, but they are not convinced.

All Nick's frights started with that V1 at Heathrow two weeks earlier.

The decision speed, V1, is a speed at which you have two seconds to decide whether to continue take off or abandon and stop. There are many reasons you may be faced with this decision but let us look at an obvious one, engine failure. If you are going LHR-JFK then you may stop, or you may be very heavy and would prefer to take into the air, settle down and dump some fuel, then return for a comfortable, frequently-trained-for engine-out landing. If you abandon a heavy aircraft at V1 then you end up with hot brakes and, in the worst scenario, the possibility of abandoning the aircraft, i.e. passengers down slides, injuries, etc.

If the engine failure occurs before V1 then you must stop because your speed may not be high enough to be sure of getting airborne and if it fails after V1 then you probably have insufficient runway and/or stopway to stop safely. Stopway is a section of land beyond the runway end which could support an aircraft and cause no significant damage and is used for considerations of stopping distance only.

There are three major considerations for determining V1: the weight of the aircraft, the altitude of the runway and the temperature at take off, known as WAT limits.

Performance is a serious subject studied for all commercial pilots' licences. There are graphs which are used to determine take-off safety and include length and altitude of runway, outside air temperature and the weight at which you want to take off. These all have to allow you to find a safe weight whereby there is an accurate V1 so that you can stop or continue in an emergency. This is why it's called 'decision speed'. Needless to say, the exams make sure you know exactly what you are doing.

If the temperature is high then perhaps your aircraft cannot provide enough power to find a V1. It could certainly be enough to get you airborne safely with all engines, but what if you lose one? It could happen halfway down the runway and you could stop, but is there enough power and speed combined to allow you to get safely airborne and achieve V2, the safe speed for flight with one engine out?

If either of these considerations, stop or go, cannot safely be confirmed then the weight must be reduced, or delay until a temperature that will permit a safe take off. This might be the choice for a freight-only flight but you will upset your customers if you delay. The usual procedure is to offload freight.

There is also a way you can reduce weight by taking on less fuel. For example, an aircraft takes fuel to cover the distance at that weight, let's say 100 tons. You add 4 per cent for contingency: 104 tons plus thirty minutes hold at destination, say five tons and fuel for an alternate, say eight tons. So now we have 117,000 kilograms on board.

However, if we really cannot offload freight then a sneaky system is to choose a destination some distance shorter, say five tons worth, and then if en route you have saved or not used as much fuel as expected and, most importantly, if you now have enough to continue to original destination with all *legal* and *necessary* reserves you simply cancel your new plan and revert to the original. Of course, it occasionally doesn't work and you have to land early but it has been proven that overall the company can save fuel if they employ this method now and then but not as a regular practice.

What V1 boils down to is knowing that there is a safe speed at which you can get airborne and fly or stop safely. This also shows you nervous flyers that every time you fly, an engine failure during take off has been computed for. Talking of which, all this stuff is now done by computers and you have to accept the V1 they give you because we no longer have to do it ourselves.

I find that a shame because on the VC10 and initially on the TriStar the pilots and engineer would go through the charts, not graphs as in the exams, but lines and columns relating to all the WAT parameters and could actually find a range of V1s as the aircraft might be very light, the runway more than long enough, the temperature fine and variable weight choices. What we found perhaps was that V1 could vary by as much as 30 knots. Whereas the computer probably gives the only one available or half of the variables, we could choose what we wanted. You might think how can it be variable?

Well, you could find that you were light and had lots of runway so could easily get airborne after engine failure anything above 130 knots but could stop at anything up to 150 knots, so you now had a safe range. What do you choose?

Probably the middle position, but what about other factors?

Say you've got nasty weather after take off, it's night and raining. Well, if things went wrong I'd prefer to stay on the ground so let's use a higher V1; if all is fine let's use the lower one and so on and so on.

Say you're going home to Bahrain from Muscat and lose an engine. Well, continue, if possible, because the new engines are at base and we can re-arrange our flight plan to keep close to Ras-al-Khaima, Sharjah, Dubai, Abu Dhabi and Doha en route in case we decide later that we *must* land.

There are so many variables, but that is why pilots and crews have full briefings before flights. Usually it's a self-briefing with all the appropriate meteorological info, Notams (Notices to Airmen) which advise you of unserviceable aids along the route, limitations to equipment en route and destination, military exercises and anything and everything that can affect your flight. You would choose a fuel figure but if there was room for a little more you might add a bit if you were going to an awkward place like Newark, New Jersey, which has frequent traffic delays.

On arrival at the aircraft you say hello to all the cabin crew who have been checking all their safety equipment, catering etc., then on to the flight-deck where the handling pilot (HP) takes his seat and starts the full check list and the non-handling (NHP) pilot puts on his reflective jacket and goes outside to do a thorough external examination of the aircraft. The ground crew have done everything, but are not offended by this final check. Actually, on rare occasions it proves most fruitful; I actually found a crack on a section of undercarriage which necessitated a replacement part. It was so fine that it was easy to miss but I just happened to stare straight at it.

Back on the flight deck the handling pilot will check all the computer and navigation settings and the ground staff report to the captain for the paperwork, technical log and load sheet. The signing of the tech.

log indicates that the captain is now in total command of the aircraft and from that moment everything is his responsibility; a lovely moment.

The L1 door closes and we get the before start check-list finished and call for push-back. When cleared the tug pushes, we start engines and then call for taxi. We advise the ground engineer we are ready to taxi and he disconnects and shows his head-set plug and nose-wheel locking pin. We wave and we're off. If the first officer is the HP this is where he takes over and does everything; the captain should now only intervene if safety is in doubt or non-standard procedures are used.

Regrettably, there are too many captains who love the sound of their own voices and cannot let the first officer do things without nagging away. They are so annoying and very few people can do their work properly, even when fully trained, when some fool won't let them get on with it.

Oh, if only I could throw a few names in here!

You're ready for and cleared for take off and now there is one thing paramount in your mind – V1. The decision is already made, if you lose an engine before V1 you *stop*, if you lose it after V1 you *continue*. The latter is not so difficult because at the call 'V1' the captain positively takes his hand off the thrust levers.

We're on our way!

When we trained for auto-landings in bad weather the subject was covered really thoroughly and many faults were entered via the simulator controller so that we could cope with all events. The decision was to land with more restrictive criteria or do a go-around.

The basic instrument and equipment for an autoland˙ requires ground equipment maintained to the highest standard for the most difficult approaches.

The equipment on the ground is the Instrument Landing System (ILS) which projects a radio beam straight down the centre-line of the runway and another beam to direct you on a normal descent with no wind at 600 feet per minute to touchdown.

CAT 1

Category one is an approach using ILS and pilot handling or autopilot. The pilot as often as not flies the aircraft on instruments and either way the limitations are that you can see the runway clearly enough at 200 feet attitude and have a visibility of 800 metres or a Runway Visual Range (RVR) of 550 metres. The 200 feet is the decision height (DH) to land or go-around.

RVR is the enhanced visual ability given by the ATC taking into account the power of the runway lighting.

CAT 2

Is usually flown using the autopilots (APs); two APs are acceptable and onboard computers compare the APs and confirm their agreed accurate performance. If there is a problem it will be shown to the pilot who decides to continue or go-around.

The limits are 100 feet AGL and an RVR of not less than 300 metres.

CAT 3A

Decision height (DH) less than 100 feet and RVR at least 200 metres.

CAT 3B

DH less than 50 feet and RVR of at least 75 metres.

CAT 3C

No limits, i.e. O/O

All Cat 3s have to be operated by autopilots, two but preferably three.

Some aircraft have just the two APs but can engage an extra module to give the control to three, cross-talking and cross-checking appropriate equipment.

The training is carried out regularly and as you progress and get the hours and the actual handing down the line (i.e. doing a Cat 2 or 3 even in good weather) so your clearance is raised. Since autoland is a full team effort, the approach limitations would be based on those of the least qualified crew member. You can do almost anything in the simulators, the instructor has a huge panel enabling him to give every emergency possible and, among other things, he can reposition you anywhere in seconds. Thus, take-off emergencies can be carried out and you immediately return to the runway for another. All of this is seen on excellent video filmed in such a way that you have the normal all-round visibility.

Whilst training for autoland Cat 3s one day the instructor was taking us immediately from touch-down or go-around back to 1,500 feet on the approach. This happened many times and is very practical. Each time the video would be switched off. At the end of one go-around we got to 1,500 feet and the instructor said 'Okay, let's start take offs again' and put us back on the runway. He did not turn the video off and instead of seeing runway appear we saw the aircraft roll on its back and dive straight into the ground. This type of intensive training eventually makes you believe you are in a real aircraft.

This dive into the ground was one of the most frightening experiences of my flying life. The first officer and I looked at each other and I could see he was as shocked as me. The instructor said 'Okay, let's go' and the first officer and I said 'No'. We were so shaken up by our experience we insisted we had to have a break – outside the simulator.

I guess it depends where you live and what your regular destinations are as to whether you use Cat 3s very often. I used Cat 3B a very few times and Cat 3C a couple of times. The lighting carpets from approach lights to runway surface lights are so strong it is quite difficult to miss making a satisfactory landing at most International major fields.

The certificates are checked and renewed at regular intervals.

By early 1979 we had started a Bangkok-Hong Kong service and it was lovely, not only to visit Hong Kong again, but to do the approach into Kai Tak itself; the long steady descending turn over Lion Rock Road known by the locals as (Rion Lock Load), counting the pegs on the rooftop washing lines and finally seeing the runway whilst still turning at 300 feet. If you even slightly misjudged the turn and there was a crosswind you had little time to sort out your misalignment. Go to Google and search Kai Tak landings for a bit of fun.

Bangkok was new to me and immediately I was intrigued by the number of strange aeroplanes, obviously abandoned, which was the result of people fleeing Vietnam with anything they could get hold of. Also, most intriguing was the golf course situated between the runways.

The town was full of great bars, restaurants and the entertainment, for what it is most well-known, girls and more girls. Although I never indulged in some of the pleasures offered (honest!), my eyes were happy enough. Mind you, a large number of the beauties had quite prominent Adam's Apples!

My greatest pleasure was in finding Thai food. I had never thought about it before, but now I was hooked and it remains my absolute favourite. Both Jaki and Gemma grow lemon grass and Thai coriander.

When I had been on the VC10 Jaki would meet me at the airport for all my arrivals with a small thermos containing two gin and tonics which made the return most pleasant. However, once there were four of us she would park our orange Volvo estate by the chain-link fencing around the airport, put the children on the bonnet and they would wave as I came into land. I would wave back by turning the landing lights on and off a few times.

Because I was a Line Training Captain I never did standby duty which, because pilots are very honest and loyal, meant it was the equivalent of a day off because people never pretended to be sick. This meant I was mostly on minimum time off with plenty of overnight flying. Furthermore, there was a drinking culture in Bahrain among the ex-pats so I was always tired. The drinking stopped well before flying but was, nevertheless, tiring.

On top of all this Jaki kept telling me I was grey all the time and my sleep pattern was further interrupted by constantly waking up because my nose was blocked. This all contributed to me making an absolutely stupid decision; I was passing the offices of Saudi Arabian Airlines in London and thought I could see what they might offer. I knew most of it anyway which was an increase of 30 per cent in salary, six to seven days off a month in one block, during which you could have a free-space-available seat to anywhere in the world on their network and training captains always got the best trips.

I went and asked for an application form or whatever and, entirely by chance, the chief pilot was on the premises and we chatted. He offered me the job on the spot including training captain. I went back to Bahrain and talked it over with Jaki who, although she was reluctant, said okay. I gave GF three months' notice and when I look back I'm horrified, but it all seemed a good idea at the time! No, the sand wasn't greener!

I booked a place in a training school at Peabody Airfield in Atlanta, Georgia, and set off to work for my ATP (Air Transport Pilot) licence. The same as the UK but without the L on the end. En route with Pan Am, I had a row of seats to myself so enjoyed a good rest/sleep lying down. I noticed a bit of a twinge in my side but thought nothing of it. I arrived Friday morning in time for the forty-eight-hour course starting at 1400 hours.

The Americans had a different way of training and examining so I had a lot to absorb in twenty hours of classroom work; they were still using feet and statute miles for visibility. I ate at the airport restaurant that evening as my convenient hotel, Days, had only rooms. I swotted until about 2300 hours and went to sleep. Suddenly, I awoke with a terrible pain in my side. I could barely move and, try as I might, I could not reach the telephone or roll over.

Eventually, I left the bed by gritting my teeth against the pain and throwing one leg over the other and falling out of bed. I was now on all fours but could not reach the 'phone, so I pulled on the cord until it fell on me. Upon dialling the desk I was told to stand by. After five minutes the door opened and ten feet appeared, the desk clerk, two policemen, one paramedic and a fireman.

The first question was 'Have you been mugged?' I explained my dilemma and a stretcher appeared but when they tried to move me the pain was so severe they lifted me on and carried me down to the ambulance with me still on all fours. The rocking of the ambulance was awful and I was taken into the hospital on a trolley (gurney) to await a doctor. After some time a lady doctor appeared and asked me if I was insured then, when satisfied, she injected something in my backside which was still conveniently placed to make it easy for her. Soon I was okay and it appeared that my sleep across the seats had allowed the metal section in between to push into my ribs and created the situation for muscular spasms later.

That morning, Saturday, I turned up bleary-eyed, much to the amusement of my fellow students, and we set off again. By Sunday lunchtime I had had enough of class and swotting for the 150-question exam the next Wednesday. I wanted to get home, so I was allowed to take it on Monday morning. The flight back to Bahrain via Dhahran arrived on Tuesday morning. Quite a lot to get in in 108 hours.

There were twenty on the course, all first officers apart from me, and most of them were from Delta Airways as Atlanta was their hub. These guys all flew on American commercial licences, knew the regulations, but only I and two others passed. To get the ATP I now had to pass a flying test, which would come later.

The chief pilot, by now Len Prudence, gave me a glowing report as captain and line training captain and then the family went to stay in a flat in Windsor belonging to Geoff Gray. Fortunately, my starting date was changed from March to late-April so I was able to look after the family whilst Jaki went through a serious bout of chickenpox.

We were able to enjoy the area as it was a massive change to see springtime in England after years of sand.

Saudi-Arabian Airlines, Jeddah

Jaki, Gemma and Josh stayed in Windsor until I was allocated an apartment in Saudi City, a complex a kilometre long by 600-metres wide in which all the Saudia expatriates lived. The community comprised eight sections of accommodation, North West (NW), where we lived, NC, NE, E, SE, SC, SW and W. Each section had its own swimming pool and six of them had two or three tennis courts. The centre was for shops. The set up was very comfortable and the entrances were well guarded. The SE section was walled off and this is where all the cabin crew lived with men separated from the women. Our place was the ground floor of a duplex but there were many blocks of six or seven storeys and even small individual houses. Parking was plentiful, either at your place or in the immediate vicinity.

The original airport at Jeddah was right on the eastern edge of town and all the Saudia offices were close by. I, and all the other newcomers, were billeted in the hotel opposite where I noticed a dead cockroach behind the lavatory bowl. The room was regularly and reasonably serviced but it was still there when I left.

The first week or so was refresher technical training – we were all L-1011-qualified – and the introduction to the SV (Saudia) way of operating. They had been developed and run by TWA (Trans-World Airlines) the American company, so we had to learn the US way of doing things. There were no real differences in aviation but some countries at the time used metres instead of feet for altitude and varied altimeter settings. The altimeter is a device using air from a static port outside the aircraft and as the aircraft climbs so the air pressure reduces; this is sensed by the aneroid barometer in the instruments and converts to an indication of height above mean sea level (AMSL).

However, this can only be construed as 'accurate' if the altitude is set to show AMSL at time of departure, i.e. airfield height 300 feet, altimeter 300 feet. The setting is called airfield QNH. At regular intervals as you passed through the different air traffic regions you were given a new QNH to reflect local known pressure. On the other hand QFE can be set to show height above the airfield from whence you departed but QNH has to be set later so that all aircraft are using the same setting. The foregoing was all very well but the early altimeters were not as 'accurate' as later ones and the system of keeping aircraft from banging into each other had its weaknesses, e.g. the quandrantal altitude system.

The system was that, above 3,000 feet, aircraft flew odd heights from a track of 000 degrees (N) to 089 degrees and 090 degrees (E) to 179 degrees at odd plus 500 feet. Then even heights from 180 degrees (S) to 269 degrees and even plus 500 270 degrees (W) to 359 degrees. This meant that aircraft were often passing each other with 'only' 500 feet between them. If the aircraft were on different QNHs because they were at an information changeover point (i.e. FIR, or Flight Information Region), and there was enough plus or minus in the differences, then the aircraft could easily be less than 500 feet apart. All this was done on the three needle altimeters.

Later the semi-circular system was introduced which was much safer with the plus-500-feet eliminated: so 000 to 179 degrees was odd numbers and 180 to 359 degrees was evens.

Eventually, the safest solution was to have all aircraft in the UK, and most areas with no great peaks, to have the same altimeter setting above 3,000 feet AMSL. This 3,000 feet varied up to 4,000 or 4,500 feet for various airfields or unusual pressure changes and was known as transition level. We now spoke of heights until we went above transition when they became Flight Levels (FL). The odds and evens still applied, so the eastern half was odd FL and the western even.

However, as altimeters were still liable for larger errors the higher we flew then the eastern half was FL290, FL 330, FL 370 etc. and the western FL310, FL350, FL390. Hence the glorious sight of aircraft trailing all four engines and passing above or below you by 2,000 feet. The standard setting for the altimeters using the International Standard Atmosphere (ISA) was 1013.2 hectopascals (millibars previously) and the US used inches of mercury, e.g. 29.92 inches.

The ISA is the standard mark for all performance related speeds, heights etc., saying that at MSL conditions are 15 degrees C, 14.7 pounds per square inch pressure and dry adiabatic lapse rate (i.e. rate of temperature loss as you climb in dry, or clean, air) is 1.98 degrees C per 1,000 feet. So an altimeter showing 35,000 feet was stated as FL350 and, as all aircraft were on the same altimeter setting, we were safe.

Anyway, back to SV; we Brits had been used to QFE for a long time but we now found we were to use QNH and 29.92-inch mercury above 18,000 feet. This height served the USA well because of so many mountains and was right for SV also, so get used to it!

All aircraft charts for performance start on the premise of the conditions being ISA but contain the complete means of adjusting all performance figures for conditions different from ISA. So, in the spring and autumn in the UK there may be not too many differences but summer and winter certainly gets you using the charts more thoroughly. Obviously, long-haul flights go north, south, east and west into hot temperatures one day and freezing the next.

Hence WAT limits whereby airfield height (i.e. air pressure) and temperature are all constantly variable and using performance charts was essential. I say 'was' because nowadays the airlines use computers – what else? – and, I suspect, V1 is either the only one available or more usually the mid-point of the choices. I always felt that the captain should have been appraised of the available range so that he/she could have made the decision.

All the group of pilots with whom I joined did their simulator training in Jeddah but a few brand-new trainees as first officers were required to do their simulator training at Palmdale in the Mojave Desert, which was the Lockheed factory base. To ensure they had continuity with the captain I was assigned to do the full course with them. I was a bit miffed in view of my time on type but it was good fun really. I stayed in the town of Lancaster nearby.

The end of the Lockheed course was to fly out to Kansas City in a TWA L-1011 and train at Topeka. We did four two-hour sessions to get the new first officers some handling, especially landings. The opportunity was taken to license me for the L-1011 on my new FAA ATP and we did the usual stuff, except for one thing which was never a requirement for the CAA ATPL.

The test included a go-around at 200 feet, then complete a tight constant turn circuit at 200 feet for a landing. This meant that you were rolling your wings level at 100 feet just before the runway end. I had no idea this was about to happen and I found it positively hair-raising. All was well, though, and I got my endorsement from the FAA.

On the way back from JFK to Jeddah in a TWA 747, I could not sleep so went to the galley and asked the lady there if there were cards on board for the passengers. She was making a coffee but said she would get me some. The chief stewardess passed by at the other end of the galley and said, 'If he's bothering you, honey, let me know and I'll sort him out.'

Charming!

The service on most American aircraft companies is normally bloody awful anyway, but really!

Saudi Arabian Airways (SV) operated the Lockheed L-1011 TriStar 200: Engines were the more powerful RR RB211-542B.

Wing span, length and height were the same as the 100.

Maximum weight 211,374 kilograms, 466,000lb. The rest was as per the 100.

Jeddah was in a state of great expansion of both buildings and infrastructure and driving around you could see nothing but mess. There were building materials everywhere, just abandoned, cars were left where they stopped or broke down – it was quite dispiriting. This combined with my 'training' left me hugely regretful of my decision.

Despite my hours, experience and hours on type. I had to go through the full training course, as did we all. This comprised an initial check-ride followed by *fifty-eight* (the first fifteen as observer) sectors. My instructor was Russ Handy, a TWA captain working for Saudia keeping his TWA salary and being paid a training captain's salary by SV! The idea was that we had to see every airfield on the SV L-1011 schedule before being cleared to operate fully-fledged and get the star with the epaulettes and a special pair of wings to show you were no longer in training. What I and others found annoying was that anybody in the airline who had a uniform, such as gatekeepers, guards etc., also wore wings. You had to decide if a chap was a pilot by his smartness and the cut of his jib, as it were.

Russ Handy was a nice enough guy I suppose but did not have the respect of one experienced pilot to another. He was only too happy to teach me to suck eggs and criticise anything and everything he could. Fortunately, I did most of what he expected well enough, but I had to bite my tongue often.

On one occasion at the end of the runway at Karachi I was cleared for take off. However, as I started to increase power I saw a Land Rover appear close to the aircraft and go directly behind. So I delayed increasing thrust for a moment as it would probably have blown the vehicle over. Russ yelled 'You're clear for take off! Why are you being so slow? Get the power on!' He was lambasting me all the way down the runway even to beyond V1; it was a stupid and dangerous thing to do and he was unimpressed by my explanation.

Just to add to the joy of this occasion we were cleared to FL100 and, as normal, I climbed at 250 knots which, unless cleared otherwise, was the maximum speed below FL100/ or 10,000 feet in the USA as their transition is 18,000 feet, not 3,000 to 4,000, as in the UK. The reason is that they have so many fields higher than 4,000 feet that they need a safer nationwide transition altitude.

I levelled off at 10,000/FL100 and maintained 250 knots. After a few seconds Russ asked me what I was doing. I advised that I was maintaining 250 knots, as required at 10,000 feet and below. He reminded me in a very sarcastic manner that the requirement for 250 knots was below 10,000 feet and not at 10,000 feet. He was right but what a way to do it.

The places SV L-1011 went to at that time were Riyadh, Dhahran, Taif and Abha, all in the Kingdom, and the overseas destinations were London (LHR), Paris (CDG), Rome Fiumicino, Geneva, Karachi, Athens, Frankfurt and Bombay (now Mumbai).

Halfway through my training I met Captain Bruce-Souster in the LHR hotel quite by chance. He asked how I was getting on and I said that I'd made a massive mistake leaving GF. He said to come back as they had not found a replacement for me. I jumped at the chance and a couple of days later I received a telex inviting me to return to my old position. I went to the chief pilot on L-1011s and advised him that I was resigning which was accepted. However, dirty work was afoot.

The normal procedure with most airlines is, regardless of your hours and experience, that you start at the bottom of the first officer list. However, I was being taken back straight into the Training Captain position again. There had been a first officer in GF to whom I had given some captaincy training and, in particular, found I had to boost his confidence as he was nervous of his new role. I set his mind at rest and he was eventually a good captain. Later on he treated his wife in a terrible way by leaving her at short notice, shacking up with his new woman, and refusing to talk to his wife when she was at his hotel room door. He was with his new woman at the time. His wife was in a really bad way and Jaki and I gave her help and support and I gave a message to him from her to which he did not take kindly.

When he heard of my likely return straight back as a captain he went round with a petition stating that I should have to start as first officer. This was absorbed by the management and Peter Bruce-Souster advised me that the offer was withdrawn, but would I come back as a first officer?

Before replying I checked that SV would accept my withdrawal of resignation, which they did, and then rejected the GF offer. Pride comes before a fall; I found out later that I would almost certainly have been back as a captain within two years. All companies demand a certain number of hours before a first officer can become a captain so more experienced first officers jump the queue; this would have happened in my case as there were so many young first officers.

I finally finished my 'training' on 2 September, having started in mid-April. What a waste of resources. I had 118 hours of training on an aircraft on which I previously had 1,300 hours! Upon completion of training I received my stars which went on epaulettes and sleeves, my captain's wings and a new hat with scrambled egg.

Flying with SV was quite the international scene; the majority of pilots and flight engineers were American (who incidentally got about 40 per cent more pay than the rest of us) but we had Brits, French, Spanish, German, Swedes, South African, Australian, Danes, Pakistanis, Indians, Italian, Belgium and Zambia. Probably more.

Life was harsh on the wives because they were not allowed to drive, so when we were off on our trips they would have to ask other ex-pats for help if there were difficulties. Added to the burden was the fact that no woman could travel with a man who was not a family member. This was ignored on the whole but incidents with the police did crop up from time to time.

One of the US pilots crossed the lights on yellow one day and was arrested for jumping the lights. He politely pointed out it was yellow but, on the authority of the policeman, he was jailed for a week on the spot. His wife was frantic in his absence for about two days. Eventually SV employed a man whose sole task was to call round the prisons looking for SV foreign personnel who were missing.

One day a pilot off to work was cut up on a roundabout by a fifteen-year-old boy driving a flash car. He remonstrated and waved his first. When he landed the next day he was put in prison because he had been rude to the mayor's son. He was released next day after intervention by SV. However, the police went to his apartment and re-arrested him on the mayor's orders. Another guy was put in prison for a week as his number plate was missing at the rear. Not one of the above appeared in court, they were there at the whim of men who hated infidels.

All three of them resigned from SV and went home.

Most of us always had a lot of money with us, as bribes were a favoured way of solving problems. It didn't help my friend Geoff Kiernander who was in the supermarket car park, leaning against his car in a proper parking slot, when a local reversed into him and called the police. Geoff was put in prison for the night. When Anna, his wife, came out, nothing. They panicked and called the special man in SV.

It takes a leap of logic to understand how these incidents happen. A captain (GF) was fined in Abu Dhabi after his taxi crashed, a flight engineer was fined and spent a night in prison when someone ran into his parked car.

The leap of logic is that all this odd behaviour is based on the simple premise that if you were not in his country this could not have happened. Therefore, it is your fault. I was only just learning to understand this when I finally left the Middle East for good.

The roster system entirely favoured the training captains and the most senior pilots. Each month we received pages of 'lines' which showed the flights, standbys and days off. Many of these lines had no overseas flights at all and those were the ones the new boys got.

My first two months were regular round-the-houses flights to Riyadh, Dhahran, Taif and Jeddah. However, I was called out of standby for a Rome-Paris in late September and later on a round trip to Cairo. Life in the air was getting very monotonous and it became obvious that my resignation and withdrawal had scotched my chances of being a training captain.

The round-the-houses flights would have been okay under the CAA rules but they were much harder under the FAA as we would sometimes arrive late at night and after seven hours (!) in the hotel set off again.

In November I actually got a line with an Athens-Frankfurt flight. This was terrific. The lines had numbers and we all bid on prepared sheets and submitted them to ops. As I said, all the best went to training and seniority but sometimes one's luck was in, as in this case.

The first couple of years were bad from a flying point of view as nearly everything I did was internal flying much more suited to a B737 than a TriStar. It was not able to be 'thrown around' like the nippier smaller jets. It was hard on Jaki, too, because, although we could use my days off to travel, it just was not practicable with two small children. We did, however, take a holiday to Nairobi using our privilege seats. We managed a safari with the children and got to see everything except leopards.

We now started to go to Karachi, Bombay (Mumbai) and Abha in the Kingdom. Abha was most interesting as it was 8,500 feet AMSL and, therefore, although using normal indicated speeds for the approach we were going much faster than normal. If the approach and touchdown were handled correctly, reverse thrust used properly and sensible braking then it was not a problem. I used to pride myself in not having hot brakes after landing.

In May 1981 the new airport at Jeddah was opened – it was named King Abdulaziz International Airport (KAIA) – with parallel runways and all the modern facilities. However, as a passenger, once inside, you are trapped. All the doors leading to the balconies are chained as are all emergency exits. The only exit was back through security and immigration or to the aircraft when the door is unlocked. What a death trap. The operations block was

283

super-modern for the time and very roomy with offices upstairs and check-in, accounts, operations, cafeteria et al on the ground floor.

Not only did I do my normal crew and captain's checks and inspection, of weather charts and Notices to Airmen (NOTAMs) for problems en route but I also had to meet the cabin crew and monitor their briefing by the senior cabin crew member. I then had to add my comments.

I may make the odd observation about what had been said or answer a question or two. However, what I always briefed on, even if they had all heard it before, was handling of trays, plates and cups on the flight deck.

My rules were:

1. Make your presence known whilst still at the door.
2. No drinks on trays.
3. Drinks to be delivered separately and *never* between the pilots.

If fluids landed on the radio and computer controls on the centre console there could be fire at worst and loss of essential equipment. I wrote about this in the company magazine and it was incorporated in the rules and regulations for cabin crew. This was, or had been, regular behaviour in many airlines.

When you were ready the crew would embark on a bus to the aircraft a mile or so away. Unfortunately, being under American overall supervision we used American school buses. The luggage space at the back was very high and the women had trouble getting their bags up there. I used to help – no Saudi ever did – and the women were grateful. On boarding the bus I was often frowned upon and asked why I helped them. I would be glared at and advised that it was demeaning for a captain to help women. This would be the reason I was to eventually leave Saudia. More later.

On arrival at the aircraft it was usual to find one of the foreigner workers cleaning the windshields (windscreens, in English), usually Filipinos, Thais or Bangladeshis. He would be on a cradle on a crane-like object and the first thing I did was to pop my head through the escape hatch in the roof and say 'Hullo'. They looked all over the place but rarely upwards for some reason. I'd speak again and they would see me and laugh. I enjoyed giving them something to laugh at and realise that some of us cared how badly they lived.

Once airborne, at prayer times, you would advise passengers in which direction to be facing Mecca. The first officer and engineer would take it in turn to pray; some of them had their own prayer blankets with them. Only about 30 per cent of first officers and 60 per cent of engineers were non-Muslim and probably 50/50 on captains.

Flying was still new for many Saudis, so care had to be taken by the cabin crew when dealing with wives. No man could help them with seatbelts other than male relatives and some men objected to females serving them. There were no Muslim women in the crews.

On flights to Europe many of the Saudi Arabian ladies in first class would take it in turns after we left Saudi airspace to use the rest rooms and re-appear in the most expensive clothing and jewellery imaginable.

I enjoyed my flying with SV because there was a lot of it and that suited me fine; I would have liked more overseas trips but I was working up the seniority ladder and occasional tit-bits came my way. Layovers in Paris, Athens and, especially, London were much appreciated. I would go to London sometimes on my days off so that I could see Andrew and Nicholas as I had done when with GF.

In early 1982 Delhi became a destination, twice a week I recall. That meant you had either a three- or four-night layover. The hotel was magnificent with two floors just for crews. The heavily-carpeted corridors had regular signs asking for silence for colleagues who all had varying sleep times because of scheduling.

On one of the floors was a huge crew-room with draught beer, a cabinet where you could leave a bottle for your next visit, a lady at a desk to answer all questions and arrange tours. There was table-tennis, cards, board games, dozens of books and a TV. There was even a separate crew menu with prices much less than the restaurants but the same quality. Give the lady or barman your order and it would arrive at the crew-room. Just to add the final touch there was a great golf course over the road.

Fuel in Saudi Arabia was so cheap that to save money on international flights we would carry as much fuel as possible so that we would land at, or near, maximum landing weight (MLW), so that uplift of fuel would be reduced. It was a massive waste of the world's resources as to carry the extra fuel it was necessary to burn more, approximately 4 per cent per hour extra. That explains to passengers why there is a limit on baggage weight because, apart from restricting maximum take-off weight, it all costs extra fuel to carry. The extra paid for excess baggage weight is not as unreasonable as you might think, although some airlines cash in on the captive passenger.

I have an amazingly lucky facility to never having a hangover which used to upset my mother-in-law, as she did. This was not a problem in Saudi Arabia, allegedly, as alcohol is not available. My first week in the hotel on arrival I missed the occasional beer but found that the local supermarket sold non-alcoholic beer, so bought a six-pack. I was studying hard and during the evening drank them all as they tasted nearly genuine. In the morning I had a splitting non-alcoholic headache! I never touched the stuff again.

In theory there is no alcohol in the KSA (Kingdom of Saudi Arabia) but many of the senior and wealthy families have it available. If you could afford it there was a black market of ordinary whiskey at £40 a bottle or more. On one occasion, at top of descent into Jeddah from London, my first officer said to me 'I'm looking forward to my first whiskey, aren't you?' I replied that I did not know how to acquire such a pleasure and he offered to give me access to his contact. The first officer had been a policeman, so I guess he would know a thing or two. Anyway, I declined, not because I would not have liked access to such sources but as an outsider (i.e. Infidel) I would be in trouble if found out.

Actually, everyone who wanted to made their own beer and wine in their second bathrooms, and the Saudis knew it. Sometimes, though, they would check up on different people and heads would roll, not literally on these occasions as that was reserved for 'justice', but by banishing them from the Kingdom after a bit of jail time.

Both the beer and wine were a bit of a hit and miss unless you took it really seriously. Mine was so-so but on one occasion, after two hours of tennis in 35 degrees C, Geoff Kiernander, my regular partner, and I retired to my kitchen and tried my new 'lager'. We supped, looked at each other, supped again. The beer/lager was fantastic and, although they would not agree, it seemed as good as Amstel, Carlsberg or Heineken. It was excellent. I was never able to produce such quality again.

My wine and bubbly however, was more successful, especially when I used real grapes instead of grape juice. The trouble with one of the grape juice bottles was that they would not fit into the fridge door as they were too tall. I was talking to one of our German captains, my neighbour, and complained about this. He knew, or just got in touch with, the owner and suddenly the bottles were shorter and we were all happy.

Later on, I tried Siddiqui, having always decided it was unsafe or unreliable and found it fantastic. It was basically neat alcohol although it had a nutty taste, as I recall, but with the addition of fruit pieces or other items it was possible to adjust the taste to other liquors, notably gin. I only acquired mine from a chap who had access to a real chemist who checked and certified it safe; not in writing of course. I stopped using it after a couple of months as it was very strong and I was concerned at the possibility of being caught in possession as it was taken much more seriously than wine or beer.

SAUDI-ARABIAN AIRLINES, JEDDAH

On 13 April 1982, just after the news that Mrs Thatcher had decided to save the Falklands, I was to fly to Khartoum. The first officer was late, so the rest of us took the bus to the aircraft and I, having advised ops about the first officer, got on with the pre-flight checks. After thirty minutes a very embarrassed and agitated first officer turned up full of apologies which I accepted. We all have problems sometimes.

Anyway, he thought I was American! Excuse me? We did, after all, have more American captains amongst the non-Saudis. As he strapped himself in he said, 'So what do you think of all these stupid Brits trying to rescue the Falklands? It's madness!' He was a Belgian fellow, so I said, 'Tell me, when we Brits helped rescue you from the Germans were your parents happy?'

This shut him up big-time and the whole flight was conducted professionally but without chat. Weeks later in a UK newspaper, I saw a lovely letter from a Belgian couple who said how wonderful that Britain still stood by those whom she would protect. I cut this out and put it in his box. I had no response but I think it was point made.

Khartoum gave me two particular memories with SV and the first was mangoes. The Sudan produces some of the best I've ever eaten and they are Jaki's favourite fruit. Every flight was to freight fruit and vegetables into the KSA and every time the station officer would come onto the flight deck and put a tray of mangoes on the jump seat and say that they were for us. Lovely. I even sometimes had the whole tray if the others wanted none. Happy Jaki.

One trip it was near departure time and, not wishing to be rude, I carefully asked the station guy if there were any mangoes this trip. He said, 'Oh my goodness, I forgot!' I followed him down the steps and watched him take a tray of mangoes off the loading ramp. I said, 'Thanks', but was astonished to realise that what I thought were gifts from the company were actually just stolen for the crew. I have to admit that after that I still accepted our 'gift'.

The other memory of Khartoum is more serious. I was making an approach to the northerly runway in very bad visibility; it was bad as the aids were unreliable, no radar and the visibility was about 1,000 metres. I was advised that there was an aircraft on such and such a turn-off and I would have to use the other one.

This was irrelevant because I could not stop in time for either of them and, as usual, we would turn round at the end and back track. After I touched down and already had selected reverse thrust I saw the tail of a Handley Page Herald poking out into a quarter of the runway width. I could not take off again, I could not fly over it and I knew not if my wing tip would miss it so I used maximum braking. It was not enough and, 200 metres or so from the obstruction, I swerved to avoid it. This was a most unnatural manoeuvre and quite unrehearsed or trained for. Anyway, it worked.

I turned round and my brakes went into the red, i.e. very hot, and special procedures apply. I cleared the runway as ordered and parked as ordered but near other aircraft and, despite my warnings, people were putting in chocks and generally going about their normal business.

We had no skilled person to assist us as our ground engineer, having seen our predicament and driven onto the runway to connect his headset and talk to us, had been arrested as his pass did not include outside the parking area. So, all the time we were there the flight engineer had to do all the work. What a shambolic place! Those who fly to such areas have to be very careful of reactions and words..

Meanwhile, an extraordinarily unpleasant man appeared on the flight deck and asked if I was going to write a SOR (Special Occurrence Report) on the incident. I advised him that I had to and he told me that that would not be wise. This was the second time I had been threatened by Middle Eastern 'heavies' (viz., Paris 1977) and I was really annoyed. As I said after writing of the Paris incident, only those who have worked in this environment will understand why I complied. If you want to work as a 'mercenary' then you play by the local rules, even if it upsets you. Anyway, I got my mangoes.

Shortly after the Khartoum incident I had my 747 evaluation ride as had all others. Why, I don't know, as I was either a good enough captain for them or I wasn't. I passed.

The next 747 course came up shortly afterwards but no big deal that I wasn't on it as I would obviously be on the next one. The last name on the list was a South African who was proud of the fact, seemingly so anyway, that he had falsely stated his number of hours to Saudia. In other words, I was deprived of a place on the course by his cheating. Anyone reading this will know about whom I am talking.

A man's problem is that he hates to identify cheats. It goes back to school days when you didn't sneak. I do wish I had because the next course was not for another *three* years. The company now had enough captains for their Boeing 747 fleet. Unfortunately, there are quite a few cheats and not enough checks. Saudi was particularly lax.

Mind you, when GF was establishing its seniority system and I was a new first officer there was another first officer who claimed more hours than me. Since he had been a student pilot, during my second tour as an instructor, since he had flown Lightnings (lucky chap) which do quite short trips, and as I'd done Transport for many years from where did his hours come? He was trying to cheat, but in the wrong company. He lost his case.

Nowadays, most cheats fail because all companies are wise to the situation and do proper checks (don't they?). It's not just to do with honour and integrity – flight safety comes into it. Who would you rather fly with: a pilot with 10,000 hours or one who claims 8,000 but only has 6,000? No brainer.

Because fuel was so ridiculously cheap in SV we always landed at overseas airports at maximum landing weight or just under. This meant quite simply that we were tankering fuel and had to buy little or none for an onward short leg, i.e. Jeddah-Paris-London, meant no need to refuel in Paris. This was a wizard wheeze seemingly but all this extra fuel needed extra fuel to carry it. Fuel consumption is very much affected by weight; the heavier you are the more power you need to maintain speed and also perhaps you cannot climb to a higher and cheaper level. This practice was actually a massive waste of the world's resources and contributed that little bit extra to pollution of the atmosphere.

Each month each captain would be allocated a first officer to fly with him on most of his flights which added a certain comfort to the immediate continuity. Also, one felt it helped the first officer to thoroughly study that captain for those things he would use or discard in the future.

One particular first officer always liked to do the landing at Jeddah as he'd really buttoned up his skills for a hairy descent and landing. By hairy I don't mean it was unsafe by any means but he loved to cut it really fine and only just get the power on around 1,000 feet before touchdown. I would say 'You're not going to make it, Mohammed' and he'd laugh and always make it. He never missed but I always thought he would.

Throughout my civilian career, more so than my military career, I gave many and certainly the majority of the landings to the first officers. These guys needed the experience and the confidence to progress to be good, confident captains. In particular, if I had never been to a place before I always gave the sector to the first officer. The reason is actually simple. When the captain is flying he has to concentrate on the charts, the instruments and the radio traffic. Whenever ATC calls and the first officer feels the captain should respond, or he doesn't know what to say, then the captain has to tell him his answer.

If the first officer flies the aircraft then the captain can be the manager. He answers and talks to ATC without hesitation, he can peruse the charts and monitor the first officer's handling and, of course, monitor the instruments at his leisure, albeit frequently. The captain is totally aware of all that is going on without all this flicking eyes from instruments to charts to controlling the aircraft. He is still in command but relaxed and it is the safest way to proceed. As captain it is your responsibility to take control should you feel it necessary; this rarely happens as the first officer is trained and competent.

In late 1983 I was doing an NDB letdown into Karachi. There was no radar that day so we were back to basics. The weather was 1,000-foot cloud-base and 1,000-metres visibility. As we passed over the NDB outbound we had a fire warning in No. 1 engine. I immediately initiated the fire drill: cancel the bell, identify the engine and waited for the first officer to agree, but there was no response as the first officer and engineer were just staring at the red warning light. I continued alone and closed the throttle, switched off the fuel supply, pulled the fire handle which automatically isolated fuel (again), hydraulics and electrics. I twisted the lever which fired the first shot of extinguishant and hit the clock button to time the thirty seconds before the second shot, should it be necessary.

I had to hit the first officer on the arm to read the check list and shout at the engineer to carry out his checks. During all this I had to follow the letdown procedure for landing. The first officer woke up and carried out his proper duties from then on. The engineer, however, contributed nothing until landing, despite my demanding his attention. As we turned off the runway, accompanied by a fleet of fire and rescue vehicles, the fire-warning stopped. For the third time in my life I had been frightened by a false fire warning.

On inspection it was identified as a technical problem, rectified, and the aircraft made serviceable. We returned to Jeddah on schedule. The engineer was given some time in the simulator and proved his abilities. They were not in doubt, but what about his control under stress?

The range of experience across SV was amazing; most airlines had contributed one pilot at least. We had GF, QANTAS, BA, AF, KLM, Lufthansa, Condor, SAS, SAA, Zambian Airways, and so on. The mix was so interesting. My next-door neighbours were American left and right and upstairs left and right was a delightful Zambian family and an Irish family.

On the night I moved into my duplex I had yet to unpack my tools so at 2100 went next door to the US family and asked for a couple of items. He had been in bed – admin started at 0630 – but kindly lent me the items.

The next day I flew to Karachi and returned with a bunch of flowers for Jaki. I took one of the roses next door with the tools and a Mexican lady came to the door. I handed her the tools and rose and said thank you and

SAUDI-ARABIAN AIRLINES, JEDDAH

I was sorry I had 'knocked you up' the night before. When she stopped laughing she explained that in American that meant 'made you pregnant'. Live and learn.

In the early days in Saudia City we had no phones (pre-mobile) so there was a Saudi in a car with a radio in contact with ops and if it was necessary to call someone out he would drive to the house, knock and advise you to report to ops. This was okay in its way but not if you were on a day off.

So, if you saw the car anywhere near your apartment you told the kids to keep quiet as Caspar was looking for you. Caspar the ghost referring, of course, to his totally white garb of the robe and headdress. When we finally got proper phones we all invested in answer machines to which the Saudis never became comfortable talking. So if you answered your phone on your day off more fool you. If you wanted someone then you drove there – it was no distance.

On Christmas Day 1984 I was off duty, having returned from Madrid the previous morning. I received a call to say they had nobody to fly to Islamabad and I had to do it. I asked why and was advised that the American captain had called in sick. I could not get out of it and went to ops via the 'sick' captain. He was playing with his kids and I asked him how he was. He was fine and said he called sick because Muslims don't celebrate Christmas, so one of them would be called out.

I pointed out that my kids were now short of a Daddy for Christmas and I made sure his wife, not his children, knew what I thought of him. He had, of course, bid the line knowing there was duty on the 25th. All month he must have known he was going to call in sick. I got back late on the 28th only to set off for Athens on the 29th as per my roster. Thank you, you bastard!

Interestingly, on arrival at Islamabad, the weather was heavy rain, low cloud and poor visibility. I saw the runway at 200 feet but there was another runway heading off to the left but sharing the same threshold point; this was not shown on the chart for the airfield. I immediately called, 'We are at the wrong airfield!' even though we had used the correct frequencies, etc. The first officer assured me it was correct as he knew the airfield so I landed; it was a nasty shock. By chance, I was in Frankfurt a few weeks later and went to the Jeppersen HQ where the charts were printed. I recounted my experience and they agreed to fix the problem. I never saw it amended up to a while later.

Normally the Saudis were very generous over Christmas. Whilst they had no interest in it they filled in most of the work and during Ramadan we, the foreigners, did extra for which we were given an extra month's salary! We were always paid at the new moon so whilst the Muslims rejoiced in the new moon as part of their religious meaning we all rejoiced because that was pay day.

The cheques were paid promptly into our mailboxes and that evening there were long queues at the currency exchange houses from where we sent our money to our own banks. If you were in there when prayers were called you had to leave quickly or the doors would be locked for fifteen to twenty minutes and you could not leave.

Meanwhile outside if the traders who had blankets on the sidewalks on which they had their wares did not immediately stop trading the Sharia Police would appear. There was no subtlety here, no please stop chaps and attend to your wares. The police had five to six-foot-long whippy canes and they would wade into the 'offenders' and administer some pretty unpleasant wheals.

Prayer times are taken very seriously, as are the end of the day cannon which signify that during Ramadan, the breaking of the fast may begin. On more than one occasion I have taxied onto my stand only to wait ten to fifteen minutes whilst the ground crew sat on their blankets and ate. Meanwhile, the passengers are all agitated because they wish to break their fast but cannot.

Around 1984-85 we actually had arrows, controlled by the flight engineers, which pointed at Mecca to assist those wishing to pray in flight.

Sometime in 1982 Jaki's maternal grandmother, Nanny, had a stroke and was hospitalised. Irene, Jaki's mother, said all was going well and not to rush home. However, Jaki, having reached the age of nine, had been sent to boarding school in England and Nanny became her second 'mother'. She had to get back.

By chance I had a trip to London and said I'd pop in to the hospital on my way to Uckfield where we had recently bought a house. Normally I would drive home, or anywhere, after landing with my uniform on, not the jacket. I arrived at the hospital, put on my hat and jacket as I knew she liked uniforms – her husband had been a Second World War submariner – and went to her bedside.

She was completely out of it, dribbling on the pillow and never responded to touch or voice. I talked about Jaki and her great-grandchildren for a while and left. I immediately called Jaki and said to come as soon as possible.

This meant that she had to get urgent assistance to obtain an exit which was always needed, other than for aircrew on duty, and to obtain three tickets at crew rates for Jeddah to Heathrow. This was all done thanks to help from some of the guys and the three of them eventually joined the queue for space available seats. As it neared departure time, she said in desperation to the station officer that she was desperate because of Nanny's condition. He said he'd double-check everything and said that he could just squeeze them in.

At this point a Saudi behind Jaki said he was senior and demanded a ticket, if necessary one of Jaki's. At this point the station officer washed his hands of the affair by withdrawing the three tickets. Jaki was so angry that she swung round and floored the guy.

In the ensuing brouhaha Wayne Cunningham, one of the US flight engineers who also had no seat, ushered them out and hid them in his apartment. The next morning he got their tickets changed to Jeddah-Riyadh-Heathrow and no one made the connection of name and situation.

Jaki got to Heathrow just in time to see Nanny before she died. Incredibly, Nanny was sitting up, lucid and explained all that I had said to her and that she was so pleased that I was in uniform. That was a further lesson that you must never assume anything about people who seem lost to you, in a coma or, even apparently dead. I was astonished because I was absolutely convinced that she neither heard nor saw anything.

Meanwhile, back at the ranch I was being hauled over the coals for my wife's actions. I was advised that if I wanted to keep my job I had to write a grovelling apology to he who had been felled. Jaki had only clobbered the rostering officer, hadn't she? The letter was received and acknowledged and I heard no more about it. Jaki, however, entered into the folklore of SV.

There was one hijacking in my time. An aircraft en route to Jeddah had a man or men come into the flight deck, put a gun to the captain's head and demand he flew to Tehran. The captain, an American, said that he had insufficient fuel to make it. He was ordered to shut up and go to Tehran and too bad if they ran out of fuel. The captain did as he was told, but was frightened because he was in a no-win situation. Furthermore, there were no charts on board for the route or destination. We had charts for everywhere we went and for fields near our regular routes but not Tehran.

After much stress and excellent captaincy they made it to that most difficult airfield despite the awful terrain. The fuel gauges showed empty and one engine flamed-out after landing due to no fuel.

The crew was flown back next day and the TV News was full of the facts of the heroic first officer and engineer who were Saudi. No mention was made of the captain. The King gave the two Saudis a stack of money and a large piece of land each. The captain had nobody, yes nobody in SV to praise him, thank him, reward him or even send a letter. Just to add to the insult he was expected to fly his normal roster the next day. He refused as he was still shaken by the event. That's what you get if you are a mercenary in that region!

As a visitor to Saudi Arabia it was wise to keep criticisms to oneself. The family ties are very strong and all Muslims are well aware of their extended family. For example, one of the catering staff in the ground school had a very direct blood-line to the top man in SV.

There was an ex-GF captain in SV who was not above offending his first officers rather more than they could take. Many complaints had been made and one day, on a departure from Paris during a check ride, he completely messed up his departure procedure. He was adamant that his radio aids and other equipment were set correctly but, when he was trying to settle down, he realised that his No. 2 VOR was on the wrong frequency. He knows his set-up had been correct and now realised he had been set up. Somehow the frequency had been changed, so he failed the check ride and was sacked. He was a good aviator and captain but learnt too late that you should be kinder to the first officers.

The day of one of my check rides I had to have a lipoma (big fatty lump) removed from my back so I asked the doctor if the local anaesthetic would stop me from flying. I did not wish to miss the check flight and give any grounds for problems with rostering, etc.

The discomfort after the op was okay, but I could put no pressure on it so Jaki disinfected a saucer from a flowerpot and I placed it over the wound and taped it to my body. It worked a treat and I could sit comfortably in my seat.

The trip was Jeddah-Rome Fiumicino-Frankfurt and during the Rome turn-round the check pilot, a Saudi, wandered off. The first officer and I discussed the departure as a couple of aids were unserviceable and our routeing would change. This information was in the NOTAMs given to us in Jeddah.

As I carried out the amended route the check pilot started haranguing me and demanding I follow the published route, etc. This in the middle of an international airport departure. I explained but he would have none of it. Fortunately, the first officer explained in Arabic and he settled down, but had lost face in front of two fellow Saudis over a foreigner. He hadn't absorbed, or even read, the NOTAMs and he had not taken notice of my pre-taxi briefing. I was concerned for my future but I heard no more about it. Such incidents can strongly influence a foreigner's standing, even when said foreigner had done no wrong.

Like most fathers in SV I tried to take a Christmas tree home from the UK for the normal festive pleasures. On arrival at crew customs I was horrified to see a corner full of said trees. Mine was duly confiscated and I said this was unfair as it had no religious significance but was for children to have their presents underneath. It cut no ice, of course.

On Christmas Eve the British Embassy opened its doors to the British ex-pats where we attended a carol service after being given a beer, or wine, or two. The carol service was held in the open and I like to think our voices carried over the walls. Incredibly, the grounds contained a 9-hole golf course.

In theory there is no alcohol in Saudia Arabia but the hotels we stayed in in Dhahran and Riyadh liked to go through the motions. On arrival in Dhahran the crew received *chitties* to be cashed for a drink in the bar. The bar was like normal bars but only served non-alcoholic drinks. We could cash our *chitty* for a pineapple juice.

There was no such bar in the Marriott Hotel in Riyadh but, as in Dhahran, you could have non-alcoholic wine with your meal. This was shown to the guest, opened in his presence and then a little poured as a taster. It all looked so normal.

The Marriott was a good hotel and their food was excellent. The best dessert was a tall glass and a long spoon to extricate two brownies, two lovely vanilla globes and a huge covering of chocolate sauce! Fantastic! It was called 'Chocolate Devil'.

Sadly, the hotel was closed and developed, or intended to be developed, as a hospital. However, planners blew it. The central structure could not be changed; it housed the shafts and supports for four lifts which were not big enough for stretchers so the plan fell through as to change them would be horrendously costly. It was still closed when I left four years later.

Jeddah is, of course, on the coast, so many people enjoyed sailing, swimming and especially wind-sailing. I was one of a group who used a beach house to the north of town where the girls could wear their normal bikinis, we could have BBQs and generally relax. Not only are women not allowed to show any of their bodies but neither are girls over the age of seven. So, no father could have the pleasure of taking his kids to the beach even when still really young.

My sport was tennis. I had tried my favourite, cricket, but opposition was quite unsporting. The only competition were Pakistani teams who took delight in bowling dangerous deliveries to low-order batsmen, and, as in Bahrain, they would never give a decision against one of their own.

Tennis was not something I had played all that much but I took to it like a duck to water. More or less every day, I would play whilst in Jeddah and quite frequently in Dhahran and Riyadh. Each section of Saudia City had its own tennis club so competitions were a regular feature.

My main partner Geoff Kiernander and I played hard, never giving up on a point. We each had half- or one-gallon chilled water containers and would play for ages. Our record was three and three-quarter hours in 39-40-degree C heat. We were really fit. I was in my late forties by now.

In 1982 Jaki decided she'd had enough of no driving and having to rely on others for help when I was away. So we found a house to rent in Paphos, Cyprus. It was on a quiet street away from the centre, so we bought a car and she was more relaxed. The children went to the local Greek school where Josh rapidly picked up childish Greek and learnt songs for the playground. Gemma was a little slower but still chattered away.

Josh was quite irritating as he would listen to the locals chatting in the supermarket, or wherever, with a knowing grin on his face. When questioned he would never tell us what was said. He wasn't fluent so I guess he only got the gist of it.

Unfortunately, the only way to Cyprus from Jeddah was via Athens which took a huge chunk of my days off to go there and back. There was an Austrian Airways flight direct but they were not allowed to sell tickets due to cabotage. However, I visited the station officer for Austrian and he said he was sorry but he could not bend the rules. But, he said, I can give you free travel. Wow! Thus were my commuting problems solved.

Meanwhile, we'd bought the house in Uckfield, East Sussex, and soon it seemed right to let the kids go to school in England. They all went home to the UK in late 1983 and my visits were now much easier.

I now had three houses: my new one in the UK, my apartment (free) in Jeddah and a derelict house on a hillside in Tremithusa, north of Paphos. We never did find time or real opportunity to rebuild the latter, so we sold it. I sometimes look at it on Google Earth and realise that the new owners have done a good job with it. It looks beautiful.

We now added Dhaka in Bangladesh to our destinations. We stayed in a luxurious hotel called 'The Sonargaon' but you stepped one yard outside the grounds and poverty was everywhere. They were so poor that nothing was wasted; there was no litter as there was a use for everything. To be in this hotel and then walk or go in a bikeshaw outside caused some quite guilty feelings.

Then Casablanca came on the list and this was a terrific destination. I think the hotel was the Hyatt and they had the inevitable Humphrey Bogart bar, which had life-sized portraits of the stars and real drink. The rooms were magnificent.

I arranged for Jaki to meet me there one visit and, as usual, I had a suite. They put beautiful roses in three areas, the two bathrooms were immaculate and there were mirrored screens everywhere, vertical I should add, and, silly as it seems, it was easy to lose your way around the bedroom, bathrooms, sitting-room and dressing-room because of the mirrors. Quite the most exotic suite I've ever had.

The added interest was the super quayside fish restaurant, the splendid souk and shops selling leather jackets. The jackets were made for Paris but any fault and they were retained. I never found the fault on my leather jacket.

The flights to Casablanca, and later Madrid, all went through Tunis where the cabin crew changed each way. Many of our stewards were qualified doctors who couldn't find work.

The cabin crew system in SV was different, at the time, and very practical. When they joined SV they were based in Jeddah but there were many other bases and when a vacancy occurred then they could transfer. The bases, as I recall, were Jeddah, Tunis, Madrid, London, Paris, Frankfurt, Bombay, Athens, Delhi and, when the 747 arrived, Seoul, Manila and Singapore. Naturally, many of the crew members chose their own country but they could be based anywhere and after an interval move on to another base.

Pilots: Jeddah – take it or leave it.

Again, the cabin crew had come from many different airlines and countries, the crews fore and aft being positively multinational.

Life in SV was fairly boring in that most flying was around the country with only a few international flights here and there; one a month if lucky. Although I saw the family more or less every month, sometimes twice, and they came out in school holidays, it was a little lonely. The tennis became my hobby and sport of choice and I played every day in Jeddah.

I was seriously bent on finding another airline who would employ me when it was announced that new courses would start for the 747. As I was still top, or close, I decided to stay so that I could get the type on my licences. By this time, I had British, American, French, Saudi and Omani licences.

Meanwhile I had another 747 evaluation trip (Why? They now knew me well enough!) and passed and was given the date of July 1985 for the ground school in Jeddah.

In May 1985 I had an amazing escape from terrorism. On the 11th I flew to Colombo where I was to stay for three nights; there were only two flights a week. The name of the hotel eludes me but the Oberoi or Marriott comes to mind. They had a great system for service at the pool whereby each table had a foot-high flag-pole with flag. When you wanted a waiter you simply raised the little flag and waited your turn.

On the morning of the 13th I decided it was time for a bit of culture and tourism so I booked a car and driver to go to take me to the religious centre and beautiful gardens of Anuradhapura. I booked the car for 0700 and a wake-up call for 0600.

That evening I got involved with a few members of the crew from HMS *Gloucester* which was visiting for a few days. She was the sister ship of HMS *Sheffield* which was sunk in the Falklands. We had a great evening and as I convinced them I was cleared to Top Secret I toured the ship. It was amazing, as was the amount of booze we managed to get through.

At 0600 when I answered the call I asked them to call their car-hire department and cancel my booking. They had a good deposit so no problem for them. I was just too tired.

This turned out to be an amazingly lucky decision because, at the time I would have been enjoying the beautiful grounds, the Tamil Tigers machine-gunned and shot 146 people dead and injured countless others.

My last flight on TriStar with SV was the night of 21 June 1985 which was Jeddah-Riyadh and return as passenger on the deadhead special. This flight was 0300 every day and positioned crews to Jeddah to avoid all the hotel bills. It was a B737 with about 100-plus passengers. It was a good idea but not nice for those of us who did not celebrate Ramadan or generally lead the Saudi style of life. In Ramadan, the fasting month, the Saudis would usually end their fast at dusk and then enjoy the evening even into the night. Well, many of us were aware that our B737 flight-deck crew were probably very tired; this is when I learnt to sleep on the aircraft. Sleeping was easier than feeling uncomfortable with the situation.

The Boeing 747 At Last!

At last, three years late, I began the ground training on the Boeing 747. I had never flown a Boeing before but the rest of the course had all been on the SV 737 or 707, so, frequently, the instructors would say, 'That's standard Boeing so we won't go into that.' Much to the instructor's annoyance and, probably, the other students' I would remind him that I did not know about Boeing. He then had to explain the full systems to me but I'm sure the others benefited from the reminder.

The final exams were, of course, in the American method which is multi-choice. Actually, CAA use that now and have done for some years. Having passed the ground exams on the aircraft systems we had thirty-two hours handling in the simulator and then a three-hour oral. The oral is done with an FAA ([American] Federal Aviation Authority) inspector on the flight deck. He starts with one or two simple questions and then proceeds to touch every gauge, button, switch and light and you have to explain their normal and emergency functions. Then you have to sit in the engineer's seat and every gauge etc. is again discussed.

At the end Captain Kellum said 'and now just a few limitations' and asked many performance, speed and engine limits questions. Prior to all these exams I had written many flash cards and always carried them with me and tested myself at every opportunity. He asked me the take-off weight of the Boeing 747-300 first and I gave him the full six-figure number 377, ??? tonnes (I've no record of the final three figures now) and he said 'Don't bother with all the numbers, just the first three will do.' I replied, 'Look here, Tom, I've learnt these numbers for weeks and you're going to get the lot!' 'Okay,' he said and so it was.

So to the first flight to do circuits and landings, let-downs and so on. The Saudi check captain said these are really strong aircraft and proceeded to turn the control wheel left and right rapidly. I was really upset as this was a crazy thing to do as the wing has barely responded to the first demand before it has to reverse. This caused awful vibration and when I saw the wing during a later demonstration, and I was in a passenger seat, I was horrified. The wing was bending and twisting in a frightening way. They are tested in Seattle to destruction, so it is known how tough they are, but this was awful abuse of an aircraft.

I then did a check-ride with Captain Kellum and was cleared for line training. This comprised seventeen sectors using the 747-100 and 747-SP and I was cleared to the line to include the 747-300 as well.

> We operated the Boeing 747-100, -300 and -SP (special performance)
>
> | 100 and 300 | Wingspan | 59.6 metres | 195 feet 6 inches |
> |---|---|---|---|
> | | Length | 70.6 metres | 231 feet 7 inches |
> | | Height | 19.3 metres | 63 feet 4 inches |
>
> 100 powered by Pratt and Whitney JT9D-7 and 300 by RR RB524-D4
>
> Maximum weight 100 340,194 kilograms (750,000lb) and 300 377,842 kilograms (833,000lb)
>
> Maximum speed Mach 0.92
>
> SP Special Performance. Fewer passengers, and lighter.
>
> | | Wing span | 59.64 metres | 195 feet 7 inches |
> |---|---|---|---|
> | | Length | 56.31 metres | 184 feet 9 inches |
> | | Height | 20.06 metres | 65 feet 1 inch |
>
> Powered by RR RB 211-524B2-D4
>
> Maximum weight 315,600 kilograms (695,779lb)
>
> Maximum speed Mach 0.92

Although we usually started with a short sector in-country it was only to collect more passengers for the final leg. The 747 fleet covered Cairo, London, Delhi, Singapore, Bombay, Djakarta, Seoul and Manila. It was a wonderful experience and a real ego trip. Here was the biggest passenger aircraft in the world and I was in charge. Wow! Just a small indication of its size is to note that on touch down in the nose-up condition the pilot's backside is seventy feet above ground. When you turn the nose-wheel to take a corner the main wheels turn in the opposite direction thus making it a very ground manoeuvrable aircraft – essential at JFK where nearly every turn was at right-angles instead of a gentler turn. JFK was never a comfortable airfield for taxiing.

THE BOEING 747 AT LAST!

En route to Delhi in early October 1985 I had bad communications on entering Indian airspace and they were unable to give me my codeword or clearance number for entering Delhi airspace. All went well, communications were restored and we landed on schedule.

The next morning, I was ordered by a military major to report to ATC at Delhi airport where I received a dressing down from another senior officer. He advised me that I should have used my password on contacting Delhi ATC and my failure was a security breach. Although I pointed out that I had not received it due to their poor equipment and that Delhi had not asked for it he was not appeased.

How daft! Here they are giving you a password on open radio and using it as clearance to enter a restricted area. As they had no area radar I could easily have been intercepted by a 'baddie', shot down and the 'baddie' taking my place and they would have known no difference. Weird!

Then came my downfall in standard SV fashion. I was on a live check with a Pakistani checker from Jeddah to Riyadh. The weather at Riyadh was below legal limits but I made an approach anyway just to see if we hit a lucky break. There was nothing wrong in doing that so long as you don't exceed permitted limits. Although in real life I would have let the three auto-pilots do the approach and our accuracy would have been spot-on, the checker said to do a manual approach, i.e. hand-fly. This was daft because the manual limits were 200-foot cloud-base and the reports were 100 feet.

I carried out a good approach and, as expected, we saw lights at 200 feet which were good enough to continue. Unfortunately, I was slightly off centre-line and decided there was insufficient time to jink right with such a large aircraft and make a safe landing from such a low altitude. So I carried out a go-around and, before I could do another approach, ATC declared a further deterioration in weather and I diverted to Dhahran.

The check pilot never shut up all the way and said I should have tried to jink right, I could have landed, etc., etc. We returned to Jeddah where he reported that after take off I had raised the flaps at too slow a speed. This was a lie, as neither the first officer nor engineer would have allowed me to do it or order it. He claimed my flying was inaccurate and also that I could have 'easily' landed at Riyadh.

The writing was now on the wall but nothing happened for a week, and then on Christmas Day I flew to Riyadh on another check-ride and on to London, arriving on Boxing Day morning. The ride went well and the first officer, Eric Sondrup, the engineer, a 6-foot 4-inch black American, and I went for a beer at the local. The locals were most confused as Eric was short and thin, I was 6 feet and not too thin and the engineer, Geoff Layne, was huge. I had no festive spirit in me.

We returned to Jeddah where I was told I had passed and actually was rostered and did a round trip to Bombay. Upon return I was given a three-month notice but with no flying. The notice period was generous but I could not work out the machinations of all this. The chief pilot was very kind but said that, in view of my go-around at Riyadh and the check-pilot's write-up, I was to leave. This made no sense in view of the fact I had been back on the line with no restriction.

Nevertheless, it was a great relief to be leaving, especially with such a generous amount of notice. I quickly restarted my search for another airline. This search ended with a visit to LTU in Dusseldorf with an interview with the chief pilot. After a reasonable time he offered me a job with them, talked about the duties as a first officer and gave me a book on their current navigation system as I had not used it before.

It was agreed that I should return the next week to sign my contract but just before I left the UK the chief pilot called me to say the deal was off. The reason was that the German pilots said they would go on strike if any more non-Germans were employed. This was crazy as we were all in the EU by this time. It was a great shame as not only did they fly the best-equipped L-1011-500, but their route structure as a charter holiday airline was worldwide. It was a great disappointment.

I was entitled to a free TWA ticket Jeddah-JFK return so I went to visit an airline employment agency with whom I had been in touch. The only opening was an internal Japanese airline based in Kyoto, I think. Anyway, the children were well into their schooling and I did not fancy such long absences and distances from home and family.

It was a bad time for work in aviation; there were few pilot vacancies in 1985-86. However, whilst still in New York, Jaki called to say Air Lanka would like to interview me in London in three days' time so I shot off home.

Air Lanka, Colombo

The interview went well and I was offered a post as captain L-1011 immediately. I have to admit that their terms were good but the salary was poor. However, no one else was offering, so I accepted and was in Sri Lanka a few days later. There were three new captains – me, David Hawkes and Roy Copeman (both ex-BA). After initiation rites, i.e. paperwork, uniform, measurements, licences issued, medical etc., off we three went to Hong Kong with our check Captain John Aston (ex-BA). The hotel was attached to the terminal building and access was via an over-the-road walkway with a moving baggage ramp. Accommodation was excellent and, to cap it all, the underground bar had two great snooker tables. Bliss!

Actually, we went there to undergo aircraft familiarisation and checks on the L-1011 in the Cathay Pacific simulators. We were all qualified but had had time away from the aircraft. John was an excellent instructor and we were soon up to speed again. John and I were well matched on the table so we had a few good beers and games. We were there for about a week and returned to Colombo on an Air Lanka scheduled flight. Next was the usual three or four trips with a training captain to get signed out on to the line and then we were free.

During our line training period terrorists blew up one of our aircraft on the ground. It was the Tamil Tigers, of course. They had threatened a cargo man with the death of his family if he did not put the bomb in a box of fruit en route to Malé in the Maldives.

The aircraft was late, otherwise it would have happened in the air. As it was many people died and one or two were never even found; having been sitting directly over the bomb they were vaporised. Two Indian Airways pilots were walking under the tail at the moment of the explosion, having just left duty-free, and were killed when the tail fell on them.

David Hawkes was just about to get airborne and I checked with ops to confirm it wasn't him and then rang Jaki in the UK and gave her David and Roy's home numbers so that she could phone Hilary and Liz to catch them before the early morning news.

By now David, Roy and I had become known as the three musketeers. When training finished we were off on our own, on 2 June 1986. It's a wonderful feeling to be let free as a commander of a large aircraft with the responsibility of the safety of so many people.

Many people feel that it must be daunting and/or weigh on the mind but that is not so. Yes, of course you are aware of and respect the serious responsibilities you have but were they to be daunting you could not make important decisions at times of stress, or emergency, or in dozens of situations, including the effect of weather on your route and destination. The task is quite simply satisfying, truly enjoyable and fulfilling.

Air Lanka's route structure with just four L-1011s was amazing; one hiccup and the domino effect could be felt along the routes from Tokyo-London. Our destinations were Malé, Dubai, Dhahran, Muscat, Kuwait, Paris CDG, Frankfurt, Zurich, Rome, Amsterdam and London to the west and Bangkok, Kuala Lumpur, Singapore, Hong Kong and Tokyo to the east.

The aircraft were the TriStar 200 and, later, the 500. This was a great leap from the others:

```
    Engines RR RB211 54B
    Wingspan    50.09 metres      164 feet 4 inches
    Length      50.05 metres      164 feet 2 inches
    Height      16.87 metres      55 feet 4 inches
    Maximum weight 231,332 kilograms (510,000lb)
    Maximum speed Mach 0.95
```

It was a fantastic airline to work for, the people were friendly and kind, the rosters were well organised so that we ex-pats had five or six days off in a row so that we could get home. Whenever I was in Rome, Frankfurt or Paris for two days or more I could get free tickets to London and back to see my family.

Regrettably, the salary was nowhere near enough to keep Gemma and Joshua at school, run a house and mortgage and pay my guesthouse bills etc. As a result, I had to keep digging into savings and look for better conditions elsewhere. As I said earlier, times were difficult in the aviation world but Emirates were hiring so I applied and failed.

Never mind, I was really enjoying my work after six years of no particular pleasure. The weather in the area was always a challenge as all year round there were bouts of heavy rain from cumulonimbus clouds, strong winds and turbulence on approach.

Colombo International Airport, Katunayake and previously known as RAF Negombo now had a runway long enough for all types. You will recall in my Comet days that PSP (Perforated Steel Planking) had been used to extend the runway to accommodate us. That had all gone and I was delighted and enchanted to see it had been used to wrap around the trees on the road to the airport. This both supported them and protected them from free roaming cows removing the bark whilst having a good scratch.

You may also recall that the take off to the east was quite scary as you flew at a rising hillside covered in trees. Well, this hill was still there but all the trees had gone. It looked much better now.

On the other side of the passenger terminal at Colombo was the old RAF base, now owned and used by the Sri Lankan Air Force. They had an old wreck of a Tiger Moth, the type on which the three musketeers had trained, and David was most keen to get it in the air again. Well, it was in such a bad state that it did not seem possible but he was allowed to try. David spent all his spare time there with a few air force volunteers getting it fit to fly. David had been an engineer with de Havilland before becoming a pilot, so he was in his element.

I'm pleased to say that I was able to watch David do the first flight of 'his' rebuilt machine. What an amazing chap, engineer, BA captain and as a nice a man you could ever wish to meet.

Actually, David did upset me once. He had decided to save this kitten he had found abandoned and had it in his chalet at Brown's Beach Hotel where the three of us were in chalets. He was hand feeding it and being generally very motherly. He was off on a trip for two days and asked if I would take over and, of course, I agreed.

I had split my thumb and had an open wound which somehow got this cat's saliva in it. David returned the next day and the cat died. David thought it may have had rabies (quite likely) so we were sent into Colombo for treatment, taking the cat with us for an autopsy. Naturally, this was a Friday afternoon and no autopsy could be done until Monday morning. We were both put on regular anti-rabies injections which lasted until Tuesday when the cat was declared free of rabies. Apparently, the brain carries the evidence.

Brown's Beach had tennis and squash courts but because of the injuries to my leg in the past I found, once again, that squash was not really for me. The constant stopping, setting off in the opposite direction and the hard surface made my tibia ache for days afterwards. On the other hand, my reasonably good tennis was put to use; Roy, David and I plus whoever was around would play all evening and often during the day, even the days were always around 84 to 88 degrees F and barely less at night.

At each end of the tennis court were roads and on the north side the squash courts, so any balls over the netting was no problem. However, the south side was undergrowth with a narrow path through it. The entrance was guarded by a four-foot-high gate with spikes and if a ball went in there the hitter had to get it. The reason was that in the heat and with sweaty hands the balls did not last long and we had to buy them en route as there were few in Sri Lanka.

Getting over the gate was easy enough but required concentration. However, the big problem was – where is the cobra tonight? It was seen occasionally and known to live there and also known that they can be quite grumpy as the late, great Steve Irwin would say. So, with much noise and hitting bushes etc. with the tennis racquet, one advanced into the den to retrieve a tennis ball. Crazy!

Roy and I spent a lot of time together when not rostered. David was always with his beloved Tiger Moth and used a favourite bar where we sat on the terrace playing cards or backgammon. From this vantage we saw the worst evidence of all of the local poverty. Paedophiles would wander by holding hands with little boys; the paedos were invariably in flip-flops or sandals and a sort of loincloth in muslin. They were all white and smirking at the disgust on our faces.

The threat of the Tamil Tigers was always present in Colombo but less so outside. However, one night there was a gunfight outside my guest house, the Starbeach, but no one was hurt. Later on, one of the English captains, Graham Swanson (ex-BA) was in his car with his wife and daughter on their way home from dinner when they were machine-gunned. He put his foot down and, incredibly, only the car was hurt. Generally, however, we in the village of Negombo had no real problems.

On school holiday periods the family came for a couple of weeks to the chalet in Brown's Beach and we decided to go to Kandy for a couple of days. So, we set off in my regular taxi with driver Sam Godopal and checked into a hotel and I paid for Sam in a guesthouse.

The next night we went to see the Temple of the Buddha's Tooth. We queued at the entrance for a couple of minutes, there was a maximum number of people allowed inside, and entered this incredibly claustrophobic, narrow-corridored, dimly-lit and hot place. We saw the tooth and went for dinner. We had queued at the Temple from 1900 to 1905. We left the next morning and that evening, at 1903, the Tamil Tigers exploded a bomb at that same entrance and killed three people. That's twice they've missed me and, more importantly, they missed my family.

Sam was a great guy, a good driver (necessary in Sri Lanka) and very reliable. He had my schedule and he always picked me up on time for my flights, operating or passenger, and was always there for when I returned. He never tried to make money out of me other than fair fares. Such people are so important when you are far from home and it gave Jaki and I great pleasure to pass on Gemma and Joshua's outgrown clothes for his children.

Brown's Beach Hotel was my first abode but I ended up in Starbeach Guest House which was cheaper, friendlier and I had air-conditioning and my own balcony from which I could pick fresh paw-paw. The local kids had a great cricket field, I couldn't say pitch, where they played cricket enthusiastically but with appalling equipment. I had a word with Josh's sports department at his school and managed to collect plenty of balls, cricket and hockey and tennis, and other paraphernalia to give to the kids. I fear many of the younger ones were bullied into handing theirs over. The kids milled around me whenever they saw me.

The walk home in the dark from tennis was somewhat unnerving as there were no street lights but plenty of snakes. My journey was slow and my torch batteries numerous. At the time the country with the most deaths, pro rata, from snakebite was Sri Lanka; it was always wise to take care.

The first officers in Sri Lanka were a very friendly and competent bunch of guys and I had the pleasure of flying with one of them who could trash me at tennis. He was Sunil Wettimuny, the opening bat for Sri Lanka. He was in the first Cricket World Cup in 1975, which was held in the UK, and he faced Lillee and Thomson at their fastest. Both he and his captain ended up in hospital due to Thomson's aggression at Lords.

We used to play all our tennis on the rooftop court at the Intercontinental Hotel Dubai. He was very athletic and charming and I was not surprised to hear that, long after my departure from Air Lanka, he had become Fleet Captain (i.e. chief pilot) L-1011.

Sri Lankans speak excellent English but emphasise different syllables on long words, so sometimes they are a sentence ahead by the time you've worked out what they've said. I think their surnames may have led to this strange emphasis; e.g. Kumarasinge, Kuranayagamm, Phampapillai, Karunatilleke. They all had the same habit on the flight deck if they wanted to leave: they didn't ask permission, they just said, 'I'll go and come.'

Fortunately, I only had to say such names as Kira, Taj, Johan, Prasuna, Freeman, Ramsey, i.e. nearly all short. The island has much influence from the various countries who have occupied it or passed through. Freeman was never called anything else, so I'm not sure whether it's his first or second name.

He and I were passing through immigration at Dubai to operate to Frankfurt and I saw a huge man. I was unaware at this time that he was the tallest man in the world; I said to Freeman, 'Look' as I pointed in the direction. Freeman said 'Oh, yes', but I could tell by his blank expression that he did not know what I was talking about. It's not surprising as the mind has difficulty accepting the impossible. The man was a Pakistani and his height was 8-foot 3¼-inches and he stood proudly as very rude and ignorant people just walked up to him and had their photographs taken. No requests made and no thanks given. His manager was really small so they made an intriguing picture.

Dubai (DXB) airport had changed only a little since my GF time but the departure area had been enlarged. Also, I noticed that the runway no longer ended at the road with the beach beyond. The beach was now a couple of hundred yards away and soon to be nearly half a mile from the runway end. I last landed in DXB in December 1988 and went as a passenger in 2012. The difference was staggering; it was now a huge airport with massive facilities for passenger-handling, aircraft parking and so on. The original building was no bigger than a three-storey block of flats 100 yards long!

Muscat was little changed from GF days to 1988 when I left UL (Air Lanka).

Dhahran was as dismal as ever but the fighter aircraft lightened the scene.

Kuwait was as hot and ugly as ever but we enjoyed a really pleasant hotel to the south which was very crew friendly. We would arrive very early in the morning and get up at 1300 for a really fine buffet lunch.

Paris CDG was a massive place and for aircraft and ATC excellent but for passengers was frustrating. The interior of departures was always too crowded and you had to work your way through queues to get to your queue. These queues were at the foot of escalators leading to one departure lounge for, perhaps, three or four gates. So you queued before you queued.

The city, of course, was wonderful and, as with all other cities I visited, I walked and walked miles just admiring the architecture, feeling the ambience and popping into bars and restaurants as the mood took me. I was never without a book and, indeed, when someone mentioned me to another and there was doubt as to who I was it was 'You know, the captain, who always has a book with him.'

My usual way to London from CDG on my layover was via British Caledonian to London Gatwick but there was a long wait between arriving and leaving. In the departure lounge on one occasion I was taken by this tall, athletic woman, striding around; it was Virginia Wade.

By chance I was sitting next to her in business class in my uniform; I said that, as it was obvious I recognised her, could we chat. She was absolutely charming, especially when I told her I had been in this uniform for about twenty hours and hoped it was not disturbing her!

The flight went well and seemingly swifter than usual and we ended up in the baggage collection area. A man came up to us and without any preamble said, 'Are you Virginia Wade?'; she said 'Yes', and he turned round and said to his travelling companions, 'See, I told you!' No words of thanks or greeting – what an ignorant man.

She said she was used to it and took it in good heart. Lovely woman.

Sadly, although we visited Amsterdam, Schiphol, often it was only to refuel, so I was unable to renew my acquaintance with this lovely place.

Rome was just a fuel stop and passenger dropping point en route to Frankfurt.

We only had one flight per week to Frankfurt (FFM) and when I arrived I would have a ticket waiting for me to get to LHR!

I would get back the night before the next day's evening flight. All very civilised.

Frankfurt had an ATC somewhat like many international airports, especially Tokyo, Delhi, Paris, and even London once. However, computerised planning has made it more difficult viz. giving priority to your own national airline. This often meant that on a long-haul flight the early aircraft would get the best fuel-saving altitude. Hence this true story: BA and LF (Lufthansa)

'FFM tower, BA123 request push-back.'	'BA123 Clear push back.'
'FFM tower, BA123 request engine start.'	'BA123 Clear start.'
'FFM tower, LF456 request start.'	'LF456 Clear.'
'FFM tower, LF456 request push.'	'LF456 Clear.'

'FFM tower, BA123 taxi.'	'BA123 Hold position
	BA123 Roger.'
'FM456 taxi'	'LF456 Clear to R/W 18
	LF456 Roger'

'FFM tower, BA123, I was ready first and some time ago. Why have you given LF456 priority?'

Before the tower could answer the LF pilot jumped in with an accent mimicking our way of speaking English-German with, 'Because vee had our towels on the runway first.'

Malé Airport on the Island of Hulhule, a kilometre from Malé, was always a pleasure, just an hour away in the Maldives and all our passengers were on holiday or honeymoon. For security reasons on Malé the ladies were boarded at the front left door, a metre behind my seat, and as we had completed all our checks we would watch the passengers board. It was an absolute delight as there was this long line of young women, mostly, dressed for holiday and comfort. It was a most pleasant turn round.

NOTAMs on one of my trips to Malé showed that a ship had run aground 3,000 metres from the extended runway centre-line. On arrival we looked for it but could not see it. However, on final approach there it was dead ahead only *300* metres from the runway. It was quite a height to the top of its aerials and was only just below us as we crossed over it! I sent an urgent message to ATC to advise them to get its NOTAMs amended as soon as possible.

Another interesting trip was the afternoon of 1 November 1988 when we had No. 4 hydraulic failure on landing. It was found to be a leak in the system. The ground engineer (GE) said he needed a spare part which was not available in Colombo but could be sent from London, arriving next day and sent out to Malé. I asked the GE if he could affect a temporary fix just to get us airborne as the problem was a no-go item, i.e. you could not depart carrying this fault.

Strangely No. 3 engine hydraulics had virtually no special work to do. Poor old No. 2 engine performed half the work and No. 1 a lesser mount. No. 4 hydraulics share a bit of duty with the lower rudder section, a back-up to another system for one aileron, a paired piece of flap and a paired piece of elevators. That was all. For a one-hour flight I really did not need it, but I could not flout the rules.

Bearing in mind the 'domino effect' of unserviceabilities down the route I asked the GE to fix it as best he could and we would hope to reach V1 on take off and then it would be sort of legal. In the event it failed just before V1 and I called 'Continue'. It was too small a problem to abandon the take off.

We landed in Colombo one hour later perfectly safely and with no problems. Had we waited for the spare part we might still have been on the ground in Malé as a rival faction to the government staged a *coup* that same day. We would have been stuck there for some time because, although the Indian paras rescued the president of Malé, it was some weeks before we would have been allowed to leave. The Tamil Tigers had apparently been involved with others in the coup, so now they had failed to kill me on two occasions and capture me on another.

Our trips to the East were very special to me as I love Asian food, especially Thai, and I enjoy Japanese as well. I visited one restaurant in Narita on a regular basis and thoroughly enjoyed their spicy 'river-and-reek' main course. It was ages before I realised it was a Chinese restaurant. It was the habit of the local crews in Air Lanka to carry their own food with them, so most trips I was on my own. This actually suited me well as I could eat where and when I liked, especially sushi and other eateries, but also eat and read my inevitable book.

Up the road from our hotel was the Boston Bar, specializing in whiskey. I rarely drank it but the beer was good. The lady behind the bar spoke no English and I said to the English chap next to me that she should learn it as I was sure many crews came there. He explained that he was actually her English teacher.

Sure enough, she improved rapidly and, as I spent a lot of time in Narita, Narita Airport being the main airfield for Tokyo, I found out that she wasn't just the bar-lady and waitress but co-owned the place with her brother Shingo, who was the cook. Her name was Suiko. I would walk in and she would call 'Hurro, Blian.' I would spend ages getting her to say it properly and she really had to concentrate. One day I walked in, in mid-winter, and she said 'Hu...llo...B...rian.' She never got any other Ls or Rs correct, hence the following accurate story.

I said, 'Where's your car, Suiko, it's normally outside?'

'I clashed it.'

'What happened?'

'Well, (Ls at the end of a word are rarely pronounced) you know the blidge on the main load? I clashed it there.'

'What happened', or 'Why?'

'Load sripply.'

She made my time in Narita really pleasant but left to marry an Air Alaska pilot and, after having two daughters, died of cancer. So sad.

In the hotel I was writing to my son, Andrew, who lived in Keighley, Yorkshire. As I finished the address the 'y' continued to the left-hand side of the envelope and I was astonished to find that I was at the left-hand end of the table. It dawned eventually that there was an earthquake in progress! I grabbed the bag in which I kept money, cards, passport, et al and, as I knew it was raining, my umbrella (I am English after all!). I fled into the corridor to find it empty and no sense of panic sounds, I then sheepishly realised it was all over and, as the building was built to withstand earthquakes, no damage was done. I returned to my room.

I have always carried a small man-bag in my flight bag so that if I ever had to abandon the aircraft in a hurry I would have my essentials with me. Furthermore, to this day I wear a money belt and/or a bag on my trouser belt whenever I fly. Personally, I feel that is good advice. After the crash in Cyprus in 1979 it took four hours to retrieve anything.

Over the last two or three years we have seen aircraft evacuations with people actually carrying, or wheeling, hand-baggage. Have they no idea how much that can delay evacuation and even create such a delay that people die? The Emirates crash at Dubai in September 2016 shows nearly everyone going to the overhead lockers even though there was smoke everywhere! Madness.

Singapore had changed so much from my RAF days. Whereas, in many areas there had been those lovely covered arcades and walkways in the shopping streets, so typical of colonial times, there was now just one of about eighty metres in Tanglin Road. Tanglin Road started at the top end of the famous Orchard Road, which was totally built up, not with houses but a few skyscrapers. Tang's, a single-storey store for all sorts of stuff Chinese, was now several storeys high and also a hotel!

Although it had been refurbished, the only constant seemed to be Raffles Hotel; you could buy the UK papers of the day which were printed there. Mind you, it took ages to get the print off your hands or clothes.

The old RAF Changi was no longer there but the westerly right-hand runway was an extension of our old runway and so much land had been reclaimed they had been able to build an airfield bigger than Heathrow.

The new Changi International also had fantastic passenger buildings with all the usual retail outlets. For me, however, it was the communications shop that I headed for. There, you could call UK for about a quarter of the cost from Sri Lanka and with total clarity. It was a great opportunity for a chat with home.

Bangkok, as always, was fun to visit and especially to enjoy the food. Outside the hotel was a pavement cobbler who did brilliant work so I used to take my shoes to him and one day, whilst Jaki was visiting, I took a pair of hers. He could not fix them before my departure so I said I'd collect them next time. We both forgot, so not only is a pair of her shoes floating around in Beirut, there's now a pair in Bangkok.

Hong Kong was much the same as it had always been, except that as Air Lanka was somewhat poorer than most major airlines we were in a hotel in the New Territories. Actually, you could go for a quiet walk, the views were of hills and the accommodation and food excellent. There was also a regular bus service into Kowloon.

One night, 18 August 1987, I was en route from Tokyo to Bangkok and experienced a seriously higher headwind than expected and realised we could easily be on minimum fuel, or worse, on arrival. Also, the weather at Bangkok and the alternate at Chang Mai was not so hot either, so I tried to contact Hong Kong early on and ask for fuel and handling. We had to use HF (high-frequency, long-range) radio but could make no contact. When we got into VHF range (200 miles at height) they had received our earlier calls and were ready for us.

The problem was that they closed at 2345 and resolutely refused to allow any landings or take offs after that time. We landed at 2320, the load sheet was ready for signing (they had signalled for a copy from Tokyo), the fuel was put on board and we taxied out at 2343. We were airborne 2345 on the dot. What service!

In January 1988 I decided to leave Air Lanka and try again elsewhere. I was too far away to negotiate easily. I went to see the Chief Pilot of Paramount Airways at Bristol which would have been good for us as we were living close to Taunton at the time. We got chatting and when he realised I was from 10 Squadron he said, 'Oh, one of the Shinies! I was on Hercules.'

It was said with a little bit of an edge so I thought, 'Oh dear, that's my chance down the tubes.' So it seemed to turn out as, having heard nothing, I called his secretary who advised me no decisions had been made yet. Nothing happened, so I re-applied to Air Lanka who seemed happy to have me back.

Meantime, I had been keeping in touch with Virgin Atlantic (VS) and Jaki, whose ex-Laker friend was in the ops department, kept reminding him that I would love to join them. On a trip to London later in the year I was interviewed by the Chief Pilot/Operations Manager, John Hayward, who agreed to my joining.

I did my last flight for Air Lanka on 9 December 1988, Frankfurt-Rome-Dubai with passengers, to Colombo and left for the UK.

It had been a wonderful experience and, much as I had loved Gulf Air and, later, the 747, I have always held Air Lanka in my thoughts with great affection.

The Three Musketeers are still in touch.

Virgin Atlantic (VS), Gatwick

On the morning of Monday 19 December 1988 I reported to the BA training school at Cranebank with two other newly-employed first officers to study at a 747 AVT (Audio-Visual-Trainer). As we had all flown 747s before this was to be a week-long refresher.

The AVT was a mock-up of the 747 flight deck with full instrumentation but only a few instruments adjustable or made to work. The lessons could be selected in any order by the students and consisted of a large TV screen and appropriate voice recordings. It is a very effective method of brushing up on a subject.

As we were living in Somerset by now, having left Ponts Green (as I always say, 'with a T') in Sussex earlier in the year, it was too far for daily commuting so I was doing B&B in a nearby guest-house/pub. On the 21st I arrived in my room at 1800 and put on the news on BBC 1 and heard about the Pan Am 747 which crashed on Lockerbie.

I actually managed Christmas at home that year. We were in a property which had been three farmworkers' cottages made into one house. It was on the road more or less opposite the Norton Manor Royal Marine base just past Norton Fitzwarren en route to Taunton-Minehead. The area was called Fitzroy and the houses were well spaced apart. Gemma and Josh were at Taunton School nearby

Life was good but I was still haemorrhaging money as a first officer's starting salary was quite low. Virgin Atlantic (VS) had started by hiring retired pilots, mostly BA, so, as they all had healthy pensions, the salary was low. Also, the retired guys were happy with their one flight per week to Newark, New Jersey, the only destination for a long while. As I joined with the second aircraft Miami was added to the list.

After eight hours in the simulator as a refresher I was released to the line training captains with whom I flew six sectors before being released to the line.

315

VS had one Boeing 747-100 previously owned by Qantas which had the peculiarity of not only having a circular staircase to the upper-first-class cabin but a circular stairway down to an underfloor galley. I never saw that before or since. The other aircraft was a -200. I'm no longer sure of which was which but their registration letters were G-VIRG and G-VGIN.

By April I had only flown ten sectors (i.e. five round trips to Miami or Newark) as there was a lot of first officer training taking place as VS expanded its crews ready for more aircraft. I was feeling somewhat bored and unfulfilled so, with the Chief Pilot's and CAA permission, I applied for a secondary job flying Jet Provosts for the RAF ATC School at RAF Shawbury near Shrewsbury in Shropshire. It also had to be cleared with the CAA.

At first they did not want a spare-time pilot but a permanent one. I pointed out that as they were closing down in a year they would be pushed to find a pilot for just a year. They agreed and I was hired. Although it was based at an RAF Station and flew RAF aircraft it was actually run by Marshalls of Cambridge. All bar one of the pilots were civilians but mostly ex-RAF.

I started in April and finished in June fitting in RAF and VS operations. Initially it was most embarrassing as I could not land this aircraft on which I had several hundred hours! In the 747 your backside is seventy feet off the ground at touchdown and I could not bring myself low enough to land. I was flaring, i.e. raising the nose to reduce rate of descent (ROD), before touch-down) and, of course, I was levelling off too high. Eventually, much to my mortification, the ground crew were coming out to watch!

Anyway, the RAF pilot who was a current qualified flying instructor (QFI) flew with me and said, 'This aircraft is designed for students, stop trying to land nicely, just fly it on.' It worked a treat and after a couple of hard landings and a good view of the runway from just a few feet I landed well.

The procedure for training was to take off using normal radio but to listen out on another which the trainee air traffic controllers were not monitoring; on this frequency you would receive instructions for your detail. These situations could be engine failure (assumed!) after take off (EFATO), radio failure, either no transmission or no reception, getting lost and one or two other scenarios. The trainees then had to assist in your recovery to the field, simulate crash procedures, etc. These trips were called 'Trucking' but I don't know why.

It was all quite tiring, I'd forgotten how uncomfortable ejector seats were whilst wearing all the paraphernalia necessary, or perhaps it was an age difference as I had last flown the JP at age twenty-seven and I was now fifty-three!

During this period and in July I was mostly flying shotgun to new first officers at VS under training or observing new captain training. Again, I was a bit bored so when Park Aviation (a pilot hiring agency) called and asked if I'd like to do a four-month contract in Paris I jumped at it. I went to see the Chief Pilot John Hayward but his deputy, the senior flight engineer Alan Bonnick, was on duty and said yes.

That night I was in a simulator in Paris doing a check ride on the 747-SP. The company for whom I was working, as a first officer, was Luxavia and the aircraft was a 'white tail', i.e. no emblems or colour scheme. We were to operate schedules for UTA, the French No. 2 airline, on routes to Cairo, Johannesburg via Nice, Kuala Lumpur and around West Africa. It wasn't until a while later I realised we were actually strike-busting but by then all the contracts were signed.

John Hayward returned to the office to hear requests from other crew members to take up the Park offer but refused them. I got away by the skin of my teeth.

Eventually there were just six crews and we were based in a ghastly hotel near CDG airport. After many complaints we ended up with a room each at the Paris Hilton for the entire contract which included seven days a month off with free travel to your home city. We had Spanish, English, French, Italian, Thai, Americans and Australians.

Unfortunately, the senior captain in charge of the crews chose me as his first officer; I was the most experienced so perhaps that was the reason. He was Bruce Crosbie, an Australian, and very mean. After several sectors I demanded to know why I was not getting any sectors myself; I pointed out that I was probably as experienced as he. He said 'Later' so I got quite snotty, not on the aircraft of course, and he gave in. It was awful, it was into Harare en route to Jo'burg and he couldn't stop advising what I should be doing and generally interfering; what a rubbish captain. On our return to Paris I advised him that I would not be flying with him again. He took it in good part as I suspect this had happened to him before.

He had worked for Air Lanka before I arrived and he had been mugged and beaten up one night whilst out walking. I found out during my time there that his appalling treatment of the first officers had caused them to hire three or four thugs to do the needful (as Indian sub-continent people say!). I can understand their chagrin and wish I had had the opportunity to contribute to the kitty.

On my last trip with him we were deadheading Jo'burg-Kinshasha-CDG when the captain did an abandoned take off in Kinshasha. The Italian captain explained his reasons but they did not convince us of the necessity of such action. However, we burst six tyres as a result of over-heating and were there for thirty-six hours waiting for fresh wheels from CDG.

On one of my periods of days off one of our aircraft was assigned a trip to Africa and return. At the last minute UTA replaced it with one of their own and, on the way back, it exploded in mid-air; a bomb had been placed in the hold. The chief steward was on his last rostered flight before retirement.

Later I went to Abidjan with a load of Muslims returning from the Hajj and we parked overnight for return to CDG empty the next morning. On arrival the next morning, the gate guards were both asleep as were the aircraft guards. We were not happy and the whole crew spent an hour or so security checking every nook and cranny as we had no idea what to expect. It looked okay so we got airborne with no ill result.

We always had UTA cabin crew on board and at each layover I was given a bottle of my favourite champagne, Laurent Perrier Rosé. Their uniform was not as startling as yesteryear but they were still lovely.

After that I flew with most of the other captains who all gave me sectors and had nothing to say or do in the way of interference, i.e. normal.

Sadly, on 16 October, Jaki called me in Jo'burg to advise me that my father was very ill in hospital in Eastbourne and to get home fast. Jaki had called the hospital and she had been advised that he was 'poorly'. She demanded to know what that silly word meant and should she recall his son from South Africa. She finally got the nurse to agree that it was a good idea.

I told Jaki that I was leaving for CDG first thing in the morning; that was the best I could do. I eventually arrived that night to find my father being spoon-fed but not wearing his glasses. His moustache was quite messy. I took over immediately, put his glasses on and cleaned him up. He was so unwell that he could barely smile but it was obvious he was happy to see me. They could not find his hearing-aid, i.e. it was misplaced, but his lip reading was good. He could not talk. On the doctor's rounds I asked how long my father had left and he said about forty-eight hours.

With that information I left my father at 2330, as I was now very tired, and went to a friend's house where Jaki, Gemma and Josh were staying. At midnight plus four minutes my father died and I have always regretted not staying with him that little bit longer. My family believe he was hanging in there to see me and then he let himself go.

My time with Luxavia was more or less finished so I stayed in the UK to sort out my father's affairs, including his will. It was time to return to VS.

Back to Being A Virgin

On 2 November I continued on a -200 for a refresher check-ride with Mike Dearden to Orlando where we stayed in the famous Peabody Hotel. At that time there were only two Peabodys, this and the original hotel. Every morning the Peabody ducks were shepherded (?) into the lift from the roof and at the ground floor a red carpet led from the lift to an ornamental pond with fountain in the entrance foyer. There they mounted steps and all twelve or so splashed in. They remained there until 1700 when the reverse process took place. Once a cabin crew removed a duck from their air-conditioned quarters on the roof and ransomed it for a crate of beer. They got the beer which was very sporting of the manager.

Shortly after arrival one day I stood in my hotel room watching lightning striking all over the place and with very heavy rain; I was thinking thank goodness I wasn't late arriving in this. The storms there can be horrendous. This first trip on my return to VS was also the first time I had seen an MX-5 sports car, Miata in the US; I was determined that I would have one as soon as I could afford it. It was/is a little gem.

On 22 April at the hotel on the New Jersey turnpike Richard Branson, who had flown with us to Newark, stopped chatting up our lovely girls and asked Bob Petley, the flight engineer, and me if we had any good ideas for the about-to-be-started Heathrow-Tokyo flights.

I suggested that, as the Japanese were avid shoppers, why not take their duty-free orders inbound to Heathrow and have them suitably packed and waiting for them for the return to Tokyo. He wrote my suggestion down on a used brown envelope and trotted off. I should have discussed some form of remuneration but I'm too naïve and simple for real business which is why I was a pilot and not a millionaire. Mind you, I probably would have been if I'd gone to that Cathay Pacific interview in September 1975.

319

Fourteen years after I retired from VS and, wishing my two annual guaranteed tickets were firmly first-class (Upper-Class at VS) instead of space available, I contacted Richard via letter and e-mail suggesting that in view of the money I must have made him with my idea for Tokyo flights perhaps he would consider making my ticket firm. I asked for nothing more. He said they offer remuneration now but I was too late. He said that even he had to travel economy now. Pull the other one.

In my absence in France VS had consolidated their Tokyo flights on Narita/Tokyo. Haneda was no longer the main airport, but, to get permission to fly over Russian territory, Moscow insisted on a landing at Sheremetyevo airport so they could make some money out of us. For the crews it was fine. We positioned via BA to Moscow the day before our trip and took our aircraft on to Tokyo the next day. Then another crew would do Tokyo-Moscow and DHD Sheremetyevo to Heathrow which meant that, as passengers, they could have a bottle and 200! We were now operating from London-Heathrow and Gatwick.

It was on my first Moscow-Tokyo flight that we had a most remarkable young lady in the Cabin crew. She had been with VS a short time and her reputation had preceded her.

Chris Fallon had applied to VS in the usual way and was accepted for interview and assessment. Having met the company requirements she was sent for the usual full medical. Later, the doctor called the chief of cabin crew and asked if she was playing games as he had an applicant before him with a false leg below the knee!

Chris was recalled to HQ and asked why she had said nothing and, furthermore, she was told that she could not be considered for employment in the cabin. Chris defended herself vigorously, pointing out that no question had ever required her to mention the leg. Plus, as she could do anything everyone else could do, she believed she should be employed.

After a lot muttering and discussing it was agreed she would be enrolled for training but if, at any time, she could not perform equally with her fellow trainees, she would be suspended. She accepted the challenge and passed; the training included being on her feet a lot of the time, swimming, righting dinghies which were made to inflate upside down, lifting heavy baggage into overhead lockers etc. The real test came as a junior when she was looking after the flight as she had to go up and down the steep spiral staircase to carry trays of drink and food to the crew. At the end of each sector she was grey with pain and fatigue.

What a woman! Chris eventually became a cabin crew chief and quite right, too.

Eventually, I believe they cancelled the requirement to land in Moscow but charged an overflight levy. It was a shame because it was an interesting layover. The time from landing to driving away could vary from one and a half to two hours as we were gathered in police immigration and identified and our passports were held until departure. Customs were pretty slow too. Chaos reigned as we left all this checking and hoped to meet up with our coach. The drive to the Cosmos Hotel took quite a while on roughish main roads and with dubious drivers.

The hotel was no better than three-star but the highlight of the stay there was dinner. The crew all sat round one table and we all chipped in £10, which delighted the maitre d', and he provided a simple but adequate meal of salad, potatoes and some sausage. However, the rest was amazing; we had Russian champagne (they call it that) which was okay and as much excellent vodka as we could handle. Upon leaving the table we were handed more vodka to take away with us.

Each floor had a lady at a table (always known as the Dragon Lady) selling cheap, nasty stuff and some cigarettes. If she felt there was too much noise she would take us to task. She was obviously there as an informer and general spy, I guess.

In those days life looked a bit sad there as buildings were ugly, shop windows had little in them and the people seemed not too happy. Many seemed to trudge rather than walk. I believe it is all much better now.

Russian ATC was very serious and deviations were hard to get for avoiding bad weather. It was usually grudgingly given but there were many military and other areas near our routes and we felt they feared some sort of secret photography or some other digression. At the time, 1989, we had to operate in metres for altitude but this was okay as we had another altimeter on the centre panel calibrated in metres. Because we were so far north over much of Russia we experienced the unusual situation whereby, in summer, it was quite usual to be in daylight or dusk conditions throughout the night.

In the winter we took off from Tokyo at 1000 and by noon, over Khabarovsk, we were in the dark. Throughout the traverse of Russia we would often get glimpses of the sun to the south as little sunrises. The most interesting of these sunrises would come from the west! As we approached Amsterdam from Helsinki and headed south-west for London we would see the sun appear as if in a sunrise, dead ahead of us. By the time we reached Heathrow, usually around 1700, the sun would have set again.

The Newark trips were always a little uncertain for fuel as it was a very busy area, it was just a short distance from JFK and LaGuardia, so we usually carried a little extra. It was not unusual to arrive in the area on time and then be sent all over the place. The Atlantic crossing was occasionally different from forecast in that the headwind from London-Heathrow west could be stronger than expected. The crossing routes were determined by Shanwick (Shannon and Prestwick) in conjunction with Gander or New York ATC.

The winds vary greatly, sometimes on a daily basis, over the North Atlantic and each day the five or six routes are decided during the night before. East-west aircraft from all over Europe, not just the UK, head across through the lightest headwinds available. The west-to-east are routed with the strongest tailwinds. These routes can take you as far north as Iceland and over Greenland and Canada's Northern Territories if you are going to the west coast of the USA; for JFK, Washington and Boston you could still pass south of Iceland and clip the tip of Greenland. You could be given similar routes on the way back if the wind has changed sufficiently.

This route gave rise to an amusing conversation between two US captains; I think one was TWA and I'll call the other ABC. American operators are always checking on route conditions because they are concerned about turbulence. The pilots aren't worried personally but if someone gets hurt then, as you know, it's lawsuits all round. There are loads of foolish passengers who think they know best so don't have their seatbelts loosely fastened as advised on PA and safety pamphlets.

Well, ABC123 asks the Northern Territories controller (NTC), 'What's the ride like ahead of us?'

NTC, 'Standby ABC123. TWA123, OK what's the ride like where you are TWA456?'

'Well, NTC it's a bit rough; our FO's eating and he's just put the fork up his nose!'

'Okay. What's the ride like where you are TWA123?'

'NTC it's difficult to say as our FO hasn't eaten yet!'

Many of the aircraft trailing over the UK heading north and north-west are quite regularly from Paris, Frankfurt, Amsterdam, Geneva, etc. The routes out of the UK have various departure points from Prestwick down to North Devon. Once on the assigned route and altitude you would report every 10-degree longitude to Shanwick and at 30 W you would advise Shanwick and be transferred to Gander or New York, depending on how far north your track was. Again, reporting every 10 degrees.

The reports would be on HF radio on a frequency appropriate to distance from receiver and/or day/night. Reception was usually excellent. It would consist of present position, time, flight level, next position and time and any weather condition you considered relevant, i.e. turbulence. If ATC designated you as the weather reporter you would also give wind velocity.

This was a vast improvement on the days when weather ships stayed on station in the North Atlantic and you reported your details to them. These chaps were out there for a considerable length of time before the relief boat came so, in my RAF days, we used to get the lady quartermasters to do the position reports. We understood that it was much appreciated.

Even going to Miami or Orlando way down in Florida it was often quicker going north via the lesser winds and then routing down the east coast. It made a better trip, too, as the views down the coast were most pleasant. The southerly route was likely to take us close to Bermuda for both destinations, and the Bahamas for Miami.

Miami was a very busy airport and it was not unusual to be given an approach on one runway and then be given a last-minute change to another. It was my habit to do a visual approach onto the assigned runway and have the ILS set for the likely alternative – only in good weather conditions, of course. On one occasion when I was captain of the aircraft I was given clearance for RWY 26, changed to 27 at six or seven miles and then, at the last minute, sent to RWY 30. The 747 is a bit big for hurling around but we managed.

The Marriott Hotel, the VS crew hotel, was in direct line with RWY 27 so a bit noisy. Along the quay from the hotel about sixty yards was our watering hole with good food, beer and ambience at half the price of the hotel. In the other direction was a bar-cum-nightclub but, as the route was alongside parkland, you had to be wary. One night returning from there a crew was held up at gunpoint by a single man and ordered to hand over their cash. The cabin flight supervisor lady was having none of this and she harangued him to boredom and he left. What a brave girl!

From the hotel you could reach a huge shopping mall via a bridge from the third or fourth floor. The bridge crossed the road and was wide, with roof windows. One of our captains was mugged by a knife-carrying piece of trash there, and not a soul took any notice; they had seen the situation and just walked by.

We rarely walked anywhere as it all felt so unsafe with so many lonely and seemingly angry men all over the place. Fortunately, VS provided cars for us at some of our layover bases including Miami which sounds okay but if you were the guy who was there when it needed new insurance, MOT or servicing then it had to be sorted out by you. Some of us just preferred to rent cars.

After forty-eight sectors with VS in fourteen months, remember I did four months with Luxavia, I did my check ride for captain. The last four had been check rides and now for my final check on 26 February 1990 to Moscow with Dudley Broster, deputy chief pilot. It went well and, in the bar later, he said I had passed and that he would fly back as a passenger. As always on a check ride, training or final, a first officer was carried so Ted Quiggan (ex-BA captain) was my first officer back to Gatwick.

It was normal when any captain was being checked, or a first officer being trained, to carry a fully qualified first officer. If, for example, the captain failed and the crew were away from base then the training captain would move to the LHS and the first officer would take his normal place. The trainee captain, although recently a first officer, was considered to no longer be qualified in the RHS as his flight-deck orientation would have changed. And, of course, if it was the first officer who failed then the other first officer just moved in.

An amusing incident occurred when we were all in the hotel bar. Dudley told one of the prostitutes in the bar, normal Russian social life, that the flight engineer fancied her and took her across to introduce them. The flight engineer was horrified when the girl said, 'I understand you want to sleep with me.' Eddie, that was his name, said, 'Good Lord no, not at all.' She said 'Well, I don't care, I am young and beautiful, and you are old and ugly.'

In case you are wondering, I've only ever known one flight-deck guy who happily employed 'the ladies of the night' although I guess there are a few others.

So, captain again and so soon. VS had been expanding fast and we now had three 747s. G-TKYO was our latest. My second flight as captain was into Narita/Tokyo on a day with crosswinds on the limits and occasional gusts. We were landing on the southerly runway, 16R, which took us over a valley and hotels and other buildings. This meant that the wind was not only strong but could cause much more turbulence than normal. Runway 16L was built but for a plot of land halfway along it. The owner refused to sell it as it was his ancestral land and relatives were buried there. When he died his family sold it.

Although I was an experienced pilot I was conscious of the fact that I was a 'new' captain and was lucky to have two very experienced BA crewmen with me. I was very careful to make a good briefing advising them that I considered this could be very uncomfortable and we must seriously be prepared for a go-around. We had not enough fuel for a lengthy departure and another attempt (it was very busy) so in that event we would go straight to our alternate, Haneda/Tokyo.

The approach was dreadfully turbulent and I doubted our guarantee of a safe touchdown. In the event we did a good job and landed safely. Two aircraft later, a Qantas DC10 (or TriStar?) landed badly and actually drove one of the undercarriage legs into the wing. It was the pilot's first flight as captain. It could have happened to anyone in those conditions and I understand that after a couple more check rides the pilot was released again to the line.

On that flight the engineer was Dave Grimstead and I flew with him three or four more times in the next couple of months and then we never saw each other again for two years, neither on the aircraft nor on the ground. This was not unusual in our line of work.

Shortly after I got my command we added Los Angeles (LAX) to our list of destinations. For me this was the best of our work at that time. One of the advantages of Narita/Tokyo over all other destinations was that, not only were things expensive, Jaki had no shopping list for me. LAX was different; our hotel was called the Pacific Shore, and it was in Santa Monica just north of Venice Beach. It was not a four- or five-star hotel but the manager, Anthony David, was a great host, breakfast was excellent, the rooms were fine, but for some reason the cabin crew were not content. When we arrived, we were given *chitties* for a free drink in the bar.

The security of the hotel was such that after 1800 hours the only entrance was through the main doors, all the emergency exits were secured against entry from outside and every door was checked every hour by a security guard with a computerised check instrument which recorded time and door.

Nevertheless, one steward on VS claimed that he had been mugged in the hotel one evening. The police were called but as his watch and wallet had not been stolen and any injuries seemed extraordinarily minor, they left it as if it were a hoax. David Anthony was distraught as their security was excellent; nobody could get in or out, except in an emergency which set off alarms, and every door was checked by computers at regular intervals. Therefore, it seemed impossible for this to have happened.

Sadly, VS decided, after a bit of snivelling from the cabin crew, to change hotels. This was a blow to David because VS had a minimum of around forty rooms a night and the financial loss in the end I believe cost him his job.

The new hotel was up the road, nearer the shops, next to a motorway and had as much ambience as railway café. Well done the muggee, I wonder if the cabin crew were happier now.

The shopping centre was actually a huge mall and to the north of it there were three streets of shops with no vehicular access. It was a great place and, needless to say, this was where Jaki's shopping lists were aimed. Being a good chap, I always tried to complete the list but in forty-eight hours (our layover period) much of it was spent walking the streets. I always used the crew car, if it was available, for a visit up into the San Bernardino Mountains, or Malibu or just a drive along Mulholland Drive. Never into the city. Why? It was a dreadful trip. There are traffic lights at every block, i.e. each 100 to 200 yards, and to get anywhere takes forever. We in the UK should be so grateful for roundabouts. I once set off to see the Spruce Goose, about nine miles south of the hotel, and after one hour and only halfway I gave up and went back.

The Santa Monica police had an easy time, I think, as I never heard of a serious crime there. It was easy to walk the streets and feel comfortable. However, one day I was walking down 3rd or 4th Avenue towards the mall and I saw five police vehicles, three police motorbikes and about fifteen to twenty police. There was an elderly chap on a bench being interviewed by a policeman and another elderly chap in the back seat of one of the cars and in handcuffs. I asked a fellow spectator the score and I was advised that one of the old guys had had an altercation and hit the other. Someone had called the police and this was the pathetic response. Not only were the police milling around but most of them were talking on their phones/ walkie-talkies. It was a farce.

I used to always have my breakfast at the same diner and it was the favourite of the police as well. The Santa Monica police were nowhere near as fit or tough as the Los Angeles police. They were truly fat; their buttocks literally spread over the chairs – men and women. It was quite obscene, especially watching them eat.

On one occasion going into LAX we had an obnoxious passenger in Upper Class. He was obviously uneducated but was one of those awful passengers who think *'I've paid the money, I can do what I like'*. He was giving the cabin crew a hard time and using really bad language. Normally, captains leave this sort of problem to the cabin crew, not because they are afraid, but pilots should not risk being attacked by an aggressive passenger. However, I went back as we were a three-pilot crew and advised him that unless he treated the crew with respect I would have the police meet him on arrival.

He continued upon his obnoxious ways so I asked for the police to meet him, which they did. They let him go about thirty minutes later and he joined

326

the crew and passengers in the baggage area. He was positively crowing and leering at us as he had obviously won. However, as I went through customs I advised the officer that that man, pointing to Mr Obnoxious, had been so odd and erratic we thought he might be on drugs. I was later told that it took him four hours to get away from the airport. Serves him right – tee, hee!

Those crew members who skied used to visit Great Bear Mountain to the north in the San Bernardino Mountains and the rest did their own thing. For me it was shopping to order and the occasional beer. That word occasional seems odd for me but, frankly, American beer has no appeal. Since Schlitz was not available I couldn't be bothered.

The Huntley Hotel in North Santa Monica had about twelve floors and an outside glass lift. At the top was the best bar in town. It was packed every evening; the tables were all in the north with views of Malibu and aircraft approaching and to the south was the actual restaurant. The ambience was terrific and most tables had jugs of Margarita on them – their signature drink, as it were. In one corner was a regular supply of free food snacks including shrimp, fish, rice, chips and succulent sausages. I visited in 2012 and the place was dead compared to before – it had been tarted up and its soul had gone. It reminds you of quite a few destroyed UK pubs, does it not?

As stated earlier the route was normally south of Iceland, across Greenland between 60 and 70 degrees N., Baffin Island, Southampton Island in the Northern Territories, across the western edge of Hudson Bay then down through Manitoba to Winnipeg. Then it could vary but definitely we passed through North Dakota, clipped Montana, through Wyoming to Salt Lake City in Utah. On to abeam Las Vegas, we nearly always had a good view of the huge Hoover Dam and then either to north of LAX and north of Santa Monica or south over Great Bear Mountain for a let-down from the east of LAX for a twenty- or thirty-mile-long approach in a westerly direction. Apart from the one landing I had with the RAF I never saw another easterly landing.

The departure was straight out over the coast into the blackness of the night, followed by a left turn over the Santa Catalina Island, and then varied tracks across America to join the Atlantic crossing using the faster winds. Although one filed a flight plan using prescribed routes, once you had departed LAX, area radar would give you direct headings or simply direct to a known point and so on. Also, as it was the middle of the night and less traffic it was not unusual to be given a 'direct to' somewhere 200 or 300 miles ahead. Normally we would reach the Atlantic around the New York, Washington, Boston stretch of coast.

As new routes were added and VS acquired more aircraft the registrations reflected the changes; eventually all our 747-200s had G-VIRG, VGIN, TKYO, VOYG, VJFK, VLAX; our only -100 was changed to G-VMIA.

Virgin Atlantic and Virgin Holidays were different companies but, of course, the V. Holidays always used VS aircraft. On one occasion my total souls on board that VMIA from Orlando to Heathrow was 510. The passengers must have had their knees behind their ears for the whole seven hours thirty-five minutes.

Sometime in 1990 Boston was added to our destinations and most welcome it was too. The city is so different from most of the USA I had seen up to this time; although it had some blocks it was mostly quite different and appeared more European in layout. The library was a wonderful place to browse, the John Hancock building had a viewing floor at the top where you could see aircraft taking off towards you from Logan International. The view of the aircraft was accompanied by loudspeakers giving ATC and pilots' messages.

In the winter the main square had huge blocks of ice being worked upon by sculpterers with chisels, hammers and chainsaws, creating full size replicas of polar bears, Santa Claus, reindeer etc. I actually had Jaki and the children there for one pre-Christmas flight and they were enchanted.

JFK is a very busy airport and its design has been enlarged over the years but they seemed to retain far too many 90-degree turns where the two taxiways actually had 90 degrees between them without any curve on entry to make it easier. In snow conditions they were marked with little flags and, in view of the conditions, you had to be very cautious.

There is an approach onto 13L where there are no landing aids and only one beacon over which you fly to start the procedure. The route leaves the Canarsie beacon outbound on about east-north-east and then you have to keep within the Belt Parkway (a motorway) and keep turning until you see the runway. There are no guidelines for height except the Mark 1 eyeball. There is a limiting height of 1,000-feet cloud-base (perhaps a little lower). It is known as the famous Canarsie 1 approach, famous because it's quite a tricky approach in rain, snow, turbulence, bad visibility, etc.

Anyway, one night in great conditions the first officer was doing the approach and handling it as well as any I had seen, including my own. Sadly I was late realizing that he had not flared correctly at fifty feet. I shouted 'flare' and took control – too late. We hit the runway really hard. To make it worse we were being given our annual line check with a training captain behind us. It was a very firm to hard landing. In aviation terms a 'hard landing' means the aircraft has to have certain checks carried out in certain areas of the airframe. We all discussed it; the flight engineer said he'd had harder landings training with Dudley Broster but, in the end, I declared it 'hard'.

When we were parked and talking to our UK ground engineer I said I was declaring a 'hard landing'. He said to hang on while he had a quick check around. He was back quickly to advise us that it was not only hard but we had a flap section bent and penetrating the aircraft skin.

As is normal after an incident we were all grounded and returned as passengers next day. The cause of the damage was that one of the flap screw-jacks (i.e. the means by which the flaps are operated) had broken and, as only one was working, the flap had tried to return to normal position but could not.

We, the crew were eventually seated in the Chief Pilot's office with a member of the Air Accident Investigation Department (AAID) of the CAA and we went through the details of my report in which not only had I explained everything but naturally accepted full responsibility.

The first officer and I separately did some exercises in the simulator where I was given some surprising landing emergency scenarios and the first officer was given further landing training. It was necessary that this was seen to be done, even though this incident had been a one-off and I had never believed the landing was hard enough for the damage sustained. The first officer had always landed well, so this was all a one-off occurrence.

It was a huge relief to hear later that we were exonerated of blame, despite having had a heavy landing which all pilots experience at some time or another, because forensic evidence showed that there was a long-standing crack in the screw-jack shaft and it could have failed at any time. Had it failed in flight, just after take off or on approach, it would have given the pilot quite a handling problem, albeit not too dangerous, maybe.

I had no idea what happened to the first officer following the incident but one day another FO said what a shame it was about him. It seems he had been made to feel he was to blame or he just felt bad about it and he resigned and went back to his old company. If only I had known, then I could have helped him. The first officer who told me this said that he should have been okay and the captain should have been responsible. Much to his surprise, I said I was the captain and wholeheartedly accepted full responsibility. Except in exceptional circumstances the captain has to carry the can; I fully accept that and was totally in agreement with that.

Throughout my time on 747s our destinations remained JFK, Newark, Orlando, Miami, LAX and Narita. Initially our main servicing was carried out by Aer Lingus every six months or so as we still had no full engineering base of our own. Some of the trips were to arrive very early and leave late but occasionally the trip was an overnighter which enabled us to have a Guinness or two in the best place to drink it. It is unquestionably tastier when it hasn't travelled or been produced under licence.

On one occasion I was called late in the evening and asked to do the Dublin run as the rostered captain was sick. I accepted and said my father-in-law, J.K. Webb, who was visiting us, would love to come for the ride. This was no problem so off we set for Gatwick very early in the morning in pouring rain and, listening to the radio, we heard it was St Patrick's Day! We arrived in Dublin about 0800, had a quick snooze and were in town by midday. First things first, a Guinness, then a snack, then a Guinness and so on. The revellers were out in force and it was a great atmosphere.

In view of our mid-morning departure the next day we had an early dinner and bed but, boy!, had we had a great time. J.K.W., as he was known, was mighty impressed as he had last flown in a VC10 en route to Jaki's and my wedding and before that in a Lancaster at the end of the war. He was wireless-operator/gunner but luckily, his words never saw action.

During my entire flying career, I was able to ask people onto the flight deck and I always enjoyed doing my PR with the passengers. On one occasion my first officer was a recently retired BA captain and when the chief cabin crew asked if we could take visitors I said okay. The first officer was horrified. He explained that he never allowed passengers on the flight deck!

Anyway, two young hippies arrived much to his dismay and, eventually, mine. The man had really dirty hair, was obviously uneducated and spoke really badly. The lady was obviously educated and with a voice adjusted slightly to please the man, presumably. She was scruffy and her blouse was practically fully open. This, I must admit, was a great compensation.

I pointed out the south-east coast of Greenland and all the icebergs and he leaned over me with his hair touching mine and my neck and said, 'Nectar, innit?' At this point I politely advised them that others were waiting and off they went. The FO, John Sherwood, looked at me and said 'See?' I had to agree he had a point but I never changed my habit. As soon as I arrived at the hotel I had a shower, and then a second one. That hair was terrible!

Throughout my flying career I was always happy to go back and sit with nervous/terrified passengers and try to calm them down. I have quite a few letters of thanks. The usual fear was of having no control over their destiny which was not only with someone they did not know but couldn't see either, so, having chatted a while, I would take them to the flight deck and show them how calm and controlled everything was and, I firmly believe, most of them lost some, or a lot, of that fear.

Another fear was turbulence and the awful sight of the wings bending and 'flapping'. One such lady was at an overwing seat in mild turbulence and the wing was having a lovely time. She was clutching her baby tightly and said she was frightened that the wing would break. So, I went into my usual spiel about the wings being taken to breaking point before being released for passengers and that if they didn't flex then they would break, wouldn't they?

The little story I told all those who disliked turbulence settled most people down. I asked if they had been in a row-boat or sailed and, if not, could they imagine being close to shore, or rounding a jetty or leaving a bay where water was choppy? Everyone answered yes in one way or another, so I pointed out that as water and air were both fluids they both had waves and choppiness. Air had temperature changes as different sections moved around and this caused waves – that was all it was. It was all very simplified but worked more often than not.

The lady with the baby came to the flight deck, had all her questions answered and left a happy lady. Shortly afterwards I received a lovely letter of thanks and the information that she now had no fear of flying at all and enjoyed helping others who were nervous.

One US lady who had been in an emergency landing after engine fire was terrified of flying. However, after thirty years and desperate to see her grandchildren in England, she contacted VS and asked for special help to overcome her fear and fly. The family were not too well off, so she had saved to afford her fare.

VS laid it on with a trowel; she was driven to LAX, escorted personally through check-in, immigration and onto the aircraft. She was accompanied on the flight by a personal friend. I and the cabin crew had been forewarned by letter of this passenger. During the cruise I went back to visit her and received the usual question: 'Who is flying the plane?' After a while I convinced her to visit the flight deck and she agreed. The crew had made sure it was spic-and-span (no coffee cups etc.) and we proceeded to make her at home, tell her about the work, the instruments, the rules etc. and answered all her questions. She seemed much relaxed.

Later I received a lovely letter from her and from the CEO who had also received a very complimentary account of me and my crew. All part of the service ma'am!

All captains were expected to attend a series of briefings by the Chief Pilot regarding fuel costs; this was October 1990, just after Saddam's invasion of Kuwait. The price of fuel was quite high and we had to cut down our consumption. It was not unusual for most of us to add a couple of tons occasionally for imagined or real problems ahead. The company had done a long and huge survey of how much extra fuel had been carried and how many landings had been made at alternate airfields. It was found that the cost to the company of carrying extra fuel far outweighed the cost of the occasional diversion to an alternate field.

The reason the cost was high was because you have to burn extra fuel if you carry extra fuel. It is extra weight in the tanks: extra weight = extra power = extra fuel consumption. The outcome was that if we carried extra fuel we had to explain fully or, better still, just take planned fuel, i.e. fuel for trip plus 4 per cent contingency, alternate fuel plus 30 minutes holding.

Well, the next day off I go to Newark (EWR) and am tempted to add two tons as that airfield is notorious for sending you round the houses. I got airborne with planned fuel and ended up with stronger headwinds over the Atlantic and lost fifteen minutes. Furthermore, EWR weather was getting bad and there were delays. Our alternate, JFK, was in bad weather causing delays so, although I technically had enough to continue to EWR, I considered Boston as an en route alternate for fuel. As time went by, it was obvious the weather was deteriorating in EWR and JFK causing further delays, albeit of only ten to fifteen minutes. I decided to pop into Boston for refuel. The weather there was dreadful too.

So, had I put on my extra two tons for EWR as usual then I would have made it. Anyway, despite my personal diversion there were very few over the coming months and VS saved a lot of fuel and money.

In the early days of Narita/Tokyo flights, there were only two a week, so on arrival the first officer and flight engineer would be given seats for the return flight and a first officer and flight engineer would fly out by BA to Narita the day before the next Tokyo-Heathrow flight. On 6 July 1990 I flew with a female pilot, Yvonne Kershaw, for the first time. She had arrived in Tokyo the previous day and she and the replacement engineer, John Peale, joined me for a few drinks at the 'Truck'. The Truck was actually a mile up the road from our hotel and comprised a large oceangoing container converted into a bar. There were a few chairs either side and a counter at the end. The entrepreneurial owner had to bring the beer from the entrance to the bar, carrying it over his head as he could not otherwise find a large enough gap as it was packed. The music was loud.

BACK TO BEING A VIRGIN

It was entirely peopled by crew and no one else. The only competition was Betty's (?) Bar in town where you could get draught beer and meals. Towards the end of the evening we all gravitated to the Truck. I say 'all' as there were many airlines going through Narita, VS, BA, Cathay, Qantas and many others, including two US airlines. Gradually the Truck got bigger and bigger until it had a stage for Karaoke, proper toilets, tables and chairs. The area went from about 300 square feet to 1,200 square feet.

Unfortunately for Betty's (?) Bar, a chap called Hiroshi opened up in competition just along the road from her and captured the aviation market. He only allowed aircrew in the bar with the exception of the European golfers on the Japanese circuit, including Laura Davis. The music was good, the beer was really fine and he played videos continuously in a top corner. They included such greats as Roy Orbison's 'Black and White' and Barry White, etc. However, the videos were predominantly aviation orientated, especially towards spectacular crashes. These videos were reacted to with much banter and laughter. The bar was decorated with donated photographs, bank notes, hats, wings etc. The place was the place to go.

On one of the trips, Gemma was with me and asked Hiroshi if he would employ her during her university holiday. He was delighted as were the crews over the next few weeks; she is clever, funny, chatty and beautiful. Hiroshi paid for a local hotel and escorted her there and back. She had a ball and, quite often, crews would know me better as Gemma's Dad!

Later on VS opened a bar and restaurant just down the road from Hiroshi's but did not attract too many flight crew; it was used more by cabin crew. Sadly, Hiroshi upset the Japanese Mafia in some way and had to close down. By this time the Truck had a nightly coach service from the town centre via various aircrew hotels to the Truck and then at 2300, midnight, and 0100 he would set off via all the hotels again. What a clever guy!

The police and others in Newcastle had acquired about a million pounds worth of aid for Romanian orphans and VS was to deliver the goods to Bucharest. So, on 23 March 1991 I flew G-VRGN to Newcastle with Richard Branson and the Press on board. Before landing I was asked to fly around the city as so many had contributed to the cause and it would let them know the aid was on the way.

I eventually approached the airfield from over the sea and thought how small it looked and how short the runway. Last time I was there it was with Jimmy Hill and the 'Match of the Day' crew and it was fine for a small twin-engine Piper Navajo.

In the event I carried out one of my better landings and actually had to keep rolling to the end of the runway to turn off. Awaiting us at the terminal were local press and my brother Barry and his wife, Judy. She was involved in an orphanage in Bucharest which was also a school and a home for the children.

The next morning we set off to Otopeni Airport in Bucharest with all the goodies. The pilot for this sector was Alex Bjoness who had joined at the same time as me. Alex had an amazingly powerful handshake; one always greeted him with slight trepidation! We unloaded and returned to Gatwick. I was going through immigration with Richard Branson and he said he'd forgotten his passport. Anyway, at the desk he said, 'You know me, chaps', and they let him through immediately.

VS had a wonderful system, whereby any spare seat on the flight deck belonged to the captain. This meant that if I wanted to take a member of the family with me I could guarantee them a seat. I would pay the normal privileged fare but, in the case of a younger child, it guaranteed that I could keep them with me.

It was quite usual to be given a call, prior to a trip, from a crew member asking for the seat for family or boyfriend etc.; for me it was first come first served. On one occasion the lucky man was Aled Jones, the famous boy soprano and, later, celebrity. He was charming and happy to discuss church music with me, a much lesser performer. We even had a drink together that evening.

Carrying famous people or celebrities allowed an occasional interesting interlude in the cruise if they wanted to come up for a chat. Many showed a different persona from their public one, the most frequent and obvious was a better speaking voice. Sadly, it seems showbiz celebs think they have to mask their proper voices to appear more 'wiv' it' for their fans.

I never saw Yuri Geller on the flight deck but his ability to bend spoons and do other amazing things seemingly meant he had some unusual aura, for want of a better description, because on two or three occasions whilst on the flight deck he had affected the instruments. He was a regular flyer with VS and on one of my trips he asked to come on the flight deck and the captain said 'No way!'

Some of the interesting passengers I flew and either went to say 'Hi' to or invited to the flight deck were Sir Terry Wogan, Judith Chalmers (should have an R not an L!) Billy Connolly, Jerry Hall, Phil Collins, Charles Aznavour, the Duke of Kent, and many others I can no longer recall.

All the first officers and flight engineers on the 747 were great guys and the old expression 'Be nice to people on your way up because you may meet them on your way down' was appropriate. One of my first officers on two or three trips was Robin Howden who had been my training captain on the 10 Squadron VC10 trip to the States, i.e. he who lost his voice with all the singing in all the 'Your Father's Moustaches'.

We got on well and he easily accommodated himself to the role reversal. Fortunately, he had been a good guy including his time as my squadron commander before I went to Air Support Command Operations.

One day in 1992 (?) there in the crew-room was none other than David 'Paddy' Hipperson from my training days in 1954-56. We went through the usual greetings and he said, 'Why weren't you at the MD-83 course in St Louis, Missouri?' I said, 'What do you mean?' and he explained that I was on his course for Paramount Airlines. I had received neither letter nor phone call despite my couple of calls asking them if they wanted me. What a messy administration – no wonder they went into liquidation so quickly. Paddy and I did just one trip together and that was Orlando in June '93.

In early 1993 a circular went around all captains to ask if they wanted to fly the newly-ordered 747-400 or newly-ordered Airbus 340. The proviso was that at the beginning of the course you should not have reached your fifty-seventh birthday, thus giving the company three full years on type. I could not make the deadline for the 747 but had a month to spare for the A340 and duly requested that. I was to be on the first course at the end of August – one month inside the limit. Phew!

From 12 January to 9 February 1993 I flew twelve sectors totalling eighty-two hours and forty minutes plus a Heathrow-JFK return as a passenger and drove approximately 2,000 miles, some in America attending a wedding in upstate New York. The outcome was a deep-vein thrombosis (DVT) and I was told by the CAA that I could no longer use the privileges of my licence until further advised!

I was put on Warfarin, and regular blood tests eventually established the correct dose for me. I eventually obtained clearance to fly after three months off. Apparently, seven of my eight return lines in the right leg had been blocked.

On 30 April I was checked by Captain Mike Vardey to LAX and return and was released to the line. It had been a worrying three months, not just for my licence but would I be fit in time for the Airbus 340 course? In the event, it was delayed beyond my fifty-seventh birthday, but either no one noticed or it was not considered fair to cancel me as it had been a company decision.

Airbus A340

I landed in Heathrow from LAX on 9 September 1993 on my last-ever 747 flight and, a couple of days later, No. 1 Course A340 set off for Airbus Training Centre, Miami. We comprised six VS captains with me as senior member and six newly-appointed first officers. We were accommodated at the normal VS hotel, The Marriott. I was paired with Phil Rose and each crew of captain and first officer was given a car as we would not all be doing the same things at the same time. Phil and I got on well and settled down to the usual massive hard work to prepare for the inevitable exams.

The training took place at the Airbus training centre in the northern area of Miami. We were all issued with the aircraft operation and technical manuals and assigned a room full of AVT (Audio-Visual Trainers) machines, one each. There we all spent the time from 0800 to 1700 matching the information in our books with TV screens, mock controls and model and TV systems layouts. Two instructors were available at all times to answer questions.

Many of us stayed on longer to avoid rush hour but, upon return to the hotel, the studying continued well into the evening. We usually all appeared between 2130-2200 in the usual great bar-cum-restaurant fifty yards from the hotel and stayed until midnight.

Up again for early buffet breakfast, then off to Airbus for another day exactly the same. The weekends were used for a little relaxation but mostly studying. We were lucky because, as the aircraft was new to the British register, the CAA were still compiling exam papers and they were not ready by the end of the second week, so we had an extra week to get ready. Subsequent crews had to cope with only a fortnight's study.

The exam was multiple choice but for every wrong answer a point was deducted so guessing was no option. It was the usual 100-plus questions with a modest amount of time allocated. We all passed bar one who managed it when sitting the exam again at the same time as the second course going through.

For me, now aged fifty-seven, I found the course quite hard as, yet again, I was learning about an aircraft from a company totally new to me. Furthermore, the aircraft was so advanced, so computerised and so complicated, to me anyway, I had to put in maximum effort.

We started the simulator flying immediately after the exams, including the guy who had failed first time, only to find that the absence of a real control column did not faze us at all. The little SSC (side stick controller) worked in such a natural fashion that we took to it very easily. The space where you would normally find a control column, or yoke, was now available for the table which for take off and landing was stowed under the instrument panel and at all other times pulled out. The table also contained all the normal checklists such as take-off, after-take-off, top of descent etc. Perfect for writing the log, reading the maps etc., and, of course, meals.

There was one problem, the overhead light was so badly positioned that when you leant forward your shadow obscured it all. It was eventually changed but not for seven-plus years.

Apart from the standby instruments, an old-fashioned altimeter, artificial horizon and air speed indicator, all the other instruments were displays on glass. Hence, the 'glass cockpit.' The two pilots each had an altitude display, called the PFD (Primary Flight Display), and a ND (Navigation Display); each could be swapped around according to the pilot's preference or even swapped from side to side, i.e. captain's altitude display down then he could replace it with a copy of the first officer's.

The attitude indicator was actually known as the PFD (primary flight display) as it also showed heading in a strip window at the bottom, indicated air speed in knots on the left in a vertical display and altitude on the right. The altitude could be changed to read metres, if necessary, i.e. in Russia and China.

The ND (navigation display) showed ground speed, TAS (true air speed), wind velocity and time to next reporting point in numbers around its periphery and the central part, graduated from 15-300-nautical miles, selectable, showed the route with waypoints and your position relative to the desired route.

Better late than never, perhaps I should explain the difference between *Indicated* and *True* airspeed. The pitot tube, either side of the nose on big aircraft and sometimes on the wing of fighter aircraft, has the air jammed into it as the aircraft proceeds through the air. At 200 knots, say, at 15 degrees and sea level, X molecules of air are rammed into the tube and the pressure is calibrated to show 200 knots on the *Indicated* airspeed gauge. The aircraft and, especially, the wings react to this flow giving lift and manoeuvrability.

However, the wing needs the same number of molecules flowing as at sea level to have the same lift etc. at higher altitudes, i.e 200 knots *Indicated*. The only way to achieve the same number of molecules as before in this thinner air is to go faster. The *True* speed is now faster than the indicated speed. The aircraft is happy and you will get to destination sooner.

The weather radar could be superimposed on the ND to show any significant weather ahead, such as heavy cumulus or worse. This meant that, even if you were in cloud, you could still manoeuvre safely and see exactly where you were in relation to the desired track.

TCAS (traffic collision and avoidance system) is also superimposed on the ND. This is a system which 'talks' to other TCAS and decides if there is any likelihood of a collision. If so, then one TCAS orders a climb and the other a descent. Should you be taking too much time the voice becomes strident and orders more effort, i.e. 'Descend, Descend. Increase Descent! Increase Descent', etc.

Aircraft appear as white hollow diamonds if the range is less than thirty nautical miles and the height difference is 1,200 to 1,500 feet. Once within a certain range the diamond fills in and if even nearer and there is a threat then a voice calls 'traffic'. Should it start looking really bad then it changes to amber and, then red, at which point the aircraft are told what to do. I'm sure it's even more sophisticated now.

The problem is that within all modern large passenger aircraft there are three INS (Inertial Navigation Systems) supported by three GPS systems. This means that aircraft maintain exact tracks and it is quite normal for aircraft to pass each other directly above or below, so if there is a climb or descent error by ATC then the aircraft are in danger. TCAS solves this and makes flying very safe.

Personally, in areas of much traffic or areas of poor ATC (yes, they do exist) then I would set the navigation computers to fly me one nautical mile right of track. Many, many pilots do exactly the same, just in case.

Having finished the ground school and exams, we progressed to the simulator which allowed a more relaxed day. Each exercise was two or three hours and never more than once a day; however, from 13 September to 21 October 1993 we only had seven days off. We did sixty-three hours then a three-hour Instrument Rating Test, followed by the final test known as the 1179 which is the form on which the results are shown.

As I've said earlier, I find tests very unnerving, even when my experience on type should give me all the confidence I need. However, the A340 1179 test on 21 October 1993 was really difficult. There were four other British pilots qualified on the A340; Larry Rockcliff who flew the Emir of Qatar, the VS chief pilot Tony Ling and the two VS designated instructors, none of whom had done the exams or an actual final handling test. This was fair enough as a fleet has to start somewhere.

So here we were, Phil and I, about to do the first ever FHT and be the fifth pilots to qualify on the A340. The trouble was that not only were the aforementioned four on the flight deck with us, but also the chief pilot of the Miami Airbus Training Centre!

Larry was the check pilot, and very pleasant too, but I was rather overwhelmed by so many experienced observers. It was quite daunting but, despite a rather 'scruffy' flight, we were passed.

When we checked in at Miami Airport for the return flight we were all expected to pay excess baggage on the amazing number of extra manuals we had acquired. After much arguing and telephoning it was decided not to charge us.

From now on I would only operate from London Heathrow.

There was a long delay in getting our first aircraft into service, so it was not until 29 November that I did my 1179 in G-VBUS at Manston. Lufthansa, who had operated the A340 ahead of us, provided an experienced instructor to do all our handling checks. I was first to fly and he was most unpleasant; despite a good enough circuit or two he was quite rude and off-putting.

Fortunately, our A340 fleet captain, Robin Cox, was quite unimpressed by all this unnecessary behaviour and Lufthansa changed their instructor. Anyway, I now had the aircraft in my ATPL and was the fifth British qualified pilot on A340.

Again, there was a delay before getting the aircraft into service but on 31 December I started my line training: to Orlando once and Boston three times, followed by another check to Shannon-East Midlands-Gatwick. Then I was released to the line.

Our A340 was powered by the CFM 56 5C4

Wingspan	60.3 metres	197 feet 10 inches
Length	63.6 metres	208 feet 8 inches
Height	16.85 metres	55 feet 4 inches
Maximum weight	275,000 kilograms (606,272lb)	
Maximum speed	Mach 0.86	

From mid-February 1994 onwards the A340 operated only to Hong Kong (HKG) with our three aircraft, G-VBUS, VAEL and VSKY. At that time

Kai Tak was still the only airfield in Hong Kong, so we had that wonderful approach and landing that all pilots enjoyed. It had, however, changed a little because there was now an ILS (Instrument Landing System) aimed directly at the hill on which stood the chequered flag painted on the flat face. Obviously, you could not use this ILS to land, so it was known as the IGS (Instrument Guidance System) and we started the turn onto the runway when we followed the guidance lights. This turn started at 540 feet – good to know if you really had to do an approach below official limits – 800 feet, I think.

Now that we were into normal airline flying and meeting varying crews I never actually saw Phil again until late March.

We continued with the three aircraft throughout 1994 flying just to Hong Kong, although we had the occasional back-up trip elsewhere. In 1994 I went to Hong Kong with two back-ups, one to JFK and one to Boston. In November we took on another aircraft, G/VFLY, and also took over the Narita/Tokyo service.

In 1995 we added a couple of JFKs a week, so we were pretty stretched but the aircraft was so reliable we achieved a high percentage of on-time departures.

We still had permission to overfly Russia without the proviso of a landing, so the flight to NRT was quite straightforward: across southern Scandinavia to Helsinki and St Petersburg, then Vologda-Kirov-Nadym-Olyokminsk-Khavarousk and over the Sea of Japan, abeam Vladivostok to Niigata in Japan, then north of Tokyo. The time was rarely outside the range 11.45-12.30 hours push-back to shut-down.

Once the Russians were okay with us, we changed our Hong Kong route via Russia and China. It started the same but after Vologda we routed Novosibirsk-Irkutsk-Ulaanbaatar (Mongolia)-Hengyang-Hong Kong. This particular route meant that we were traversing the Himalayas and, although we were at 33,000 feet and, later, 37,000 feet, they looked damned close. We had strict procedures should we have an engine failure; depending where the failure occurred we had well-defined routes in one direction or another. These were all clearly identified with heights, tracks and airfields to consider for landing. These charts and instructions were on the console between the pilots throughout the period over the mountains.

The view was awesome on a clear night and the tops seemed a very short distance below. Come to think of it, they were!

On one occasion when we were routing Hong Kong-Myanmar-Calcutta-UK, our original route before permission to overfly Russia, but the headwinds were so strong that I was routed Hong Kong-Tokyo-Khabarovsk and the usual Russian route. It was much longer, but we should just have been able to make Heathrow. If not, then a crew would have been sent to Helsinki to await our possible need to refuel. In the event we made it with the exact amount of reserve fuel remaining after sixteen hours and ten minutes flying. My longest flight ever.

I think we practically exhausted subjects for conversation on that trip or maybe we were the exhausted ones. Anyway, I recall mentioning the chap at RAF Chivenor with the car registered as RAF1 and the station commander's unsuccessful attempts to buy it. I was driving home to Somerset that morning after arrival, half-asleep, and exactly abeam Stonehenge, passing from the opposite direction, was an old car registration RAF1. I had not seen it for forty-plus years. What a coincidence!

In the early days of the A340 our cruising speed was Mach 0.82 whilst all other aircraft were cruising at Mach 0.84. This meant that if other aircraft caught us up, i.e. ten minutes behind us at the same level, then they had to slow down which cost them fuel. However, they could then usually climb to the next permitted flight level and when we wanted that level the other aircraft was still not ten minutes ahead, so we were stuck down and using extra fuel. VS decided that, where possible, we would carry a little extra fuel and cruise at Mach 0.84. It worked well, we used barely any extra fuel and it stopped irritating other crews all the time.

Hong Kong in the 60s and 70s, when I was in the RAF, was a shopper's paradise but, whilst still good for bargains, had become pricier. I was not a good haggler, so had less success for bargains than most other crew-members.

Jaki being an excellent cook, especially of Asian dishes, was pleased with my regular arrival with plates, bowls, spoons etc., with the Chinese style of dragons, etc. Each trip, and there were many, I would wrap three or four items in my clothes and bring them safely home. We ended up with twelve small, medium and large bowls and plates and many spoons and one or two accessories for the kitchen.

Years later, when living in France, we went into a cheap store called Bagi and there were hundreds of all the items I had carefully carried from Hong Kong, and they were much cheaper! I always found Narita better because I had no shopping list. As the years passed with all the extra destinations the shopping lists grew, but not for Narita. Oh, bliss!

In early 1996 Air Mauritius were a little short of pilots so a few of us had the opportunity to work for them. Unfortunately, I only had two sectors, Zurich-Mauritius and return three days later to Charles-de-Gaulle, Paris.

We flew as a VS crew, Cliff Newton and I, but with an Air Mauritius first officer to assist with the company procedures and information about the airfield. My two assisting FOs were Nick Kapoor and San Vaitilingon.

The layover was lovely; the hotel was on its own small peninsula next to the airfield, there was a wonderful 9-hole golf course and excellent bar and restaurant facilities. All the guests were couples, some with children, and Cliff and I realised we were getting some interesting looks. We guessed some thought we were a couple too, so we acted strongly to disavow them of these thoughts. I could have done with more of these stand ins for Air Mauritius.

The A340 had so far provided many happy and interesting memories. Not the least was the fact that, in its early days, it gave so many surprises as all the new and tested computer-ware came up with many sudden surprises, most of which simulated real problems. The initial response was 'What's it doing now?' and then sit on your hands and wait. Like many computer problems they wouldn't go away unless you did something, but what?

Sometimes careful watching and muttering would be enough but, occasionally, a small press on a nearby button would sort it out. Slowly but surely all problems were ironed out and it performed perfectly. In the early simulator days we were advised that, whatever happened, we were to get on with it and were allowed only three 'What's it doing now?'

By mid-1996 the A340 expanded its routes into the more usual VS areas such as Orlando and Washington Dulles (IAD). Orlando was a wonderful place to take Gemma and Josh and IAD was perfect for spending hours in the Smithsonian Aviation Museum. Once I was so engrossed in there that, when I glanced at my watch, I found I had only forty minutes to pick-up at the hotel. The taxi ride, shower, shave and dressing allowed me just enough time to pay my hotel bill and step into the bus dead on time. Phew!

One of life's great disappointments occurred around 1995-96. I was playing golf when Jaki received a call for me to fly to Hong Kong that night and to please call immediately. Jaki called the golf club and the lady in the pro' shop said she would go and get me if it was urgent. She could see me on the 15th fairway at Long Sutton Golf Club, but Jaki said not to worry as I would finish shortly. As soon as I got to the club house I received the message and immediately called John at ops. He said he was sorry but he had needed an answer urgently so had contacted Laurie Knight and found him available.

The callout was to fly Princess Diana to Hong Kong and return. I was so upset and, to add to the gloom, the Princess always asked for Laurie Knight for her other flights. Good for him, but I like to think she and I would have hit it off also.

We had a first officer who had recently retired from the RAF with senior rank and interesting experience but not transport. He felt that these qualifications should put him higher up the seniority list and, therefore, accelerated promotion to captain. Like so many of us when we left the cloistered confines of the services we were not fully aware of how civilian life worked.

Shortly after this he flew with me in February 1996 to JFK. Our departure was hectic and it took all my experience to cope with it. That day snow had fallen continually, the taxiways were mostly covered but the runways were semi-cleared. It was snowing as we sat on the flight deck planning our departure. First, the aircraft had to be cleared of snow and hosed down with anti/de-icing fluid. This had to be planned precisely because the combination of fluid temperature, OAT (outside air temperature) (ambient) and time from application to departure, i.e. lift-off time, are all interwoven variables. You cannot learn these figures, you have to read special instructions, use graphs and liaise all the time with company and ground crew.

All planning done, icing considerations planned, fluid sprayed and off we went. It had been non-stop hectic. As we taxied out our way was blocked by a BA 747 which had taken the wrong turning. I was now down to only five to six minutes before I would run out of safe time with anti-icing and have to return to the terminal.

The problem was sorted out and we got airborne with two minutes to spare. The take off and climb was uneventful and we broke out at about 6,000 feet into the most beautiful clear and starry night. The first officer was exhausted, as was I, from all the concern, paperwork, manual work and doubts about timing.

We were one of only a few aircraft that departed that night; it had never occurred to me that there was a problem as long as we played by the book and it worked. I heard that after this trip, and having seen what captaincy involved, the first officer withdrew his claim to early command and decided to get the real experience.

Captains and flight crew always know if anyone of any special interest is flying with us. One evening out of the USA (I can't remember where, but probably East Coast) we were advised that Monika Lewinsky was in the second row of Upper Class, aisle seat, right-hand side. Well, naturally we all went for a peek round the front galley area but she had reclined her seat and was totally covered by a blanket, head to toe. We always know our passengers, famous, infamous and the rest.

Later on, Zoë Ball had asked if she could visit the flight-deck so I said, 'Of course.' She appeared and the first thing she said was 'Do you know who you have on board?' We said, 'Do tell.' She said, 'Monika Lewinsky but you can't see her and she seems to be asleep.' One of the FOs, Bob Ilett said, 'Yeah, she's had her head down all night.'

We all laughed out loud except Zoë Ball – so it either went over her head or she plays a damned good straight face.

By mid-1996 the A340 started joining in with 747s doing Orlando from Manchester and also LHR-IAD (International Airport Dulles) Washington. Indeed, my last flight as a captain was to IAD with Nigel Holden as FO, and my daughter, Gemma, in the flight deck. Normally I headed straight to the Smithsonian Museum for all of my layover, but for Gemma I stuck to more mundane things like touristy stuff and shopping.

On the way back to the hotel I saw the worst wig I have ever seen. This older chap had exited his car and was assisting a lady from the rear. He had normal hair as in monk's arc from over the ears and dipping to the neck. I surmised the rest of his head was bald. His own hair was grey/dark and his wig was orange! Also, it was perched on his head in such a way that the back of his head was as a big smile with a ginger moustache and a goatee beard. It reminded me of one of the great Tom and Jerry cartoons.

Sadly, I was approaching my sixtieth birthday which meant I could no longer be a captain of an aircraft over twenty-five tonnes, so I could apply to be a captain with one or two of the commuter airlines or act as an executive pilot on Gulfstream, etc. *But*, I was much happier flying long haul so asked VS if I could stay on as first officer. They kindly retained my services as a contracted Senior FO. This was most useful as Josh was still at Holloway University doing his Masters in European Business Studies so the salary was gratefully received. Mind you, I would have carried on anyway, I didn't think of my job as work, it was a way of life.

On 10 September 1996 I landed at Heathrow from Dulles as my last flight as an airline captain. I was sixty the next day and, although it was on the horizon to extend the age limit, I was 'too old' to fly heavy jets. This was crazy because I was permitted to fly aircraft under twenty-five tonnes which, in some small airlines, meant the pilots did the paperwork for each flight, sometimes carried or hauled out baggage and freight and could legally do three or four sectors a day at mid-levels and, therefore, have weather problems all the time.

But I could not sit in the sunshine at thirty-odd thousand feet on one sector per duty period and let computers smooth the way. *Crazy*!

On 14 September I went to Berlin where I was converted to the RHS (right hand seat) by a VS instructor in the Lufthansa training school simulator. For the rest of the year I flew nearly all my trips as first officer to captains who had been my first officers. The old saying came to mind, 'Be kind to people on your way up as you may meet them on the way down.' I must have done something right as all my trips were calm and courteously run.

I had always enjoyed all my flights as captain and now, surprisingly after so many years (twenty-seven) in the left-hand seat, I was happy as an SFO. As you would expect of people who command airliners, not one captain showed any nervousness or deference to me because of my recent position but they were all very courteous.

For my part, I revelled in doing a good job as FO but without any side or implication that I could do better. I had firmly determined to be an FO and nothing else, to be correct in my respect for the system. On rare occasions I was asked for advice over and above that requested normally and it was given freely and with respect.

My life as a first officer settled down to being happily freed from all the responsibility, the signing of everything and making occasionally very difficult decisions. Of course, as a first officer, it was my duty to question something if I felt a doubt about it, but those occasions were, and are, quite rare.

The one thing I particularly missed from my captain days was the occasional suite and/or better rooms given in many of the hotels. The 'captain's room 'in the Hotel Tokyo, Narita, was on a 45-degree corner of the hotel and was larger than the other rooms. It was sited such that you enjoyed a view practically straight down the runway only a mile away. All pilots love watching aeroplanes so this was a great spot.

Two or three months into my SFO days VS added Johannesburg to its destinations. The fifth A340 joined us registered G-VSUN.

VS placed many items at the various hotels for crew use, such as bicycles and helmets, golf clubs etc. The JNB (Johannesburg) hotel was the Sandton Sun, undoubtedly the best hotel we used. Here we had eight sets of golf clubs which most of us on the flight deck used every visit. JNB is surrounded by great golf clubs, most of which were championship courses, and I'm pretty sure I played all of them.

The lifts inside the hotel were all glass, except for the floor, and they gave a lovely view as you went up, even though there were only seven or eight floors. One day I got into the lift on the third floor, the VS floor, to go to the Mezzanine floor. As I entered I came face to face with the England cricket captain, Nasser Hussain, and realised that the other six or seven occupants were English cricketers. I said, 'Good Morning' and received not a single acknowledgement. Nasser just stared at me with his usual gormless open-mouth appearance. I left two floors later and said, 'Goodbye, good luck for today,' and just one person grunted 'Thanks.' I think it was Darren Gough.

How rude and stupid to behave in such a boorish manner. Of course, they get pestered and are tired of being harassed but in a lift with three floors to go? I have detested Nasser Hussain ever since. Mind you, they had no trouble fraternising with the general public when it came to the evening when we and all our VS ladies were in the bar. The girls were more than welcome into their circle, which was quite natural, of course.

VS was now employing more female pilots, which was a good approach to balancing fairness and acceptance which had been lacking in the past in aviation. They were a good bunch of ladies and performed exactly as the rest of us. It was a pleasure to fly with them. Our two female captains at the time were Yvonne Kershaw and Camilla Daser, with both of whom I had flown when they were first officers but strangely, and sadly, I was never crewed with them as captains. I was really disappointed.

One of the new first officers had a remarkable story of determination and dedication. She had been a secretary (?) with the Chippenham Council and saved every penny she could to get a PPL (Private Pilot's Licence) and, having achieved that, continued to get her night rating, instrument rating and then instructor rating. Instructors got abysmal payment for their work but she ploughed on. Later she got her twin-engined rating and, finally, managed to get a job as first officer with some small passenger or freight outfit. As the hours progressed, she moved on and on until she was flying twin jets, 737s probably. Eventually she was taken on by VS and made the grade as A340 first officer. I flew with her many times and was always in awe of her achievement. Sadly, I cannot remember her name, even after poring over my logbooks.

It was decided that brakes were cheaper to fix than engines, in particular the mechanical parts for reverse thrust, so all deceleration was with brakes and, if necessary, reverse thrust. So, we became so used to just braking that reverse thrust was relegated to the back of the mind.

This mindset contributed greatly to one of the worst arrivals of my life. We were coming from the north to fly past JNB airport, turn left and approach the runway from the south. When we were about ten to fifteen miles to the airport, the ATC asked if we could come straight in and land from the north. The captain, Adrian Grantham, and I looked at each other and agreed we could do it. Well, as pilots know, if you are going to change prepared procedures you have to be sure you have things right in your head.

I used speed brakes, flap and undercarriage as early as speed limitations allowed but we crossed the runway touchdown a little high and fast. The indicated landing speed would always show less than the actual speed (True airspeed) of the aircraft as JNB is 5,000 feet-plus above sea level.

I crawled all over the brakes, as they say, and we came to a safe stop short of the end of the runway, but it was all rather poor handling. Adrian looked at me and said, 'You had reverse thrust available, you know!' I was mortified but I must congratulate him on not interfering, as he had the right to do. All good captains let first officers make fools of themselves as long as safety is not a problem. A young first officer would have learnt a lot from that. So did I, although I had done high-altitude landings many times.

After a couple of years at SFO on contract I was advised that I was now on one month's notice and to be paid by the hour. Fair enough, especially as I was now earning more money. This was eventually reduced to being rostered for one flight per month, but I still got called out and it was quite usual to do four trips a month, seventy to eighty hours paid by the hour is hot stuff.

There were strong rumours in 1998 that pilots were going to be allowed to fly beyond the age of sixty-five and that there would be no restraint on captains' age, so long as they met the six-monthly medical criteria and had a first officer aged sixty or less. I knew bureaucracy would not work quickly enough for me but had high hopes. Meanwhile, on with the job and enjoy it for as long as I could.

The joy of flying, especially military and airliner work, is difficult to explain easily. One of the great joys is the amazing sights that present themselves; the three or even four aircraft crossing within a short distance of each other and trailing (those little lines you see from the ground) are actually quite spectacular when they are within 1,000 feet (300 metres) of you; the size of the aircraft so close is pretty awesome too.

Other sights are the myriad variations of sunrise and sunset, the moon seems so much larger, the stars brighter. Why, well there is no other light anywhere, it is pure darkness. The fun (not always, actually) of avoiding serious clouds and especially cumulonimbus using radar and Mark 1 eyeball is satisfying. More so when your passengers have no idea how hard we try to give them a good ride.

The really sad business of long-haul flying is that if a passenger wants to look out of the window and raises the blind all the TV watchers make him close it again.

The modern passenger is missing icebergs in the North Atlantic, the glaciers of Greenland, the wildness of the Northern Territories, the Hoover Dam, Las Vegas at night, the Rockies, the Alps, the Himalayas (including Everest), the Mediterranean, the view of Vancouver as you approach from the east, the plains of Africa, rivers, islands, thunderstorms, the Northern Lights, the lines of volcanoes on the east coast of Japan and so on and so on.

When I am sad at being out of aviation I dwell on so many wonderful experiences flying has given me but, apart from a few exciting or worrying incidents, the greatest sight of all was on a LAX-LHR overnighter.

The captain was in the bunk behind the flight deck and the other first officer and I were in awe of the constant brightness and changing patterns of the Aurora Borealis. As time went by and we flew farther and farther north the lights were above, below and around us. I had never experienced this before and we both rested our chins on the glare-shield (i.e. keeps the sun from shining on the instruments during the day) and stared outside, with the occasional glance at the instruments, of course.

Suddenly, the lights were denser and started to curl over us and for about a minute or so it was just like Waikiki or Bondi Beach! We were actually surfing the lights. I would have no argument with anyone having trouble believing me, but it was thus. Surfing the Aurora Borealis, it was exactly as you see real surfers being in a tunnel of white water. A quite phenomenal experience!

For reasons I cannot fathom, I have never described this to another long-haul high-altitude pilot, so I don't know if it was rare or old hat. Whatever the answer I will never forget it.

I remember once flying in first-class as a passenger with Gulf Air, having been up to the flight deck for a chat with the chaps and finding they had an electrical and hydraulic problem, the weather was bad and Heathrow was in poor visibility and rain.

We arrived at Heathrow and the landing was quite firm. This enables you on a very wet runway to immediately break through the water and touch the runway. If you try too hard to make a smooth landing in these conditions it is possible to 'ride' the water for a moment, the wheel doesn't spin up and the tyre overheats and could burst.

After the firm landing, the passenger next to me said, 'He's not much of a pilot, is he?' I thought that if he only knew the work that goes into a comfortable and safe flight he might think otherwise.

All pilots have good and bad landings, probably 95-per-cent-plus good and sometimes, despite experience, you manage a rough one, through either having a bad hair day or even a weather cause such as gusts or variable crosswinds. Any pilot who's sitting in the front of a passenger aircraft should never be judged on his landings.

By the year 2000 we had ten A340s, the last five being G-VSEA, -VAIR, -VHOL, -VELD and -VFAR. Also, there was planned the introduction of the A340-600 which was twenty-eight feet longer and with real engines instead of hair-dryers, i.e. really powerful Rolls Royce Trent 500s compared to CFM 56s.

With the introduction of the -600, and retaining some of the -300, we needed many new pilots, so courses were arranged to train newly joined first officers on the -600 with a two- or one-day extra course to include the -300 which they would fly whilst waiting for the new aircraft.

I found out that I would soon be surplus to requirements which I could understand. I requested a return to the 747-200, but there was no opening. However, I never received anything in writing, so just carried on flying. In December I had four trips, including my one and only to Shanghai and when the January roster appeared my name was not on it.

I took this as confirmation that I had retired! My last flight was to LAX and I finally went off duty on 31 December 2000 at 1559 hours. On 6 January I received a letter to advise me that my contract was finished. Nice!

Parking Brakes Off. End of Check-List

I felt a bit let down as it was a sad way to finish forty-seven years flying, which included twenty-seven of them in the left-hand seat of multi-jet passenger aircraft. Taking average speeds and logbook passenger numbers I reckon I flew 6,282,386 nautical miles, i.e. 251.3 times around the world and carried 768,038 passengers. Actually, I have a sneaky idea I went a bit further and certainly carried a lot more, but I started quite late in logging the numbers of passengers. As I only had 5,500 hours in the Royal Air Force I worked hard to finish with a reasonable 22,500 hours total. Sadly, I never recorded any time as a passenger, deadheading crew or paying. I recommend all young pilots reading this (hopefully) to keep a full record. When you reach my age, eighty-two, you will wish you had. I must have well over a thousand hours as a passenger.

Retirement

It has taken a long time to get accustomed to the idea of never again enjoying the responsibility, fun, frights (rarely), camaraderie, sights from *the* front seat and the massive satisfaction of a job well done. Fortunately, as at Taunton, I'm still on a military low-flying route so get some thrills; mind you, I seem to be the only one. Also, the Airbus 380 was flight-tested all the time over our house which, at first was fantastic, until I became 'Disgruntled of SW France', as most of the testing seemed to be at night!

It seems strange not to be in uniform; I started at seven years old in cassock, surplice and ruff, continued in blue with the Air Cadets and Royal Air Force, green in Gulf Air, then black from then on. That's fifty-seven-plus years in uniform. Crikey!

My damaged left leg finally caused me to give up golf but I have a three-acre garden which forces me to 'enjoy' gardening and my sixth gorgeous Dobermann, Tallulah, and wire-haired Dachshund, Archie, to ensure I retain fitness and have fun.

All in all, not a bad life, eh?

Afterword

I Don't Like Flying

Don't you? Why not? My guess is that you're frightened because you don't like your destiny being held in the hands of someone you don't know and may not even like. That sounds reasonable to me. If it's any consolation, there are occasions when I can be a little apprehensive, but never in a British registered aircraft or an airline from a country that has the same, or very similar, regulations. I can be uncomfortable in an aircraft crewed by people for whom 'face' is a way of life, where the first officer is loath to question a captain's decision, even though he's sure it's wrong or not the wisest choice. On a British and similar registration system the crew are a team, with a captain in overall command who is prepared to listen.

Let's have a look at the people who may be looking after you.

A commercial licence qualifies a pilot to act as pilot-in-command of those aircrafts best suited to single-pilot operation, and to be first officer on bigger aircrafts. The ATPL (Airline Transport Pilot's Licence) holder may act as pilot-in-command of all types of aircraft. The subjects on which they are examined include:

- Air Law.
- Airframe, aircraft systems and powerplants (engines).
- Instruments and how they work.
- Weight (mass) and balance, to be safe throughout the flight as the balance moves due to fuel usage.
- Performance, i.e. take-off figures, in-flight heights safe to use, and approach and landing planning.
- Meteorology.
- Navigation, using charts and radio.
- Operational procedures in general (all companies have their own but they only differ slightly).

- Principles of flight (aerodynamics).
- Radios and telephone procedures, for which you receive a separate licence.

Before being ready to fly you, the pilot first has to sit in on lectures and AVTs (Audio-Visual Trainers) from 8am to 10pm, learning everything about the aircraft that you are sitting in, which they are examined on. The pilot will then learn the handling and idiosyncrasies by spending up to 70 hours in a very realistic simulator and be tested again with emergencies, bad weather, engine failures (rare nowadays) and anything the examiner wishes to throw at them.

After a few days off, they fly with passengers and a fully qualified instructor in the flying officer's (F/O) seat. The pilot's overall hours and whether they have had time on this aircraft before will determine their time spent under training. It will also depend on their final check with another training captain.

The pilot is then released to the line and is in command. It's a wonderful relief after weeks of sweating away (literally) and, if it's their first command, they will feel very proud to have made it.

So! How do you feel so far? Perhaps a little more confident in your pilot?

Pilots undergo many checks throughout the year and some can be stressful because they are constantly defending their licence (read—livelihood). These checks include:

> Medical: Full check every 6 months, including an ECG and blood test. Hearing tests and chest x-rays vary according to medical history or age.

> Simulator: Every 6 months a captain and a first officer are checked at the same time. They are put through 4 hours of emergencies; situations requiring urgent but proper decisions, totally unusual and sudden problems and even some 'normal' problems. The next day they do the same again but with a serious check on our flying instruments whilst in emergency conditions.

> Safety equipment training (every year): Dinghies, fire (including the real thing at the local fire training centre), oxygen for pax and location of all items for survival, special training on doors in view of their importance in evacuation and the fact that the slides are also the flotation devices (dinghies really). Exams to follow!

Technical: Every year two days are spent ensuring that we have all maintained our four large volumes on handling, technical, navigation and company regulations. These all get amended regularly, especially technical. An exam follows.

Just to add spice and surprise to all that, the CAA (Civil Aviation Authority) designate one or more qualified pilots to be attached to each British airline. Their responsibility is to watch over the rules governing the standard operating procedures (SOPs), crew training and company regulations. To this end they can appear unannounced anywhere in the world and climb aboard to check that the crew are conforming to all regulations and that their performance adheres to company SOPs.

There is a touch of whimsy here because, as with all personnel, they have to ask the captain's permission to enter the flight check. To my knowledge nobody has dared to refuse entry. Once there, of course, they've got you.

Have you decided that your flight deck are a pretty well-trained bunch of professionals yet? Wouldn't you be happier if doctors and lawyers went through these rigorous tests?

Now that I've explained that the flight deck has some pretty good talent up there, let's look at the cabin crew (CC).

Most European and Asian airlines have excellent service for their passengers. They are appreciated for their hard work and consideration to all. However, what you see is the result of a lot of hard work and what you don't see is far more important. This is all to do with your safety and requires a lot of training.

Cabin crew have to know the location of, and how to use, every bit of equipment on the aircraft. This includes oxygen, extinguishers, first aid, door safety and use, evacuation conversion of escape slides into flotation devices, smoke and fire. They join with the pilots to learn how to fight real fires and how to act together as a team. The chief and one other person are fully trained on defibrillators; both when to use them and how. All CC members are trained to cope with births on board. Their exams are rigorous and regular. Furthermore, they have a basic understanding of passenger psychology and learn to look for signs of agitation in probable wrong-doers or people who are just worried.

PLEASE watch and listen to the safety briefing before take-off, even if you're an old hand at this flying malarkey.

While you're milling around in departures, being ripped-off buying things in Duty-Free that are sometimes cheaper in the shops where you're going, the flight deck are meeting in company operations, greeting old friends and buckling down to learn of any changes or problems down the route. Is the aircraft top notch? (yes). They will read info on their aircraft of the day and, not least, check the weather en-route and at the destination; even if conditions are good they still select, and carry enough fuel for, an alternate airfield. They check all the numbers; weight, surface conditions and speeds. They agree and accept the computer's decision for now, knowing that when they have final weights they can confirm or change as necessary. The cabin crew will have finished their briefing from their chief and will be on their way to the aircraft, as will the flight deck, once they have completed their reading and planning.

The handling pilot (HP), the one who will be flying you, will settle into his seat and start the internal pre-flight checks. One of the first things he will do is set up the navigation equipment, as this needs time to get up to speed and many instruments rely upon it. The HP puts in the accurate latitude and longitude, which is usually painted on the information board at each parking place, and, of course, in all the aircraft charts. All systems will be checked and all knobs, buttons and switches correctly set.

Meanwhile, the non-handling pilot (NHP), wearing his yellow safety jacket, will start at the bottom of the front steps and proceed in a clockwise direction looking to see that all is well. The ground crew do not regard this as showing doubt in their proficiency and realise its value.

The NHP will return to the flight deck (FD) and cross-check the accuracy of the position and routing put into the navigation equipment, plus a few extra checks concerning his own side of the FD. Once you (and all of your fellow passengers) are on board, the cabin crew chief (CCC) advises, 'All present and correct according to expected load'. The traffic officer hands the captain the load-sheet which confirms people on board (POB), the weight, and the balance, whilst the duty engineering officer offers the technical log for inspection and acceptance. Once the captain signs for the aircraft, he is in command.

The doors are now about to be, or are, closed. You are being your usual nervous self, but the crew are exhilarated: WE ARE ON OUR WAY! The NHP calls for pushback, the captain (HP or NHP) advises the person on the headset by the nose wheel and the tug starts the push; this is the departure time and, hopefully, matches what it says on your ticket. At this point the captain or F/O will give the spiel over the passenger address system (PA) regarding route, weather, etc. and repeat what the CCC advised you regarding keeping your seat belt comfortably fastened whilst in your seat. This is very wise advice, more on which later.

Now the NHP, having seen the ground crew and tug clear of the aircraft and the nose wheel locking pin being waved at the FD, calls for taxi clearance, which will be given with appropriate routing to the runway (r/w) in use. During the taxiing the NHP carries out the pre-take-off checks, which include setting the wing-flaps to the correct angle, and all actions are cross-checked by both pilots. This device changes the apparent shape of the wing to the air as the engine power accelerates the aircraft. This shape provides better lift than a 'clean' wing. However, it can be noisy and depends on the type of aircraft, or even a particular one of the same fleet, because it's a lot of weight to be moved and the system usually uses a screw jack.

A what? Imagine a nut and bolt where the bolt cannot move except to be turned. Imagine also that as the screw turns anti-clockwise, the bolt, if held, will slowly wind along the bolt. Ok, now think big screw and big bolt, or some attachment to the flap, and as the screw turns then the 'bolt' has to move. The flaps are heavy and the screw jack does a lot of work, hence some noise.

Now for the time you have been looking forward to...or not! Cleared to take-off, the HP advances the thrust levers and you hear the power increasing as the aircraft starts to roll. When the power is set the captain takes the levers whether they are HP or NHP.

At 80kts the NHP will have called the speed as it is not a good idea to continue using nose wheel steering above 80kts. Now the rudder comes into play to keep the aircraft on course. As you go along the r/w you may hear a regular thudding noise that gets faster. This is caused by the nose wheel running along the centre-line lights; some pilots like to stay in the centre, some try really hard to get each wheel either side of the lights or, like me, keep to the upwind side about a yard.

Remember, V1 is decision speed and if anything occurs which means the captain does not wish to take into the air, or there is an engine failure, then he calls, 'Stop', 'Abandon' or 'Reject', whatever is the flavour of the month or airline. 'Stop' is now the thing, I believe. He has 2 seconds to mull this over and if the decision is stop he will immediately close the levers and apply full braking; nowadays braking is automatic when the thrust levers are closed.

If you are in an aircraft which abandons t/o then you can be sure it will stop in the right place.

At V1 the captain will release the levers if they intend to continue and now, whatever happens, you are going to get airborne. If an engine fails it matters not as the aircraft is at a satisfactory weight and speed and can accelerate to V2, the speed for safe flight.

The NHP calls VR after V1 when you are continuing. VR is the speed at which the aircraft is ready for comfortable flight and the HP simply raises the nose to convince the aircraft of this and it soars aloft like a homing pigeon on a promise when released.

Oh dear, more noises: you may sense a surge of air as the air conditioning units start to force enough air into the aircraft for you and make enough pressure to keep you comfortable and alive at high altitude. How? There are valves at the back of the aircraft which control the outflow of air so that the pressure inside is at or about 8.5 pounds per square inch (P.S.I.) more than outside, thus maintaining cabin altitude at around 8,000 feet.

What's next? Well, the undercarriage (gear) has to be put away until needed again. 3,000 P.S.I. of hydraulic pressure opens the doors, unlocks the gear and starts to raise about 6 tons of metal and wheels. This is no mean feat so there will be noise; especially when it thuds into the wheel-bay, as it's called. Brakes are applied before it gets into the wing and you may hear a smaller thud a little earlier as the nose wheel is stopped by a pad in the roof of its housing.

Nearly there; when the aircraft is at a safe height and speed, the flaps are selected up and that noisy screw jack sets off again. When they are in and flush with the wings, the aircraft is now 'clean' and is accelerating to climbing speed. Sometimes you will hear the power reduce as air traffic control (ATC) hold the climb for other traffic and then, at the top of the climb (TOC), the final reduction is made on entry to the cruise.

You spend longer in the cruise than climbing or descending, so turbulence (eek!) seems to happen more often. It can make you feel queasy or, more probably, frighten you. I don't like it much either when I'm a passenger, but only because it sometimes makes reading my book difficult. Air is no different from water, it is a fluid and, therefore, moves around easily.

Most of you are fine on water in a gentle swell, in a biggish boat, or even a bumpy ride in a dinghy. If you go past an outcrop of rocks, a headland or a jetty, then the water can get choppier; do you panic or take fright? Probably not. Well, an aircraft is subject to identical movements of the air. Normally the air is a moving mass which does move somewhat like a gentle swell but is so slow that you cannot sense it. However, all clouds can provide some, or lots of, air movement, otherwise they couldn't form. Aircraft radar identifies the really bad areas and the crew avoids them, especially those towering cumulonimbus. Whatever turbulence you have cannot even remotely harm the aircraft. Modern aircraft manufacturers actually build an exact aircraft hull to which exact wings are attached in the normal way and are tested to destruction by having their wings bent up to an angle you cannot believe. Certainly way beyond anything you will experience in flight.

Just to add to your woes there is also Clear Air Turbulence (CAT). Again, this is just air movement but, as its name suggests, you can't see it coming or guess it will happen. However, all pilots report such areas as they experience them so that others can put the seat belt signs on. Now you know why you are advised to keep your belts comfortably fastened whilst in your seat.

By all means dislike turbulence, but don't fear it. And by the way, there is no such thing as an air pocket.

During the cruise, if you are one of those who like to look at the beautiful world around us, you will often see an aircraft so close that you wonder what is happening. Simple! The system used to avoid messy collisions is for the aircraft going on along the airway to have one set of heights 2,000 or 4,000 feet apart and the aircraft flying the other way will then fly in the gaps. Except under close ground radar ATC, you will never be closer to another aircraft than 1,000 feet. Furthermore, as I said earlier, all aircraft now carry a TCAS (Traffic Collision Avoidance System) which was excellent in my time so must be superb now. The really close view of the contrails will thrill you.

At the end of the cruise you have to descend if you want to land at your destination, right? This simply means reducing power to flight idle, i.e. minimum, and lowering the nose. You may notice this but that's all that's going on. Actually, I used to be a bit sneaky at this point and disconnect the height lock on the auto-pilot and lower the nose the tiniest fraction and, at the same time, reduce the power a smidgeon. I'd keep doing this a bit at a time until at correct descent speed. The idea was to wonder how long it took passengers to realise we were on our way down. Well, we had to get some fun somewhere: keeping passengers happy with smooth flying has its boring moments. Following this the cabin crew start clearing up, so there's the giveaway. The seat belt signs will be on soon and the toilets locked.

If your destination is busy you may be held over a radio beacon or a specific position and circle around for a while. The wings seem to 'tip' up and down a long way but, in fact, the angle is no more than 30 degrees. In the hold, or approaching the airfield, those wretched noisy screw jacks have more work, so expect the noise, and if you have a wing view out of the window then watch them. As more flap is used for landing you may hear them three or four times. Between flap movements the gear has to go down, gravity does most of the work but hydraulics take some of the strain off at their lowest movement. As it is, there is quite a lot of noise for two reasons; the rush of air over the opening gear doors and then 6 tons of stuff seeming to bang into position. You are now lined up with the runway, a bit more screw-jacking takes place and you are set.

The pilot flies down a gentle slope at a safe speed, dependant on weight, and makes allowance for any cross-wind. This explains why you feel as if you are going sideways; you are a little bit sometimes. Never fear because the pilot straightens the aircraft at about 10 feet from the runway. At 50 feet the nose is raised slightly to reduce the rate of descent onto the runway. At 30 feet the power is slowly reduced to be at ground idle as you touch down like a feather on the runway (or not!). I mentioned flight idle earlier; it is higher than ground idle so that if you need power suddenly in flight then it is immediately available.

All pilots have a firm or hard landing occasionally, usually they know why, but other times not. A less than gentle landing only matters to one's sense of pride; it certainly does not upset the aircraft. As I said earlier, a good landing is one you walk away from and it's an even better one if you can use the aircraft again!

I realise that I have treated the subject a smidgeon flippantly, but the emphasis has been to show what happens on board and why. You have the most amazingly well-trained flight deck and cabin crew who take immense pride in what they do; trust them and enjoy the flight. Look out of the window, please, see sights you may remember forever. Some sunsets and sunrises are spectacular, although flight deck have no special love of dawns; after a few hours of low lighting and watching the stars I'm afraid the sun hurts.

The old but accurate cliché is true: each year more people are injured or killed on the roads in Britain than in all the aircraft operations around the world put together, honest!

On behalf of the captain and crew I wish you a pleasant onward journey and we look forward to you flying with us again.

Index

360

INDEX

INDEX

INDEX